Robert Payne

The talent revealed in Mr. Payne's writings is not altogether an autochthonous one. It is, as well, the result of much traveling and an almost unbelievable variety of occupations that have increased and sharpened his sensitive perception of the contemporary scene.

Born in England in 1911, he has attended the University of Liverpool, the Sorbonne, and Capetown University. He has lived all over Europe, from Poland to Spain; in Africa and Asia, and has been variously a shipwright, an armaments officer, a news correspondent, a translator, a professor of English in China and a pilot (receiving his flying license when he was 18). He is a prolific and prodigious worker and has lately been devoting all of his time to writing. Both his fiction and non fiction reveal the deep feeling and sensitive emotion of a mature nature that is essentially that of a poet. At present, he is in America and is working on several new manuscripts which are to be published in the near future.

CHINA AWAKE

By Robert Payne

Author of FOREVER CHINA,
DAVID AND ANNA, ETC.

WHEN FOREVER CHINA was published two years ago, Orville Prescott said: "The best book I have ever read about China. A literary event of the first magnitude."

This new volume is sure to achieve the same acclaim. Like its predecessor, CHINA AWAKE is a record of the fundamental qualities and eternal truths that are much more the history of a people than their political and military exploits. It is broader in scope than the earlier volume, for in the intervening years the pattern of China's destiny has been changing and Mr. Payne has followed the course of that change.

In its pages he visits Red China twice, wanders over the ancient hills of Yunnan and falls in love with that most enchanting of all cities—Peking. But above all else he has been concerned with the lasting spiritual values which China has to offer the West. In his political discussions with leaders throughout the country, in his work with students at the University, he has come to believe more strongly than ever that Asia and the West are complementary rather than antagonistic.

As in FOREVER CHINA, the author has used the journal form, written with originality and great beauty of style. Here are stories of war and civil war, portraits of Madame Sun Yat Sen, Dr. Sun Fo, General Chu Teh, General Marshall and a host of others whom Robert Payne met on his journeys. Here are tales of ghosts and high adventure, pictures of Chinese landscapes and Chinese faces, and, most poignant of all, stirring accounts of the heroism of students and soldiers. To read Mr. Payne's journal is to travel with the heart and the mind and to return, like him, with increased faith and hope in China's future.

Also by
ROBERT PAYNE

—

CHINA AWAKE

by ROBERT PAYNE

DODD, MEAD and COMPANY, NEW YORK

FOR WEN YI-TUO

poet, scholar and lover of America
who died gloriously

INTRODUCTION

THIS is the story of the Chinese students seen through the eyes of a foreigner, and how they behaved through the last years of the war and the first year of peace. As in *Forever China* I have been more concerned with the colours and shapes of people and things, the permanent landscape in which people move and have their being, than with the political implications of the struggle which is now going on. I went twice into the Communist areas, and learnt only what I knew before—that among the young in China there is a vast hope, and among the old there is no hope at all.

Inevitably the political struggle is reflected in these pages. We were faced with civil war, the murder of students, the concrete menace of the secret police, poverty so great that it remains to this day one of the greatest plagues known to man, and though I lost faith with the old and found them incapable of exerting even the moral pressure that was demanded of them, I hope that the young have come clear through these pages. They were times that tried men's souls, but the young did not falter. In Yenan, Peking, Shanghai, Nanking, Kunming, wherever they congregated together, they planned their secret conspiracies, which were no more than conspiracies for democracy and lasting peace. To them therefore, and to the youngest of them all, this book is dedicated.

In those five years in China, I watched a revolution taking place in the hearts of the young. There was bitterness sometimes, and much agony. There was the sense of insufferable strain, and even at times a sense of futility; yet they would say: "These things have happened, but they will pass. One day we shall have power." Sun Yat-sen, dreaming in London of the day when the Manchus would be dethroned, thought it might take a hundred years. Time moves more quickly now. The over-lords will not always have power. Though there is still civil war, a new element has entered the scene—the massed desire of the people for peace and justice. The old feudalism is at last crumbling, and those of us who saw the hammering at the walls can only rejoice. Because the stage is set and history has never enjoyed such exciting moments as the present, the old tumblers and actors still played their parts, but in the new China they will have no part to play. Out of the misery and distress of all those years only one thing is clear: China is awake, with blood-rimmed eyes, a young lion going in search of her freedom and still shaken by the agony of her birth pangs. There were times when one wished it otherwise, times when the agony seemed too intense to bear, and the treachery too evident, times when one even forgot the beauty of the landscape and the people (who are as beautiful as their landscape), times of utter remorse, when it seemed that no bitterness was too great, no scruples were too keen-edged, no horror could surpass the horrors we had seen; but in the end we came back again to the students in the classrooms and the peasants in the fields. There is a phrase which is often used in China —"the worst is over." It is said very often when the worst is still a little way ahead. But this time we knew it was over, and in spite of the civil war the aftermath of the ten-year war could not be worse than what had gone before. The corrupt, the malingerers, the millionaires and the men who believe that democracy is implied by secret prisons and secret police and arbitrary power have had their day; now, almost at the moment when they have succeeded in obtaining absolute power, they will pay the forfeit.

While the war was going on, a necessary silence was imposed on most of us in China. The country was so near defeat that to have spoken out at such a time would have made for greater cruelty. In that sense we were dishonest; we knew the risks and we were pre-pared to pay them, but now that our responsibility is to the whole Chinese people, and to peace, we dare no longer hide the corruption which exists in the country. It was Wen Yi-tuo's wish that these things should be made known. Wen was the greatest scholar of his time, and much of this book inevitably concerns him, and our great love for him. He half-guessed he would be killed; and this meant nothing to him as long as his great country survived. There are good elements in the Kuomintang, but the worst are so much worse than we can imagine that we are at the mercy continually of those who, believing that the Kuomintang represents the interests of the west, are prepared to despise the achievements of the agrarian revolution in the North, and the leadership of Mao Tse-tung. It would be well to state here that the best among the Chinese want neither the Kuomintang nor the Communists in power, but a government of the talents, learning from both.

My main interest was the Chinese student, whose courage in

viii

December 1945 filled me with alarm, for though I had expected it, I had not expected so great a devotion to the principles which are enshrined in the *Declaration of Independence,* and saw no hope in courage so absolute, fearing that it would betray itself in a thirst for martyrdom. Yet, though they desired martyrdom more than they desired anything else at that moment, they were aware that life was most precious to them, and knew that victory was near. Those who died died willingly; those who remained were consecrated to their task. "The revolution," wrote Dr. Sun Yat-sen, "is not yet over." With the help of the students and the peasants the revolution may yet be successful.

In the chronicle that follows, I have tried to show all facets of the Chinese scene. I have often used initials rather than names only because Chinese names are confusing to the western reader. The letters of Bergery have been quoted because he more than anyone else I ever knew was conscious that Asia had so much to offer the West, believing that each was complementary to the other, and lasting peace could only come from a richer understanding between them. I had thought once of calling this book *Hope out of Asia,* till one evening in Kunming a Chinese pored over the manuscripts and said: "You must call it *China Awake.*" The diary begins in the days when the Japanese armies, after the fall of Kweilin, were crowding towards Chungking and Kunming; it ends shortly after the assassination of the greatest Chinese I ever knew. Here is the rough sketch of a landscape written while China was in anarchy, but never—in spite of so much oppression and hunger—had she been more awake.

ROBERT PAYNE

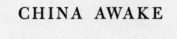

CHINA AWAKE

1944

December 6th . . . Even though the sun had set, the waves of the sun beat against the earth, and there was no moon, and the lights had gone out. In some of the shops greasy candlewicks were shining, mirrored against dusky silver; and we had passed the shops selling dragons' eyes, noodles and boiled eggs in sweet milk. There was an air-raid, and the air was hot and moist on our faces.

Liu Lien was talking excitedly as he always talks; we had been down to the centre of Kunming, and suddenly he remembered that he had to attend a meeting. He shook his head, and I saw him clearly as we passed the dimly-lit noodle shop—the beard like a lion's and the black hat jammed over his high forehead. I've forgotten his exact words, but there was a conspiratorial air about them. It was something like: "I should have remembered—you know, we're going to blow China to smithereens tonight." I remember it seemed an odd thing to do during a Japanese air-raid. We passed down a side-street towards the lake, stepping carefully over oily stones, and in the faint light we could see the old ceremonial China before us—the stone archway, the camel-back bridge, the golden-roofed hotel in the middle of the lake now occupied by soldiers. He was speaking rapidly and a little hoarsely, following his ideas at the run or gathering them together as one gathers snowballs, then hurling them into the air, delighted when they exploded into soft powder—the finest white dust. We passed students—they were everywhere at night, and you would find

1

yourself wondering why their hot blood could never be stilled as they sat on the stone benches on all the parks of the world; and sometimes even in this faint light we would see someone detaching himself from a stone bench and bowing to Liu Lien. "It won't last much longer," he said. "The days of bowing are nearly over. They are all Americanized now." "And then?" "There is no *then*. It will be one world—Willkie's one world—and I'm glad it has come. Better that we should all be alike, and dress alike, and think alike, than that we should be always at one another's throats." He said a moment later: "Let the differences between us become smaller, but let the heart grow larger." Then I lost him; he had disappeared to talk to some students beside the lake.

I am always afraid of losing Liu Lien, but he returned some moments later and the conversation went on as though there had been no interruption. We could see the great dark walls beyond the lake, and sometimes a fish would stir, or one of the lovers in the boats would make a little scream, and somehow it no longer resembled Kunming—it was the dark night of the world, waiting for the dawn. I asked him where he was taking me. "Haven't I told you enough? We're going to blow China to smithereens." He laughed, and in the darkness I thought I saw him drawing his ragged patched coat more tightly around him.

I said: "I still don't understand."

"Oh, but you will. What was Bergery always talking about?"

Bergery was my friend; he died more than a year ago.

"Peace," I answered, knowing that Bergery would have been ashamed to hear the word without qualifications, himself the least peaceful of men.

"This is what we are going to talk about. Peace in China. No civil war. A lasting peace, and if necessary the scholars will have to fight for it."

In China a scholar has a right to be ignorant of politics. Politics are for those who have put aside scholarship, or for historians dealing with the politics of another age. We have no time for them in the university, just as we have no time for war. The Japanese are supposed to be less than two hundred miles away. We have reached a state of crisis, and half the businesses in Kunming are prepared to pack up and go. The Japanese are trying to wedge through to Kweiyang and Chungking and there is no evidence that either the American aeroplanes or the Chinese army can prevent them. The students have asked for guns. They have been re-

2

fused—Liu Lien says that the government does not trust the students, and would prefer to see them massacred. I doubt it—there are probably insufficient guns to go round; but though we are rarely compelled to believe in the necessity of politics, we are beginning to realize that the Japanese are nearer than we ever imagined. What happens now?

I could see the face sometimes as he puffed at a cigarette, and all the time I was afraid a soldier would shoot at him—you are not allowed to smoke during an air-raid.

"Does it help?" I asked. "There's panic everywhere, and you talk of a civil war? There are Japanese aeroplanes overhead——"

He said: "The important thing is that we should change quickly under the stress of war. We have not changed. We thought we would open out the West of China, but we have not opened it out. We failed in this, and this is one more reason why there will be a civil war."

"There are so many reasons——"

"Far more than you can imagine. This is the last wave of the Japanese—they won't have strength for much more. How do I know? Good Heavens, when you teach students you know everything. They have relatives everywhere. Students come from Siam, Indo-China, Japanese-occupied China, even India. They are coming all the time. So we know better what is going on than the Foreign Offices. The peasants and the business men don't panic in the same way—the students never panic, or else we have worked in vain. The thing is to understand that."

"I have faith in the students, but not always in the professors," I said, and then more softly: "And in many of the students I have no faith at all—they will take the jobs which will give them most money. I wish there was more sense of dedication. It exists, but not always."

He smiled: "What is dedication? To be out on a dark night, and to have faith in China."

I pondered this for a moment, then he explained: "The poor are so wretchedly poor, so inconceivably badly trained, so miserable with the sickness of their souls that they will come and stick a knife in your back for a thousand dollars. You must have some faith to be walking with me now."

It was dark in the side-streets, and perhaps the siren had gone off, for no more candles gleamed in unpolished mirrors, and we thought we heard the putter of anti-aircraft fire at the airfield.

3

Suddenly a searchlight sprung up, a solid shaft of ivory, the elephant's tusk leaping out against the strange enemy of the sky; then another tusk; and then another, till the whole sky was full of the battle of the elephants, silently probing for the gnat which would soon appear. We heard the gnat rumbling. Liu Lien said: "I have half a mind not to take you there. You see, they don't trust anybody, but the civil war . . ." And then we came to the house, knocked and entered into the large courtyard, lit with the tusked moonlight from the moonless sky. Still there was no one. It seemed a strange meeting, for he had been hinting at revolution. A marble lion, chipped, looked up at us, looking like an inflated pekingese in this misty light, and then the putter of anti-aircraft shells came closer; somewhere behind the white tusks were the red sprays of tracer bullets. Liu Lien was singing softly:

> *"A woman never knows*
> *What a good man she's got*
> *Till after she turns him down . . ."*

"Where did you learn that, Liu Lien?"

"I was at Yale," he said, and it seemed strange in this half-darkness, the grey beard flowing over the patched gown, the eyes sparkling.

We could hear voices, and I think we were on edge, because the Japanese were still close—they said Kweiyang was in flames, but no one knew for certain, and then he knocked on the door and we were blinded by the sultry smoking candles. The house belonged to a professor of French who knew Gide and Valéry; there were photographs, great shelves of bookcases, laboriously transported from Peking. Clean-faced, sombre, with unshaved cheeks which seemed greenish-blue in this light, the professor came to welcome us.

"You're late," he said, motioning to a servant-girl to take our coats, and this was perhaps the oddest thing of all, for none of us could afford servants.

"We got lost in the moonlight," Liu Lien said.

"There was no moon yesterday, nor is there a moon tonight," the Professor went on. He looked hopeless and helpless, standing there; then his head shot out, you saw the fine lines of the cheekbones, the helplessness had gone.

Two generals, in full uniform, came out of the glare of the candles. I recognized a young poet, with glasses, the face with-

4

drawn, a modern Buddha; there was Wen Yi-tuo, the greatest of all; they said Lo Lung-chi might arrive, but no one knew whether he would arrive for certain. There were perhaps twenty or thirty professors, no students. The servant-girl brought in cups of hot tea, the leaves spinning on the surface of the water. Liu Lien rubbed his hands. We could hear the distant rumble of aeroplanes through the paper windows, and the courtyard outside was brighter than the candles.

Liu Lien said: "It's odd how one talks quietly during an air-raid. Do we think the Japanese can hear?"

There were prints on the wall, scrolls, uncomfortable cushions, bamboo chairs. The French professor's wife came in, wearing a slit skirt, walking delicately only in the places where there was a carpet, because she was going to have a baby. The conversation was desultory, and then Liu Lien stroked his beard more dramatically than ever and said: "Are you waiting for me, or am I waiting for you, gentlemen?" and I wondered why he spoke in English.

He went on, for they had suddenly become silent: "There is nothing exciting. We want to bring out a new paper. It will be about art—about the things we stand for. We have invited you because we want your help."

At any other time in the world's history, the statement would have meant little; but it meant a great deal tonight. We are being attacked by the Japanese; we are blockaded; the government has openly deplored the activities of this University, in spite of the fact that Lienta is the greatest University in China; we are the seat of a provincial government which is fighting against the Kuomintang, we are the headquarters of the largest American force in China; the students are openly demanding arms to beat off the attacks of the Japanese against the University, knowing that they will attack the University and destroy it before they destroy anything else, as Nankai was destroyed in the past. Even if there was not one word of politics in the paper, it would have implicit in it an attack on the government, of all Chinese governments. The legendary qualities for which the University stands, only because it harbours the greatest intelligence of China—these will be the subjects of the paper, for here we have men who have studied abroad and yet retain a consciousness of the value of Chinese civilization for itself, seeing themselves more clearly than the uneducated soldiers or the bureaucrats see themselves.

Liu Lien went on: "This is all, gentlemen. We can have our own

5

paper. We have reason to believe we can have our own paper. I want suggestions for the title, if you agree. I would like to know your views. I won't tell you of the urgency of the matter—there are some views which it is necessary that we should say aloud. Things are happening—it is unnecessary to go into details—which cry out for our voices." And then he was silent, and we heard the patter of anti-aircraft shells against a neighbouring roof.

More tea was brought. They were all talking at once, discussing it among themselves, the two generals leaning forward like children who have been allowed to stay up and hear their parents talking. The conversation had left Liu Lien, who brought some strips of paper out of his pocket and showed them to me—they were painted red and blue, and showed friendly Japanese offering to protect Americans. They had been dropped over Cheng-gung airport three or four days previously. An American soldier had given them to him, saying: "They're worth a buck each." "They've got a nerve," Liu Lien said. "They are playing psychological warfare, but it's much more complicated than that. It has no effect on the Americans, but it has a great deal of effect on the Japanese. They think they are playing the American game. Yesterday, when an American bomber flew down, it was followed by a Japanese fighter. The Japanese dropped a few small bombs, and now the Americans are annoyed —not at the bombs, but at the thought that the Japanese could follow them down so easily." Then he said: "If the Japanese come, I'm going to take to the hills—there's no life like a guerrilla fighter."

The lights went on suddenly; we all blinked; and it was odd, then, to notice how the colour was drained out of the faces of the impoverished professors by the electric light. In the candle-flames they looked better, the redness in the faces showing, but in electric light all the shabbiness of five years of exile came to the fore. Liu Lien was speaking to Wen Yi-tuo. They were strangely similar, talking forcibly, without gestures, trained by centuries to habits of calm; in their force there was calm. Wen's heavy black hair caught the electric light, and shone silver. He has killed the marionette. The fame he could have had, the fame he possesses, they seem to mean less than nothing to him. And like Liu Lien he must struggle for every penny he earns, knowing no greater bitterness than that he must be taken away from his books to carve seals at night for gain. Liu Lien has private pupils and does no teaching at the University, though everyone in the University knows him. One of his

6

pupils is the daughter of the Yunanese general who so inexplicably appeared tonight.

They were talking about the details of the paper. Liu Lien was asked to be editor-in-chief. Will there be articles on politics? There is some dissent, but gradually this disappears. Who will write them? Will they be signed, or anonymous? Will each professor take it in turn? There are so many things that must be said, so much cruelty which must be stamped down, so much justice which must be invoked. And then where will the paper be bought, and who will print it, and will it come out every week or every fortnight or every month, and how far will it represent the Democratic League and how far will it have a policy of its own? But the Democratic League has almost no policy, except the traditional liberalism of the Chinese scholars; they will build up their policy from the beginning, against all the nonsensical insults of Kuomintang tutelage—how long must the Chinese be under a reign of tutelage?—and against all private interests which insist that scholars shall have no right to speak, though traditionally they alone have the right to speak on all occasions. Essentially, it will be a paper representing the University. But how much of the University? How many of the professors are wise enough to realize that they have a part to play? Some, very few of the professors, are paid agents of the Kuomintang, editing Kuomintang newspapers, transposing all errors into the justice of a cause, bitterly conscious of their errors, yet hiding them. And so it goes on, backwards and forwards, conversation weaving through the cigarette smoke, the birth of a new paper. Liu Lien rubs his hands and puffs at his pipe, the same bulbous pipe which has long since turned his beard the colour of tobacco. He counts the number of people present. "Twenty-seven." Then he nods, the tremendous headshake, and says: "It's enough to start a revolution." Everyone smiles. More tea is brought in. An hour later, in the darkness, for there is no moon and no light in these dark streets behind the lake, we go out.

Someone said: "Have you thought of a title for the newspaper?"

Liu Lien laughs: "It will be the Awakening of China, or China Awake—something like that. Well, it's time."

Then we go out in small groups, back to our dormitories, hearing the plump rats squealing across the road, past the lake now empty of lovers, empty of all things, even of elephant tusks. It is three years since the Pacific War broke out.

7

December 8th . . . READING Katharine Mansfield's *Journal,* observing for the first time that all those who write journals are singularly and hopelessly in love with life: and the journals are written so that life can be lived again. Have you noticed how Katharine Mansfield writes with the sharpness of a blue-bird's wing, cutting into the sudden air the emotions of a motion? And then, too, though she was quiet and had about her the air of a nun at the perpetual sacrament, her extraordinary self-dedication. To remember this, and to dedicate oneself always.

December 10th . . . COMING away from the city, in the little cattle-truck that goes down to Indo-China (or would go down if the bridges had not been blown up), what relief, what delight in being away from the town. Here everything sparkled, the grass was greener than on the hills, the dewponds were full of ducks, the peasants walked hopefully again, attending their business, no longer screaming in the market-place. We found the professor at last in a small mud-hut in a mud-walled village, a short man with the inevitable blue gown, fresh-faced, happy in the comfortless house where there were too few chairs; but there were wall-paintings of Thibetan snows and animals, there was a carved Miao chest, there were his own books, and there were all the books he had forgotten to return to the University library. He entertained us happily, breathing in great gulps of air, forgetting if he ever remembered the small turmoils of the campus. Here there were no students to disturb him, no professors to talk to him—with his wife and his children he formed a self-contained world.

This was good, but even better was the journey on train at night, wedged up on the box-car, seeing the smoking dusk on the Serpent Mountain, not able to see the faces of the farm-boys and farm-girls who came into the cattle-truck, but knowing they were there—their laughter and their songs, but as it grew darker the songs ceased, there was a terrible silence, and soon we were passing near the airport, seeing the red flashes of the beacons, the black hulks of aeroplanes on the grounds, the silver mists and the revolving searchlights; and somehow, in the very intensity of the darkness and light, this western airport at night seemed perfectly appropriate to the setting. In the night it was easier for them to accept the presence of the airport. And then gradually they all turned slowly round, peering at the aeroplane slowly coming out of the clouds from India.

8

But most of all I remember the immense plain, like a plain in Hungary; the vastness of the sky; the clouds like smoking castles. . . .

December 14th . . . THE danger from the Japanese has gone. Somehow, no one knows how, all our fears have vanished, and we seem in spite of the government and in spite of the knowledge that the Japanese are near, and may come nearer, in a state of extraordinary *quietness*. Liu Lien says: "We know from the merchants. Prices have gone up again. So there is no danger." He said there was panic on the market when the Japanese were near Kweiyang, everyone was selling, only the most astute were buying. "Yet little was lost—the main thing is that we have faith in our mountains." I asked him what he meant. "Oh, it's such difficult country—they can hardly get through, and they are so tired of China."

Dreamed of Verdun, which I once visited. In Verdun there were legends; every battle produced its legends, and this was inevitable and necessary, for until the present wars there had never been so much suffering as at Verdun. Bergery was a reporter there; we would often discuss it together. He said: "It was vastness—the greatest imaginable vastness of suffering. It was then that I grew accustomed to blood. There were whole villages, whole towns of which nothing is now known. We do not know where they were, for every trace of them has been obliterated. This is the kind of thing that has not happened in China—the fighting has never been so great, and the villages were nearly always abandoned when the Japanese came near." But tonight I dreamed of the trench of bayonets, the trench of which nothing remained after the explosions except the bayonets which formed a long line above the earth.

December 15th . . . CHIANG SHIH-RO takes almost no part in politics, yet he remains among the greatest of the scholars here. It is perfectly possible to be a great scholar and at the same time to be disinterested in politics, on one condition: that the man should by his example give freely his criticism of the turmoil around us. And this Chiang Shir-ro does to perfection.

He is more sturdy than Wen Yi-tuo, more brusque, the brain less complex and passionate. He was educated in America, England and France; and seems to have learned most from France—certainly he speaks of France with greater affection. He lived in poverty and hope; now at last he has been given a small house in a garden full of

9

camellias, a perfect setting for a sociologist. Once he lived in a house outside the city, in the "bad lands." There, because the landlord wanted someone else capable of paying higher rent to take over the house, and he refused to leave for three weeks, he was beaten over the head by the landlord's hired thugs. He complains gently: "There is no law in this country," or still more gently: "Where have we come to, with our great civilization? Are we becoming animals?" He will talk for hours about the dying soldiers we see all day, the mismanaged hospitals, the corruption which hurts him as though it was a wound on his own body; and by loving him, one learns to love China. More and more I believe that the best remains in the more upright scholars, but what is disturbing is that so many professors have thrown in their lot with a government which possesses secret prisons; and very rarely nowadays do the professors talk of this great University as "a bulwark of democracy." But the students talk of it.

Wen Yi-tuo and Chiang Shih-ro are the two most popular professors. They are popular because their learning is profound, and also because of the example they set to others—fearless and ashamed, with no bitterness and great love for their country. While they are here, I shall stay. If they went away, I would feel that the main pillars of the University had gone—there would only be the threats from the government, the carefully rendered attacks by the Chen brothers of all that the University stands for. I would prefer Lienta to be bombed, as Nankai University was bombed, than that it should become the centre of a reaction. And yet every day the reaction gains in strength, and an uneducated militarist government pretends to give orders to the scholars. Wen Yi-tuo said this morning: "Oh God, if only the government had been to school. . . ."

December 16th . . . Hsun Tzu wrote: "All rites, if for the service of the living, are to beautify joy; or if to send off the dead, they are to beautify sorrow; or if for sacrifice, they are to beautify reverence; or if they are military, they are to beautify majesty." I fear it is only too true, but the ceremony for the dead soldier which one of my students observed last week was hardly in keeping with the ancient adage. Before he died on the Kweichow road, they stripped his clothes; then, because they were on a high hill, they simply rolled him down until his body reached the flooded fields. There was a small splash. "But it's better," the student said. "One should be buried in rice—then one grows again."

10

December 18 . . . CONTINUALLY talking with students and professors, seeing the shame in their faces, and then listening to the apologies that are made so often—we are weak, we haven't deserved this, but we must go through with it—knowing that the real China remains in the faces of the peasants and in the face of the land. So one lives out one's life in intolerable bitterness and hatred for those who are dragging China down, with pity for some, and no pity at all for others, believing always that the best must be upheld. . . .

December 19th . . . I AM beginning to lose my faith in many professors, though it is impossible not to reverence them. The breaking strain of a man can be calculated as one calculates the breaking strain of steel; and too few are possessed by those rare elements which make steel stronger. S. is the editor of a Kuomintang newspaper; he is also a follower of Sprengler, yet in the past he has written things which are abundantly clear, with vision and insight. He is still probably the greatest authority on the Chou Dynasty. But I like to think of him now, knowing the treason that goes on in his soul, as an old man with a fine taste in orange brandy which he distils himself, so that it tastes like Cointreau. Weary beyond words of the effort of making expenses meet under an inflation, he is beginning to dislike the students, to hate the hours necessarily passed in their company. He will say the strangest things of the students, he will curse them because the standard of education has gone down, because they are no longer so attentive as they were, nor so learned. "They don't attend lectures to understand," he said. "They are beginning to attend because it is something that has to be done. Pure scholarship is doomed." He said: "How right they were in the past to burn the books. The mountains of books—you cannot possibly believe how terrible is the sheer weight of books done by Chinese scholars." I can believe it is terrible in its sheer weight, but at the same time I cannot think of anything more terrifying than that someone should want them burnt. I argued for a while. He became quieter, more suspicious, and his eyes looked dreadful with worry. He complained of the latrines, which are so badly arranged that anyone who lives for long in his house inevitably becomes sick. His gown is faded, yet he is still strong. He said: "Scholarship—it is very nearly at the end. There is only one great historical scholar, and he is nearly blind. You think the Universities are the beginning of things, but I think they are the end of a long historical evolution —strength will come from somewhere else."

11

"Where will it come from?"

The eyes became glazed, and he said: "The peasants and the soldiers."

I left shortly afterwards, drunk almost with his orange wine, and more perturbed than I have been for a long time. I cannot see how or where strength can come from the soldiers.

December 20th . . . BUT when the sun sank and the lake was quiet, the day began. The whole street was alive with lights. There were the buddhist priests beside the coffin, the abbot on a raised red dais, candles everywhere; there were small stalls with acetylene lamps; there were the sounds of shouting and laughing.

I do not know why, but in China more than anywhere else there are nights like days. Inexplicably, a street that has been dull for weeks will suddenly take it upon itself to show its extraordinary delight in life and colour. There is no street in Kunming more unprepossessing than the Pei Men Kai. There, because it is near the North Gate, soldiers pass all day, and the Governor's horses are led out to pasture, and muddy jeeps will come to the American Consulate; but there are few shops, the street is hardly more than ten feet wide, there are almost no houses, only great barricading walls which shut out the sunlight, horse-droppings, dying soldiers. Yet tonight it blazed. There was a marriage in one house, a funeral in another, for some reason there were acrobats, and all the way down the street you heard the chink of mah-jong tiles and the songs of a flute-player. Most beautiful of all was the funeral. The priests wore red robes painted with gold characters, they rang bells, they lit candles round the coffin, they waved their wands and in the light of the red candles their faces were more than life-size. It was not a rich funeral, and perhaps the person who had died was of no importance; there were hardly any mourners, and as usual in China the mourners were only vaguely interested in the actions of the priests. Yet, where there had been darkness before, there was a blaze of red and gold light. And you heard the bells ringing and the drums playing all the way down the street, and this sound, mingling with the laughter and the songs of the wedding, seemed perfectly appropriate; it was as though the street had suddenly taken to itself the attributes of the gods, who take pleasure equally in the wildest joy and the most solemn grief.

12

Tomorrow there will be little festoons of coloured paper in the rain, there will still be a coffin and the boy who is married will still be in bed with his wife; but we shall know that once in our lifetime this street has been perfectly alive.

December 21st . . . THEY were talking of the rape of Nanking. There were three students, two of them girls. One wore her hair in pigtails, yet she looked older than the others, with a long mouth, thicks lips and heavy eyebrows. She moved gracefully, and I have noticed that she seems to move cautiously, often looking back over her shoulder even when she is on the campus. I remembered, too, that she was not a very good student, her essays were singularly sentimental and I think I have read altogether eight of her essays in which she describes her native village in Shensi. The Communists are there now, and it may be that like all students from Communist-occupied areas she is continually under suspicion. The other girl was eighteen, incredibly beautiful, looking more Spanish than Chinese, her face red and her body unbelievably lithe under the blue gown. The boy was a young engineer from Fukien, handsome in a pale way, without much expression in his face, and he possessed a singularly determined desire to please.

"The rape of Nanking was nothing," the girl with the heavy eyebrows said. "Oh, it was terrible enough. No one expected it. The Japanese said nothing would happen, and the people foolishly believed them. But in Shensi, if they come to a village before the villagers know they are there, then it is truly terrible."

I thought she wouldn't want to talk about it, for she must have known much about these places, yet she went on:

"I was fourteen—they came very early in the morning. I was sleeping, and suddenly my grandfather came to where I was sleeping and whispered: 'Don't say anything, don't speak,' and he put a handkerchief over my face and carried me quickly to the tunnel. There was an escape tunnel near the wall. He dropped me down—about ten feet, and I remember I groaned, and at that moment there was a tremendous hammering on the door. I thought my sisters were in the tunnel, but there was no one else except me. I could hear everything that was going on.

"I could hear things, but I couldn't understand them. The Japanese talked such bad Chinese. I heard the sound of wood breaking, and then screams—they were my elder sister's screams. I knew they were hers because she had once cut herself with a chopper.

13

And then she was begging for life. There was no sound from the other sister. I thought she was safe. There were only my two sisters, grandfather and grandmother—mother had died, and my father was in the army. But the screams went on. She was fifteen, and at fifteen you know how to scream loudest. I heard my grandfather's voice, very low and muttering, and then a shot and a great gasp of pain, and I knew it was my grandfather's voice, and still the screams went on. I wanted to get out of the tunnel. I could hear the floor-boards creaking rhythmically, now a creak, then another creak, and sometimes laughter, and once I heard a bottle being broken. Once, too, they threw a heavy lead weight down into the tunnel, but I was hiding under the shelter of boards and they did not see me.

"I went to sleep at last. The air's bad there, and you sleep a long time in tunnels. When I woke up it was night. There was no sound from the Japanese. I climbed up the tunnel. My grandfather was dead, shot through the temple. My sister was lying naked on the floor with blood all over her legs; she was alive and shaking her head from side to side like a mad woman, and there was no sign of my other sister. I started to whimper, she woke up and I helped to dress her, but she was very sick; and you could hear the sounds of people weeping in the next village. We never found my other sister. What was strange was that even when the Japanese were defeated, the girls would hardly ever go out of their houses, they had all been raped and they did not want to see each other. They preferred only to speak to old men."

December 23rd . . . THE dawn grey, chilly, the birds like razors cutting through the air. One of those rare days of our summer when the day opens like an unbelievable torment of greyness; and then the sun came through very slowly.

There are four cold days a year in Kunming; there are eight days on which the sun never shines; there are perhaps twelve days when it rains for more than half a day. But today seemed the worst of all days, with threatening clouds and the peculiar grey doom in the air. So we shivered, and those who had come from Peking remembered the little bronze foot-warmers, and the fur-lined coats; but most of our fur-lined coats have been sold for whoever benefits by the inflation. Yet suddenly we heard a bird singing, J. ran out into the courtyard and you could see all the greyness vanishing, pushed resolutely away by the sun which looked more than anything else

14

like a golden brush. And all day it was spring.

The weather is treacherous in China. The peasants know when it will rain, but they are not infallible. There was drought this year; they had predicted a year of plenty. There is supposed to be a Miao tribesman in the hills who controls the weather, there are almanacs which foretell when the rice should be planted and when it should be reaped, there are always villages which produce abundantly, and five miles away you will find a village where half the population is starving. J. said: "I asked the Miaos why they wore their colourful costumes. They say it is to make the plants grow— for rice and cabbages like bright colours. They have a story that when you are working in the flooded fields, the rice is admiring itself in the mirror of the rice-lake, just as the young people admire themselves; but if you wear bright colours, then they seek to imitate them, and if you are strong they seek to imitate your strength. So they do not allow the dying or the very ill to walk in their pastures."

In the old Chinese *Book of Songs* the pure enjoyment which the men have for working in the fields seems to come from the novelty of it all; only a few hundreds of years before these songs were written, the men were hunters of the stone age, and agriculture was something so new and beneficent that it turned them into singers. And looking at the Miao girls who ride down from their mountains to sell vegetables on the Kunming market, one wonders what songs they sing in their fastnesses, and how much more we should benefit if we heard them.

December 24th . . . Liu Lien was saying: "The revolt of Asia has assumed unimaginable proportions, and this time it has come to stay. We are tired to death of hearing what the west has to say about our revolt—they cannot understand us. We are revolting against our own feudal past and against the future which the west has to offer us. We are nationalists who are prepared to throw overboard our eastern nationalism at the first sign of federation. There will be large federations in the East. Asia for the Asiatics! Certainly this will come, but it will not come with any overlordship from Japan, nor from Russia—it will come of our own will, because we desire to be free. The Chinese Communists are Chinese first, Communists later—it would be the greatest mistake to underestimate the nationalism of the Communists. In its more intense form the nationalism of the Kuomintang is only one more example of the disease, telling us nothing of the patient, the boil erupting and the

15

sickness increasing. The important thing is that we know so little about nationalism that we are prepared to squander it in exchange for an understanding with other countries."

He went on: "Tell them that what is happening in Asia is a huge sociological experiment, and we shall never understand the present situation in Asia unless we realize that the peasants are sick of their insecurity, sick of their helplessness, sick of their lack of political consciousness; the young peasants are trying in every way they can to understand what is happening around them. You will see it in the army, where they ask questions fearlessly of their officers; you will see that they are reading more newspapers than ever, and they are trying in every way to discover why they are fighting. Their loyalties are small; their greatest loyalty is loyalty to their villages, their wives and children. Never have they been so badly treated, never have they suffered so much. Please do not believe that the peasants are patient. In ten years they will have political consciousness on a scale which has been absent from China for over two thousand years. Then, when they have political consciousness, things will begin to change—a change which will grow up from this generation, and owe its origin to the circumstances of the war."

I asked him about the newspaper. He said they had found a printing press, they had even obtained a permit from the Governor, and if one printing press was raided, they would find another easily. The first number of the paper had been announced and would come out in three or four days. There would be some trouble, of course. The paper was liberal and democratic. Simply because it was these things, the government would attempt to prove that it was communist. "We cannot write one word against this atrociously corrupt government without being accused of being communist." He smiled, and then he said: "You know—this government cannot go on much longer. There has been so much crime in its name," and then suddenly, as though he was still following the same line of thought, speaking in the same voice, he said: "I am following your Mr. Churchill. There is nothing—not even poetry—so delightful as painting. In painting one can forget everything—everything without exception."

December 25th . . . Perhaps because it is Christmas Day, I have been going through Bergery's letters. One day they may be published in full, for he was a prolific correspondent, and believed that his letters were more true to himself, and more justifiable than

16

the impersonal things he wrote for the newspapers.

As the war goes on, many of his statements seem to lack the emphasis they would have acquired later. Occasionally he was wrongheaded. He believed in the Kuomintang till late in 1939, and even up to his death he would speak of some Kuomintang members like Wang Wen-Lao with an affection which seems dubious now. He knew Gandhi, and found himself attracted and repelled, and something of the same magnetic reaction occurred apparently during his many interviews with Nehru—a great love for the man, and an incapacity to subscribe to the man's beliefs. He drew an unforgettable portrait of Chiang Kai-shek in the confusion of battle during the 1927 campaign. He reverenced Roosevelt, though he would say that power had corrupted him as it corrupted all others. He corresponded for years with Luce till one day a gap, which had been there from the beginning, broadened; and distrust began, yet five years later he would speak of Luce affectionately, saying that he was at least more human than most power-gatherers, and generous in most of his impulses. The long gallery of the great people he had known sometimes confused him; it pleased him to remember that they were less important than the peasants, the students and the professors he met in his wanderings. Fame had never touched him. "The first step to hell is to be famous; the second step to hell is to use your fame to increase it. And the third step is to believe that it is enduring." He was charitable in all his judgements, even to those who were least charitable; if you knew the man's heredity, you could forgive almost anything. Once he made a list of the crimes he hated most. The first was: distortion.

"Life is so easily distorted, we are such slender reeds, so easily twisted." The theme recurs often in his letters, and his fear of the power-gatherers lay precisely in their power to distort the elemental things of life. He kept copies of most of his letters. There was something of the priest in Bergery. The huge face, the heavy brooding shoulders, the suggestion of tragedy written on the unchanging face—one saw them and kept faith with the man. "I have been through battles," he said once. "Neither the publisher nor the news-editor has been through the things I have seen—how dare he distort what I have written? The distortion goes on. It is illimitable. Nothing one says or writes has the direct honesty I demand of it any more. Men write for Hollywood, or worse, but what can be better than writing for our times, for the people? The American journalists are responsible for the war, as the British are responsible, and the

17

Germans and the Russians. If there had been no dishonest reporting, there would have been no war." And again: "I am growing old, and do not care any more, but of one thing I shall care always, and that is the charity of youth to the old. The old sicken me. Look at the photographs of the famous, and then look at the photographs of young boys and girls—are they the same animals? Youth—yes, but to old age an unforgiving No." I remember I asked him why he was impenitently resolved to hate age, and then he laughed a little and said: "Because I am growing old."

I would argue with him for hours on the nature of love, for this was the abiding subject of his thoughts, perhaps because he was divorced from his wife. Again and again there would be the hammerbeat of the New England voice: "There must be innocence and praise and great patience—in this complex world we must act like lovers at all times, with a lover's patience and a lover's hate, but always with the lover's sense of praise." I would grow impatient; beginning to wonder whether love was enough, whether youth was enough, I would fling at him some wounding retort, saying that it was easy to love but infinitely difficult to understand. We lived in a world of complexities divorced from the simplicities of youth. He would answer: "Nothing is more complex than love, and love is the reason for its own existence, and for the existence of the world. Oh, I don't mean puppy-love. There is the love of a father for his daughter, and this is perhaps the most holy love. Or perhaps in middle age you meet a young girl, you know she is going to be married, and suddenly, quite inexplicably, you find that all your happiness depends upon her happiness, and yet you have never touched her and but rarely seen her. That may be more holy. There was comradeship in the trenches during the war, and that may be holier still. But of all loves the most holy is that of the old for the young." And now, while I hear the tone of his voice, I can still see him present by my side, the huge face noble in candlelight; but I see him less clearly as time goes on.

One reads old letters with a heart-breaking sense of detachment. These things *were*. They lived, and are not, and even if they were to be published, they would hardly live again with the intensity of their first writing. Now, while the war-light thickens, it is best to leave them alone—perhaps they will hurt less after the war, and certainly one will read them with less sorrow.

Yet it is worth while reading them, occasionally listening to the voice now dead, the lips now muddy, seeing the eyes which are no

18

longer eyes. I have no grief for him; so complex a person was immune from all personal sorrow, though his nights were nightmares of battlefields and hospitals. He liked to believe that he was immune from grief, for the same reason that he liked to believe that he was immune from old age—both hurt too much. Now, during this festival, reading over his letters, some of them I shall write down:

. . . As I see it, we have been torn too much by the luxuries of living; the invention of steam in 1750 has brought us to ease too easily. Better if like the Athenians we lived on "three or four olives, a dash of garlic and the head of a fish"—things would taste better, and the richness would remain. I know now that the only times I have felt the sheer glow of life was when I was starving; in New York, I eat too much, think too little and feel almost nothing at all. So I would have the young especially realize there are virtues in a *minimal moderation,* and I would have them remember too that all great men are libertines of the spirit, and chaste in their physical bodies. The church was chaste for good reason—I cannot think of any modern system which places the same significance on chastity. Yet chastity is a necessity always.

. . . Or else, like the lemmings, let us all drown in the midnight seas. We have gone far enough, God knows, so far that we have forgotten our heritage. Who, living in this century, knowing the accursed invention of steam which has paralysed all our lives, knows what the heritage is? What Europe was in its glory is foreign to us now, and yet the old China is still living and can be understood by the Chinese, it is in their blood, they know instinctively how much suffering, how many centuries of striving brought that civilization about. What can we know of Europe except by refining our sensibilities to the uttermost, developing our taste to the uttermost? I would have all children know what Europe was. More important than the kings of England or Denmark are the rose window of Chartres, the Apollo on the Parthenon, the suffering face of Akhnaton (where the disease was first visible which conquered Hamlet), the Ara Pacis in Rome, the small figures carved over Athenian tomb-stones, the knives and spears of the Saracens—perhaps a hundred other things. Over them all the brooding Beethoven and the liberated Bach. These they must know, or Europe will

19

perish. And they should know their own countrymen the peasants, and listen to them, and travel over Europe. For if history were rekindled in their minds, they would know the value of themselves. But midnight comes, the lightning flashes, the SS troops in black with the jagged lightning on the collar—these must not be remembered. . . . Oh, but above all remember the Greeks, not because they were possessed of a classical feeling, but because they reached the greatest heights, and suffered slavery, and yet saw clearly. I praise Apollo, the only god, for he is hardly a god, hardly more than a man singing, but so beautiful in the sun. And we should remember that our thoughts were pure then, not muddied over and confused with Lebanon and Christ—I as a Christian have the right to fulminate against Christ, and to wish he had been born nearer Mount Olympus. Then, then, Europe would have been stronger, richer, infinitely more *convincing*. And yet Christianity has taken so much from the Greeks that we have not lost wholly; even in the hymnal there are Greek hymns, the orphic spirit remains, they too knew the service which is perfect freedom, the bondage which is fashioned by breaking bars. Praising Christ, I curse Paul, who knew too much of Athenian dialectics, and I remember St. Jerome, who believed like the Greeks in the heroes, for he said the saints were nearer to God than the angels. Men! The value of men—this is what they believed in, not the power-gatherers, not the headlines, not the machines—men, men, men, men, men!

. . . My dear Robert, I have said so much about love in my previous letters, and it is time we defined our terms. By love I mean the "unwilled and necessary delight in others." I mean that when we see a man, we should have on our mental faces the expression of a hungry gourmet. "Here is a feast," we should say. "Let us eat it up, and let us remember our table manners. Let us gorge on him, swallow him, make him a part of ourselves, let us know him, let us above all find those places where we have common ground." The main task of the generation which confronts you will be the understanding between Asia and the West, and how shall we understand unless we love, unless we go to them humbly, unless we sincerely offer them our own wealth of technological knowledge in exchange for their vigour, their sympathy and their more sensual and mystical knowledge. We cannot go on as we are, and between the East and the West there is only one common meeting-place—the undiscovered territory of love.

Oh, this is trite—it has been said so often, and yet it is necessary that it should be said continually, and in the loudest imaginable voice. There is no mystery in the East. Somewhere, Joseph Conrad says: "The mysterious East, perfumed like a flower, silent like death, dark like a grave." Nothing could be more erroneous. There is no mystery, for their faces are open to us; there is no perfume, unless as I truly believe there is something pleasing in the smell of human sweat; there is no silence, for nowhere in the world are men more noisy than in the market-places of India and China; and there is no darkness, for the sun shines always. Let us at least not start from false premises. Let us at least begin at the beginning, in the places where men can understand one another. Let us be dedicated to the understanding of the East, for no task could be more urgent. And though we may not have love, then by dedicating ourselves to the greatest of all problems confronting us, love may come.

I say now very quietly, almost in a whisper, that we are in danger of losing all if we forsake the East at this hour. They may turn against us. They may realize how shoddy are the premises under which some of us believe in ourselves. Jawaharlal Nehru, Gandhi, Sun Yat-sen—those names which are instinct with life, which blaze like the eastern suns, these are the things which move the East. I say "things" advisedly, for they are almost impersonal. And on what slender threads has developed their hatred for the West. Once in a train Jawarharlal Nehru overheard General Dwyer recounting his successful massacre at Amritsar. On such slender threads we have our being in the East. Always we are overheard, always they see us when we think we are invisible, always we give ourselves away; and if we have no love, how shall we endure there? You may say: "We cannot help ourselves." Then I say that if we do not help ourselves in time, the East will rise up against us, and in sheer man-power overwhelm us. And let us not blind ourselves by believing that we do not deserve to be destroyed. If we continue as we are behaving now, we deserve to be destroyed.

So, though not many years are left to us, at least we must make our choice—and the choice is between love and the opposite of love, which is not hate, but indifference. You say in your last letter that "love and hatred are both a weariness to flesh and spirit—better that there should be detachment." How wrong you are! What is important is that we must endure, and by enduring love; and hatred is a kind of love; and detachment was well enough in the East four thousand years ago, when there were few enough people, when there was not this desperate need to love. Our cities are Buddhas. New York is detached. London is nearly detached, and Shanghai is wholly detached; but for ourselves we must love from the very core of the heart or perish. And you ask, too, how one should show one's love, and surely there is nothing simpler—one must help all those with whom one has any contact, be charitable and merciful always, be understanding, seek to see the spirit which is in all people, and the beauty which is in all people, and never to hurt either the spirit or the beauty, and always to praise it. For people are the things of which our lives are made, and nothing is more holy than the community of people except perhaps the community of children.

I have been sick. The same old devils plague me; and the most ferocious of all devils is the thought that because we have not in our generation loved enough, the generation that follows will not even understand that such a thing exists and is necessary. We go by thin threads. For a thousand years, following Lebanon and Greece, we had this vision; now it seems that we have come to the end, and must begin all over again. *Ora pro nobis.*

Sometimes he would send these strange tortured letters, but more often they were parts of his unwritten autobiography, descriptions of the early days of mobilization during the first World War, a journey through Spain under Alfonso, some scandal or other he had picked up in Nigeria or America. He had a particular passion for the Negroes, and made a prolonged journey through the deep south. He admired people who "were in possession of the fountain of life," and praised the Russians and the French and the Chinese for this reason; he found as he grew older less life among the British and the Americans, but this was perhaps due to his inveterate habit of distrusting his own stock. He was proud and haughty in some moods, saying that since he was himself descended from princes it was understandable that he found the aristocracy

22

intolerably weak-willed; the strains had crossed too often. He envied those who were descended from yeomen or peasants. Most of all he envied musicians, and he said once: "I would prefer to live among the Balinese—the rest is idiocy. One should live in conformity with nature and the physical body, for there is no other happiness." But towards the end of his life the moods and vapours vanished completely, and when he died on his mountain-top in Szechuan there was composure and serenity in his face, and it might almost have pleased him if he had seen himself dying.

December 27th . . . SHE was a girl student, wearing a jade necklace, and I think I have mentioned her before in this diary. Even now, though she will soon be married, she can hardly be more than eighteen, very lithe and slender, with blue-black hair and cherry-red cheeks, walking with an animal grace which is common among the peasant-girls but rare among students. She had been a murderer. Once when I asked her about it, she very naturally burst out crying; but this evening the whole story came out, not from her, but from a boy who had taken part in what later came to be known as the Tientsin massacre.

"What you must understand is that in the early days of the war, terrorism against the traitors was unorganized, and the bravest of the terrorists were the young students from middle-schools. Perhaps they were brave because it never occurred to them that they might be arrested, or perhaps they were more cunning—knowing they were young and the police were sympathetic sometimes, they preferred to do the killing rather than allow others, who would be tortured. At that time Chen Ti-kung was the Salt Collector in Tientsin. We knew he was working with the Japanese, and this in itself was not perhaps sufficient, for thousands of people were working with the Japanese. What made him dangerous was that he was in a position of great responsibility, very close to the Japanese general staff, and he had given orders for the arrests of some Chinese.

"It was decided to murder him. This happened one day when the students were eating ice-creams. We were eating, and then someone said, 'Oh, we must kill him—it is intolerable that we should breathe the same air with him.' So it was decided. We followed his movements, and we bought guns and ammunition through our house-servants. You ask them to buy something, and without batting an eyelid they will always obey if you have the money. They

23

said we could buy three revolvers for thirty-five dollars. We gave them thirty-five dollars, and they bought us six revolvers. We were ready then. We would send guards to wait outside his official mansion, and we would spend hours in the ice-cream shop mapping out his movements, so that we knew at every hour of the day or night exactly where he was.

"Then one of the students saw his car outside a cinema. The cinema was showing *Gunga Din*. We had seen the film, and we remembered that towards the end there is a prolonged burst of gunfire between the English soldiers and the tribesmen. This gave us time. We telephoned to all the other students to come, and mapped out a plan of campaign. The campaign was very simple. All of us were to enter the cinema armed, and all of us were to try to shoot Cheng Ti-kung during the time when there was fighting on the screen. It was as simple as that.

"But it was very dark inside the cinema and we couldn't find him. Then K. decided there was only one thing to do. You know that on the side of the screen in China there is another oblong screen where the speech appears in Chinese words. One of the students went to the cinema telephone and called up the manager. Would he please insert into the slide the announcement that Mr. Cheng Ti-kung was urgently wanted in the manager's office. The student spoke as though he was speaking from the Salt Commissioner's own office. The manager complied. The slide was put on. Still no one came to the manager's office, but it was noticed that a man in the third row had half reached out of his seat. His wife had pulled him back. We couldn't be quite sure whether this was our man. We telephoned the manager's office again, asking that a more urgent notice should be thrown on the screen. We were lucky, because at the moment when he rose from his seat there was a fusilade of machine-gunning on the screen. Three of us shot at him. The back of his head was blown off. His guards began firing. The whole place was in confusion. One of the girl students found herself trapped into a corner by a foreigner—a Swede. She brought the butt-end of her revolver down on his head, and they say he was killed—he had a very thin skull. Half the audience was struggling to get away, and this helped us, because all the students managed to escape; and we were not so stupid as to throw our revolvers away—they would come in useful afterwards. I remember the smoke and the fumes and the film still going on, and then two minutes later we were out in the sunshine. The Japanese never found us. They arrested hun-
24

dreds of people. If they had looked in the ice-cream shop, they would have found us eating ice-creams."

December 28th . . . READING, and suddenly realizing that the old mediæval words: *oil, bread, hunger, frost, lumber, birth* and *death* retain to this day their Biblical flavour and resonance, so that we read in two languages, one which was common to Shakespeare and to his ancestors and the other which is more nearly our own. Weary of our library, we are beginning to use armed services editions, finding there nearly everything we missed before—a wider choice and a more excellent text of the classics. And then, this afternoon, during one of those visits which are the plague and delight of professors, a student said: "What does 'what the heck' mean?" Mercifully, I was just able to recall Hecate, the Goddess of Darkness, but if he had asked a moment later I might not have recalled. He smiled, a smile so delightful than all goddesses of all darknesses are banished for ever.

December 29th . . . THE sun set slowly, with virgilian splendour, with a kind of relentlessness which I have never seen before. The shadows were thicker, the red scarps of the mountain more wildly restraining the sun, as though they alone of all things in this valley desired to be remembered; and because the peasants say the mountain is like a dead man lying on his back with his face to the sun, it seemed all the more proper that it should exert itself against the sunset. The whole sky was a sheet of luminous purple clouds; the birds were silent; avenging angels were awake; all would be destroyed. But no, the red scarps lingered. The whole of Kunming, all the biscuit coloured walls, all the green lakes and marble stones, all had disappeared into the frost of night; and long after the mountains had really disappeared, their fiery redness was visible on the retina of our eyes.

December 30th . . . A FAILING sadness as the year ends. This is the last page of one of my notebooks, and there is room enough only to quote one sentence of Bergery's, to be remembered always: "Love, love, love—how often have I rejoiced in these words, repeating them in all the languages I know, a word which sounds admirable in every language except English, and most admirable in Sanscrit—*ananda*—a word which alone should be sufficient to exorcise war."

25

1945

January 1st . . . ALL things are hungry: the earth is hungry for rain, the moon for the tides, the sun for colour and the young for each other. And then, this evening, sitting down to the table for dinner, noticing how hungry was the white porcelain bowl for the goldfish painted on her.

January 3rd . . . As USUAL the new year was a riot of green and yellow splashing over the lakes and willows, turning them into crystallized rainbow colours. We had half-heartedly expected it; there were storms yesterday, the aeroplanes circling low all night, and sometimes through the breaking clouds you saw their green and red lamps, but more often you only heard them—those broken roaring sounds which are the signs of our coming victory. We have, I am afraid, little enough hope in the victory. We talk all night of victory this year or the next, and for ourselves the only hope is that it will bring us to Peking; and even then we know that Peking has nothing to offer us except skyrocketing prices. We shall be as lost in Peking as we are in Kunming. Will they never realize that what we want is not peace, but the place which holds all the associations of our youth and happiness?

And then think of this in terms of the millions who have been uprooted from their homes; how eagerly they dream of returning to their scarred and bombed houses, how devoutly they pray for the small orchard which they saw through the tears of their paper windows, the rivers where they swam, the places where they have left their faint marks on the earth. We are featherless chickens who

27

sigh for the places we knew and the corn we pecked in the past. And everywhere, all over China, there is this desolate dreaming for a past that will never return. I wrote once in a book written on the eve of the disaster in Europe: "We must be stern, unsentimental, rigorous . . ." I doubt it now, remembering that the only happiness comes from sentiment, and rigour and sternness are both vices to drive us away from ourselves.

I remember reading somewhere that Conrad had a certain scorn for landsmen, saying they did things badly because there was too much safety in their lives and not enough responsibility. They knew that whatever they did, their little boat was not going to capsize or spring a leak and sink with their wives and families. He could not have written this today. We are seamen now, or if we are not seamen, we are conscious of being at sea. There are elementary lessons to be learned, but we have not learned them. We have not learned this: *We must be stern, unsentimental and rigorous to ourselves, but not to others.* For ourselves there is one law, but in our relations with others there is a simpler law which overrides everything else—kindness. It is, and will be, as simple as that.

January 4th . . . AMAZED, as always, by the differences between the thought of East and West. The Chinese love the sun so much that when they make paintings there are no shadows—everything is seen at high noon. No Chinese would say, with Sir Thomas Browne: "For the world, I count it not an inn, but an hospital; and a place not to live, but to die in." Hence their industry, their tireless enjoyment of life, even the worst forms of life. Hence, too, and this is more important, their delight in human intercourse, their belief that nothing is of greater importance, their regard for the family with all its attendant evils. I remember once coming across a river in Szechuan with the poet Liang Tsong-tai at sunset and being delighted because a student called from the bank a line of Liang's poetry: "Our happiness is to ride in the setting sun." I thought the sentiment was Chinese, but even in the later ages of the T'ang Dynasty, when poets were obsessed with "the tears dripped by candles," no Chinese could have spoken in this way without having lived in Europe; and Liang Tsong-tai is essentially a Frenchman writing in his mother-tongue. The Chinese have no love for shadows. For them life remains simple, a thing which obeys the seasons and refuses obedience to anything else. They have not the depth or complexity of the Indians, who are in love with darkness; they

28

are the children of high noon, seeing everything clearly against the burning sun.

January 8th . . . I HAVE never met anyone so dedicated to scholarship as C. He has a devotion which is almost frightening, he spends nearly every hour of the day on his books, dreams of books, dreams of calligraphy, dreams of the university. He deserves the assistant professorship which has just been given to him, but precisely because he is a scholar he is beginning to be afraid of his responsibilities.

"In the first place it is highly unlikely that I shall be able to wake up in time for the seven o'clock classes. The landlady will wake me, there is an alarm clock, I have asked the student next door to wake me, but think what would happen if the landlady were ill, or the student somewhere else, or the alarm clock failed to go off. I am at the mercy of my surroundings. There is a man upstairs who scrapes with his hob-nailed boots on the floor—I cannot work when he is there. Or the wind blows through the paper windows—impossible to work. Or someone comes to see me. I go to sleep, I wake up, I read, I write. I have come to the stage when the only thing that matters is books; I can defend this belief; there is surely nothing so important as producing perhaps a few poems, a few pages of good criticism, and yet it is a terribly empty life."

I suggested it would be good to fall in love.

He thought for a while. "Yes, it would be good, but try to imagine a young Chinese scholar falling in love when he knows everything about it from books. There will be nothing new. It's terrible. I know everything, and I have suffered nothing except the wind and the hob-nailed boots."

January 9th . . . THE imperial minister Tso Tsung-tang during the Ch'ing Dynasty was asked by Sir Robert Hart what he thought of western influence in China. He answered: "You are all too anxious to awake us and start us on a new road, and you will do it; but you will regret it, for once awakened and started, we shall move faster and farther than you think; much faster than you want." But is it true? We have heard so often that China absorbs everything—customs, ways of thinking, peoples and even whole cultures. We are reminded that the Chinese are the oldest nation on the earth, but are they? Like every other race, they are a medley of all races, with here a face which is essentially Turkish, there a face which comes from Burma. China is not homogeneous: each province has its own culture, its own way of looking at things, and none of them have understood or absorbed the west except in the most superficial way. The whale can swallow everything except the west, but the west sticks in its mouth and will not be absorbed without a revolution; and it may happen that the whale, with the west in its mouth, may die of hunger.

Helplessly, in the last two years, and mostly in the last six months, we have watched China or rather the Chinese Government incapable of solving the simplest problems. There is resolution, but nothing with which to resolve. The government is run by a single family; the old classic virtue of family affection has become unalloyed nepotism; the best are hindered; the merchants unbelievably corrupt. All this has happened at the time when the country could least afford the luxury of the old virtues. Efficiency is at a discount. In the greatest days of our danger, there is a supreme carelessness over the fate of the people. In the days of the Chou Dynasty Po-yi dwelt on the shores of the North Sea and waited for the world to grow clean. But we cannot wait any longer.

China is awake, but still stunned. For the Chinese the best thing that ever happened was the defeat of the Americans in Hawaii and of the British in Burma and Malaya. For a while, after so much weariness of battle, they sat back and preferred to see the allies lick the wounds inflicted on them by the Japanese, conscious that China could still withhold the Japanese by doing nothing; till the best among them revolted and attempted to make China independent of foreign aid. The self-reliance, which was vanishing or had already vanished, returned again among the technicians, and it is to them and the universities that we owe the best things in China. The war has shown one thing: China cannot live with her old virtues as a major power. In this new world nearly all her virtues are vices.

January 10th . . . THE fantastic confidence which the Americans have in the Generalissimo. . . . But why? I have no confidence in him. I have no confidence in one man, and least of all have I confidence in dictatorship. The dictators are like the Egyptian statues, so much larger than life that we assume they are permanent and all-knowing. But does he know that for the seven hundred millionth time a soldier has come up the Burma Road to die in rags and filthiness, his body like a bone, wracked with malaria, with pus
30

coming out of his eye-socket and moving so slowly that he seems to be someone moving through a nightmare more terrible than any invented in this war. "We have ten million soldiers," an official told me, when I complained that these men from Burma should not be left to die. "Does it matter about one soldier?"

No, it doesn't matter. In the long run there will be no changes in China because he has been abandoned. The land will still be the same, the people will be the same, countless millions will still be born, there will still be smoke from the chimneys and the fields will still be reaped. But when it happens that officialdom is utterly divorced from the people, when the food of soldiers is taken from them by their officers, when the people have no more confidence in those who have raised themselves to power, when nepotism and corruption are the rule and the best are starving, how can I praise an incompetent government and pretend to admire it? In this country I admire only one thing: the overwhelming greatness of the people who have suffered too long.

January 11th . . . WE LIVE near the Thibetan border, and sometimes we are reminded that we are not far from Lhasa. Pierre Goulart has come down from Lichiang, and all evening he has been talking about the grace of the tribesmen who come to market. He stutters in broken English, and simply because his English is broken we are conscious of his excitement, so that even when he talks of the monks running their prayerwheels by electricity, tapping out prayers on typewriters, of cabarets in the holy city of Thibet and of highwaymen equipped with the latest Bren guns, it is difficult not to disbelieve him.

"Ah, but the best time of all is market day. The Thibetan boys come and get drunk round the fires. They sing. They dance through the flames. It is camaraderie—the real camaraderie. I have gone with them. I, too, sing. They come to my house, and sing for me, and sometimes they bring girls, and they sing for me. It is better in Thibet. If you look at a girl, her lover does not knife you. In Lichiang it is terrible—one look, one knife. And then in the evening, the dancing. It is endless. Such grace. Such beauty. The cities are terrible. In Lichiang all the races of the east come together, and they tell stories to one another, and the women run after the men."

More and more often I find myself dreaming of those snow-white mountains near Thibet where no one ever thinks of the war, because the war is so distant, and even irrelevant. According to

31

Goulart there are almost no traces of the west there. They live their lives simply and naturally, so that he too lives simply and naturally, saying that he is afraid of only one thing—there is a tribe ruled by women who lust after white men, and he is in danger of being seduced by them; and when we burst out laughing and wonder why should he be afraid, he talks endlessly and charmingly of the feats of the Thibetan monks who can remain naked in the coldest weather, of the footprints of giant bears and the blue wines of Lichiang, which are like fires.

January 12th . . . A NEW letter from Bergery, perhaps the last that I shall ever find, written when he was in India in 1940. I remember I read it through, and then forgot about it, and tried to find it later when odd phrases kept recurring to my mind:

"We are, my dear Robert, standing on the edge of time looking out over eternity. You may not realize it in Singapore—it must be difficult to think of India in Singapore—but after being here, I can only say that the first tremblings of the new order are visible here. It is not the fear of Japan which has caused this, nor our failures nor even our successes, it is something which goes beyond all these which has caused *the contempt for the west.* We have failed, but not where we think we have failed. We have failed precisely where we thought we were most strong. We have failed because we have never, except in rare moments, understood the East.

"They cry out for independence, these Indians, and their present government is in no sense capable of understanding their desire. They can say and do say that if India were independent now, it would be wide-open for invasion from Japan, it would no longer be a fortress for the allies, Hitler is advancing across Europe and hopes one day to meet the Japanese in India, the Indians are incapable of forming their own government and the communal quarrels would remain unsolved. All these things are true, but for the Indian they have no shadow of importance. For them the important thing is that they have learned that our scientific experiments, our ways of thought, our accounting, our insistence on a special kind of efficiency and management have not produced the kind of happiness they want. God knows what kind of happiness they want, but it is not ours. They are in love with sex, with the earth, with high mountains, with the dust and smells of India; they are not in love with the west. This is why Gandhi is so great a power. To everything we have brought to India, he raises a quiet protesting Nay.

32

"This is all I have learned, and perhaps it is enough for the moment to realize that we are hopelessly lost in this country. I went to India first when I was twenty-four. It was like paradise. It was paradise precisely because it was incomprehensible. But now the things we do not know are immeasurably more important than the things we know. It is no longer a question of the Indian soul, of the Indian way of thinking, of the Indian interpretation of the world: it is a question of how we shall use the vast powers we possess in a world where the peoples are unknown. I insist on this. *We do not know peoples,* we do not even know persons, and the major task of your generation will be to return to the simplest and most difficult of all things—the understanding between a man and a man. And precisely here lies the difficulty, since we have confused ourselves with other issues—we are endlessly confused, because we insist first (such is our tragic heritage) on believing that the greatest problem lies in the understanding between a man and a maid.

"We cannot have peace unless we understand one another, but how shall we understand one another except by sacrificing ourselves in the attempt? To climb Everest, to travel to the Antarctic is easier than to understand a man, and when we have understood a man we cannot express our understanding in words. How shall we say that a man is naked before us, and we are naked before him? How shall we say we have stripped ourselves to flesh and bone? How shall we be sure of our understanding? We, who have lost the power of receiving the sudden naked impact of *things,* are still more lost when we consider the sudden naked impact of men. I do not want to torment you with the endless difficulties involved, except to say that the first of all difficulties is that men are so rarely naked: they are clothed in history, customs, manners, the habits of their ancestors, the inviolable laws of their temperaments and approaches to the world. We deal with men too roughly. We have lost those delicate antennae which once must have been ours. We are resolved to short-cut all problems, since we are conscious of the difficulties; and we have no humility. I came across long ago a phrase of Dino Campagni, which I hope I can remember accurately: *Niente vale l'humiltà contra alla grande malizia.* Humility is of no avail against sheer evil. This is true. We have no reason to be humble before Hitler. But we have every reason to be humble when we are faced with our fellow-men.

"The island of Elephanta has been taken over by the Royal Navy, but by luck I was allowed to wander into the famous caves and see, by the dying light, the three-headed God who stands with his immense shoulders in the darkness between the pillars. I cannot convey to you my wonder at its perfection. Art had not reached such sublimity before or after. Here is the impersonal raised to the sphere of ultimate abstraction, and yet how delicately he gazes at us, and forgives. No bombs can destroy him. He is shielded for ever. On the left is the Destroyer, with the cobra in his raised hand; on the right is the Preserver offering nothing except the remote benediction of a smile; and in the centre is the *Trimurti* himself, the great head weighed down with thoughts of creation. Of this I am sure. The act of creation is continually about to be performed and in a moment will continually reveal itself, and what is wonderful is that the conception of the act of creation should have been endowed with so much majesty and repose.

"India gives me hope for the world. There is a vastness in this country which is not terrifying; on the contrary it is delightful beyond words to come upon men who realize their insignificance and immaturity when they are surrounded with such visible evidence of the splendour of creation. If there were Himalayas in America, no one would dare to build skyscrapers. In India the rains are torrential and sweep the land into the sea; the sun burns you till you scream for mercy. Perhaps it is the same in Malaya. But let me say that it is in these countries of great extremes that I have the highest hopes for the future, for in those countries men must realize their essential and necessary humility.

January 15th . . . HE IS tall, well-formed and he has one of those long sensitive faces that you find in portraits of the *boddhisattvas* which Sir Aurel Stein discovered buried in the Gobi. He has come back from America, where he spent a year at Yale delivering occasional lectures on Chinese philosophy and amusing himself vastly. He is one of our most senior professors, and one of his eyes is nearly blind, for which reason he wears a black patch, but when he removes the spectacles you do not notice that he is blind, you notice only that one eye looks innocent and the other superbly wicked. He smiles often. He speaks English better than most Englishmen, and writes it on the rare occasions when he writes anything with fiendish command of the medium. He likes telling stories. He lectures abominably. He sleeps through faculty meetings with the felt hat which he always wears tipped over his eyes. He flew back yesterday over the Hump, sick and weary after the long journey, but before he went to bed he had time to tell one story of his wanderings.

He was delighted with America, even though every eye specialist gave him different opinions about his eyes, but what delighted him above everything else was going into a restaurant where, since he wore a black patch and was wearing clothes which remotely resembled military uniform, he was taken for a Chinese guerrilla leader on holiday. The restaurant keeper refused to accept his alibi. Unthinkable that he was not a guerrilla leader. Speeches were demanded of him. He made them. The drinks were on the house. He was tempted to describe impossible adventures. He was asked to sing the Chinese national anthem. And then, as everyone came round afterwards to congratulate him, he slipped quietly out of the restaurant forever.

January 18th . . . How in God's name does one teach English prose? We are still on holiday, but it is time to prepare lectures for the coming term. There will be few lectures: you cannot teach English prose by standing in front of a blackboard and scribbling with chalk. There will be tutorials, of course. Out of our mythical library, we shall find some books for them to read, and somehow it will be possible to convince them that there are good prose-writers and bad, and it is better for them to read the good.

Yesterday I came across in one of those voluminous notebooks which follow me round the globe almost the finest of all the prose passages I know; but I do not know whether I dare quote it to them. It was written by an illiterate lover and was found on the sands in Sidmouth in 1887:

> *My Dearest Marey,—i be verry well and appey to inform you that i be very well at present and i hope you will be the same dear Marey—i be verry sorry to hear how as you dont like your quarters as I chant be able to look on your dear face so offen as i have done dearest Marey, pure and holy meek and loly loveley Rose of Sharon. Dear Marey, dear Marey i hant got now know particler noose to tell ye at present but my sister that marryd have got sich a nice lettel babey, and i wish how as that our littel affare was settled and we had got such a nice lettel dear two.*
>
> *Dearest Marey I shall not be appey till then Dearest Marey pure and holy meek and loly lovely Rose of Sharon. Sometimes*

35

i do begin to despare as i am affraid our not will never be tide but my Master have prommist i how as that when i git ye he will putt ye in the Darey yard to feed the Piggs and ge ye atin pens a week Dearest Marey puer and holey meek and loly loveley Rose of Sharon. i be coming over to-morrow to by the Ring and you must come to the stayshun to mete me and bring a pese of string with you the size of your finggar and be shure you dont make A miss take dear Marey.

Father is A going to ge us a beddsted and Granny a 5 lb. note to by such as washin stand fier irons mouse trap and Sope, and wee must wayte till wee can by carpetting and glass crackery ware and chiny. Dearest Marey pure and holy meek and loly lovely rose of Sharon, i be very appy to say our old Sow As got 7 young uns laste nite and Father is a going to ge us A roosester for our Weding Brakefast Dearest Marey pure and holey meek and loly lovely Rose of Sharon. So no more at present from your fewture and loving husband.

But how can one convince a Chinese student, brought up on obedience to grammatical constructions, to write with that immediacy and brilliance?

January 19th . . . THE fear has gone. Though the Japanese are still near, and more airfields are being blown up by Americans who are retreating through the incompetence of the leadership of the Chinese army, for some reason we are no longer afraid. We know in our bones that the Japanese have lost the war. They can build their railway from Singapore to Peking, but we know that the railway will never assist them to defend their continental empire. The fear went as suddenly as it came. It may come again, but it will never come with the same force or authenticity. We felt in December that the Japanese could do with us as they pleased. With ten more men at the right place they might have thrust down to Kunming; with another ten men they might have thrust through Szechuan; but they failed to take advantage of the masterly inaction of the Chinese. The Chinese peasants and soldiers are blameless. They did what they could, and died by the hundreds of thousands. But for those who led them, for the merchants who filled up their cars and made their plans to escape to Kansu—but what would be the good of escaping to Kansu when the rest of China had fallen? —for the unthinking and the unspirited, and the careless above all,

36

there should be no mercy. Nor will there be any mercy in the hearts of those who fled from Kweilin.

We know that the people can stand intolerable strains, we know that there is in them an unyielding strength, but these things give us no comfort. It has become a *cliché* that the Chinese can bear everything without complaint. It is true that they do not complain. They have learnt over the centuries that complaint leads nowhere —there is no one to complain to. But what if they should ever find someone or something to whom they could complain? What if they, the most democratic of all people in their daily behaviour, should find a government *responsible to them?* (Then the prizes of government would be less, the responsibilities almost intolerable, but at least there would be an end to their silence, and their unendurable sufferings.)

January 20th . . . STORM. The lightning reared above the mountains; the rain emptied itself; everything blue, silver or jet black, the trees and buildings black, the lake the clearest imaginable blue. And afterwards, when we were shuddering and licking our wounds, the memory of the clear colours of lightning, which are clearer than anything seen in sunlight. . . .

January 21st . . . HE IS a young student who talks very slowly, not because he does not know English well, but because he likes the sounds of English and is anxious to pronounce them as perfectly as possible. He was in Burma before the war, and therefore knows more about English ways, and is not often critical; it amuses him to compare the English with the Chinese, and somehow he has managed to see us both from the heights of his impassivity.

"In Burma it seemed to me that the English were perfectly just— they were almost inconceivably just—but they were not human. If you are human you are not just. The Chinese are human, therefore they have no conception of justice at all. A merchant was arrested. It happened to be a Chinese merchant. He was put on trial for some offences I have forgotten—probably something connected with the customs. The trial continued. It was certain that the merchant would not be acquitted. He sent a message to the judge offering a large bribe. The judge mentioned this in his summing-up, and said that the four years imprisonment that he had originally contemplated would be increased to six years because the Chinese had offered a bribe. It was not just, but it was justice. A Chinese would

37

either have accepted the bribe or forgotten about it altogether; an Englishman refuses and remembers.

"We have no belief in law—hence all our troubles, all our civil wars, all our corruption. But how shall we escape this? The Chinese are democrats in their private behaviour to an extent unknown abroad, but in their public behaviour they are all anarchists. And this is the problem—to make out of the anarchy we instinctively desire a state of law.

"So all the way through Chinese history we have had the *Fuhrer-Prinzip*. Power has come from the top, from the Emperor or his ministers, from the Generalissimo who has acquired in his old age something of the terrible efficiency of the Emperors. To us, the Soong Dynasty is a reality. But it *must* end. If the Soong Dynasty lasts out this war, then we shall have learnt nothing from America or Great Britain. Hideously, incompetently, we try to struggle on in the manner of our ancestors. Somehow we must strike a balance between justice and humanity, and the odd thing is that in all our philosophies it is not justice which is studied, but something infinitely remote from justice—the conception of Heaven which obeys its own laws."

It took an hour for him to say this. We wandered down many long roads and went across many fields, but there was no shelter in any of them. These young Chinese, with no experience of democracy except in the election of their student officials, have a desire for democracy which is like a great hunger. They do not understand it. They do not know the patience which is required, the almost illimitable forbearance which is necessary. But like hungry animals they go in search of their watering-places, and they know that in the end there can be no hope for their country till the government is responsible to the people, and to the people alone.

January 22nd . . . THE storm continues. Black lightning against a white landscape. The thunder rumbling against the West Mountain, which was no longer bright red but a kind of fluorescent green. And sometimes, inexplicably, in the silence after the thunder, the birds screaming madly and the streets deathly still.

January 23rd . . . THE storm ceased suddenly at two o'clock in the morning. Lying awake, listening to the dying patter of the rain on the tiles and suddenly realizing that the Chinese love the sound of the rain on leaves and stones for the same reason that they
38

love calligraphy. The sound is colourless, music reduced to its essentials, the music of the earth and water and the clouds. In China water is the dominant element; and it is the flow of water over stones which has given the patterns for their calligraphy. There are different stories about how the calligraphy arose. Some claim that it came from watching the stars, others that it developed from the footprints of birds in snow, but the oldest story of all explains that the famous trigrams were seen on the back of a tortoise rising from a river. Wherever you find yourself in the ancient legends of China, there is always water—the floods drained by the Emperor Yu, the tortoise rising through the river, the Tung-T'ing Lakes where Chu Yuan was drowned in his grief. And tonight, looking out in the clear moonlight, and seeing all China as one vast silver lake. . . .

January 26th . . . THERE has been some kind of entrance examination half way through the academic year, and some new students have suddenly appeared. Damn! They make me nervous. For a week these new students will look like expressionless muttonheads. For another week I shall suspect them of glimmerings of intelligence. After the third week I shall know them well enough to know that they understand far more than I do. There is always at first that unbreakable iron wall; and then gradually the wall breaks down, we take our courage in our hands and somehow, without knowing what we are doing, we find we have broken through. In three months four or five of those new students will have become closer to me, and dearer, than if they were my own children.

What pleases me above everything else is that they are at last looking healthier. There was a time when they all looked sick and pale—not all, but so many of them that the others were coloured by their prevailing sickness. The school infirmary was full. They were going down with typhus every day. They returned with bruised eyes, and a great weariness, unable to concentrate, unable to read by the dim electric lamps. The standard went down. We began to lose hope. We said it would take twenty years to build up the standard again, but now we are more hopeful—in five years they will have regained all that they lost during the war.

It is so difficult to speak about the students without emotion, the tall thin girl with the eyes which notice everything and seem to record everything, the boy who resembles a musician and who is in fact a fiddler who scrapes out on his violin beyond the grave-mounds the harmonies which give him a curious settled peace,

39

the basket-ball player who looks like a Greek god. There are only two Yunnanese in the class. The rest of them have escaped from the north; almost none of them ever hear from their parents; yet though they are the flotsam of the war, they are the only stable things left in this country. I have no hope for China unless the students, the professors and the technicians get power.

January 29th . . . THIS morning there was news from Yenan. To these who have never heard of Yenan it must mean nothing at all, but to us it was an event of astonishing importance. There is a vast area of China which to us is called simply Yenan. We hear little about it, and of the little we hear we are immensely critical; but gradually, out of the welter of criticism and propaganda, we have formed a picture which cannot wholly be wrong. There is another government in China which exerts vast powers. It has said to the peasants that the livelihood of the peasants is all that matters, and all other problems are small, even insignificant, in comparison with their livelihood. And in this the majority of the professors and the students are in perfect agreement, without being in the least Communist. Also, we know that they have been fighting vigorously, with inadequate equipment, we know that there have been full-scale battles against the Japanese in which the Communists won. We know this; we know little more. Because we accept this, and secretly praise the Communists, it would be absurd to call us Communists. We are lost. We cannot go on with the authoritarian government we have. We cannot endure for one moment the thought of the secret police continuing into the peace. We are weary beyond words of rule by the military governors. The Generalissimo has outlived his usefulness. For a while he represented the forces of goodwill; now he represents the forces of evil. It is as simple as that. And yet we do not want the Communists in power. We want only that this war should be fought to an end, and afterwards there should be a government of no party, no affiliations, no beliefs except the belief that China shall disappear, for nothing is so dangerous as the name, and in its place there shall be only "the Chinese people."

The message from Yenan was brief: "We are well. J. was captured by the Japanese. There has been tremendous fighting."

February 1st . . . AT LAST we have left the theatre where we have lived for a year and a half. A few, but not many of the best professors of this University will remain, cooped up in the shallow
40

theatre boxes looking down on a stage where there is nothing at all except bare boards. We were lucky to have lived there at all: there are places infinitely worse. It was never uncomfortable. The misery will wear off. We shall forget the dirt, and the falling plaster and the broken tiles; we shall forget that we never dared invite anybody to see us; we shall forget the mud and the smells of Peimenkai, the half-open graves outside the North Gate, for next to us there was one of the most amazingly beautiful gardens in Kunming and not far away was the Green Lake and twenty minutes' walk away lay the University.

The oddest of all things is that we are going to live in the house of a Russian vodka-manufacturer, where the smell of vodka hangs in the air, where the great brown jars lie in rows downstairs and GI's come roaring in at all times of the day and night for their vodka poured into gasoline tanks. Nothing could be more different from the theatre than this wide-open spacious courtyard, with its pale red poinsettias and the faintly bitter-sweet smell of vodka, which must surely be among the most pleasant of all smells.

I have turned traitor. It cannot be helped. I did not even fight against it. When the offer came, I accepted it eagerly. I have spent four years with the professors, and of those four years one and a half were spent in conditions which made the t.b. worse, so that the little calcined spots in the lung opened and bled, and I lived too long in a state of tubercular excitement. I confess I am grateful for it. There are things I would never have dreamed of without t.b., and since everyone around me was suffering from the same disease, I learned to understand them better. The spots have healed now, as we expected they would—we are six thousand feet above sea-level, the air is clear and there is an enchantment in Yunnan, where the streets are filthy beyond words, which cures all disease. The theatre was dangerous: cold, damp, insufferably oppressive with the high walls all round it. I comfort myself by saying that we can now at last entertain guests.

But there is the Russian landlord and vodka-manufacturer to be dealt with, a huge man with a keen brain and a ferocious temper. He lives in a world which is not unlike my tubercular world last year, incessantly stimulated by vast quantities of vodka, a giant who has stepped straight out of Dostoievsky, ruthless in his determination to make a fortune, suffering from a disease of the spleen, impatient of all restraint and five times larger than life. His father was a station-master in Manchuria. He will talk at the flop of a hat of the

41

great forests and the great cold. For him Manchuria is not a part of China, but Yellow Russia—*Zhelto-Rossiya*. He has the utmost conceivable contempt for the Chinese when he is drunk, and the greatest admiration for their business abilities when he is sober. He took me into a corner of the courtyard this evening. "They're always playing tricks with me. Look at that." *That* was one of the bamboo-covered cases in which crude potato-alcohol is brought to the factory before being distilled. He kicked it. A false bottom fell out. "It's always happening. God damn them. They don't know what's good for them." Then he grinned like a child. "But I always find it out."

He has a peasant delight in life, and the quickest brain I have ever known—no nobility of manner, but a kind of desperate good-temper. He puts a whole bottle of vodka on the table. "Drink as much as you like. You'll have a clear head in the morning. It's not like whisky—the crude oils have been taken out. Well, what the hell are you waiting for?" He drank down half a bottle, for a moment his face clouded and he looked tired, then suddenly his face resumed its normal appearance of benevolent savagery. "Why don't you drink it. It won't hurt you. You're weak. Do you have to give a lecture in the morning?" I nodded. "All right, take it easy." There is a hammering at the outer gate. "The GI's have come. They can bloody well wait. I'm not going to open the door for them. I like them, but I am going to have my privacy. I'm a merchant. It's not the kind of thing I wanted to be, but I'm a merchant and even a merchant has the right to have some time of his own." There are moments when he looks almost crafty, when you realize there is some deep-seated passion of remonstration in him. He wanted to be a scholar. He has an excellent mechanical brain. He was a White Russian, but it was inhumanly difficult for a White Russian to receive any University education. He wanted it beyond anything he has ever wanted since, but from the very beginning he was cursed with his insecurity and had to struggle for money. For a while he managed a third-rate boarding-house in Chungking. He opened a restaurant. Then early last year he came down to Kunming on business and discovered there was room for a vodka-factory. He bought this building from a retired Yunnanese general who lives nearby, still retaining his old bodyguard. He refuses to go out at night. He has explained very carefully that he must keep his money in American dollars under the mattress, and he dare not leave the house. He distrusts his servants, probably for good reasons. He is supremely dictatorial, and cares less than nothing for the opinions of others; but he gives a curious impression of goodness. I realize we have fallen from the frying-pan into the fire. He has suggested very gently that sometimes there may be a little drunkenness at parties— nothing very special—a little breaking of glasses. Does the professor mind? The professor, looking at the wide space of the courtyard, is secretly delighted. "And then of course there are my Russian friends. They are terribly talkative. They like to pick quarrels, and sometimes the GI's are troublesome. You are sure you won't mind?" I nod vehemently. "Like hell you don't mind. You wait and see," he said darkly. All the while the hammering at the door continued.

It is going to be a game of wits. He cannot "place" me, but it is not in the least difficult to place him, for he comes straight out of a Russian novel. He has the goodness, the occasional cunning, the delight in losing himself in drunkenness, the fierce casual temper of one of the characters of Dostoievsky's novel. Above all there is the goodness. Tonight, half an hour ago, he was playing Russian love-songs on his mandolin. It was utterly delightful. More and more vodka bottles appeared on the tables. The large room downstairs, with its tapestries on the walls, its inverted paper umbrellas for lampshades, its hideous furniture which he designed, the flowers and the tablecloths became a scene of magic. We were in Russia, or rather we were in Zhelto-Rossiya in a small house among the forests. He sang endlessly. He needed no audience, and it was a good voice, even when he was hopelessly drunk, and he had a perfect sense of time. "I used to play the trumpet at Shanghai," he whispered. "Do you know what I would like? To be rich enough to have a large house and a private orchestra. I could shout to the *chef d'orchestre* and say, 'Play this,' and by God they would play it, and then I'd throw some coins at them. I don't want to be a damned merchant. Yes, that's what I'd like." There is nothing in the least outrageous in his desire for a private orchestra; it is the reverse of all his sufferings, the dream of his childhood which has almost come true, and yet has not come true—there is a lurking suspicion in his eyes that it will all fade into nothing and leave him, a young poverty-stricken boy somewhere in one of the coastal ports of China.

I have known him now for three weeks, but this is the first time they have been singing. I went downstairs again to find they had grouped themselves perfectly on the floor, their faces were flushed and I have never seen people so happy, and conscious of their happiness. The songs went on, a slow-rising flood, so that as time passed you were no longer conscious of people enjoying themselves, only of the enjoyment. Song is the only arbiter. It is more powerful than vodka, more heady, there is more pure delight in it—and how strange that those last dying notes should be so similar to those of Chinese scholars reciting their poems. I have read somewhere that the Navaho Indians finish all their songs with the words "All ends in joy and beauty," as we would say "Amen" at the end of a hymn or the old Hebrews said "Selah." So it is here, though the joy is disguised in sorrow. And so it must be: for so much joy would be unbearable. It was the same in Elizabethan times. The happiest songs and ballads are laments. And something of the same sort happens in the greatest epics, which describe the most bitter defeats in terms of victories, yet knowing all the while that the defeats were there, turning the conquest of Troy or the Grail or Rome herself into defeats, not so much of nations, but of men's happiness and delights. Does Virgil celebrate the achievements of Rome? Hardly— the Aenied is nothing but a series of laments; yet there is joy in lamenting:

Free suffering for the truth makes sorrows sing,
And mourning far more sweet than banquetting.

It is useless, then, to lament that we lament; this is how we are made, and how we have seen the world through all ages. And what is consoling is that the Chinese and the West, so often at odds with one another, in their deepest moments of grief and joy, see the world in the same way. The weeping has joy in it. I doubt whether it could be otherwise. Except for this we could not bear our sorrows, our griefs and the hideous ways in which we die unless by some transmutations of the mind the horror of it became in the end something else—a kind of sweetness. So Shakespeare, having seen a dead man floating in the Thames, transformed him into coral and pearls. "Full fathom five thy father lies. . . ." And this is what makes China so much beyond all our efforts of imagination: there is so much starvation and degradation, so much inconceivable horror, that in the end we turn away and see only the abiding beauty of the landscape and of those who are still living.

February 2nd, Re-reading yesterday's note . . . I think what I have written is true, and in a sense it is the only truth that can be said about China. But it is a dangerous truth. It is necessary to say, as often as possible and as loud as possible, that the degradation, the filth and the corruption exist. The landscape is there; the peculiar brightness of the air is there; but the suffering is unbelievably horrible, and all of it is unnecessary. It is not only the soldiers who come back from the Burma Front to die. There are the chain-gangs, village magistrates who wield powers of life and death over villages; there are the endless corrupt officials and officers, who by being corrupt are endlessly lowering the standard of the poorest; there is the absence of justice, since justice is bought and sold almost openly; the absence of any democracy. There are the starving who are left to starve, the rich who are left to enjoy their riches— the ease in which one can avoid taxation—the horrors of a Chinese prison where you starve to death. And there is almost nothing except the incredible patience of the farmers and the scholars to put over against these things. Liu Lien says: "We do not deserve to win this war, but we do not deserve to perish."

I have seen farm-boys whipped and sabred for running from the chain-gangs. I have seen them led off with ropes round ankles and wrists. These things happen. They happen even in England to deserters, and in a sense these farm-boys were deserters; but an English deserter does not suffer from the caprice of the officers. Caprice rules. If you hate a man you arrange that he is arrested on a trumped-up charge. It will cost him two million dollars to regain his freedom. It is perfectly permissible to share this with the police. It is equally permissible to allow him to die of slow starvation. There is no law. The Legislative Yuan is utterly ineffective. There is *habeas corpus* on the statute books; it is on the statute books, but it is nowhere else. The salaries paid to the police and the judges are inadequate; bribery follows, corruption follows, the vicious spiral is endless and the poorest of all suffer most. And yet all these things are unnecessary. It is perfectly conceivable that in China in our lifetimes there will be an independent judiciary. The police in Peking before the war were renowned for their fair-mindedness. Thefts and murders were punished; they are not punished now, for the police themselves are thieves and murderers.

You may say: "Why does not public opinion put an end to these horrors?" Sometimes it does, but public opinion depends upon the press. A little while ago a newspaper was courageous enough to point out that the woman who had beaten her slave-girl to death hardly deserved acquittal. There were exactly two reasons why she should not be acquitted. The first reason was that it was il-

45

legal to possess slave-girls, the second reason was that it was illegal to murder. The case had to be re-tried. The woman was rich, but she was not influential. She was shot after a protracted trial not far from the place where I am writing this. But how often can newspapers, where there is no free press, take their courage in their hands?

There is a deep-seated bitterness in nearly all the Chinese I have met when they speak of law. The law is a thing that rankles, a hideous thing. It gives neither protection nor hope; it is the scene of their gravest disaster; it is black as the uniforms of the policemen.

February 5th . . . THINKING of England—always the same parts of England, Cornwall, Rame Head, Cawsand, the white towers of kaolin, the lakes in the north and the mountains of Wales. All my moods and vapours come from this—that I was born on the edge of Cornwall, that little tongue of England which juts out towards the sunlight and America. The heavy mists, the bright beaches, the white cliffs, the consoling greenness of grass. . . . The Cornish are proud and insular; dark-skinned often; as swarthy as gypsies with their Spanish blood. They are Gaels, but unlike the Welsh they are not tormented by a sense of guilt, and something of the legendary grandeur of the past clings still to their mountains, where Arthur fought interminable battles, and the air is softer than anywhere else in England, and flowers grow more abundantly. That the Scillies, the ultimate islands of Britain, should have vast flower-beds pleases me enormously. The Americans may not understand us, but we do not welcome them with a metal goddess— we offer them *an island of flowers.*

It is odd how one thinks of England, for in all China there is hardly a single landscape remotely resembling an English countryside. We do not decorate our mountains with pagodas or ricefield terraces; we leave them severely alone, or else we draw on them in chalk a white horse, or hope to find flowers on them. We are not conscious, as the Chinese are conscious, of scenery as a vast perspective to be dominated quietly, on the highest places, with a spire. Our churches are in valleys, and have been always; and in this we are unlike the Spanish or the Chinese who love to arrange citadels on high hills. Most Chinese temples are half-way up hills, and from there the priests look out upon the world, seeing it at a distance, untouched by its ceaseless troubles; but no one in England goes to church to look at calm valleys. We are both in love with valleys, but the English prefer to live in them and the Chinese to look down at them.

February 6th, Self-discipline . . . THE unknown, the unenviable yet perfect martyrs of this war—not to be forgotten, to be called to mind often. Lidice, the Jews in Poland, the soldiers in France . . . The Jesuit retreats, when the priests call to mind the *details* of Christ's suffering. But now—today—not with passionate hunger to imitate, but to have sympathy. To remember when I return to Europe that a wheatfield may have seen a scene of mass-suffering. And to remember the roads of China.

To be free above all; not to become a part of any machine; never to lie, because they did not lie; to know that the state is a machine for producing human agony or human happiness, and that agony must be destroyed. To speak to my friends, to M., to S. and all others without dissembling, because there is no time left for dissembling.

February 7th . . . BUT why should the martyrs be asked to pray for us? It is inconceivable that they are angels. They are not mediators. The boy in Paris who was thrown from an ice-cold bath in mid-winter into an empty cell, where there was only a trap-door, cannot pray for us; nor can the men in the salt-mines pray for us; nor can the Jews. Prayer like love is useless. Better the steel-cold brain, the determination that it shall never happen again, but it must go with the determination to build something worthy of the people who have gone through this hell. No election promises. A promise made by all. The end—that people should be humanly happy, that children should laugh and the young be satisfied with each other.

In all these things our only guide is the greatest art. (The world of the politicians and the world of art are no longer contiguous, but they must be brought together.) This alone. No other sanctuary, unless by accident or cunning we break through the walls; and there is art in young children and lovers, for they are unconscious of their surroundings, find happiness only in themselves, and need nothing to support them except themselves. To worship the permanent and to love what is fleeting. . . .

And then, too, always to remember the sources from which we are sprung. . . .

And beyond that—nothing, since we know we are not permanent and cannot see more than a generation ahead.

What changes will take place! We see the world as it is, not realizing that the maps will have changed in twenty years time, and we also shall have changed, changed beyond recognition, as a meteor changes colour in its downward flight.

There is no direction. There is no progress. There is not even a sense of direction, a signpost. We have invented, as our greatest treasure, the sense of morality, and when we argue so bitterly about east and west we should remember that the highest ideal in China, India and the West has been the contemplative scholar. It is from him, and not from our suffering, that we have acquired our love for peace.

Beethoven wrote to Bettina von Arnim: "I have no friend, I must live alone with myself; but God is nearer to me than others in my music, I accompany Him without fear, and always I recognized Him and heard Him. I am not anxious for the fate of my music, no evil can befall it. He who understands it will be rid forever of misery. . . ."

The search for the magic spells. . . .

February 8th, A strange story . . . K. TOLD me the story yesterday evening, while we were sipping brandy. He has been with the Americans in Burma, and yet when you look at him, the pale egg-white skin and almost feminine lips, it is impossible to imagine him as a soldier.

"I was a liaison officer, and so I came to know both sides of the conflict, for there was a very real and at times bitter conflict between the Chinese and the Americans. It was not so at higher levels, though there was conflict again at the highest levels of all. The Americans were tough. They were the finest soldiers imaginable, but they had no patience with our old-fashioned generals, whose armies were often paper armies—that is, perhaps a quarter of the troops on the roll had no existence at all except to provide lists of names, and for each of these names there would be a certain amount of payment from the Central Government. And then another quarter perhaps were dying or suffering from sickness, and of the remaining half perhaps not more than a quarter were active combatants—the rest were officers, servants, orderlies, foragers, stray boys who had joined because they had nothing else to do.

"The army in those days was under the direction of General Wei Li-huang, but the strategy was largely in the hands of the Americans. The final decisions were usually made by the Americans.

48

In general the Chinese were perfectly content that this should be so, but among some of the minor generals there was a great deal of criticism.

"One of these generals, who belonged to the old school, believed in charms. He gave charms to his officers—it was, of course, unnecessary to give charms to his soldiers, but occasionally he would order the priest who accompanied him to make sacrificial offerings. The priest was theoretically a taoist priest, who wore an oiled top-knot and a long black gown. He was usually barefoot, and though he ate sometimes with the general, it was quite clear that the general despised him. Whenever there were visiting officers, the priest was put away.

"I was a major in the army commanded by this general. The colonel befriended me, and we made various plans by which the soldiers could be given better blankets—you know how thin a Chinese soldier's blanket is—and we did everything we could to improve their lot, even to the extent of depriving the general of some of his proceeds from the War Department. We made it clear that we were determined that the soldiers should have a new deal. We improved their pay—partly out of our own pockets, partly out of the commanding-general's; and we arranged that their rewards for capturing enemy rifles, flags, swords and so on should be increased. The Chinese soldier lives for these things. He will attack a redoubt with astonishing bravery simply for the sake of the rifles he captures, and for which we pay a few dollars. He has no final loyalty to China; his final loyalty is to his commanding-officer. And usually it is the young commanding-officers on the field who win battles and try very often to improve the lot of the soldiers.

"We had been teaching the soldiers to read one afternoon—it was a few days before the coming battle, we were resting just outside some farm-houses. Then the general came along in a sedan chair. There were two sedan chairs, and in the second was the taoist priest. The priest stepped out and stood by the general while he made a speech—the perfectly normal and inevitable speech, imitating the Generalissimo's voice and accents, about our duty to the country, our passionate desire to rid the country of the Japanese and the need for the most implicit discipline. We noticed that the taoist priest was smiling and stroking his beard, and was behaving with unusual familiarity with the general, even occasionally winking at him. The general smiled and asked my soldiers whether they were prepared to die for China. The soldiers answered in chorus,

49

the general went on with his speech. At the end there was a short silence, and suddenly the general repeated in a much graver voice whether we were prepared to die for China. All those who were prepared to die for China were ordered to step forward. All stepped forward. The general smiled to the taoist, and was about to step back in the sedan chair when an idea occurred to him. He smiled gravely, contemplated the soldiers for a long time, rubbed his cheek and said: 'This is very interesting, but as a test of your loyalty to your general I have one more question to ask. Who will sacrifice his life for me?'

"You would have expected perhaps that all the soldiers would have stepped forward, but in fact there was silence. No one answered. If they had known what was about to happen, and if there had been time for them to discuss the inevitable consequences, they would have stepped forward faster than they had ever stepped forward before—they would have rushed the general and perhaps killed him, and they might even have killed the taoist priest. Instead, they stayed where they were. After a while a curious fluttering movement occurred—there was indecision—there was a kind of deep-rooted tantalizing uncertainty—no one knew what to do. The general—and this is what made matters worse—continued to stroke his chin, looking at them, saying nothing, making curious movements of his hands towards the taoist priest. And the uncertainty of the soldiers deepened with their increasing boredom, for they had no idea what to do or what was demanded of them, or of their consciences, except that they should stay where they were in order to avoid the most terrible catastrophe.

"Death is not so bad as boredom and uncertainty. A soldier, after being asleep all night, lying on the wet ground, covered only with his thin cotton uniform and his thinner blanket, fights because the nights and the days are an infinity of boredom. We engage battle at dawn, at the moment when boredom has reached its maximum, and more often than not we exchange battle at the moment before dawn, when the interminable boredom has reached a point of excruciating intensity. We fight, then, not for our country, but because we are lonely beyond words, because nothing is left to us, because it seems to us at that moment that life can no longer be endured unless we make a noise, run, shout and murder.

"For perhaps five minutes the soldiers stood there. I assure you there are times when five minutes are endless. And then suddenly and unaccountably, from various places, soldiers stepped forward
50

tentatively, not knowing what they were doing, unable to stand quite still, saluting the general, but not in the usual way—they saluted him as though they were saluting someone they had seen in dreams. They were like people dazed. There were cries from the soldiers at the back: 'Don't move! Come back!' It was like when you throw a stone into a pool. You notice the same thing sometimes in crowds—an inexplicable uneasiness which slowly accumulates and pervades the whole crowd—not panic, but the heights and depths of uneasiness.

"We knew, I think, what would happen; but we couldn't foresee how it would happen. Five had stepped forward from the front rank—five people standing alone in deathly stillness. The general asked: 'You are prepared to die for me?' There was no answer, but they threw up their heads in the manner which means in the east either a deliberate 'yes' or 'no.' Then, walking slowly down the line, pausing before each one, he shot those five who were prepared to die for him. A pause, and then he said: 'Dismiss,' and that was all.

"But in a sense it was only the beginning. There was no sign of revolt; there were not even the faintest mutterings. The general returned to his sedan chair accompanied by the taoist priest, and smiled at the soldiers, showing his teeth. Perhaps he would be alive now if he hadn't smiled at them; but there was so much triumph in his smile that the soldiers immediately understood that he had scored a victory over them and they had lost 'face.' The most extraordinary thing was the way he remained there, offering no resistance at all when they suddenly rushed towards him. I could not see the general. I had no desire to see the general. I remember wondering how he would die, and what would happen to the soldiers who were responsible, and whether we would all be court-martialled and shot out of hand. But we were not court-martialled, and the general died because they trampled him underfoot, trampled to death by these young farm-boys who wore only the lightest of cotton slippers."

February 10th, The Beauty of Chinese Women . . . THERE are many reasons why one stays in China; the best of all is the vision of Peking which we hold before us continually. We cannot live without this vision, and probably we have all coloured it so heavily that we shall never be able to recognize the image we have created out of the despair of war. We are people of instinct; and our instinct is to return to Peking for the same reason that the lemmings leave the coast of Norway and wander into the North Sea.

Who are we? Where do we come from? Where do we go? For us all these questions are answered simply, with an almost intoxicating lack of chiaroscuro. We see ourselves clearly, and we know we are wanderers who have come from nowhere and will eventually reach Peking. The yellow-tiled roofs, the broad smooth streets, the monuments beyond the earthwork walls, the quietness and dignity and composure of an imperial city—these are the things which keep us alive, though some of the students dream of their native villages, the mulberry-trees, the quiet evenings beside the village pool with the caged birds and the girls beneath the evergreens. For foreigners it is the same—the disease of Peking is contagious, and we wonder how long it will be before the famous poet Wen Yi-tuo leads the long march of students and professors to the north, just as he led them south seven years ago. One year? Two years? No one knows.

But there is still another thing that keeps us here—the beauty of the women, the sloe eyes, the small waists, the smooth skin and those mouths which have the sharp edges of petals. Above all—the eyes, and the extraordinary grace with which they walk. They do not carry pitchers on their heads, yet when they walk you remember their ancestors who carried them. They sway very slightly—the skirts are tight, and it is necessary to sway—and they do not seem to be entirely of this world. And so many of them look like young Florentine princes or like the youths who lean negligently on their spears in Giorgione's paintings. And yet by some odd and malevolent destiny the girl-students are far less handsome than the girls from the tribes who come down from the hills.

You can rarely tell a man's age in China; it is infinitely more difficult to tell a woman's. M. is sixteen. She has all the maturity and grace of a woman of thirty. K. is thirteen, and may well be a witch a thousand years old, riding on broomstick and bucket, for her face is so changeable, so many ages are contained in her, so many lanterns glow behind her eyes, that I am at a loss how to speak to her, and blush sometimes as though she was at an age when one could fall in love with her. She knows this—the Chinese child is at least conscious of the moment when a man looks at her with something more than curiosity—and how perfectly absorbed she is in the contemplation of her own beauty! how delighted she is when you speak to her! how quickly she perceives the moment when you are absorbed in contemplation of her, and how smoothly (as with a

52

turn of the wrist) she perceives that she perceives!

One day I must try to paint her at the moment of her complete self-absorption, the moment when she admires herself and laughs at herself, and by laughing sees herself more plainly than ever. She is beginning to read *The Dream of the Red Chamber,* a book which describes with infinite grace and malice every possible intoxication which occurs in romantic love. She identifies herself with all the characteristics of those lovers, and at the same time she sees herself magnified like someone on a screen. Meanwhile we wonder, with a half terrified sense of our own inadequacy, how beautiful she will be when she grows.

And perhaps this is what is consoling and at the same time bewildering—Chinese women never go through adolescence and they remain like children, with a child's tantrums and a child's clean-cut beauty. The sharp edges remain, as sharp as the edges of petals. . . .

February 15th . . . There, on the edge of the Green Neck Lake, bathing after the rain, were the children. They were perfectly content. The plum-trees are still in flower, and all over the lake floats the frosted crystal light of the small buds in the rain. There was even a rainbow, a great band of vermilion and blue-green, and all the white rocks and all the pathways were shimmering, and in this acqueous light, which is like the light of coming storm, the duckweed was bright and purple.

It could not have been better. They splashed and twittered like birds, and sometimes they ran back to the small huddled pile of clothes they had left on the shore, and then again they would return, because it was more pleasant to break up those long plains of duckweed than to flounder through the streets at sunset. It was like a Yuan Dynasty painting; one even regretted the absence of the solitary heron or the pony which is usually to be found in those paintings; and there should have been beetling cliffs above, and a river winding milk-white below. It was not to be, but afterwards when I thought about them the cliffs and the ponies appeared from nowhere, and for hours afterwards I heard the twittering of the children. And last night, when I was in bed and thinking of them, it was exactly like turning slowly over a long Chinese scroll.

February 16th . . . To remember always the things the Taoists worshipped: clouds, floating duckweed, the moss at the

53

foot of rocks, the valleys where no one ever enters, the peach-blossom gardens and the short stalk of a rose. . . .

To remember their three greatest desires of the Chinese: to live long, to be unhindered and to see the light at the bottom of the well.

But how in God's name, and at this hour of the world's history, to follow those counsels when we are faced with such despair?

February 17th . . . He came out of the rain, the thin small rain which has been falling all afternoon. His blue clothes were smoking with the damp, and he looked, as he always looks, like someone who has stepped out of a painting. He brought an essay on early Elizabethan poetry? Would I look at it? I did, and it was incredibly bad and wrong-headed, and half of it had been copied from a miserable text-book—a list of names and dates, and a professional text-book inncompetence overlaid everything he had written. "Where the devil did you get it from?" I shouted at him. He lied delightfully—the essay is three weeks late, and he was at his wit's end to produce it. "But surely it is not like this? You write poetry yourself. Why must you write this nonsense?" He sat down and gazed out of the window. "There is so much to read," he complained. There was a long argument. What had he read? He had struggled with some early plays. They meant nothing to him. He had found some lyrical poems, and been lost in admiration of them.

"Which one did you like best?"

"There's a very short one. It's indecent, but I liked it."

"How does it go?"

"I don't think I ought to recite it—it's about the rain, and something else."

And then at last, after half an hour of special pleading, there came from him the most innocuous and delightful of all songs, a song with so much ancestral innocence and modesty, so much understanding and youthful desire that it was almost like the last act of a tragedy:

> *O western wind, when wilt thou blow?*
> *The small rain down can rain.*
> *Cryst, if my love were in my arms,*
> *And I in my bed again!*

February 18th, The Secret Police . . . There seems to be no way out. We live, in this age of nightmare, with the secret police all

54

round us. A student has disappeared. No one knows where he has gone, or whether he will ever return; no one doubts that he has been spirited away by the secret police. There can have been no trial, there are even very good grounds for believing that the student who has disappeared has been mistaken for someone else.

You can see them sometimes hovering round the University gates, men with lawless and broken faces, the excreta of prisons, the refuse of this civilization which is in danger of making us all refuse, men with American guns in their pockets and a price on their heads. It is easy enough to understand why they are there. Of all places in China this University is the most glorious, because it is dedicated to democratic government, and believes in democracy, not knowing what democracy will bring China, because it has never been practised. One of the presidents of this University has called it "the bulwark of democracy." Probably he was wrong to use these words, for ever since then we have been conscious of being disliked. Universities, democracy—the two words most disliked by the soldiers who are in power. And what is so ghastly is that one can do nothing, absolutely nothing, to convince anyone outside China that this is true, that we live from hand to mouth, not knowing what further onslaughts on freedom are in store for us. I said once, and still believe, that whatever is good and new in China will come from the Universities, and whatever is bad will always come from the soldiers; the longer I stay, the more evidently true it becomes, for the soldiers have no understanding of the problems of the country, the merchants have even less and least of all in the future government of this country will the officials have any sense of what is due, since they more than any others have grown to despise the peasants. The peasants and the scholars can be despised, yet they remain.

The voice of the Chinese people is not yet heard abroad. We are confused and shamed by the picture that has been drawn of heroic China. No one speaks authoritatively for China abroad. The chaos is all round us. By the barest margin the Japanese failed to capture Kweichow and Szechuan, and no one is blamed, and no one will ever be blamed, because history will be written by the official historians. But at least there must be a footnote to describe the misery under which one lives with secret police and racketeers in power. And perhaps there should be another footnote which will say that in spite of all this, there was a heroism vaster than anything we can imagine.

55

February 19th . . . A FEW weeks ago the great scholar Wen Yi-tuo travelled with some students to see the prehistoric forest two hundred miles to the south. He has come back with his drawings, but he is thin and pale, suffering from typhus.

We know he will recover, but it is impossible to describe the fear which overwhelmed us. We cannot—dare not—think of what will happen without him. I know no one else who is so perfectly representative of Chinese culture. Liu Lien reverences him, and sometimes when I pass the mud-hut in the campus where he lectures, seeing the crowds of students who stand outside listening at the windows, I am more than ever conscious of my inadequacy. I think of his red-gold beard, the young stocky body in the blue gown, the amazingly sharp eyes, the fire and depth of his voice. I remember the first day I met him, a muddy cloudy day in September when it seemed that the whole street was falling into decay, and yet suddenly made living by his presence. At least three professors have died since I have been here, and there is no reason why, on his pitifully small income, he should be able to resist the disease.

I do not know anyone else in this University who carries such quiet authority. There are moments when his voice becomes deeply passionate, his anger ripens, the grim relentless smile becomes almost terrifyingly cold, and he will talk quietly of the corruption in the country and the responsibility of the students in the face of corruption. One thinks of people who are pure flame; he is the purest I have ever known. And everything has fitted in: the years when he half starved in Chicago, learning to paint, the years of the civil wars, when he said he became almost insane, seeing the burnt villages and the dead peasants, and knowing that he was powerless to help them. The years when he took part in the renaissant movement of poetry, and those other years when he decided to re-examine with all the artifices of modern scholarship the basic interpretation of the Chinese classics. The years of study over the Chou dynasty bronzes, and early inscriptions, seeing the vigorous life in these ancient testimonies of an earlier and better China, and being puzzled by them, and trying desperately to understand the impulses that brought them to the light. The years of suffering and near-starvation when he carved seals at night and taught in middle-schools for a few extra dollars, and always the quietness and nobility of a prince among men. I asked him once whether he would ever go into Parliament, if there was a Parliament in this country.

56

"Yes, but it's better to live like this. We are nearer the heart of the people. I have taught a few middle-school students to love Chinese literature and adore freedom."

This afternoon, seeing him pale-faced and sad, leaning on a stick, shivering a little with the memory of how nearly typhus had stricken him down, I wondered how much reserve of strength there was in him, and in the others. Surely there must come a time when they will have no reserves left at all! And this saddens me more than anything else, because I cannot conceive that China will be worth living in when the best scholars have perished in the cold.

February 25th . . . STEPHEN SPENDER's *Ruins and Visions* has at last arrived. It was the one work which Bergery wanted to see above all others before he died, perhaps because the title delighted him, though once he objected that any great book of poetry on this war should be called *Ruins and Splendours*.

I met Spender only once, but the memory of the lacquer-red face in Paris, the strident eyes, the heavy curve of the lips, the almost Jewish profile, the contemptuous way he carried his six foot of lean muscle and the extraordinary animation of the face remains so vivid and so perfectly in keeping with the poetry that it is unforgettable. I have forgotten Dreiser's appearance, though I dined with him often, and it is difficult sometimes to recall Malraux whom I saw nearly every day in Spain. Remembering the high forehead, the flabby handshake, the clean cold brain, he seems still the dimmest of all the portraits I brought back, and perhaps this was due to his weariness, a kind of elemental exhaustion that had descended on him after his last aeroplane had been shot down. He was working on a film; complained bitterly of the difficulties; spoke precisely and delicately of the heroism of the anarchists; and I remember now that there was in him a curious sense of uneasy admiration, as though he wondered whether one needed greater courage to fly over the enemy lines than to break through the lines with thin-armoured tanks. Now as I grow older, and the memory of Spain dims, I remember only the burning buildings at Tarragona, Modesto's handsome features, Lister's smile, one or two ghastly bombardments in Barcelona, and a Spanish girl called Aminta. And then, much closer and somehow more disturbing, the picture of Spender who had just returned from Spain, sunburnt, with fiery eyes, and how incredibly the man's face was symbolic of the times.

57

February 26th . . . LIU LIEN was thumping the table: "Human dignity demands that men should not live in fear of the secret police. This above all! Those who employ the secret police are the traitors—there are no other traitors compared with these. We cannot breathe this air. The police should be open and undisguised, unarmed. We are fighting for our liberties. Must we have them poisoned at the source?"

I am afraid it is only too true. The secret police is everywhere among the students, even perhaps among the professors there are one or two, and though we know their names and they have been persuaded into silence, how can we be sure that others will not appear? And what is far more worrying is that every Chinese officer I have spoken to has nothing but the most bitter contempt for the universities. . . .

February 28th, Khalifa . . . I HAVE no idea how it arose; we were not even discussing magic; suddenly I found myself talking of the Khalifa ceremony which I saw near Capetown. Perhaps it was the air as we sat in the garden this afternoon, which was so much like the air in South Africa; or perhaps there was no reason at all except that it was pleasing to tell the story.

The Chinese have no great love for the Mahometans, and find the Arabs more difficult to understand than the English. Fanaticism is not their forte. But it was odd how rapt they were when I spoke of Humudi, a young man, less than forty, with a swarthy dark face and a short trimmed beard who gashed himself with knives one evening years ago for the pleasure of Allah.

There was a small stage near the dockyard of Simonstown, and on the festival day the young Mahometans gathered, bare to the waist, singing songs, throwing incense sticks into the air and beating drums. I remember how immediately the curtain rose Humudi was standing in the centre of the stage, fingering a long sword, his love locks curled and his chest gleaming; and behind him there was some delapidated scenery painted thirty or forty years previously— a waterfall, a garden, stone urns. The singing went on, Humudi fingered his sword, there were flowers on a small altar and two yellow footlights shone up at Humudi, still chanting, still fingering his sword.

It must have been some time later that the men came from behind the scenery, beating cymbals and tom-toms. Humudi smiled and rolled his eyes, and he was no longer the Humudi I had known
58

in the dockyard when he held the sword over the smoke of the censers; and while the hammering of the gongs continued, he lifted the sword above his head and suddenly plunged it, in a single reckless sweep, into the pit of his stomach. We could see the skin parting, the knife edging its way in, the muscles inflexibly controlled, the sword quivering. Still holding the sword into his stomach, he began to dance a little. The dance may have been taken for a sign of weakness. The singers sang louder, the beating of the drums became more somnolent and more scented herbs were thrown into the censer.

Some time afterwards Humudi took the sword out of his stomach, and someone tossed him a few short, sharp daggers. These, too, he held over the censers; then, holding one dagger in each hand, he plunged them both with a single movement into his cheeks. Later he plunged them into his throat and through his tongue; it was a thick tongue, but the dagger penetrated right through. Humudi would smile at us with the daggers still hanging all over his face, though he was sweating and his eyes were rolling. Others came to perform the same miracles. A fitter in the naval yard stuck rows of skewers into his chest and then seized a long curved sword, lifted one of his legs and brought the sword with all his strength against the knee. You could hear the sword shivering on the impact, and the knee shivering, but there was no blood, only a wedge-shaped wound. So it goes on—boys and old men running swords and daggers into themselves, while the smoke rises from the censers and the singing is endless. Nothing is so magnificent as the sweep of the long silver sword with the gold etched line drawn through it. The sword sings and does not bring death; it brings to birth a kind of subterranean fleeting life, the flicker of instinctive rejoicing, the certainty that if they praise Allah nothing can wound. There are faint red marks on their arms and faces where the swords have been. To show us that no harm had been done, one of the boys brought a candle close to Humudi's face; there was a faint scar, already thickening. Humudi had carved through his stomach, now he put out his tongue, and began slicing through it, till we could see that half the tongue was cut and soon it would fall from his mouth. He was about to carve the lingering fragment of flesh when someone took the sword from his hand. There was no blood in his mouth. The teeth shone. A small boy climbs onto the stage, his body white and delicate, not sunburnt like Humudi's. He rips off his shirt, one of those faintly blue transparent shirts of silk which the Mahometan boys wear the moment they leave work in the dockyard. He holds the smaller sword at arm's length, and when the time comes to slice open his stomach, he does this negligently, smiling, with the expression of a sleepwalker, and also with something of the expression of a St. Sebastian ringed with thorny arrows. And so it goes on, with sudden pauses, exotic silences, the steam of smoke rising from the censers, the wailing of the drums, and all the time there is the patched and discoloured garden scene behind. The sword does not go deep in the stomach. He cuts across the smooth flesh, almost as a violinist cuts across the strings with his bow. Sweat, which has gathered on his heavy eyebrows, suddenly falls through them and momentarily blinds him, and at that moment he mistakes his aim, carves deeper into himself, a drop of blood forms, grows bigger, till it is as though the petal of a scarlet poppy had suddenly come out of his flesh. Later he will carve across his neck and face till there are thousands of thin entangled scorings of red upon him. He has failed. The moment of blindness has brought into being recollections of an earlier existence, when it was unnecessary to carve oneself for the glory of Allah. Humudi comes on the stage again. It is his performance. He is perfectly conscious of his mastery, smiling and exhibiting his unsullied flesh, putting out his unbroken and miraculously healed tongue, rolling his eyes, quivering with pleasurable emotion; and suddenly noticing a single drop of blood on the bare boards, looking up aghast, as though he was shocked to the core. But he is not shocked: a sword far greater than any we have seen hitherto is brought to him. What will he do? We amuse ourselves happily. We wonder whether he will cut off his own head, and replace it with the same sleep-walking gesture of defiance. It is possible. Anything is possible. The drums beat louder, the young boy has slipped once again into his silken shirt, the audience is craning forward, the sword is at least three inches wide and four feet long, curved and tapered. What will he do? But inevitably there is a sense of anti-climax when he performs a feat he has already performed before, bringing it down with all his strength into the stomach. We ask ourselves why he should trouble, even for the glory of Allah, to perform again—and then you notice that the thick edge of the sword has penetrated deep in the stomach, far deeper than before, and he is quivering there, shoulders hunched, the muscles coiled, and the drum-beats are growing louder and they are coming from behind the altar, throwing flowers on him, surrounding him, acclaiming him, in the same way perhaps that a matador is

60

acclaimed when he has killed his bull; but this time it is Humudi, the fitter's mate, the man I am accustomed to see in the main street of this small South African town every day, a man who smiles delightfully and wears a little red fez, since he has never been to Mecca and is therefore never allowed to wear the green turban. Somehow he had brought himself to the pitch where even inserting a sword five inches deep in his belly was a possibility. The silver sweep of the sword as it flashed down, the way he grinds his teeth in agony of expectancy, the sullen brooding and shaking shoulders, all these are witness of his accomplishment. He smiles painfully. He has hurt himself. Ever so gently the edge of the sword-blade is removed, and still, as we had almost expected there is no wound, only the curled pink lips of a wound. There is applause—thunderous applause, the curtain falls, someone rattles a little bronze chest already half full of silver coins, and shortly afterwards we went out into the night, with the Southern Cross spread over the sky.

And I went on to say, I remember, that it was not unpleasing, they had demonstrated by their fanaticism the subservience of the body and shown by their energy a curious sublimated beauty, the skin ravaged and torn, then instantaneously healed; and perhaps I said something of the alteration in their eyes, how the eyes smouldered with a kind of longing to escape from the encompassing body, to be only eyes worshipping Allah in the desert; and I was not in the least surprised by the Chinese who said they saw no beauty in fanaticism, for I knew long ago that they were too disinterested to worship in this way. But I confess I was delighted by the young student who remarked: "It is a very uneducated kind of thing to do. The perfect taoist can leap out of his body just by looking at a knot in wood or a blade of grass, or anything you please."

March 1st . . . Autumn never comes to Kunming, and there is no spring. The dreary disorderly leaf-breaking autumn of England is inconceivable here; we have four days in the year of ice-cold winter, the sun shines on all the other days of the year. It is unfair, of course. It means that we fall miserably ill as soon as we go to Chungking. We are so accustomed to spring weather all the year round that we are the pampered darlings of the earth.

There is better weather in Kunming than in California. I have known an American pilot to come off an aeroplane during a rainstorm, when there was mud everywhere. They had told him that Kunming had the best weather in the world, but he went away unbelieving. A pity. If he had stayed half an hour longer, he would have seen a sunset over the Green Lake of pure blue and silver.

Yet we long for winter, hornbeam fires, the leafless trees of an English autumn, with the rooks crowing and the cracked earth white with frost. The English winter is like the Arab's desert: so hopeless and bitter that it uplifts the spirit in revenge. When everything else is vain of promise, the winter blood sings and hope floods the veins. But I know now that as I grow older I dread the change of seasons, preferring Yunnan with its continual spring and Malaya with its eternal summer than anywhere else. Is there anywhere where it is continual autumn? Perhaps there is, for Dante talks of a place where the leaves are eternally dropping from the trees.

As we grow older, the seasons become our enemies. The young delight in change and do their best to contrive a thousand seasons in each year, being simple enough to absorb all that life offers them; but we who have absorbed too much prefer the comfort of an unchanging pattern, waiting for another winter, the clear outlines, the wholeness of the known in the snow and the icy fields. Who was it who said the snow was an indication of our immortality? But surely to live in Kunming, in eternal spring, is a greater foretaste of the gardens we have promised ourselves!

March 2nd . . . Why the devil does one write? Beethoven said: "My art must be consecrated for the good of the poor." (*Dann soll meine Kunst sich nur zum Besten der Armen zeigen.*) But what does he mean by the poor? Not the poor of spirit only, nor the poor of pocket, but all men, since all were poor compared with Beethoven.

And then let us set beside the words of Beethoven those others of Juliana of Norwich: "Full glad and merry is our Lord of our prayer."

March 3rd . . . Walking over to the University this morning, the earth crisp and moist after a dawn-rain, the blue haze of mountains in the distance, the road rough and uneven and yet lit with I know not what blinding green reflections from the trees, I watched the beggars in rags walking towards the lake. They must have been desperately poor, for their clothes were hung onto them with string and there were a hundred patches; they were unshaven, and they had beards like porcupines. They were not like our English beggars. They did not saunter as though they owned the earth.

62

They were afraid of the police—so much was evident when they came to the great red poles near the west station, where taxes are collected and men suffer the indignity of being gazed upon by policemen who are accustomed to the utmost licence in dealing with their fellow-men. Would they pass freely? One could almost imagine them being taken to the graveyard a little way away, forced down on their knees and shot.

They were searched roughly, the shreds of their clothing were torn and the policemen deliberately ripped up the cloth over their chests, half-expecting, I suppose, to find something hidden just above the belt—a coil of stolen wire, gold bars, anything you please. I have seen beggars clubbed and beaten, knocked to the ground and kicked dangerously even though the police wore only cotton slippers; but these were luckier. But what was more revealing than anything else was that they did not skip away afterwards, they did not laugh, they made no gestures, they did not once speak in protest to the police—they *shrugged their shoulders* and walked on with the same deliberate tread with which they had come to those red poles.

But the misery remains. Even in this continual springtide we are frightened and angered. There are the boys who come past the University to die, wrapped in their soldier's rags, white bones breaking through flesh; there are heaps of beggars in the doorways in the early morning; there are the young women who starve to death in our streets, and we are so accustomed to their starving that we hardly pay any attention to them, though sometimes the anger will flare up and we wonder how it will end. We know how it will end, or rather we know that it will never end, unless there are radical changes in this country, and the most necessary change of all is that the government should enter more sober hands. We cannot live in this whirlpool. The beggars can shrug their shoulders—they have won their victory, but the Universities have won no victory at all except the victory of their continuing existence.

There is terror in China. Just before he died Lu Hsun wrote a short essay called "The Dark Night." The dark night remains, though it is lit with lightning. He wrote: "There was a time not very long ago when a prisoner condemned to death was led through the busy highroad, and he was allowed to protest in the loudest voice against his condemnation, he could say the vilest things against his judges, he could tell the story of his brave deeds and demonstrate his courage in the face of death. At the moment

63

when he was about to be executed, the spectators would applaud. When I was young, I thought the practice was barbarous and cruel. As I grow older, it seems to me that the rulers of the past were courageous and supremely confident of their power in permitting these things to happen. And perhaps it showed that the rulers were showing their kindness and even benevolence to the condemned man. But nowadays this no longer happens."

March 4th . . . I KNOW the war will come to an end soon, but I am appalled by the prospects for China. I cannot see any hope of peace, nor is there any sign that the social revolution will be brought about by those who are now in power. There are scholars here who will say: "It is not their fault—they are soldiers—" as though that explained anything, and others who will say, with the same shrug of their shoulders that the beggars employed when they passed through the gates, "What can you expect of them? They have had power all their lives. Can you expect them to give it up for the good of the people?"

I cannot expect it, but I had hoped for better things, for a wider distribution of wealth and a greater consciousness of the evil of centralization. The Chinese soldiers have not known such power before; it has gone to their heads now, for they can kill more people and grow richer far more efficiently than before. . . .

March 6th . . . I THINK it was Liu Lien who first astonished me by saying that the Greek anthology had so much in common with Chinese poetry that he was occasionally bewildered, wondering what influence could have come from Athens to affect the wandering Chinese poets. Some influence had penetrated certainly, at second hand through India, where the Buddhas of the Gandhara epoch have the elegance and suavity of Apollos; and these Buddhas, subtly changed, elongated, made more tragic and infinitely less robust, barely recognizable descendants of athletes, were worshipped in the Liang dynasty and even into the T'ang. Alexander is known throughout Malaya, but only the barest mention of him has ever occurred in Chinese records. Greece touched China briefly; Apollo became Buddha, and Buddha himself became a wandering Chinese monk in a red robe, more taoist than buddhist, a gaunt benevolent spectre who promised men who had no belief in rebirth, that if they behaved truthfully they would never be reborn.

64

But the Greek Anthology touches T'ang Dynasty poetry intimately: the same weariness, the same decadence, the same simplicity of emotion expressed with disarming brevity. English lyrical poetry has one facet in common with Chinese poetry, the Greek anthology has another, and between them they almost express the whole. These Greek poets of the Alexandrian declension saw vividly and worshipped small things—grasshoppers they particularly delighted in, they spoke of curled lettuces and loved to describe flowers, but loved most of all to be drunk among companions. "Xenophon the wine-bibber dedicates an empty jar to Bacchus: receive it gracefully, for it is all he has." So had Li Po spoken on autumn nights in the mountains of Shensi, substituting for Bacchus whatever god he worshipped at the moment. Lucilius wrote: "Little Macron was found asleep on a hot summer's day by a mouse, who pulled him gently by his small foot into a hole in the wall; thereupon Little Macron strangled the mouse with his tiny hands and cried, 'Father Zeus, thou hast a second Hercules.'" It is the kind of thing that would have appealed to Chuang-tzu, the hoary old philosopher who told better anecdotes than anyone else in China.

But the similarities go deeper. The Greeks detested death and loved life; saw no hope in death, and infinite hopes in life. They were obsessed by the transience of life, for it seemed to them that no sooner had the bridal bed been strewn with saffron than they were at the gates of old age. "Philip his father laid here his child, who was twelve years old, his high hope, Nikoteles." We cannot write like that any longer, but the Chinese could write with an even greater brevity. For the Greeks also death is "the laughterless abyss," "the place of dust," "the house where there is no wine." Death would be bearable if there were wine-pots in Hades, and the ghosts of women and friends. They faced death and life at their sharpest points, and neither were afraid. "Let us drink an unmixed draught of wine; dawn is a hand-breadth; are we waiting to see the bed-time lamp again? Let us drink, O luckless one, for we shall sleep through the long night." *Dawn is a hand-breadth.* I do not know why it is, but this seems to be written in Chinese, by the poet Li Po, the two gigantic characters leaping from the page.

March 8th . . . ONE day in the year 353 A.D. the great calligrapher Wang Hsi-chih, accompanied by his friends, with four red-maned ponies carrying food, wandered out of the gates of the city. No day could have been finer. It was spring, with high clouds; they were accompanied by singing girls and many pots of wine. The songs of birds echoed from the cliffs above them, and they would pause sometimes over small bridges, and sometimes they would drop tufts of grass or flowers into the water, watching them sail downstream. As they left the gates and drum-towers behind them, they were talking eagerly; the singing girls smiled and wreathed themselves in blossoms, and not far from the city they asked their bearers to lift them to the ground, so that they could admire the scenery. Perhaps this was a mistake, for the men complained that the songs of the bells they carried in their ear-rings were too loud— they sounded better when they were muted by the silk curtains of the sedan chairs. And besides, they were distracted by the presence of the girls; and sometime afterwards, on some pretext or other, the girls were sent home.

There had been invasions and many wars recently, but the enemy had been flung back from the gates; they could breathe in peace. So they walked along the narrow pathways, the men in their cotton caps and their red shoes, the horses with the panniers following behind them. They were conscious of an inexplicable unrest. "Perhaps," suggested Wang Hsi-chih, "it is the noise of the ponies' hooves. Let us send the ponies back to the city." This they did, ordering only that some of the bearers should carry the pots of wine. But even then they were conscious that the unrest continued; and by the afternoon it was so deep that it could be felt.

Wang Hsi-chih paid his respects to the men who accompanied him, and said: "Let us stay here near these plum-trees. Nothing could be more beautiful. And let us drink wine till the moon rises." For he saw that the moon would soon be risen, and he thought their happiness would return if they waited patiently. And then, as they sat down, and fires were lit, and the wine was poured into little bronze cups, at some moment before twilight he was overcome with grief and took his brush and wrote: "There were no clouds in the sky; the wind blew softly where we were sitting. Above us the vast compass of the Heavens stretched from pole to pole, and around us were all the green things of Spring. There was music which pleased us, and there were all the colours of the earth to delight us. Yet we were sad. And so it is with all men; for a little while they sit by fires with their companions, or perhaps their hearts are uplifted when they are alone by some inexplicable mystery of flowers, and so for a while they are easy and forget their doom. But then the wind impetuously wanders; they grow dull and afraid,

66

and they fall to thinking of how these things that please them will, in the moment it takes to beckon to someone, be things of yesterday."

March 9th, A murder . . . MY STEPSON told me about it today, and I believe he invented nothing, but so well did he describe it, even imitating perfectly the *thump-thump* of the body falling downstairs in the ill-lit house, that my respect for him increased immeasurably. It is the kind of thing that happens rarely—a murder among students.

"It was over a girl student. She was lodging only a little way away from where I am staying, and he was keeping her. There are quite a lot of girl students who are being kept by boys, and often it is not at all what you think. He was keeping her only because he liked her, and because she had never been able to receive her money from the north. And then she fell in love with another student, and she told the boy she could no longer see him, and returned his letters, and the watch he lent her, and she knew he was heart-broken. He said nothing. He wandered away into the country, rarely attended lectures and fell to brooding. He found a revolver somewhere. He knew where the other boy lived, and last night he went to see the boy. He was quite mad. He shouted that he was going to kill the boy, and no one believed him, and it was so dark and everyone was so frightened that they failed to recognize him. He went up the stairs. He hammered at the door and said: "I'm going to kill you," and still no one took it seriously. And then when the door was opened and the boy faced him he suddenly became quiet, and said very softly: "You must let me have her back," and he took the boy's arm and led him to the head of the stairs, and took out the revolver and shot him, straight in the heart, so that he fell over very slowly and rolled—*thump-thump* down the stairs. By this time quite a number of students had come out in the passageway. It was dark. They could not see exactly what was happening. They saw the smoke from the revolver, and they saw the boy standing at the head of the stairs make a sudden leap right down the stairs, so that he fell on the body of the boy he had killed. He was obviously mad. He started battering the dead boy over the head, with the revolver, and then he looked up, saw that people were looking at him, pushed his way through them and rushed out into the street. They haven't found him yet. I don't suppose they ever will find him."

67

I said: "Why not? It ought to be easy."

"It's not easy. He can change his name and disappear. Perhaps they will never find him."

I am writing this by candlelight, and remember now that the story acquired its prodigious effect from two causes: the electric light has been cut off and the story was told only an hour after it had happened. I asked what kind of student he was. He was not an unusual kind, rather quiet, good at basket-ball, and my stepson had seen him every day in the tea-house in the Wen Lin Kai. There was nothing at all unusual in him; but what was puzzling was not that he had murdered the boy, but the tremendous leap down the stairs onto the body of the person he had killed. What frightens me now is not that this thing has happened; what frightens me is the unexpected banked fires which must lie in all these students who are impoverished still and cut off from their homes.

A night of nightmares. An American soldier came in later: "I went into a back street trying to find a pro. I found one all right. She was mad. Ripped up her skirt and kept throwing herself at me. But that wasn't so bad as what happened later. I was still in one of those back-streets. A door opened and something was flung out. I thought it was slops, it was so small and made such a wet sound when it fell to the ground. And then I saw it was a man, and someone had buggared about with him, and smashed his face in, and then a policeman came out of the dark and told me to move on. . . ."

March 10th, A Painting . . . T. SHOWED me a Sung Dynasty painting which he says is a copy of a famous T'ang painting. He has carried it all the way from Peiping, and hides it under his bed. There were high cliffs and horses and a small bridge, and there was almost nothing else; but what was surprising was that the painting came to immediate life, it was not necessary to wander in it and feel the texture of the rocks and the texture of the sleek skins of the horses; they came immediately to life, and yet it was a life entirely unlike anything we have known on earth. There was a heraldic quality, not only in the horses, but in the mountains. The colours were very pale, but the total effect was almost blinding, and as always there were no shadows, high noon among mountains.

What is the explanation of their total success in conveying a landscape? Partly it must be the insistence on noonday, the unshadowed country of the mind, the eye's quickness in catching the thing in flight and *letting it continue its journey*. Nothing is turned

68

to stone; everything becomes living, just as the scrolls of characters I hang on my wall are still living with a frenzied life of their own. Su Tung-po's famous bamboos have this quality; they are caught, but so deftly has the huntsman imitated the motion of the object he is pursuing that he has become identified with it. The artist, at the moment of crisis when the brush becomes no more than a projection of his own vision, draws rapidly and silently, with half-closed eyes, and there flows through him the green sap that flows through bamboos; and the wind flows through him; and his roots are in the earth, a fathom deep. So it is with Ma Yuan's more famous *Bare Willows*, where one is almost conscious of the painter's three separate leaps into the known—the leap into the willow, into the lake and into the bare mountains in the distance.

I have no patience with the Chinese theories of painting, which depend on indefinable definitions of terms, which can be translated a hundred ways. Hsieh Ho's famous six principles defeat analysis; I have seen six different translations, and none of them convey more of the nature of Chinese painting than we can learn if we set a painting of Chinese mountains against a painting of apples by Cézanne. We learn more by sudden contrasts than by voluminous footnotes. I have tried to translate the six principles with Liu Lien's help:

(a) the spiritual essence creates the living movement,

(b) the bones obey the laws of the brush,

(c) there is identity between forms seen and forms portrayed,

(d) colouring obeys texture,

(e) the composition must convey orders of space,

(f) the classical forms are created from the past.

But how close are we, reading the classic footnotes to a classic text, to the moment of exaltation which occurred when Ma Yuan saw a bare willow in the depths of winter and made his sudden leap into the known? Or when, looking at my friend's painting, one is conscious that the moment you have turned away these heraldic horses will climb to the tops of the heraldic mountains?

The stone-carver cannot make mistakes; the painter with the unglazed paper before him dare not erase a line. They live, as lovers do, on the edge where every false move is a catastrophe, even the slightest deviation is fraught with danger. And how much we have lost in the West, working with clay and painting with thick oils on canvas, having never cared to study a single bamboo leaf and catch it on the wing!

March 11th . . . IT WAS odd, coming round the lake this evening, our summer over and the blossoms fading from the trees, to see how much of it was snowbound. There was no snow, but the sun was white, and the trees and the duckweed turned up their leaves to the white sun. One expected sleighs, and almost we heard the sleighbells.

And then at night, when the searchlights shot up like thin splinters of ice, and the shapeless clouds turned into icebergs. In this light even the airplanes coming over the Hump, caught in the glare, were icefloes.

March 12th . . . REMEMBERING the plains of Hungary, the white bridges over the Danube, the peasants in their Sunday clothes and the quietness of the sun over the land, the two gypsy girls in the camp at Vac and the gold and scarlet clouds; and realizing now that I went to the East perhaps because I saw Arabians in Spain and Chinese in Budapest.

There are signs of the East all over Europe—in the towers and minarets, in Saracenic embroidered walls, in crusaders' castles everywhere. From the Bible we have derived hints of the East; our mediæval literature brims over with the imagined glory of countries which are not Persia or China, but remembered opium-dreams of fountains and flowers once seen by travellers. I knew in Spain two sisters, one dark and Arabian, the other with flaxen hair. In Budapest there are girls with high cheekbones and slanting eyes, and nothing was so wonderful as to see them bathing on the shores of St. Margit's island in the summer. But the gypsies, who sing their Romany way through the plains of Hungary, dark urgent people in coloured rags and silks, sultry and graceful and adoring, covered with thick dirt, with burning eyes, these, I suppose, were the first intimations of the East, the first sparks of that tinder which burns once you have passed the cedars of Lebanon, for they were as graceful as the Malays and still there was something hooded in their Chinese eyes.

I can never express my admiration for the East without a sense of shame for never having learned an Eastern language before I was twenty-seven. What are Greek and Latin irregular verbs compared with the clear energy of a Chinese character? There is shamanism in the East. You say a word, and the thing is there; and poetry lives, as a river lives. There is an old Hungarian song, sung by the priests of the plains:

70

My hiding-place is an old law,
Holla! I hide in songs!

So it was near Budapest, one sultry autumn, when we came upon the two gypsy girls, Margit and Lulugyi, which means "flower," and asked them to sing for us beside the road. They had ribbons in their hair, and the dust flashed over them, and the broken cooking-pots lay all round them, but they "hid in songs." I have seen the same thing in China, along the Chialing river, when the naked haulers rest for a while and sing in the shelter of rocks. The most primitive instinct of all is to sing, and one can sing as well along the plains of Hungary as among the cliffs of China.

As I remember her, Hungary was made for grief. Though the plains were dazzling, they were longer than anything conceivable. They call the plains *puszta*, meaning the desert, and turn their eyes to the East—the desert stretches from Hungary to the China Sea, the same world, the same horsemen in bondage to her. You see the desert again near Cracow, overlooking the Vistula, grey plains vanishing to eternity; and there too, though they pretend to fear the East and point to the Hunnish and Turkish swords they have captured, and of how Attila was driven back, yet already the East is there. We pretend that European civilization has its roots in Greece, but since Greece has its roots in Asia, and our religion comes from Lebanon, it is hardly more than a protest which will grow fainter as time passes.

March 13th . . . I HAVE been looking again, with a sense of curious bewilderment, at the small sandstone statue of Buddha with his attendants which stands in my room. It was modelled by some priestly craftsman in the Liang Dynasty nearly fifteen hundred years ago. Less than a foot square, it has a cool concentrated devotion in its archaic forms; we could not carve like this today, because we could not believe in the depths of meaning which are contrived in the folds of the gown, in the aureoles, and in the kneeling boys. The faces are not Chinese, but they have about them an expression so nearly Chinese that it is easy enough to believe they were modelled on the faces of men from Central Asia who had come for many years into contact with Chinese power. The attendants wear the same slippers which we wear today, but their gowns are simpler than modern Chinese gowns and more like those worn in Japan. There is the *bodhi* tree springing from the lotos leaf, and

71

Buddha holds in his hands a gift of fruit—perhaps Buddha is already the goddess Kwan-yin and the fruit is a peach. Here, fashioned in Chinese Turkestan or somewhere in the south, Buddha has been caught and photographed at one of the moments of his pilgrimage and change. Once he was Apollo. He travelled through India, wearing many disguises, and when at last the portrait of him reached the later T'ang Dynasty, he was already a princess from the west—in his long pilgrimage he had changed even his sex, so that today my barber still has on his walls a portrait of a willowy girl holding peaches and wearing the silks of earlier dynasties. But what is most amazing is that I noticed for the first time today, on this Buddha carved so long ago, there is incised on the bare chest the sign of the swastika, the wheel turning as the sun turns, the sign of the Nazis, which the Buddhists employed as a sign of blessedness.

So the thing has suddenly sprung into the light and become contemporary. The small carved votive tablet is still fulfilling the purpose which was announced in the inscription, an inscription which never fails to move me because the floods and calamities of the Great Liang Dynasty are the same as ours. Here it is:

> *In the fourth year, and on the third day of the second moon, in the reign period Tien Chien, of the Great Liang Dynasty, the one who believes, Meng Chi-kung and his sons, Chen Chi and Chen Yeh, on behalf of the whole family who have so often met with calamities, faithfully promised this votive offering. They have now completed their task. They hope that the dead (members of the family) will enter the Three Orders, and that the living will soon abandon the Eight Calamities and pass through the gate of bitterness.*

Almost it has the brevity of the Greek Anthology; in their own terms, and using the necessary words, nothing could be simpler; and in our own day how many echoes there are to the hope that we shall "pass through the gate of bitterness."

March 17th, The Dream of the Red Chamber . . . SOME day this book must be translated in full. It is a long novel, over a thousand pages, and yet how deftly there is expressed in it the whole of a world! Though Dr. Hu Shih, who was once Ambassador to America, has made some important discoveries, we know even now almost nothing of the author, who lived in the Ch'ing Dynasty and

72

clearly described himself in the hero, subtly changing himself into the young and most sensual dreamer Pao Yu. There are perhaps only three great novels in the world—*The Dream of the Red Chamber, The Tale of Genji* and Marcel Proust's *In Search of Lost Time.* The first has been translated only in an abbreviated version, the second has been admirably translated by Arthur Waley and the third has been translated even more admirably by Scott-Moncrieff. But how extraordinary it is that this long Chinese novel, in which a whole dynasty appears by implications, in which the most prodigious tenderness and understanding and compassion have become the tools of the author, so that he is enabled to describe everything that passes in the minds of adolescents—everything without exception, has never been translated in full.

It is impossible to quote from the book. There are splendid passages, but so much splendour is lost in detaching them from their context that they are better left alone. We had hoped so often to translate it here, but it must wait now till we return to Peking. And this is what is so desperately annoying—this most perfect of all Chinese novels could have been translated in the relative quiet of our exile, and given to the world at the moment when it enjoys peace.

March 18th . . . J., who lived for a long time in Manchuria, told me this afternoon the story of Kornilev. He told it well, for evidently he admired the young bandit; and as he described the robberies in winter, the murders, the long chase through the forests, it was almost as though J. had known him intimately; and perhaps he did know him, for more than once he suggested details that could only have been known to one of Kornilev's companions.

"It was when I was a student in Harbin. It was a long time ago, but I can remember many details of this boy's life, and I often think of him. He was young and handsome, and he had declared war on the world; or rather he had declared war on the rich, and all the money he ever took from them he gave to the poor. He had a gold medal from his school, and afterwards they said one of his uncles had promised to send him to Belgium, but the uncle died, or perhaps there were other reasons, he did not go to Belgium and suddenly he disappeared from school.

"I think we were perturbed even then, because we all knew Kornilev would do great things, but we did not know the kind of

73

things he would do. We did not imagine he had gone out into the mountains alone. There were bandits in those days. He tried to find them, and soon he found a girl and another man, and the story was that they lived together, sharing their lives, and they made plans to capture Harbin.

"That was in the days when there were Russian military garrisons in Harbin, and nearly all the merchants were Jews. Most of the wealth of the place was in the hands of two men called Soskin and Nevaroff. They were fur-sellers, jewellers, wine-merchants, land-owners. They obeyed the orders of the military garrison, but they were themselves more important than the garrison. Gradually we began to hear of high-way robberies, and a little later we heard that one of the highwaymen had been recognized as Kornilev. We could make nothing of it. We thought of the handsome young man whom all the young girl-students adored, and we wished him luck. But the highway robberies increased; at first nearly every week and then nearly every day there were stories of these robberies, which were sometimes accompanied by murder. We noticed that he never murdered the poor camel-drovers, but always the merchants. And then gradually we heard that the robberies were coming closer—there was a robbery less than five miles away from the centre of the city, and then later there was a robbery at the gates, and then a little later Kornilev had entered the city itself, disguised as a peasant, and he had put up in the market-square a notice saying that he had come, defying the police to arrest him. The police could do nothing. They arrested everyone in the square, but they could not recognize Kornilev.

"Then—I do not know how it was—we began to hear more of Kornilev; we heard the names of his accomplices, and both were students from the technical school—the girl was extraordinarily beautiful, and the man was known as a clever mathematician. We heard that he was organizing a small band, perhaps a hundred disinherited peasants were living with him in the mountains. They sent soldiers after him, but they never found him. The long convoys of merchandise coming from China and Russia were now well-armed, yet he attacked them with impunity, and it was noticed that he behaved well to the women of the merchants and rarely removed their jewels. There must have been millions of roubles in his hide-out. And now he began to announce that on such and such a day he would enter the building of such and such a merchant, right in the heart of Harbin; and though they did every-

74

thing to prevent it, on the day he mentioned he would appear and disappear with a haul of furs, or diamonds, or silks.

"The garrison commander put a price on Kornilev's head, and a week later announced that he was prepared to offer Kornilev safe-conduct into the city. He would parley with Kornilev as one commander to another. It was a trap, of course. Kornilev very nearly fell for it. Shortly afterwards some small time bandits were arrested and publicly garotted. In reply Kornilev announced publicly—in the great market-square, in letters two foot high—that the garrison commander was receiving bribes from the merchants and that he had tolerated this long enough. He proposed to capture the garrison commander and the two merchants Soskin and Nevaroff who had offered the greatest bribes. The whole military force was advised that Kornilev was the enemy, to be shot at sight. Great columns of soldiers went out after him, drums beat all night, vast rewards were offered; still the diamonds, the furs, the great wooden cases of tea, even delicate machinery, even whole con-signments of guns and ammunition disappeared. One night there was a ball at the house of the garrison commander. Kornilev came, disguised as a merchant, with two of his men, and with the girl dis-guised as a young debutante, wearing ropes of pearls and a dia-mond tiara. It was marvellous. At the height of the ball the lights went out, and Kornilev stood among the famous generals and ad-ministrators with a revolver in his hand; and he looked more hand-some than ever, clean-jawed, beautifully built, lithe as a tiger. He said nothing. There were flashlamps, and we saw by their light, and Kornilev made a little speech, asking the ugly women to lay down their jewels and the young pretty women would be unharmed. He collected the jewels and then disappeared.

"But this time he had made a mistake, for once he had gone the garrison commander ordered that the gates of the city should be closed, and a watch kept. No one was allowed to move. The whole city was kept under observation. By now so many photographs of Kornilev had been published, that everyone knew what he looked like. But even then we thought he would escape.

"At school we prayed before the ikons that he would escape. Hours passed. We knew that at the moment of his capture, the whole city would know about it. We heard that on the Saturday the curfew would be lifted; we prayed that if he was still in the city, he would last out till the Saturday, and then he could hide himself among the villagers and make his way to the hills. But it was on the

Saturday that they captured him. He had escaped into a neighbouring village, but someone had squealed, seven thousand soldiers were sent out after him—seven thousand!—and at last they found him hiding in a lavatory with his girl.

"This was what was terrible—that he should have so undignified an end. We would have not minded so much if he had died among his hills, or if he had charged the soldiers on horseback with a sabre. But to capture him in a lavatory! It was like death for us—we went to school almost crying. There was a trial, of course. He admitted nothing. The trial went on for a long time, and at last the sentence was pronounced—garotting seven times.

"Perhaps you do not know what garotting means. A seven times garotting means that you are strangled seven times, and each time except the last you are brought back to life.

"We hoped he had poison, but he seems to have believed that his army in the hills would come and rescue him. It was a winter morning, with snow on the great market-place. He was sobbing like a child. Soskin and Nevaroff paid ten thousand gold to the Chinese who performed the garotting, to make sure they would not kill him before the seventh. He was twenty-six, and the execution lasted two hours and a quarter."

March 25th, The Saint . . . THERE are still times when conversation veers round to him. We have all known him, or seen him, or heard the legend of the young Cambridge scholar who came to China before the war, before the disease set in. His highest aim was to imitate the old Chinese scholars, to live only for scholarship, living quietly and undisturbed by the things of the world. He was brilliant in everything he touched. He had written nothing, but gave promise of writing so profoundly that people felt an instinctive sense of homage towards him. They said he had been the Generalissimo's English secretary; he had translated the speeches delivered at the beginning of the war into perfect Johnsonian English. It was the time when the Generalissimo still represented the best of China. Then he disappeared. He was next heard of in Kweilin, and then he returned to give broadcasts in Chungking, and then he disappeared again and we heard he was teaching English at a miserable salary, living in the house of a workman, with a box of books, a bed, a table and a chair. We have been trying to invite him to the University, but he has never answered our letters. And this evening K., an Englishman, said: "He is quite the
76

filthiest man alive. Lives with the Chinks. Lowering our prestige. Just going downhill."

It was odd, because I remember seeing him once in Chungking. It was after the rains, when the streets were running with blue water reflecting the sky. He was wearing a blue Chinese gown and a great yellow beard, and he was lifting the skirts of his gown as he walked barefoot in the rain. His prominent blue eyes were staring up at the sky and his great chest was inhaling the warm smoky-blue air. The children loved him and followed him and splashed him, and as he walked down the road, there was simply a man enjoying the wholeness of earth and sky. It was as simple as that. He was powerfully built, nearly six foot high, and he must have had immense reserves of resistance to have lived as he did, eating the coarsest of Chinese food.

"The mad Irishman," my companion murmured, and turned away with a look of hostility in his eyes.

"Are you sure he is mad?"

"Oh yes. It's quite certain. Look at his eyes."

He was coming past us, and you could see the protuberant eye-balls, but there was no madness in them—only a great delight. He must have had the strength of a lion, for I could see his great brown calves as he splashed through the muddy water; his hair flowed back like a lion's mane, and his beard was thrust forward like an offering to the sun; but I noticed that he had a nervous smile, a quick repetitive flashing smile directed at nothing in particular, the smile that you see on the faces of people who have starved or on the faces of those who are so nervous that smiling comes too easily to them.

A motor-bus passed, with its churning blue vapoury smoke, hiding him from view. And then instead of those mirror-pure pools of blue water, there were cesspools of mud, and he was covered with mud, dripping all over. Yet I do not think he noticed the mud, he walked straight on and the children followed him screaming with joy, and above him was the blue sky of Chungking and his white teeth glittered.

He gave the impression then of being a prince among men, and the closest I have ever seen to a saint. It was like a god walking to his appointed destiny. We watched him till he was out of sight, and I hoped I would meet him again, for so had Ulysses walked to the bronze gates of the palace of Alkinous and so should one walk through life.

77

March 26th . . . THE howling of dogs at night, just after sunset; the splutter of fire-crackers; the girls from the tribes riding down from the mountains in the dawn; the mud-huts on the campus with their broken paper windows; the professors who are still starving and the students who are no longer starving, because many of them have got jobs with the Americans who are now in Kunming; the utter sadness and joy of China: these are the things we contemplate while the war goes on.

We are cut off from the war, though aeroplanes fly over our heads all day, and though we are nearer to America than we have ever been before. Every five minutes another aeroplane comes over the Hump and lands on the great airstrip near the lake, so heavily laden that the wheels throw up an explosion of white powder the moment they touch earth. Even now, though less than before, our nights are made luminous with wing-tip lights. And sometimes, on the rare occasions when there is a storm, we hear the moaning of the aeroplanes which are not allowed to land. Six aeroplanes have crashed against the Western Hills; no one knows how many have overshot the landing markers and been burnt on the field. Warsaw, Poland, Berlin, Budapest and all France are broken, but in these backwaters nothing is harmed, or rather everything is harmed by the slow, desiccating, tormenting inflation, which is responsible for all the dead bodies one sees, and all the misery. Whose fault? The merchants and the bureaucracy above all, and the idiot irresponsibility which has settled on the country like a plague of locusts. There is no "treason of the clerks," for the greater part of the clerks are innocent. Nor is it in any sense treason, when the whole government of a nation has become irresponsible. The Generalissimo says: "For the sake of the Party and the Nation." Hitler ordered crosses to be put up on the bodies of those who were slain in Russia, and on the crosses there were inscribed the words: "For Hitler and Fatherland." When the country becomes the second thing in men's minds, then we have the beginning of treason.

I still have hope for China, but less now than before. I thought there would be peace; I know now there will be civil war. With the war against Japan still being fought, there is mounting evidence that the Kuomintang is planning for a three years' war against the Communists; planning deliberately and desperately, against the better advice of their most responsible advisers; planning for the sake of planning, and for the sake of war. And this leaves us chilled

78

beyond belief, because we know that China has suffered too much, and dare not suffer more.

March 27th . . . MODERN China has nothing to teach us, but surely we have everything to learn from the old! The old sacramental life of the rituals and the seasons, of the scholars devoted to scholarship, of imperial examinations through which the most humble could rise to positions of power, but only through their scholarship, the dances and the festivals and the games, surely these are important; and perhaps it is because we no longer have any sacramental beliefs that we are at the mercy of war.

"The way of Heaven," wrote Confucius, "is ruthless: no leaf is spared because of its beauty, no flower because of its fragrance." But though the Heaven of the ancient Chinese was ruthless, it was not arbitrary; it obeyed its own laws, and those laws were predominantly the laws of ritual and the seasons. The brooding immensity of Thomas Hardy's world is alien to the ancient Chinese spirit which sees the visible heavens constantly changing, and from this constant change has evolved an austere worship of its powers. Heaven was impersonal and passionless; it was not just; it was not unjust; and men were imagined to have contact with Heaven only through the mediation of the Emperor. In this simple cosmology the Emperor claimed no power except that which was vouchsafed to him by the people and by Heaven.

So the Emperor wore the twelve emblems—the sun, the moon, the dragon, the phoenix and the mountain on the upper garment, and on the lower garment there was an embroidered sacrificial cup, a reed, a flame, a sheaf of grain, a battle-axe and some other sign whose meaning remains unknown. So deeply were these emblems engraved on the minds and hearts of the Chinese that even today the Great Seal of the Republic bears the twelve emblems.

But the Emperor himself was in theory powerless, claiming no powers except those which Heaven allowed him. Repeatedly in Chinese history he is made to refer to himself as "the only one," "the abandoned," "the lost one." If the people are discontented, he must be dethroned—by force, if necessary. In the commentary to the *Bamboo Books* it is stated that when Yao had been Emperor for seventy years, a brilliant star was seen and phoenixes wandered in the courtyard of the palace, and grain was abundant; sweet dew moistened the ground and crystal springs sprang from the hills.

This was the good augury. But when the Hsia Empire was declining in luxury several hundreds of years later, the usurper invoked the evil auguries—the blackbirds and the crows and the late harvest—and the Emperor was dethroned. So, too, in the *Book of Songs* we have some of the original curses which may have helped to dethrone the Emperors:

> *I look despairingly to Heaven,*
> *But find no pity there.*
> *For years we have been without peace:*
> *Heaven grinds me on a whetstone.*

The Emperor, then, was the mediator, but of equal value was the Great Sage, who wore no regal and embroidered gowns, and often starved as he wandered among the conflicting tribes. You recognize him by his evident authority. "Like a fathomless fountain he springs forth and waters the plains. Being all-embracing like Heaven and deep as a spring from the abyss, when he appears, the people all reverence him; when he speaks they all trust him; when he acts, they take delight in him. So his fame spreads through the Kingdom and even among the barbarians. Wherever ships and carriages go, wherever the strength of man penetrates, wherever the canopy of Heaven is overhead, on whatever spot the sun and the moon shine, this delight in him comes forth." There are other signs. There are auguries at his birth, and auguries announce his death; and in himself he is a man who suffers the suffering of the people. In this he is like the European hero—Christ and Prometheus and a million others—but what is important to the Chinese is not his suffering, but the peace he brings to the people. The Chinese are obsessed with the thought of a land at peace. The landscape they paint is the landscape of their dreams—a landscape without war; there are no recorded Chinese paintings of war (though there are a thousand Japanese paintings of war) and hardly any poems in which the poets delight in war. The unending dream is recorded in the *Ta Tung:* "When the great Tao was practiced, the world was common to all. Men of great talents were selected: virtue was respected, and brotherhood was cultivated. Therefore they did not only love their parents, nor did they love only their sons. The aged were provided for, all able-bodied men found employment, the young were cared for, kindness and compassion were shown to widows and orphans, and all were served. Men had the work proper to them and women had their homes; and
80

all hated to see their fields untilled, yet none hoarded tillage. They hated themselves if they did not exert themselves; they did not exert themselves only for themselves. Thieves, robbers and traitors did not show themselves, and the doors were left open always."

To the Chinese scholars, reading these words now, knowing that "thieves, robbers and traitors" are abroad, that nothing they can do will affect the situation as it is now, no words could be more ironical. In this most tragic of all lands, there is almost no hope that we shall come soon to a time when "the doors are left open."

March 28th . . . I HAVE heard better ghost stories in China than anywhere else. There are stories of fox-spirits and of stones that came to life, and there is the story which R. told me one evening when the wind was coming through the paper windows and rats were scuttling behind the mortar walls. "There was nothing strange. It was like every other day at Peking, and the sky was glittering. It was in the afternoon towards twilight when I went out into the courtyard, and then I noticed on the roof there were twenty or thirty blue figures walking, and I could not understand why they were there, and just watched them. They talked animatedly and walked along the roof, and the heavy blue gowns had heavy folds, and I remember I thought: 'There is wind, and it is surprising that the gowns do not change their folds.' I was disturbed by their appearance and watched them for a long time, and when I went into the house a telegram came to say that my uncle was dead."

But the best of all the stories I know is recorded in Feng Yu-hsiang's autobiography:

"My father was a very religious man. On the first and fifteenth day of each moon he would put on his full uniform and prostrate himself before a painting of Kwan-yin; and afterwards he would sit in meditation with his feet crossed, counting his beads. One afternoon, after he had returned from camp, a snake crawled into the room where he was praying. It was a bright yellow snake, seven or eight feet long, and it was crawling along the south wall. My mother was frightened out of her wits, and rushed with me out of the room.

"My father, entirely worthy of his buddhist training, showed perfect self-control; he was not in the least disturbed by my mother's panic-stricken cries. He sat there as calmly as ever, looking at the yellow snake, which he believed to be the god of wealth,

81

and then he began to kowtow to the snake, and all the while he was repeating: 'Amida Buddha, Amida Buddha. . . .' "

It is not, of course, a ghost story, but I know nothing so ghostly as the moment when this harassed old soldier kow-towed to the immensely long yellow snake.

April 2nd . . . THE conversation turned to Tsao Yu, the greatest, I believe, of all contemporary Chinese playwrights. I remembered him well, for I had taught in the same University; lean, well-formed, a long sensitive sunburned face, with impatient long hair that fell over his forehead, quiet and short, yet given to furious bursts of energy, a hater of dictatorship and a lover of beauty. I remember most the dark eyes, in which the love and the hatred were most pronounced, and the stentorian actor's voice which would call to me across the campus; and then too there were the legends of the women he had adored, and his terrible impulsiveness, the sweetness of his smile and his moments of despair. He was the first to bring the western stage, with all its complexities, to China. In his play *Peking Man* he confronted the first inhabitant of China with the feudal and degenerate descendants of old Peking families; Peking Man himself, in all his primitive vigour, leaps onto the stage. The title of Tsao Yu's plays indicate his main strength— *Thunder and Rain, Sunrise, The Wild Plain, Peking Man, The New Birth*—in the same way that Lu Hsun's titles—*Crying, Hesitating*, and there were many more—were indicative of his country's weakness. Nearly all Tsao Yu's plays take place at night and end with the dawn. An immense, desolating and over-riding pity for all helpless things informs everything he has done, but I did not know till this evening that he wrote in the introduction to *Sunrise:* "So many terrible things oppress me. I shall never forget these evils till my death. . . . One after another these errors have penetrated my heart, and I must seek some means of revenge."

April 3rd . . . THE stars came out white and clear, so many that the sky was like an immense bridal veil, not silver but pure white sheets flowing in waves across the sky, and softly undulating, a night so unlike other nights that it seemed as though it had come upon the earth for the first time. And the trees were smaller than ever, and the lake was dead black, having no existence because only the sky was alive. In this clearness, with the end of the wars in sight, what auguries are foretold?

82

According to the Egyptians, the stars were the body of a woman arched across the sky, and I confess this pleases me more than all the mythologies which give to star-shapes the names of heroes and animals. The night is feminine; the day belongs to man. Looking at the sky tonight, no other explanation was required, and all our complex mythologies seemed fruitless. China has never possessed complex mythologies; the mythologies of China are tenuous things, ever changing, the tribes came together and just as the two crowns of Egypt were made into a single double crown, so the mythology of one tribe was incorporated into the mythology of another; there are the great Emperors Shun and Yao, and before them there was Pan Ku, whose hairs became the forests and whose breath the winds; but nothing is more certain that these mythologies come from different tribes. What is delightful in Greek mythology is that it seems to stem from a single gift of feeling. There are no two-headed lambs, no monsters except the Cyclopeans, there are tombs of golden masks, there is Dodona and the unchanging sea. Men live near the shore, between the desert and the town, the gods and goddesses careless of their divinity and having the size of men, fighting among men and suffering from men's sins. Our western gods do not carve through mountains so that rivers can flow; they are more accustomed to small streams, they lift their skirts and wade across, and almost they have no magic powers. And then it occurred to me, looking at the great black deserted lake in the distance, that the Chinese gods can only have sprung from long wanderings in desert places, huge, magnificent in kindness, and always old.

April 7th . . . I MET him first half an hour after he had jumped by parachute from an aeroplane over Kunming, a huge young American, larger than life, with close-cropped hair and a German name. He said: "The thing you have to do is just go limp. Don't fight against it. Just let yourself fall." He was so heavy that they had to give him an outsize parachute; his clothes fitted tight on him, and you thought he would burst out of them; he smiled gently, and looking at these powerful shoulders, you understood why he was afraid of his own strength. I saw him rarely. He disappeared for months on end, mysteriously travelling behind Chinese lines or through the heart of Japanese country. He came back yesterday. He had been on two missions, one in Burma and another in Fukien. On each of the missions he went with millions of Chinese dollars,

83

with tommy-guns and high explosives and an interpreter, for he knows no Chinese, and he would tell the story of his adventures very quietly, without quite believing what had happened, thinking of his wife and his ranch, or of the gangsters he had once known in Cleveland. "The worst moment was in Kachin country. I was going alone—nearly alone, and we knew the Kachins were near us. We felt them. We were walking down a forest path in single-file, and sometimes we saw the glint of their knives, but there was no sound. We had gone on for a long time, and then we came upon three Chinese soldiers—but the soldiers were headless. We knew what had happened. The Kachins had cut off each head with a single blow of their long *daos*.

"There was nothing we could do. We went on more carefully—that's all, and then sometime in the evening we came upon a Kachin village. It was clear that they distrusted us, but they knew I was an American, and this puzzled them—they did not know whether they were allowed to kill the Chinese who were with me. They stood there, with their arms folded, the long knives at their sides, and they said they were pleased to see us, and they looked up and down at me, and they could not make me out—they are small fellows, though very proud. They kept on looking at me like that. I didn't like it. They came and felt my muscles, and I wondered whether they had decided to put me in a cauldron and see whether I was worth eating. But they didn't boil me alive—they asked me instead whether I was prepared to fight with their three strongest men. I nodded. There wasn't much else I could do. So they took us into their tribal temple, and all over the rafters there were heads stuck on nails, and some of them looked very new. I knew a lot about the head-hunters by this time; I was beginning to be afraid. They have guns and they are good at firing them. If I won the fight over their three strongest men, they would probably kill me; and if I lost I would be killed anyway. It was six of one and half a dozen of the other.

"It was getting dark, and we stripped and fought, and all the while I was expecting a *dao* to cut off my head, or perhaps they would simply fire at me. I was unprotected, and I liked them. They must have sensed it. I knew they were cowards. They don't fear guns, but they fear hand-grenades, and they can't make out 'stringers,' which are small things like pencils that shoot about fifteen yards. Well, I won. It was a near thing, but the three strongest men were down on the ground, and for some reason they

84

did not kill me, they gave me embroidered cloth and showed me the path to the next village. I was frightened as hell. It was dark. I set off with the others, and we had gone fifty yards down the road when there was a burst of machine-guns firing at us. Odd kind of freaks. I suppose they had a passion for changing their minds."

He spoke about other things: how nearly all the mayors in the Japanese-occupied villages were pro-Chungking. He would go there, and find that they knew he was coming, and everything was prepared. There would be feasts for him, the mayor would sometimes present him with one of the mayoral concubines, and once he had helped some Chinese to capture a company of Japanese. The Japanese had plundered and raped; mercy towards others had never occurred to them, but when they saw the American they threw themselves down on their knees. "It was indescribably squalid. They were weeping and shivering with fear. The Chinese pointed out the man who had done most harm, the man who had murdered and raped his way through this small backwater of China. It was this man who was kneeling before me. I lifted him up by the neck and slowly squeezed the life out of him. . . ."

April 9th . . . Though we dream of America, we know that China will outlive all we have produced in the West. The dream of America is very real; but we do not dream of Pittsburgh or New York or Chicago—the things that are closest to us are the goldenrod in Maine, the persimmons falling, the lean hogs rooting for them, the snow falling in the woods of Minnesota and the loveliness of the Hudson River; we dream of juleps, fried chicken and corn-pudding, of Negro spirituals and the long evenings of the south. The redwoods of the coast appeal to us like the tidewater in Virginia, and sometimes, reading a Chinese book, we find ourselves involuntarily thinking of the groves of firs and cedars in Oregon—we call them groves because in this treeless land we cannot even imagine forests. The apple-blossoms and apples of Shenandoah, the woods and sheepwalks of Maryland, burr oak and shag bark, the rustling of fieldmice in the shucked corn of Illinois. And we, who are in such desperate need for mythologies, may find at last that there is no need for mythology: it will be enough if we simply come into contact with such simple peaceful things. And perhaps this is the strength of the Chinese in the present-day, who suffer viciously as none have ever suffered before, because they have their simple peaceful things all round them and have grown through the habit of mythologies, have forgotten once and for all the necessity of demanding explanations.

April 13th . . . THE war drags to its end, Berlin on fire, Budapest in ruins, Cracow a shell, Paris alone unharmed. I have asked the Chinese professors and students what they think of this: there are two answers. The professors say: Perhaps in a year we shall reach Peking. The students say: Perhaps in six months we shall return to our villages, we shall spend a week there, perhaps two weeks, then we shall have the immense task of putting China on her feet again.

The horror has been mounting so long that the capitulation of Germany becomes only another horror, different in degree but not in kind. The horror cannot cease, cannot suddenly be changed into darkness. In the history of nations no curtain falls unless every person in that nation has left the stage. And for the same reason no curtain rises unless every person is present.

And in China they are not present; for many weary months the audience will be faced with the curtain, and from behind the curtain we shall hear the three parties howling at each other. There is no conceivable identity between the Kuomintang, the Communists and those who have lived under Japanese control. It is not only that they have no community of interest, but all have suffered in different ways, and the suffering must be exorcised in different ways. There are three diseases demanding three separate cures. We shall be in danger of forgetting the extent of the disease if we forget that a third of the Chinese race lived under the Japanese.

It is not entirely their fault, though it will be worth while to remember that there has been more treason in China than elsewhere. These last five years have taught me little except that much of that treason was justified, and will remain justified, until the Chinese peasant has an elementary chance to survive. They grew up under militarism, their villages at the mercy of warlords no better than the Japanese. They have seen their brothers starving, and they have no deep-rooted consciousness of being Chinese. Their loyalties are to their families, only because in these vast wars only the families have power to act together; afterwards comes their loyalty to the village, a long way afterwards comes their loyalty to the *hsien,* and infinitely distant is their loyalty to the state. It was not always like this. Sun Yat-sen spoke of the Chinese as "a
86

sheet of scattering sand." It is true, but there are virtues in sand—if a bomb falls, the sand rises and floats down again, and is almost the same.

But how in a world so broken can those three elements of the Chinese race come together? It would be a mistake to under-estimate the power of those who have lived under the Japanese. It was not that they were treacherous, but they grew accustomed to treason. It is the greatest wound, but who shall say it is more poisonous than the wound that has overtaken Chungking? The bureaucracy is out of touch with the people, the military organizations are out-of-date, there is so much of modern China which is hardly more than a survival of the Chou Dynasty three thousand years ago. It was said that General Ho Ying-chin offered the Generalissimo three tripods, the legendary offering which is made to the great leader of the people. The Generalissimo refused. It is to his credit that he refused, but it is hardly to the credit of the General Staff that it should have thought in the terms that were applicable in the reigns of the Emperors Shao and Yu some five thousand or more years ago. There are too many anachronisms, too many anachronistic minds. There is a broken people, starving, with almost no hospitals in the country and few trained minds. The brilliance of some scientists and teachers must not be allowed to blind us that China is on the verge of self-discovery. It is true that she is awake at last, but at what a cost have these blood-rimmed eyes been opened! Better almost would have been to sleep this western nightmare away.

In the history of a nation no curtain rises till every person is present, until there is some unity of purpose and desire. Nationalism has been achieved. It was not won by the Kuomintang, a party which made its greatest error when it placed nationalism first of the sacred three principles. It is neither the Kuomintang nor the Communists who are responsible for the scattered successes which have been won in China during the war—those successes were won by farm-boys, who fought (to their credit) for things they hardly believed in, since to them a village was greater than an Empire. And so it must be repeated, again and again, till the belief penetrates our western minds, that the government of China is nothing, and the people are everything. And this is as it should be, according to the most ancient Chinese traditions, since the Emperor was nothing but the mediator between the people and Heaven, the unmoving pipe-line, whose power was at the mercy

87

of a single flight of crows or the revolt of the people. But now that they are revolting, will the Emperor delegate his powers?

The greatest single obstacle to the peace of China is the Generalissimo. His virtues are only too well-known. No one, least of all the Communists, believe him to be in love with power. This bald, overworked, Confucian scholar with the training of a second-class private in Japan and the sympathies of a parade-ground sergeant, who has modelled himself on the most reactionary and scholarly of all generals, Tseng Kuo-fan, who loves China passionately with the orphan's love of the surviving mother, a man who is not in the least a mediocrity but one who has obeyed the hardest impulses of his heart, an ascetic and a mystic who every morning stands in silence and listens to the clear voices of dawn, an old Testament Christian who believes in a moral law, yet governs by means of the secret police, the most forgiving of men, since some of his greatest enemies have been put in positions of high power; this man, for whom I have the greatest respect and admiration, seems to be the most dangerous for the peace of China because his amazing virtues are no longer those that are required. What is wanted is the delicacy of the surgeon's hand; this Chinese wound will not heal with a knife. And he will insist on using the knife, because no other weapon is known to him. We can no longer afford to have warlords, but still less can we have this unwieldy military government, where everything is done in secret, by secret cliques, and where power goes wandering whenever the Generalissimo wanders. This is what fills me with horror at this war's end—I cannot believe that the man I respect most will have the courage to relinquish his power.

Does it matter who takes the power? I would prefer a government of mediocrities than a government of military saints, and have no hope that we shall be able to persuade one to improve on the other. The war is won, but not by China. Zhukov and Eisenhower near Berlin will sweep the Japanese from China, but they have been able to do this only because the Chinese armies kept the Japanese from Szechuan. I thought once that the final battles of this war would be fought in Vienna and Szechuan. It was nearly true, for it is certain that the end is coming not far from Vienna and on the borders of Szechuan the Japanese at last began their slow retreat. But the cost has been too great everywhere, and not least in China, where the wounds of war take longer to heal.

It is best to be detached—neither pessimist nor optimist. I have great hopes for China, but it is permissible to observe that though China is awake and the eyes are opened, the eyelids are clogged with too much blood. The best was the past, but the Chou Dynasty only existed in legend and the T'ang was a mess of wars; the scholars and the artists were greater than their governments even then. It is permissible to see in those young students, who are more handsome and clear-sighted than any students I have ever seen, a more compassionate future; but I know now their weaknesses. They live, as we lived when we were students, in a glittering romantic world. They, too, have read their Shelley and Blake, they can still see the flames which announced the French Revolution, and feel in their bones the glory of the new dispensation, before Napoleon's whiff of grapeshot broke the fine impatience of the people and turned them all to soldiers. I have no fear of a march on Moscow, but I fear the whiffs of grapeshot and the disillusioned eyes. Over thirty, we are all disillusioned in China. The illusions will come again when we are a little older, and often they return, and they return most of all in schools and Universities; but the war has chastened us beyond measure, as it has chastened and killed so many. Will they keep their promises? They desire nothing better than to serve China? Will the government allow them to serve? Will they be able to give as freely as they desire? We need some ghost of a thing to attach ourselves to, something we can admire so stringently that we can give everything we have to its purpose. But where is the thing? With China split into three and a military dictatorship, I see no signs of the China for which men can give without reserve.

This is certain: they will give as much as they can, treading the dangerous line where east and west will meet. China is not perhaps the important thing. A social revolution will sweep over the whole of Asia, and Asia itself will come into its own. An Asiatic bloc is not improbable. There are signs of its coming—stray signs, like the Indian student here who is translating Confucius into Hindustani; and it may be that the coveted nationalism of the East will be thrown overboard once acquired. Asia for the Asiatics? Power will come to the east, but I think it will be peaceful power—they have suffered too much to play with war again. To imagine that America and Russia are the great colossi is like thinking one move ahead in chess; the greatest colossus of all is the babe with the bloody eyes.

I have more than hope, but I know that the way is untried and

89

desperately unsafe. If the Chinese students and professors were in power, I should have greater hope. I should have more hope still if I could see clearly through the murk of the three diseases which inflict such terrible injuries—diseases which may grow when they come into contact with one another, as a man is weakened more than thrice if he suffers thrice. The best way was the legendary way; that has passed. The new way is harder than anything that was performed when the Emperor ordered the progress of the people with something of the instinct of Heaven ordering the progress of the stars. I repeat: the East can never be the enemy of the west—it owes too much in technical knowledge and in the technique of education ever to come into conflict with us. But the gravest danger of all is incessant, incestuous conflict with herself, not knowing the way out and therefore swinging her arms wildly. As I see it, what will be wanted more than ever is foreign teachers who are skilled in inventing techniques. What is wanted is young people, who have respect for the deep resources of Asia; the financiers and military advisers are wanted least of all. In the beginnings of our contact with Asia Rome sent Jesuit missionaries, Verbiest, Schall and others, who were wisest when they showed their respect for ancient canons, and most ill-advised when dogma entered into their plans. We should have no dogmas in Asia, and no armies. Best, too, to have no more missionaries unless they are medical missionaries. We are faced with the greatest of all problems —not the greatness of Russia and America, but the towering emergence of Asia with its untapped resources of power. . . .

April 14th . . . I SLEPT late, and when I awoke M. came in, crying. Why? Roosevelt is dead. I have never known such grief. It is on everyone's faces. It is like stumbling in snow—not knowing— The worst of it is that we knew he was frail, but we had made an image of him in which there was no place for frailty. The old charwoman has bought some spills to light before his photograph which hangs on her broken wall. The students looked apathetic, wearing their "Roosevelt issue," saying very little. J. said: "It will be delayed shock. We will realize it more deeply next week." The soldiers have gone into mourning. There are black arm-bands. One wonders when they will be taken off. Crowds round the O.W.I., just standing there, as the English stand round Buckingham Palace on days of national mourning. The misery of it goes deeper than we shall ever know.

90

April 15th . . . The failing light over Europe and the other light rising over Asia, which fails and seems to burn out, flickering horribly in the wind, but like the Chinese candle when blown out, suddenly and inexplicably reviving. There are some of us who have come to this point: our greatest hope lies in something which, at the moment when we gaze at it, shows no light.

Above all, to keep faith with this, not blindly, but because demonstrable truths are there. The Chinese and the Indians have no need for this faith: for them it is not a faith, but an elementary need, like bread.

The major task facing the West is the patient understanding of the East. We shall never understand wholly these men who in a most complete sense are our enemies, for they will take from us without ever believing in it the things we prize most in mechanical civilization. There are places in China which have jumped from the Stone Age to the age of radial engines and blockbusters. They know nothing of the long journey we have taken towards mechanization, of how our impulses sprang from Mesopotamia, Egypt, Athens and Crete and so through Rome and the Holy Roman Empire. They cannot believe that we have a history as they have a history, nor are they taught, in any of the schools I know, more than a brief summary of our ancient history, yet our ancient history is more contemporary with modern China than anything recorded in mediæval times. The great movements of Egypt, Athens and Rome are nearer to us than the wars of succession. They do not know this, and perhaps will never know it; they will take all we have to offer in their stride, and yet we, who have so much to take from them, are in the same case—with the greatest imaginable difficulty we must discover the springs of their behaviour. And these we can only find in their past.

More and more I feel that government should be taken out of the hands of lawyers and placed in the hands of historians, even of journalists. Or perhaps more particularly it should be placed in the hands of men who have been journalists and studied history. The game of words at conference tables must remain, but the highest powers must never be given to sleepwalkers, soldiers or lawyers— the three most dangerous races of all the races of men.

But now, with the death of Roosevelt, the task has become inconceivably difficult. In the East they trusted him. They believed he was simple and honest, they threw around him the mantle of Lincoln, he became in the purest sense the image of prevailing

91

justice. It may be that they did not trust him always for the right reasons, but at least their trust was justified, because it was necessary that there should be trust in the West. We pray that an image as great as his will take his place, and know there is none.

May 3rd . . . To FORGET the war, one has only to step out in the direction of the lake with its tumbling arch-ways, its gold-fish, its camel-back bridges and wooden pavilions lying above the reeds. There are small flat-bottomed boats which float on the still water like boats in dreams. This is not the picture which Chinese artists have painted for you—no solitary fisherman among mists, nor are there egrets: only a few yellow-gold hoopoes with stiff yellow brushes on their pert heads, and occasional crows. There is a legend that a fabulous battle took place not far from here in a valley beyond the red-gashed hills: the crows and the hoopoes fought a battle, and hardly a single hoopoe survived, and all over the field there was blood. It is a better legend, and probably more true than the legend of the Indian Prince who came during the Han Dynasty in search of a green horse and a gold cock; for we live in the kind of world where aerial battles take place. A wing with a star has drifted to the surface of the lake—more than thirty American airplanes have been broken on these hills. But it was the lake that attracted our attention, so inconceivably still, so full of drowsy colours, an opium-dream come to life. And there was nothing in the least surprising, even in the opium dream, to find that the lake was covered with boats with their cargo of lovers.

May 4th . . . SCREAMS at night, and then a long silence. It happens often; we shudder in bed, because we live outside the wall, in the bad-lands where until recently there were murders so often they were past counting. It was a girl's voice, and she sounded as though she was very young. I inquired about it this morning. Nothing. No one else had heard it; and I shall never know whether she was dead when she reached our door, for there they were—the tarnished red evidences of unknown horrors last night, two inches away from the great black gates which are bolted and fastened with a heavy wooden stake each night; and the dogs of the place were licking the red stains.

May 5th . . . L. WAS complaining for the ten thousandth time of the influence of the French in Yunnan. The garrison soldiers wear

French helmets, the shop signs are still occasionally in French, there are even Annamite girls whose skirts are slit higher than the skirts of Chinese girls; and it seemed strange that he should object to these things. A *poilu's* helmet is irretrievably feminine, and these handsome young soldiers, with white leg-bands and dark uniforms, plump as English chickens, were at least pleasing to the eye. Then what did he object to? Was it that half the Communist leaders in Yenan are returned students from France? Was it that in the house of a general we know there are tasteless French embroideries and alarm-clocks, and in the gardens of the American consulate there are nudes of stone which have seen better days. It turned out that it was none of these things. The thing that hurt him most was to see in the hands of all the middleschool children and nearly all the shop-clerks a book by Pa Chin, which has the simple title *Home*. I asked what this had to do with his temporary horror of France. He explained that Pa Chin (a pseudonym which derives from the first syllable of Bakunin and the last of Lenin) was a returned student from France, where he had inherited his anarchism. "And the devil of it," L. went on, "is that he is not entirely a bad writer. He says things which are fundamentally true, and his account of the decay of the old families in Chengtu I know to be accurate, because my own family decayed in the same way. But there it is! He offers, in very simple sentimental language a picture of decay, and he has put nothing in its place. They lap it up. They are indescribably affected by the picture he draws of a society which no longer owes respect to the fathers of families, but he leaves his young men with headaches and mistresses and a kind of vague belief in Shelley—for Shelley is his favourite poet. It is easily the most popular novel in present-day China. It is good, but how much better it would have been if he had had the courage to draw a picture of society as he wants it. We know that the old was bad; we have no idea where to find the good."

Soon the film of *Home* is coming to Kunming; we shall all flock to it, and we shall sympathize with the young anarchist hero and we shall hate the old patriarch who orders the servant girl to drown herself, because she is his son's lover; and however bad the film, we shall find ourselves in deep sympathy with the young and with a horror of the old. I agree that it is not fair, but I am inclined to believe that it is inevitable. *Home* will probably never be translated. It demands of the reader too great a knowledge of the complexities of the old Chinese family system, the loyalties and the fierce dynamic which ruled over the ancestors. But sometimes even the dons will admit that he writes well. I had written years ago a novel which began in a snow-scene, and somehow it seemed perfect that we should be presented first with the white page of snow, from which slowly and delicately the characters of the story are made known. And though it may be true as L. says, that I like in novels only the drama, and have less care in the slow elaboration of character, I know few things better than the opening scene of *Home*:

"The wind blew relentlessly, and the air was alive with flakes of snow, torn cotton-reels aimlessly dancing and falling to the ground. On both sides of the road, beneath the walls, the snow was piled high, so that the road seemed to be lined with two trips of white braid; in between the strips of white braid lay the muddy road.

"There they were—the people walking down the road and the sedan chairs, all fighting against the fleecy wind, all losing their courage in the effort. Incessantly and increasingly the snow fell filling the air with misty whiteness. Snow settled on everything, on umbrellas, on covered tops of sedan chairs, on the straw hats of the sedan chair carriers and on the faces of the young.

"Whirled by the wind, the umbrellas were bent to all angles; more than once they were wrested away from their possessors. Mingled with the footfalls on the snowy paths came the wail of the wind, forming a kind of ancient music, which grated on people's ears, arousing in them a sense of terror and distress. It was as though the wind said: This snow and this wind will govern the world forever—there will never be a spring.

"Dusk was gathering, clouds sagged, and in the streets you saw only the disjointed outlines of men and things, for the street-lamps were still unlit and what other lights there were had altogether disappeared in the increasing dark. Streets drowned in water and mud, air chilling the reluctant flesh; and the walkers thought only of the brightness and warmth of their homes.

" 'Oh, hurry, hurry!' said the boy with the gold-rimmed spectacles, which shone above his round frozen face. . . ."

May 9th . . . THERE was a cold wind in the air this morning, and most of the students were wearing gowns. It was time. I thought there would be no more gowns on the campus, for half of the students seemed to have taken to the blue Sun Yat-sen uniform, which resembles a bus conductor's uniform, and the other half were wearing "Roosevelt issue" which gives them the appearance of GI's.

The gown has evident advantages. It is graceful, it is warmer than an overcoat, it has heavy sleeves which serve as places where one can conceal frosted hands, it is cheap, it lasts longer, it can easily be washed—but it has one drawback, it is so long that you are continually tripping over it. The Athenian *chiton* reached to the knees; the Chinese gown demonstrates the greater modesty of the Chinese male, who prefers his feet to be concealed. Wearing a Chinese gown, it is impossible to walk quickly, or rather it was impossible once, and now the young students think nothing of striding in their long gowns, till you can hear the crackle of seams and see the thickset knees jerking against the cloth. The upper part of the gown is narrow, becoming fuller towards the base; and this too is functional, since until recently all Chinese scholars had narrow shoulders. Times are changing. The student who greeted me this morning had over his "Roosevelt issue" a gown which was slit to the waist—he kept warm, and at the same time he had freedom to move his knees.

May 10th . . . HE WAS an old *rentier* with a grey face, a stubbly beard, a faded gown with the white dribble from his opium-pipe staining it to the waist, and he moved ponderously and slowly when he came into our room. His secretary came with him. I have noticed that the secretaries of old *rentiers* have a curious depravity of feature; they seem, even when you meet them on the most law-abiding occasions, to be looking for opportunities of murdering their employers. This young man was dark-skinned and sly, with high curving eyebrows, an inch long mole on his chin from which three hairs sprung like a moth's antennae. I did not like him. He leered as he translated the old man's words, and he told us a story about a young Chinese giant from the north, from Hupeh, who was arrested for murder. He was put to jail and told that he would be executed. The young giant took his fate meekly till the next afternoon when the gendarmerie came to take him to the burial mound. He hid behind the door, he hung to the bars, he refused to be moved away, and even when they had struck him over the head with rifle-butts, there was so much life in him that he clung to his cell,

95

completely silent, throwing himself down when they lifted him up, somehow escaping from them even when they had bound his wrists with yellow cord; completely defenceless except for the strength he derived from fear, a man, said the young secretary, who was inspired with the passion of living. What was strange was that he never spoke. Like an animal at bay, he reserved his strength for the fight; and it was half an hour before they could get him, still struggling wildly, out of the cell. And as he told us all this the young secretary's face quivered with remembered excitement—it was clear that he had been in charge of the execution and perhaps also of the trial. Only once did this incredible giant raise his voice and that was when they were a few paces away from the prison gates, and he said: "I am innocent."

"Well, then, we had to carry him to the execution ground. He had no dignity. He struggled—this immense giant—all the way to the burial ground, and once he even slipped away, the gendarmerie fired after him, he was unwounded and he was only captured when he was cornered again in a pastry-shop. A tremendous man, seven foot high at least. And he said nothing. We carried him outside the Small West Gate, eight of us, all tugging and pulling, and when at last we had reached the place where he was to be executed, more and more strength surged in him, and we were afraid we would fail to execute him; we were all throwing ourselves upon him, beating him over the head with our rifle-butts, he was covered in blood, we had broken some of his bones and we heard the grinding noise, and still he fought blindly, and then at last we were able to step away, and he was lying on the ground, we took aim and at that moment he rose, he almost shot up, facing us, and he said quietly, his face covered with blood: 'Give me the sun.' And then we all fired at once, and altogether it was necessary to fire nearly forty shots before he was dead, and then we buried him." And while he was telling the terrible story, the young secretary leaned forward with excitement, his face quivering, and the three long hairs sticking to the mole were trembling with indignation.

We had forgotten the old *rentier*. Perhaps the story was too much with him, he complained of pains, his grey face became greyer, he leaned back in the chair breathing heavily. We suggested aspirins, or whisky to revive him, but he waved us away weakly. I thought he would die there, and in fact nothing would have pleased me better, but instead of dying he began to demand loudly a copper coin. We found a copper coin. The secretary took it, undressed the

96

old rentier to the waist and began to rub the copper coin over the chest and the stomach. Bright red patches appeared. His breathing became more regular. For half an hour he lay there, purring like a cat while the red patches increased in size and ceaselessly the young evil-looking secretary, with the trembling hairs on his mole, revived the old man by rubbing him with a copper coin.

May 15th . . . So THE war is over; Europe lies broken like a wound; the last blockbusters and the last V-2's have fallen; but the shock remains. It was a long war—longer than the Thirty Years' War. It ended with men fighting with pitchforks in sewers, and began with the Polish cavalry riding against phalanxes of tanks. We have expected it, and we must have realized dimly that in the very beginning it would have some of the qualities of the last war, and in its very ending it would be entirely new—the massed searchlights of the Russians blinding the defenders, so that they were compelled to fight underground, in the places where there was no light at all; and dying there, like sewer-rats, remaining unburied, the last stratagem of the defeated being to leap into his own grave. And somehow it was not related in any way to the war in Spain, which was the last war where those who were mechanically untrained were able to resist invasion. From now on it is war without passion, the war not of bayonets or knives but of the whirling electric scissors. The war in China is child's play compared with theirs. We fight with Mausers still. The impersonal electrically-driven warfare of the West has not reached these shores.

There will be American landings on the coast, the Japanese will use their tanks, and the landing-craft will appear in the bays of Fukien or Kwangtung. It matters little. They may fight for another year, for two years, or only for a single week, but they have lost their Empire already and still they will have won the obscure cause they fought for—which was Asia for those who live in Asia, the fertility of the soil for those who tend the soil. Now, in these last days of the war, we come to the critical time, when the shifting forces of the East are about to take up their positions. The magnet is attracting into alignment a million little spores of iron. In which way will they turn?

Every Chinese I know looks forward to the day when there will be no more armed foreigners on Chinese soil. I suspect it is the same with other countries bordering on China. It is not nationalism; it is simply that the people are weary of the incalculable difficulties inherent in the strain of behaving normally under the eyes of foreigners, who are still strange to them. The Chinese are not yet accustomed to our manners, our brusqueness and discourtesy. I went with a Chinese professor to a consulate where the consul was swearing at one of his servants; and the Chinese professor's face drained white in silent protest. It is the same with the American army—the Chinese cannot understand our outbursts of rage and dissatisfaction, our incapacity to think of "face." They are tolerant and lazy. They cannot understand why we are intolerant and think laziness a crime. They will learn later, but it will take longer than we imagine to teach them for their own good a sense of time; for nothing can be more important than a sense of time when you are dealing with generators.

We have to learn from the Chinese that time means nothing, and they will have to learn that time means nearly everything. There are other things we shall have to learn. The oriental knows that the road of life does not pass through grief, or sin; he has no sense of guilt, as we have a sense of guilt, no sense of things eternally undone. Therefore his wounds heal more rapidly. He can laugh off tragedy, when we are sick with savage misery: he has seen it before, and knows there is no price for suffering. They are wounded and diseased, but not as we are wounded and diseased. How to bridge these things? This is the important thing. With the wars so nearly over, more and more I feel the desperate urgency of an understanding between East and West.

June 1st . . . FROM the beginning of time the stones in the rocks, the colours in the earth, the seeds of trees and the running waters have been waiting for the moment when some artist will make out of stones a statue, out of colours paintings, out of trees paper and out of water ink and poetry, and after millions of years, and as a result of the most fortuitous circumstances, these things are made. There comes a moment when the earth has accomplished its purpose, the artist sits back and exclaims: "Behold!" This is the supreme moment of accomplishment, the moment for which all things have striven—music, the stones, colours and the printed page. And yet, I thought, gazing at all those books on aesthetics which my step-daughter has brought back from the University, with their ridiculous fine-spun theories of the nature of art by philosophers who have never made anything of any artistic worth, the whole world offers us at every moment the command: "Behold!"

Every yellow tree, every bud of camellia, every glint of flesh and cloth and sweat, they are all crying out: "Behold!" Some things cry louder than others, some shriek at you, some whisper, some complain almost with a dying voice, some even threaten, but all are crying: "Behold!" and in this sense life itself at the regarded moment is the artist, his task finished, leaning back from the easel and shouting that one word which now seems to me the most beautiful of all words, because it has about it an air of detachment—behold, but do not hold—and because somehow, in this desert of the war, the word is a magic spell, so brief and commanding that it puts to rout all the devils of the imagination. There are incantations to be pronounced at the beginning of every work of art, but there is only one incantation to be pronounced at its completion—*Behold!* The child comes running up to its mother, certain of its own charm, and says: "Behold!" The gnarled trees say "Behold" and the stunted rocks in the garden and the shining green of the Chinese tiles on the roof, they are all saying the same word, all desire to be seen and admired and understood and upheld, and all are quivering there, afraid that you may not notice them. There are voices crying in the wilderness—trees that may never be seen, women who may never be loved, shapes of shadows and colours that may never come to pass; and I believe now that it is not enough, as Bergson said, that the universe should be fashioned into a machine for the making of gods—it is a machine in which every living and dead thing is crying out to be beheld.

June 2nd, The Japanese Prisoners . . . THEY came last night in lorries down the Burma Road, but I have only just seen them. It was dusk when we went along to the school and found them there in that huge walled garden more than half a mile long. In the dusk they looked ragged and miserable, grey shapes huddled over bundles, sitting cross-legged on the earth, with the Chinese guards standing over them with fixed bayonets gleaming in the faint light. Gradually it was possible to distinguish the men from the women, but only because the women had more clothes. They said nothing. They did not complain. Someone was knocking in a post, and soon there were ten or twelve posts round that small huddled group in the dark, and then the barbed-wire was uncoiled, and bent nails were hammered into the wood to support the barbed wire, and still the prisoners huddled there, paying no attention to what was happening, not lost in their thoughts, but numbed by the darkness and the encroaching circle of people who were watching them. Then someone lit a light, and the barbed wire shone silver—two silver rings surrounding the faces of the prisoners, which were no longer grey in the darkness but bright crimson. And what was so extraordinary and delightful was that in that moment they did not look like prisoners, they came to life, they sprang out of the earth fully armed with the colours of sunlight, and though they were encircled with silver chains, they had escaped from their prison.

June 3rd . . . THINKING of the prisoners, the lorry waiting, the knife-gleam of the bayonets, the throbbing of the engine which somehow suggested the throbbing lorries I used to hear outside the Gestapo headquarters in Munich, the beardless faces of the boys and the prim fleshy faces of the dancing-girls who were captured months ago in south-west Yunnan, and then the silent guards in their heavy blue botton-padded uniforms and the school-building looking so grey and desolate half a mile away, and the guards at the entrance of the school who would not allow us to come in until we bribed them with cigarettes, the awful loneliness of it, and how those thirty or forty prisoners huddled on the grass in the darkness seemed to concentrate in themselves all the half-dead horror and boredom of war as I have known it in Spain and China, it occurred to me that we could put an end to the war just as easily—you have only to strike a match and see people's faces as they really are, in the bright flames.

What was awful was that they did not move or moan or speak to one another; they were utterly obedient; they must have been cowed until the moment when someone struck a match to light a cigarette. They did not know what their fate was. The dancing-girls, according to the guard, were not even Japanese, but Koreans. They sat there, huddled in the greyness, hidden behind invisible strands of barbed-wire, so dead with fear already that all life seemed to have shrunken from them. I have never known anything like the loneliness of those people: they were beyond pity. J., who was once a prisoner of the Japanese, said he knew what they were thinking. "They were wondering on which part of this field tonight will I be shot, and in which part will I be buried. It becomes terribly important. You stand there in the prison courtyard, and you wonder which is the way out, and you realize there is no way out, and then you wonder at which precise spot near the wall you will

100

be stood up to be shot. You always think you will be shot. You don't imagine for one instant that you will be tortured to death. You just say over and over again: 'That wall over there.' You know exactly where you will be shot, but in fact you are never shot there, and sometimes you escape."

But the most important, the most momentous thing of all is to discover at which point in the history of the world someone is going to strike a match which will allow us to see each other as we really are.

June 5th . . . I AM sure there is nothing quite like the Chinese lavatory. On those bare smeared boards with small round holes in them, you crouch with your trousers round your ankles over a green cesspool which is slowly crawling with fat sluggish-silver worms. It is not entirely unpleasant; the difficulty for the foreigner is to keep your balance, because the board is very narrow and there is danger that you will fall into a ten-foot depth of that green moiling stuff, and you will never come out of it. I suspect that there are three or four bodies in the cesspool where I go every day. I know there are dead rats, for they sometimes float to the surface; by the time they reach the surface they are very brightly coloured indeed. The wonder lies in the colour of the pool, green and silver—the brown miraculously obliterated. There are bubbles on the surface and rats, very dark rats, with bodies as long as your forearm, come prowling round the edges of the pool; and so we squat there, looking for all the world like Buddhas, while the board creaks and only a half-inch thickness of wood separates us from the worms waiting below.

There is, of course, no sanitation in these backwoods of China; we live by virtue of the anti-toxins in our bodies, and we only just live. The precarious balance between health and disease is maintained by luck: every day I see rickshas passing down the streets with some dead body or someone hidden in wrapped counterpanes on his way to hospital. These beautifully bright, silver-encrusted latrines are the home of a devil even more forbidding than the Japanese, and far more long-lived; and what is terrifying is that the Chinese seem to have come to terms with the devil, vast numbers of them possess the required anti-toxins in their bodies and somehow manage to survive. But in a country where dead rats lie festering in every street, and the drains are clogged, and in the very best of houses the latrine opens into a stream which is no more than ten

101

yards from the house-well, the miracle is that anyone survives at all. When the war is over, China will need first, I suppose, railroad engineers; but secondly, and of more lasting importance, will be good sanitary engineers.

June 6th . . . LIU LIEN was roaring round his library this morning and puffing at his pipe; "We will have to go to the roots of things. Do you hear, we are blowing civilization to pieces! Do you hear, we will have to go to the roots of things!" I did not know what was responsible for this outburst, but shortly afterwards he became quieter—the thing that had enraged him was probably some report of the bombing of Tokyo—and then he said: "I would have all politicians read the earliest books of all, so that they will be shamed. Our civilizations started in bursts of glory; they are no longer glorious. It would be easy, and not at all unprofitable, to spend the rest of one's life reading the Indian *Rig-Veda*, the Chinese *Book of Songs* and the Hebrew Bible. They are fresh, with the wetness of birth still on them, and we are all old now, and there is no dew on us. Read the *Iliad*—everything is shining, gleaming wet, blazing in the sun."

I wanted him to talk about these things because he is the only man I know who understands the three civilizations which I am beginning to think are the most important of all—the Hebrew-Greek-Christian, the Indian and the Chinese.

"One thing you might notice is the extraordinary similarity between India and the West. The Greek gods were borrowed from India—Varuna becomes Ouranos, and there are a hundred others. But please notice that the earliest surviving fragments from India and the West—the first chapter of Genesis, the *Iliad* and the *Rig-Veda* are about gods, while the earliest Chinese poems are about lovers: very human lovers. This is important. The Chinese have always been human, while the west has always attempted to be super-human; and the worst thing about the west is that it has succeeded ever so efficiently in being super-human. I assure you, you are really gods with your airplanes and your skyscrapers. What is even worse is that the earliest Indian gods, the gods of the Bible—Moses and Abraham—and the gods of the *Iliad* are all conquerors. 'I am the conqueror, supreme in conquest,' says Indra. The Indians have a legend that one day the standard of Indra will be split into a thousand pieces, and perhaps they saw the advance of power which their earliest philosophers prophesied for the West. It has
102

come now. With the very best will in the world I prefer the ancientest writings when they are about lovers."

I objected that there were love-poems in the Bible; there is Hesiod's *Theogony* which largely describes the love-affairs of Zeus; there are, for brief moments, even love scenes in the *Iliad*. But he shook his head. "In India, in Babylonia, on the Nile, in Greece there were always these terrible gods of power, brooding and malevolent, filled with ideas of conquest. They were the seeds that were planted in the west, and the seeds have come to flower in the present wars. . . . How can you escape it? There is only one way, and already it may be too late. Let all your thoughts, all your poetry, all your philosophy be concerned with love."

June 7th . . . I CANNOT believe this story, but I know it must be true. J. tells me that last Sunday he was walking in the neighbourhood of a pure lake near Chenggung, about fifteen miles from here. It was late in the afternoon. He had seen the lake, which is a kind of crystalline green in colour, transparent, very cold and, though small, infinitely more to his liking than the Green Neck Lake in the city or the vast lake which lies beneath the Western Hills outside. "And then I saw two soldiers carrying a pannier. They were walking against the sunlight, and I noticed that in the pannier there was a soldier. I hardly paid any attention to them. There are so many sick soldiers in China, and they are so often carried in panniers. The sun was going, and they looked huge against the skyline. I forgot about them for a while, but when I looked again they were not far from where they were before, and the pannier was being set down, and the soldier was screaming—not very loudly, but at least he was screaming. Then, and this was worse, I saw the two soldiers take spades from the pannier and they began to dig a grave. I thought: 'They are going to execute him, but the strange thing is that I have seen many soldiers and many men being led out to execution, but they never scream.' So I went a little closer. The grave was being dug slowly, and the voice of the soldier in the pannier was growing louder. It was like a girl screaming softly: probably he was half-gagged. And then the most extraordinary, the most terrible thing happened. They took the soldier out and laid him in the grave, and all the time he was screaming in that faint, weak voice of his. There was nothing I could do. The grave was stamped down, perhaps it had taken altogether hardly ten minutes, for the earth is soft in these places and the soldier's hands must

103

have been tied behind his back. And then, walking very quickly, the two soldiers returned with the empty pannier swinging between them.

"I spoke to them a little later; they told me the soldier was ill and dying, and their captain had ordered them to take him to the hills. This was the expression they used—'take him to the hills.' They obeyed. They could only obey, though they said they deeply regretted it, and perhaps if there had been good doctors he might have recovered." I had it on the tip of my tongue to ask J. why he did not hurry to the soldier's rescue, though I must have known that the grave-diggers were armed. As he told the story his face was dead white. "There was nothing," he said, "there was absolutely nothing that could be done!"

June 9th . . . ALMOST nothing during the last year has delighted me so much as the letter I have just received from a student. It is a bad letter; I am afraid it shows only too well that I have only barely succeeded in teaching him idiomatic English, but I find it absurdly exciting. Moreover, there are times when I become weary of idiomatic English, weary of journalistic English, weary of English-English; there are moments when Chinese-English or Doughty's Arabian-English or Conrad's Polish-English make life more enjoyable than one could have imagined:

Honoured Sir,
I feel I could hardly speak out any words to support the reason why I was absent last week and yesterday, except the reason of my wretched tooth. My tooth, indeed, was well treated the week before last week. But it ached again last week. I went to the dentist and asked for reason. He said my teeth were somewhat particular, not so normal as the common people, and his medicine still had done its duty. What a ridiculous answer is that! I suspect that I am being cheated by the dentist. To pay one thousand and two hundred dollars for the treatment seems to me not too heavy bearing, although my monthly salary, one thousand and five hundred dollars, still is poor, yet the waste of my time really is my greatest loss. The loss of my time also means the looseness of my lessons and the uneasiness of my health. Such losses are losses far beyond the loss of my money, even beyond the unbearably abrupt toothache in my dream. What can I do now? He said the only way to treat my tooth

104

well is to go to his hospital everyday afternoon regularly. When my tooth will get well, he did not tell. So I am afraid that I still could not attend your lectures this week. But anyhow I will let this devil treatment over within this week. The final way to calm myself is to pull the wretched tooth off.

My novel report on Joseph Conrad's "Almayer's Folly" will be handed in on Thursday.

I am quite sure the novel report will be handed in, but unfortunately it will not be nearly as good as his letter.

June 10th . . . I HAVE been to see the Japanese prisoners. They live now right at the end of that immense half-mile long walled field which includes the Kung-hwa Middle School, and some very small crumbling cement houses which are now occupied by a few professors and teachers. The field is in flood, though the prisoners are camping in a cluster of tents on raised ground, and their tents are infinitely preferable to the drab humid cells where the professors, their wives and their children are living. The tents are ringed round with barbed-wire, but no matter—already they have planted flowers and there are small whitewashed rockeries with inscriptions on them which no one can read and they have put up incense burners inside the tents. One of the prisoners is a graduate from a Tokyo art college, he paints admirably in water-colours and spends nearly the whole day sitting an inch away from the barbed wire, sketching a tree or a child running or one of the grotesque houses where the professors live. He is quiet and terribly withdrawn into himself, wears *tapagata* sandals with a big wooden screw between the big toe and the next and seems hardly to be conscious that he is in prison. The Chinese guards treat him with the respect which is due to people who can paint—it is a miracle— they look over his shoulder—they ask to be painted, and the presence of the painter has changed the camp entirely. Except for the painter and one young Japanese who seems to be his particular friend, the Japanese prisoners seem squat and ugly, stocky, broad-chested, thick-lipped, without waists, the bodies like chunks of wood; what is surprising is that the painter and his friend do not look Japanese at all, they look exactly like students at the University, they have the same grace, the same awareness and simplicity, the same fine ivory profiles. The painter was planting seeds when I came. God knows where he found them. Did he carry them all the

105

way from Japan, or did he exchange them for a painting? He sits there, painting slowly, glancing up occasionally with pursed lips and the faintest of faint frowns; and simply because he is painting, he is no longer imprisoned. K., a professor living in one of these houses, has had long conversations with him in Japanese. He asked him what he missed most. He answered: "Cherry-trees."

The Korean girls were in separate tents, young and husky, not handsome but hardly distinguishable from Chinese peasant-girls, with strong legs and arms. They are forever running up and down the field outside the barbed-wire in search of pails of water; four or five of them are pregnant; one is dying. They are rich. The Chinese guards are particularly solicitous about them, but it is difficult to imagine, in the strong sunlight falling on the immense field yesterday, that they were geisha girls who danced to the orders of senior Japanese generals who are long since dead. They say they were peasants, and therefore they are permanent; and against this landscape they are as happy as against any others. But not far away from them the majority of the Japanese prisoners in their dull white singlets and ragged trousers pace up and down, up and down, up and down, incapable of finding like the Japanese painter who is now painting imaginary flowers any release from their prisonment. In the hot sunlight blue bayonets gleam.

June 12th . . . THE floods have come. All over the field outside my window there is the cloud-reflecting mirror. Yesterday it was messy with pools and ruts of water; today, entirely submerged, it is a brighter blue than the sky. Going along the Burma road this morning, I saw a cabbage-field under water. There was nothing surprising in this, but what was surprising was that three naked children were running through the lanes between the cabbage fields, kicking up showers of silver water. This was not surprising either. What was surprising was their fat father, with a belly like a bronze bell, wearing a pair of green drawers, who was swimming in the cabbage-field on his back and at the same time towing a kite which was the same colour of his drawers and was probably made of the same material. He looked perfectly, idiotically happy.

June 13th . . . ONE of the Japanese prisoners was shot dead last night as he crawled out from under the barbed-wire in search of—cabbages. I am not sure that I believe he was searching for
106

cabbages, though there is a bed of vitriol-green cabbages nearby, but it seems unnecessary to shoot him dead. He had not one chance in ten million of escaping.

I discussed this with Big Bill later. He has been on at least ten secret missions behind the Japanese lines, he has jumped from aeroplanes more times than he can remember, he can hardly be accused of cowardice; but he says he fears his own sentries most. Once when he was at a training-camp in India, he forgot the password and decided it was best to stay away from the camp, though he realized perfectly that he might be eaten by tigers. He had good reason to, for a week before one of his buddies returned drunk to the camp, had no idea what the password was and walked up to the sentry. The sentry was a Gurkha armed with a *kukri*, a yard-long evilly-curved sword. The sentry said: "Halt!" The buddy went lumbering on, and apparently didn't notice the sword which curved round and cut off his head, for there was the same happy drunken smile on his face when his head was picked up. "Probably fifty thousand people have been killed already in this war by their own sentries, and sometimes, damn them, just for the devil of it, sentries will fire when they know damned well who you are!"

June 14th . . . THE soldiers were placing great baulks of timber across the flooded field. They looked happy in the sun, bronzed and clean-limbed, bare-legged and bare-chested. They splashed in the water like children and arranged that some of the baulks of timber should be so carefully balanced that when he stepped on one end, the other end would come up like a seesaw. They were amazingly happy until an old professor came along, tottering with a stick, prodding each baulk of timber until he was sure it was safe, the long blue gown wrapped round his waist, so that he looked ridiculous with his thin legs in the flapping pyjama trousers. They were hoping—they were desperately hoping the log would come up when he stepped on it, and they watched breathlessly, secretly their dark eyes looking malevolently and happily at each other; and then in that breathless and heavenly moment which occurred just before he stepped on the forbidden plank, there was suddenly the sound of an outrageous cry, the professor looked round, waving his stick and one of the soldiers lurched forward to his assistance. And then in the distance we saw the professor squatting on the broad bronze back of a soldier wading knee-deep in the mud.

107

June 15th . . . L IU L IEN was talking of Chinese poetry again.
I suspect that he hates talking of Chinese poetry, but is sufficiently
aware of my ignorance to allow me to suggest impossible solutions
for the problems that torment both of us. He insists that there are
two kinds of knowledge, which he calls "elemental" and "mechanical." "The sun is a great re in the heavens which swings in a vast
semi-circle around the earth, and then mysteriously—ever so mysteriously—appears again the next morning in the last place where
you could imagine it to appear. It is infinitely larger and brighter
than any stars, and by some perfect miracle of celestial achievement is exactly the same size as the moon." I nodded, for I could
raise no objections to the statement. "This is what I call elemental
knowledge—the sun as it appears, its first fresh impact on our eyes.
You know, or you think you know that this is nonsense. It may be
nonsense, but we cannot make poetry of the Copernican system of
the heavens, or else we see the sky as 'a patient etherized upon a
table.' The sun according to the old Indian philosophers was a
horse. The Chinese do not see the sun—there are no early poems to
the sun, for the good and simple reason that their whole landscape
is bathed in it. Then there is the 'mechanical' way of regarding the
universe, the way of knowledge, of complex understanding—I do
not see how we can make poetry out of this, or even how we can
live according to the laws of a mechanical universe. There is darkness there, no poetry. . . ."

I left him, leaning on his stick, looking out across the tangled garden rich in convolvulus and bamboos. Birds came, the sun shone,
the flagstone path was gleaming wet from the water slopped from
the wooden pails; and assuredly for him there is no mechanical
universe, and the sun rises every day from the place where you
would least expect it to rise.

June 17th . . . T HE rains had cleared, and Kunming today was
splendid. I have been out to the lake, past the wooden barges filled
mast-high with green vegetables, past the great gleaming whiteness of rock-salt which lies scattered on the shore, and there were
the tribespeople who had come down over the mountains and over
the lake, the men hardly distinguishable from the Chinese but the
girls arrayed with golden headdresses and red waistbands, with
silver pearls hanging from their ears and embroidery everywhere.
There they were, tumbling the vegetables from the boats, lifting
the gleaming rock-salt to the waiting carts, dark-faced, silent, and
108

yet with an air of gayety and dancing. They looked splendid, but perhaps that was because there was whipped cream in the air, and beyond them lay the clean sharp sculpture of the western mountains, which are naked but for their clumps of cedars hiding the distant temples. Wherever there are woods in China, there are temples. The hard and splendid line of the mountains, and the clear-cut images of these girls . . .

Now that I have lived so long in the sun, I cannot think of going to lands less widowed by her. There is such splendour on the shores of this lake that the mind reels, so clear-cut, so full of trembling thorns the air. In Peking the sun shines all the year round, and I am amazed that in this country where the sun is so continually bright that there are not more temples, not more works of great art. The prime condition of art is the clarity of the air—so did Egypt and Greece and Crete and northern France produce their great sculptures and greater temples. Wandering round Kunming, I find myself a thousand times in Greece. Here are the spectral asphodels, here are the vales of Lebadeia, here in the lonely rock-strewn path to Parnassus. There are little temples to the earth-gods which are not unlike the same temples in Greece; here too the blue of the sky at dawn and sunset is bitten into the hilltops, and the old ceremony of throwing a kiss to the sun in the morning is not forgotten, and the tribespeople still walk with grace, accustomed to running up mountains and balancing pitchers on their shoulders. Socrates and Alcibiades wander round the University, and perhaps neither would have complained of this University built on gravemounds.

June 19th . . . HERMES had entered the room. It was one of those curious moments when silence descends like a heart-throb. We used to call it angels' wings in England, and say the clock-hour pointed always to ten minutes past nine, till we learned that there were other silences than bedtime. You will come across such silences in a Chinese market; the babble and shouting all inexplicably cease, and there is not even some harried young man being led out, with thumbs tied, to execution.

We had been talking—there were perhaps twenty professors in the room—of the approaching end of the war. It cannot last—it cannot—so we have been telling ourselves, and all the while we are conscious that something even more dreadful than war hangs over our heads. Civil war is a profanation of all the temples, somehow infinitely worse than war; perhaps because we are no longer killing

109

strangeness, but ourselves. There are primitive excuses for killing the things you cannot understand; there are no excuses at all, primitive or civilized, for killing your own children.

There are rumours that as soon as the present war is over, civil war will break out like a spring which has gathered momentum by long waiting. The plans are all there. The heavy American equipment has not been used; it will be used for other purposes than smashing the Kwangtung Army in Manchuria. The lorries, the jeeps, the ammunition, which have been looted from American headquarters have gone—where? C. says: "It has gone to kill the Chinese," and he tells a terrible story about his son who in the civil war of 1927 was compelled to drop bombs on his native village. "We found out afterwards that one of the bombs had landed on the family cemetery just outside the village. How does one report such things to the ancestors?" He is a social scientist, has little enough faith in the ancient rituals and has not reported anything to the ancestor since his father died forty years ago. "It was not a big bomb, but it spoiled the cemetery, and when the rains came, where the cemetery had been, there was only a dirty pond. We found part of my father's body at the bottom of the pond—hooked it up and buried it again—it was still just recognizable. I told my son about it. He didn't care very much, and kept on saying: 'We must unite China even if all the graveyards become ponds.' But this was by no means the worst of it, for we could not find my mother for some weeks later. The village headman told me that he had done everything he could, but the dogs broke in to the place and they found her about three miles away, or all that was left of her." It was sometime after this that Hermes entered with his wings.

But the civil war is a stark reality: we have known the moment when all Chungking and all Kunming was prepared to flee, when the Japanese came so close that the big bankers raided the petrol pools with armed thugs, so that they could get away. We have seen the bandits on the road, and we know, or think we know that the Communists can come down from Sikong—they have gone on even longer marches. We are not afraid of the Communists or the Kuomintang. We are afraid of bandits, of endless marching, of the things that Tu Fu was afraid of—barren countryside, the rice black and burning, the festering and the misery of being abandoned on a Chinese road with armies all round us. We have read it in Chinese poetry, and we have seen it, or guessed at it; and though we know that the Japanese are on the verge of supreme punishment, it may be the turn of China soon. And there is nothing we can

110

do; there is not even as there was in the past any faith in the shamans who could exorcise the devil of war. Or rather we have faith in them, the shamans are people who come to tea with us, professors of law and political science and jurisprudence, but they have lost their powers. C. says: "The students are afraid, desperately afraid of only one thing—civil war. They talk about it all the time. It is nonsense to say that they are listening to Yenan radio, which is already proclaiming against the civil war. They are not listening to Yenan—they are listening to their own hearts." There are strange rumours in this country, and strangest of all are the rumours which insist that the Government is deliberately heading for a civil war. What then? Another twenty million killed for the sake of a political theory? But fascism was not killed by the armed forces of Britain, America and the Russians; political belief remains till it is laughed into nothingness, and it is only now that we are sufficiently remote from the curious senile gibbering figure of Hitler that we can laugh at it. We couldn't before, for no one can laugh at clawed fingers at the throat. Now that the claws are clipped we can; but more and more I am beginning to believe that we won the war by our own courage, and also by some benefit of providence.

I remember now the essays I have read by the students—so many essays proclaiming the end of the war. There were essays filled with the continual ringing of bells of brotherhood, of a great chastity which descended upon the world, a spiritual and effortless simplicity which would follow the end of the war. All the radio stations would be singing hymns. Sometimes I listen to an American radio and we twist the dial and reach San Francisco; and there are no hymns; and there is no rejoicing; there is only the moaning of Frank Sinatra portending the end of the world.

Perhaps we might have guessed as much. We put too high a price on our victory; we spoil too much of ourselves in these relentless bombardments, in copying the enemy's abuse of laws. We are creatures of the midnight sometimes, as black as Hitler's ganged hordes, and perhaps we shall have to pay for it, and God knows where again we shall obtain our mental balance. Force has come into the world sharper than it was in the first world war, and more obliterating. Perhaps too we have suffered too much to be able to rebel against our suffering. We shall wear this suffering to the end of time, our children will wake up at night, dreaming of the strange man with the uplifted arms who led us all to the pond where we swim with the Gadarene swine. Best of all if we could wash out this page of history, and begin again at the place where we began, for

111

we have lost our certainty and are all wanderers in the desert, and neither Christ nor Buddha nor Confucius can tempt us any more.

But is this true? I suspect that Christianity and Buddhism, with their solemnity and ceremonial, with their otherness and strength and confiding belief in striving will return. I suspect that like the *Wandervogeln* in Germany at the end of the last war we shall seek out a faith in ourselves from mountains and rocks, and all that grow on them. I suspect that people will no longer be content, in their fear of another war, to take the 8:15 to Waterloo and bury themselves coffin-wise in offices for the greater glory of someone else's deposits. It may be in my life-time that the thing I dream of most will come about—we shall all be wanderers, believing the whole earth our own, belonging to no nation, lovers of each other and even of ourselves. There may come a time when the frontiers will vanish, and then there will be no more wars and civil wars will become still more ridiculous. It was the wrath of God that drove Adam and Eve from the garden into a strange land; it may be by the wrath of war that we may turn the unploughed into the sown. We must love one another, or perish. The old truth becomes more certain now when we have seen so many perishing. The block-busters that tear down whole streets, gut out the burning hearts of vast cities have shown us that the old nationalism, which began only six hundred years ago, for previously in Europe at least there was a theoretical Holy Roman Empire from Portugal to Jerusalem, must go. We are not Americans, we are not Britons, we are not Russians: such things do not exist: they are malicious theories invented for the purpose of easy thinking: we are only people, who are born, love, fall ill and die miserably. And few of us have any delight in killing, and all of us are squeamish of blood, and there is not one who has seen a battle who hasn't felt a sinking sensation in the pit of his stomach which makes him hope that the earth will open and devour him. Then why go on? Political theories? Necessity? The eternal wavering balance of forces? It is easy enough to show that these things have no validity—one has only to point to a child new-born, which turns its face blindly to the sunlight, so helpless a thing that our own present helplessness in the face of war seems strength in comparison.

"My grandmother said that the world should be governed by women," C. was saying, after Hermes had left the room, "till I pointed to the example of the Empress Dowager, and then she said
112

it was better to give it to the young. It is no use giving it to the old, she said, because the old are so close to death that they hardly care what happens. Give it to those who enjoy life, and then there will be an end to war."

June 20th . . . A SOLDIER in the peaked cap was sitting on the kerb. He was about nineteen. He had a full brown face, thick ropes of veins at his neck and he looked like a prince among those crowds of washed-out office-boys and shopkeepers who passed him, very handsome, crouching against the side-walk with his sprung knife and the green bamboos over his knee, very delicately whittling slender little strips, out of which he made birds, grasshoppers, even camels.

There are street-stalls where these things are made out of blown sugar, highly coloured and very messy. The children like them, because it is pleasant to lick the strange creatures with your tongue, watching it change its shape until the blue fins of a fish become something else altogether. But the soldier's birds and grasshoppers have a greater validity: the weaving of the slender bamboos into the shape of a grasshopper's body is not easy, but the final grasshopper possesses an existence of its own, an almost startling *vraisemblance*, especially at the moment when he takes out of his pocket the coloured sunflower seeds which he threads together on a splinter and makes into eyes. They are grasshoppers like those in green jade which are found in Han Dynasty tombs. While the bamboo is still moist and the little springy strips out of which the grasshopper is woven retain their life, furious life flows still through the bamboo. But after I had bought one, L. told me, watching it dangling on its long silky stalk, quivering with life, that in a day or two it would be shrunken, the moisture would go out of it, there would be nothing left of it except some dried-up stalks of leaves. "How did you know?" I asked. "Of course I know—we all made them when we were children. They were made exactly like that. But now they no longer teach children how to make these things. The soldier must have come from the country—there is no doubt of it!" He told me that he could still remember his grandfather putting on ceremonial robes to ride out to the hunting-ground, but the hunting-ground was only a long field among the gravemounds where the archery contests were fought to the banging of muted drums. He had seen, as have millions of Chinese, the midnight ceremonials for Confucius, the burning braziers and the

113

incense burners and the curious dulled echoing sound as the priests prostrated themselves and drummed their foreheads on the ground. He had seen the Empress Dowager returning from Sian and a thousand other things of the past, and there was nothing to replace them except the Monday morning ceremonial of reciting the last will and testament of Dr. Sun Yat-sen. "It had grandeur," he said reflectively, "and there was something to live for, and there was great excitement when we cut off our pigtails and tied false pigtails to our heads, but we were probably wrong in abandoning the monarchy. The Russians dethroned the Tsars and made Stalin even more regal, infinitely more powerful, with statues of him in every market-place; and his utterances are the utterances of a god. Well, we have dethroned the Emperor, and there is a terrible vacuity in our lives." And then all the way home he took the little jade-green grasshopper which quivered with its immemorial bamboo-life, and gazed at it sadly. The past was reflected in this little galloping thing with the beady red eyes, more perfect than any grasshopper that has ever flown, so real that if you held it in your hand it seemed to peck at it.

June 25th . . . THERE are mornings when you wake up, surprised that you can have been born to such beauty, when the bird hopping on the bough seems to have been dipped in quicksilver and the air is a blue veil gently moving, warm and like silk; golden mornings of misty dawns, so ripe that you wonder why the fruit-trees are not bursting into instantaneous blossom, when even the mountains quiver and dance with life. I did not know before I came to Yunnan how mountains could romp and skip as they do in the *Songs of Solomon,* but they were skipping this morning through the misty veils of pulsating blue air. There is no other place in the world like this except perhaps California, though there are wet mists there and sometimes scudding clouds. Every year there are twenty days of cold weather in Kunming; on every other day the sun shines. Perhaps forty days of the year there are vast arching rainbows, when it rains over the distant hills; but though this is the rainy season, and the aeroplanes were grounded two days ago, today was a shimmering brightness so bright that it hurt the eyes.

In a Szechuan spring there are mornings like this, but only rarely: when there are glittering thorns and petals of light hanging in the air, the sunrays glancing from them. Then the mist rolled away from the gorges, from every uncarved mountain slope daz-
114

zling colours appeared and there was fruitfulness in the air. They were not many, and you knew when they would come by the thick mist that fell at night: but in Kunming you never know when they will come, and there seems to be no reason for those sudden bursts of efflorescence that come from the sky. It would be easy to live the rest of one's days in this cool-burning sunlight. I know a German who is so delighted with the place that he thanks God daily the Chinese army has taken over the only commendable hotel, and will probably keep it for perpetuity. "And thank Heaven the Indo-Chinese railway is broken, and will take a year to repair; and thank Heaven Kunming is becoming less and less an important air-base; and thank Heaven everyone will soon be going back to the coast." He assumes that the war will end soon. He may be right, but I fear that aeroplanes will soon be coming from every direction to spoil his contentment with holiday-makers. But the roads are bad, the Burma road is a monstrosity which will probably soon fall into decay, there is no sign that the Yunnanese will welcome foreigners in the future—they have hardly welcomed the "down-river" Chinese in the past. There are rich mines south of Kunming. There is a fantastic medley of tribes from Thibet, Burma, India, Siam and Indo-China living in this forgotten corner of China. There are camellias as large as a girl's face, and there are a million opium-smokers. There are Tali and Lichiang—two most unbelievably beautiful places, in the shadow of snow-mountains. And why in the name of all miracles should one ever desire to leave this miraculous place? And if you answer that the drains are bad, there are too many dead beggars and dead rats lying on the road, that plague may break out at any moment, that everything man made is shoddy and everything made by nature is unbelievably glorious, it makes little difference; for the drains are bad everywhere else in China, and there is not one square inch of China where a beggar has not laid down to die, and the Chinese themselves are perfectly delighted at the thought that their own creations are insignificant in comparison with the creations of nature—one might as well die of the plague, they say, as of a surfeit of canned goods, and what does it matter as long as one dies in the sunlight? There is no sun in Hangchow or Suchow for a quarter of the year. It is miserably cold there in winter. Peking is foul with dust storms in summer and hideously cold in winter. There is a grey slimy cloudbank over Chungking for two thirds of the year. Then why leave Kunming? they will ask, where at least we have temples and lakes, and if you

115

like hunting, there are wild-geese and mouse-deer, leopards and tigers and even elephants somewhere. And you half believe them until you start dreaming of the wet miserable splendour of a London winter, the fug of the subways, the plate-glass gleaming, the books and the theatres. The absence of books is the worst. But if the books should come after the war, I do not see any reason for ever leaving this place.

June 28th . . . "The standard," he said regretfully, "has gone down." I nodded. I heard it before, and there was nothing one could do about it. The Chinese war has produced few good books, the students are underfed and provided with poor living quarters and can hardly be expected to produce of their best. They work hard, but they are too excitable in this age of excitements to delve deep into things. They are looking healthier than when I first came to China, they suffer less from diseases, but the explanation lies more perhaps in the good fortune of the weather than in their physical resistance; also there are more tinned goods from America in this city than anywhere else in China. The standard has gone down, because there are no up to date books, because the Chinese University system, depending upon an incredibly inefficient credit-system which plays into the hands of the mediocre, is apparently unchangeable, because the professors are underpaid and have to seek other jobs, because there is corruption everywhere and we spend half our lives prodigiously attempting to avoid its influence. Power corrupts. Mercifully we have neither power nor money, though some of the professors exert a far-reaching influence in their self-sacrificing devotion to scholarship, afraid of nothing, sublimely unaware of the threats which sometimes reach them. I know a professor who has been threatened by the secret police for advancing his views on government; but he remains indomitably cheerful. Not all have his calm; a few have surrendered to the greatest vice of all, subservience to the powers which bring them money. It is difficult and unnecessary to blame them: against the forces arraigned against them, at a time of starvation and mounting inflation which no longer leaves us surprised but dumb-founded, against childbirth and death and sickness they have no remedy except surrender. It is easy enough in this modern China to obtain money: the difficult thing is to refuse the bait, though dangled ever so close. So we go on, shadows in the sunlight, accused by some of being communists and by others of being lackeys to the most cor-
116

rupt government on earth, and in reality being neither. There is devotion to scholarship still, and this must remain, for the beauty of the Chinese countryside and the beauty of her scholars are the best things in this bitter power-ridden country.

July 2nd . . . THERE is something a little bewildering in the teaching of English. You realize, after a few years of teaching English, how very little you know. You realize that all the rules of grammar are there to be broken; that the studious young student who never makes grammatical mistakes is somehow always wrong; that there is such a thing as Chinese-English which adds to the richness of our tongue, and which cannot be corrected, because you can never perceive exactly where it is wrong, for it is not wrong. You cannot translate Chinese directly and literally into English, yet the Chinese way of thought can go most delicately into an English dress; and it would be a pity to put red pencils through all those amazingly subtle Chinese idioms, however un-English they are. I used to put a peculiar kind of scrawl against all those places where it seemed the students were delighting in sheer sentimentality. I am not so sure that they are sentimental now. Though they delight in the pathetic fallacy, they know it is a fallacy and enjoy it, as one enjoys the conventions of a play; and there is a tough brilliance and resilience in their imagery.

It seems just possible that in five thousand years nine-tenths of the population of the world will be Chinese, and they will speak a debased kind of English. It is a frightening thought, for English is already so debased that I dread to think of the literature that may be produced in the future. We have been going downhill since the Elizabethans. Must we reach the stage—and it seems that we shall soon reach the stage—when English is one of those odd, brief, childish languages like Danish, where the words look more like pellets flung haphazard on the page than living voices? I used to admire the clipped languages of *Life* and *Time,* but they have grown dull with age; their forced conventions are fossilized already, music has vanished and what is left is only the strident adjective wandering lost over the page. But there are still American writers who have taken over the heritage that the English have almost lost through dullness; one can comfort oneself with the best Hemingway, Katharine Anne Porter, Muriel Ruykeyser, Stephen Vincent Benét and a hundred others, and at the worst moments of crisis, when it seems that the English language is losing its powers

117

already, there is always the amazing George Bernard Shaw, whose name should be pronounced with reverence, because he wrote English rhythmically and with skill—so skilfully that he introduced into the language an element which had never appeared before: the momentum of sheer skill.

July 3rd . . . Now that the war is coming to its final and catastrophic end, I am beginning to believe, like Liu Lien, that in spite of all these years of incommensurable hardship, we are unprepared for so fatal a thing as the end of a war. We need knowledge and understanding more than ever, we need a technique of brotherhood as efficient as the technique we have created for destroying our brothers. Christianity has lost its power; Confucianism is dead; Buddhism is a forgotten sect which exists faintly in Nepal, Ceylon, and in a few mountain monasteries in China. We have no guides any more; holiness has been blasted out of us. We shall have to begin from the beginning.

Bergery used to say that we had more to learn from the Balinese than from anyone else, but I am beginning to believe that we have more to learn from some tribes of the Pueblo Indians, who have discovered how life may be lived harmoniously. There is in Ruth Benedict's admirable *Patterns of Culture* an account of the Zuni Indians which reads almost like an account of ancient China. The word "zuni" means "middle"; so too do the Chinese people call themselves citizens of the Middle Kingdom—*Chung Kuo*. They have for rainwater the same magical respect which the Chinese possessed until recently, and sometimes still possess, for their rivers; water, indeed, is the most holy of all things, for they are agricultural people, and "to bless with water" is the synonym for all blessings. They regard the rain-clouds as their grandfathers, signs of coming fertility, and see themselves in some way like plants made fruitful by the rains. They have the Chinese scholars' abhorrence of all violence, and they have so ordered their society that there is no room for violent emotions, either of jealousy or revenge, or of any attachments which refuse to accept dismissal. Life for them is a fleeting thing made valuable by the glory of the perpetual processions of the seasons, and their own accompaniment to the seasons' progress in their dances. The Zuni Indians are so gentle that they are surprised that white men should whip their children; they whip their own children in the ceremonies of initiation, but only in mockery, causing no bloodshed or hurt. They show no
118

anger. Their priests are at all times utterly sober. They gather willow-shoots for prayer-sticks and adorn themselves in their dances with eagle's feathers and ears of corn and wave plume wands—all organically beautiful things. They ask for orderly life, pleasant days, shelter from violence, fertility of the earth. "In their strict regard for the Apollonian ethos," says Ruth Benedict, "the Pueblos distrust and reject those experiences which take the individual in any way out of bounds and forfeit his sobriety." They have no use for the peyote or the mescal bean, nor do they use fasting, torture, drugs or alcohol to induce dionysiac sensations of power, preferring to be unashamedly themselves than beholden to their own extreme sensations; and unlike the westerners they are not drugged by speed and have no craze for violence.

They have even constructed a system by which crime becomes almost impossible; adultery is not a crime, and in any case hardly ever occurs, for their marriages are held lightly, without those depths of romantic and possessive passion which have afflicted us since the days of the troubadours. There is almost no thieving, because everyone has enough to eat and property is not so much despised as held to be a hindrance in life. There are murders occasionally, but they are rare. Those who thirst for authority are disparaged, and sometimes prosecuted for sorcery. "The ideal man in Zuni is a person of dignity and affability who has never tried to lead and has never called forth comment from his neighbours. Any conflict, even though all right is on his side, is held against him. Even in contests of skill, like their footraces, if a man wins habitually he is debarred from running. They are interested in a game that a number can play with even chances, and an outstanding runner spoils the game: they will have none of him." And then again: "A good man avoids office. He may have it thrust upon him, but he does not seek it. The folk-tales always relate of good men their unwillingness to take office—though they always take it. A man must avoid the appearance of leadership." What is strange, and delightful here, is that all these qualities are those which we associate with the Chinese scholar, the same qualities which Confucius desired his disciples to possess and inculcated into generations of Chinese. The Zuni family system is matrilineal —so to a very large extent is the Chinese family system. They love painting themselves and wearing masks and have a peculiarly intimate sense of brotherhood with animals, and they are not afraid of the gods; and it would seem now, at this moment when our own

119

civilization is in such mortal danger, that we have everything to learn from the Zuni and the ancient Chinese, and nothing to offer them.

Tao Yuan-ming relates a famous story of a fisherman who wandered down a forgotten creek to its source, which was a mountain cave. Through the cave he saw a small light shining, and passed through it into another landscape inhabited by men who had escaped many hundreds of years before from the Ch'in Dynasty. They lived here perfectly content, with no desire at all to belong to the greater world outside, though they asked the fishermen for the name of the reigning dynasty; they were handsome and given to farming and wore their hair according to age-old fashions; and though the fisherman attempted afterwards to return, he could not find the landmarks, and no one ever found them again. The story is called, from the place where the fisherman saw the gap of light leading to these forgotten people, "The Peach-blossom Fountain." He noticed particularly that for hundreds of paces along the source of the stream there were peach-blossoms; and it was strange, reading Ruth Benedict's delightful book, to find that the Zuni Indians particularly delighted in their vast peach-gardens, and their silver-mines embedded in the slopes of mountains.

July 5th, Sukiyaki . . . UNACCOUNTABLY, there was a slight frost in the air, or perhaps it was no more than the *sharpness* of the sunlight which gave the curious impression that the sparkling drops of light in the air would congeal and turn into hailstones. But the sun was shining, and the students had come in their blue gowns, and the great stove lay on the balcony in the full glare of the sun, which was so bright that even when the stove was burning you could not see the charcoal flames. All round the stove were baskets, some containing meat cut into small strips, others containing rice, others vegetable oils, others all kinds of greenstuff, and still another contained bottles of wine. Lard was poured into the copper bowl, and then the huddled little strips of red meat were poured: the sukiyaki party was on. It is the easiest of all parties to prepare. From time to time one of the students would pour into the bowl more lard or vegetable oil or tomato sauce, and all the time the meat was turning into a dark golden brown. The smell was intoxicating when the wine was added: there seems to be no end to the things that can be added if one pleases. A mountain of green vegetables is mixed with the meat, and stirred; there is the pleasantest

120

of sizzling sounds. The blue-gowned students sit round the glistening copper bowl as though they were attending a sacred rite, they fill their bowls with colourless rice, they sprinkle wine into the meat at every opportunity and they seem almost to be reciting their prayers. And so it went on for nearly two hours this afternoon in the sparkling frozen sunlight which made all colours quiver like flames.

They have such things in Japan, with geisha girls proffering the dishes, but it is pleasanter to have it on a sunlight balcony with a crowd of students all taking part in the magical rite. The heat-haze dances over the copper bowl, the wine throws up puffs of cloud and we are all ministers to the flame.

July 10th . . . THERE was some urgent business to discuss with Liu Lien, and I found him in the courtyard reading St. Thomas's *Summa contra Gentiles* and surrounded by young soldiers playing shuttlecock. He had a brown horse-hair fly-whisk in one hand, and for some reason which I never discovered one of those curved ivory batons which appear in ancient Chinese paintings in the other—probably a heirloom derived across many centuries of scholars, and useful now as a rather elaborate bookmark. He complained that St. Thomas was ridiculous, but absolutely marvellous. There it was, all cut and dried into a waterproof system, but it was impossible for him to believe that sin was like that, or virtue was like that, and the Holy Ghost was altogether too pat. "There is one thing they have all forgotten, and that is that men hiccough. Life isn't—life can't be so resolutely systematised." He complained that a Jesuit had called upon him in the morning and asked him to believe that Jesus Christ created the world. He had thought about it for a long time, rejecting as inconclusive the existing data that there was a world before Christ's existence, but finding it intolerable that the Jesuit should have accused him of blasphemy when he suggested that there might at least have been two creators—Christ and Pan Ku. "Why not?" Liu Lien asked maliciously. "Pan Ku at least looks the part. His breath became the wind, his voice the thunder; his left eye the sun; his right eye the moon; his blood flowed in rivers; his hair grew into trees and plants; his flesh became the soil; his sweat descended as rain; while the parasites which infested his body were the human race. And really I do not see why they should be so exclusive. There are Mexican gods, and Hawaiian gods, and Indian gods who created the

121

earth—there should be a special pantheon marked 'gods who created the earth.' I assure you there is nothing amusing in this. It is the exclusiveness of the west which I find so demoralizing, the 'oneness' of things which is only a convenient way of summarizing a fantastic complexity. Who created the earth? The sun shrugged off a little red-hot island, but what made it shrug off the little red-hot island, and so on, and so on, till you find that a star a million million million million light-years away caught a fever and set the sun shaking, but what made the star catch a fever—until you are dizzy: it is so much easier to say 'one.' There is no such thing as 'one.' "

He was very amused with us in the little enclosed garden, shaking his horse-hair whisk, "which does no damage to the flies—they are caught for a moment in the horse-hairs but they fly away again after having had their little lesson," and though he has a deep-seated passion for the west, I notice sometimes that he treats us like small children. It is not fair. It is almost too easy, from the heights of another planet and with a mind trained to scholarship, to pick holes in our delightful craziness. Sky-scrapers make him roar with laughter; aeroplanes of course are infernally dangerous, and therefore he does not laugh at them, though he likes to remember that when the aeroplane was invented in China the reigning Emperor murdered the inventor; he likes to relate the story of the Revolution of 1911 which began in Szechuan because some peasants mightily objected to railroads, and their small uprising somehow coincided with other uprisings, equally unimportant and accidental, till someone remembered that Dr. Sun Yat-sen was in America and someone else thought it would be a good idea to get rid of the Ch'ing Dynasty; "railroads are crazy things," he will say, "it is much better to walk," but the next moment he will be praying that some book or other will come by air-mail. It never does, and he begins to calculate how long they will come by pack-mule through India and Thibet.

But this afternoon, perhaps as the result of reading St. Thomas, he was in a curiously light-hearted mood. "I hope you have noticed that all the great men in the West have been either homosexuals or men who were harried by their wives."

"I haven't noticed it."

"Well then, Plato, Dante, Sophocles, Michelangelo, Shakespeare, André Gide——"

I objected that André Gide could hardly be compared with Shakespeare.

122

"It doesn't matter—the very best men were homosexuals, and all the second best men were harried by their wives. Let me instance Socrates, Dickens, Thackeray, Goethe, W. H. Hudson—oh, there are hundreds of others—all had termagants for wives. You know this as well as I do. The implications are obvious—everyone is frightened by their wives."

I objected that Confucius was also frightened by his wife.

"Nonsense, it depends upon the interpretation of a text which was inserted into the canon four hundred years after Confucius died. The text is a forgery."

"Oh well, there must be a lot of Chinese writers who were frightened of their wives."

"Absolutely none. We love our wives, or else like Li Po we have four or five of them, and just forget them. It's all a sign of disease—homosexuality, being frightened by your wives. It's absurd! It's the kind of thing that never happens in China." He raised the fly-whisk and neatly swatted a fly.

We discussed the sukiyaki party, the brown meat, the crackling of eggs, the smell of lard and wine and the blue-gowned students all round it, and how delightful it was in the glare of the frozen sunlight.

"Sukiyaki! Good heavens, it's not sukiyaki at all—it's a Chinese invention. Everyone used to have it in the T'ang Dynasty."

I said: "You are in one of those moods where you see everything through Chinese eyes, and when you attack the west, it is just pure nationalism."

"Nonsense, I never attack the west, I have the most unfathomable worship for everything that comes out of the west, but it's crazy, and so are we, and it's much better that way—only your craziness leads to block-busters, ours to an old man swatting flies."

July 13th . . . I HAD not noticed before in the house of the President of the University a scroll hanging on the wall which is an ink-rubbing from a stone erected on the shores of the Yellow River in the Han Dynasty. It means simply "stone gate," the character at the top being a stone and the character below a double folding gate, not unlike the gates you find in some Chinese houses; but what was extraordinary was the dignity of the carving and the way in which the rubbing perfectly reflected the handwriting of someone dead more than two thousand years ago, so that you could *feel* the moment when he twisted his wrist, feel the strength of the

123

long-dead hand, the amazing virility of the man who is otherwise unknown, There were also accidental accretions to the original beauty; the ink-rubbing mirrored the broken surface of the rock, which was faintly split in several places, and the places where the splitting of the rock broke the shape of the letters were perfectly appropriate to the design—impossible to imagine where else the splitting could reinforce the original beauty of the carving. No one seems to know why the unknown calligrapher should have written these characters; it may have been part of a larger inscription, or perhaps there was a village called "stone gate" or perhaps he simply wrote the words to amuse himself. It may have been a river-marker, and it is even possible that it comes from a graveyard. But what remains is the utter simplicity and strength of the man, whose writing with a brush had been copied by a stone-mason.

Modern stone-carving is almost worthless; the carvers do not follow the calligraphy, with the result that the inscriptions you see are bastard entirely, born of debased handwriting and careless imitation on stone. Moreover, it is extremely difficult to follow the pattern on stone even when the written page is pasted over it, for the slightest slip of the chisel will lead to a shape which inevitably alters the complete pattern. Every day on my way to the University I see a stone-mason laboriously inscribing inscriptions on stone, and perhaps it is emblematic of our times that he is half-blind and allows the chisel to splutter over the edges of words. He has chosen a peculiarly friable rock; the inscriptions will have disappeared in fifty years, and no one will worry overmuch. It would be best perhaps, since modern resources are at hand, to burn out the letters electrically, but the Chinese scholar with whom I discussed this fears that the life will go out of the inscription if copied too mechanically. The joy of these rubbings lies in the perfect marriage between the writer and the stone-mason; if he errs at all, if he allows the chisel to slip for one moment, he will err in the right direction and know how to recreate the momentary balance. It is then, when calligraphy is printed on stone, that the fragile and enduring beauty of these things is demonstrated: when a split-second sweep of a light brush on soft rice-paper is made to endure for thousands of years. And just as the rubbing includes as the result of the texture of the rock many accidental beauties, so too the stone-mason should pay heed to the qualities of the rock in the same way that the calligraphist pays heed to the qualities of ink and paper; he should be able to visualize the appearance of the engraving across the years,

124

digging less deep in the corner which will receive the winds, calculating the effects of sandstorms and rains and dews.

I am more and more convinced that in the heart of everything Chinese there is the art of calligraphy. The rest—the habits, the customs, the peculiar serenity and charm of the very best of the Chinese—springs from it. All Chinese are born to be painters. You can tell more of a man by watching him writing than by watching him play mah-jong: you know his virtues from his writing, and some of his vices, while from watching him play mah-jong you know all his vices, and some of his virtues. And perhaps it is in this effortless delight in revealing themselves that they obtain their serenity.

July 15th . . . AT LAST, after months of torture and meditation, I have come to the end of the first version of *Vision of England.* It began many years ago when I was reading *Beowulf* and noticed with some surprise that the epic begins with the death of Scaef, the father of Beowulf, and his burial by sea in the dead of winter, an account made glorious by the roughness of the old Anglo-Saxon syllables; you see the ice-floes and the darkness and the ring-stakes and Scaef's body taken on the ship and the blue smoke of the funeral pyres, and you hear the lamenting. There is hardly anything in our early English tongue so fine as this, perhaps the first and oldest of all recorded English. And then, ever so mysteriously, the poem begins with Beowulf.

I suspect that there was a much older epic which ended with the death of Scaef, an epic which contained his whole life and explained how he brought the corn to England. There are brief accounts of him in the *Anglo-Saxon Chronicle*, he is mentioned in passing by Saxo Grammaticus and William of Malmesbury and one or two others, but all we know for certainty is that he drifted alone on a rudderless boat towards the shores of Schleswig, lying in the boat asleep, surrounded by armour, his head resting on the sheaf of corn from which he derived his name. "At the age of fifteen," says Saxo Grammaticus, "he possessed physical perfection, and the strength which enabled him to excel all others: the ripeness of this Skjold's spirit was such that he outstripped his strength and fought battles at which one of his tender years could not look on." William of Malmesbury describes his beauty; and this is all, or almost all we know of him. So I have imagined him coming from Jerusalem, bearing the corn from Christ, floating without mast or oars down the

Nile and across the Mediterranean, staying for a while in Greece and Crete, planting vines in the south of France, coming to Cornwall and entering into the abode of heroes in Snowdon, whence he is summoned to take part in our present wars. Then he dies, according to the account given in the opening verses of Beowulf.

But there are flaws in the poem. It is too long, and modern poetry can hardly sustain poems of great length; and what is worse for my present purpose is that the figure of Scaef remains almost unchangeable, he is always the handsome Apollonian youth who brings the corn. He does not grow old. His heroism is almost past belief. There are no tragedies except the final tragedy of his death; and though he remains in a sense the embodiment of England, the journey through the Mediterranean from Jerusalem has made him altogether too European, too saturated in the peculiar ethos of the Mediterranean, to be perfectly English, for the English are no more European than the Icelanders, to whom they bear the closest resemblance. I think I like best the concluding speeches of farewell, when Scaef takes leave for the last time of the English coast:

> *Therefore I command that all the Heroes*
> *Be remembered by adoring lovers.*
> *O heap upon their graves no wreathes of stone,*
> *Nor of white lilies nor of sorrowing yews,*
> *Nor lilies nor the scented palms of Easter,*
> *But flowering crocus from the hands of children*
> *And all the country flowers—let these be laid*
> *In silent meditation and no grief.*
> *Though they are dead there is no need for tears:*
> *God plucks the heroes as he culls sweet flowers.*
> *And listen now, a pure wind comes from the East,*
> *The doves from Hebron announce the presence of Christ,*
> *And in his merciful whirlwind let the dust*
> *Fall from our faces, and the silver dew*
> *Sleep on our eyelids; and when the evening comes*
> *Like footprints of blossoms when the broken boughs*
> *Are tossed by the March winds, then let the sleeping child*
> *Still think of blossoms. Soon, full soon*
> *The silver ghosts depart, and winter comes*
> *Bearing the blossoms on the lifted boughs.*

126

Let the dew come not softly, but in showers,
To wake the parched earth, let the violets dim,
The hyacinths and the sweet bleeding dogrose
With swift ethereal gaze lift up their blind eyes.
As flowers in summer clothe our solemn faces
And with unruly fingers pluck our heart-strings,
These flowers shall grow through all remembered winters.
Then let the wind blow softly on the rose, and let the catkins
Swing on the spring-time boughs, and let the dogrose
Set fire to briars, and where the winter meadows
Are swept with ice, let the proud naked boys
Make paper boats and dive from heaven, and let them swim
Among the flowers of Spring, and let their limbs be clean
As the white wings of birds, and let the birds sing
Trill, trill, trill over our shadowed lives.

Let there be no stain, neither let there be rust upon them,
Let the bright shields be burnished and made clean
With solemn promises and holy covenants
Of mercy like the mercy of the flowers,
Such mercy as the silver ghostly narcissus
Sings in delight of heaven, or as the purple hyacinth,
Remembering Adonis among the unhewn cedars
Of Lebanon and the misty plains of Syria,
Weeps for his youthful beauty: let us weep like flowers
When filled with dew at sunrise, and let us pray
That no flowers close their sweet eyes,
No evening falls, no starlight beckons us,
But out of brightness we may see the Sun.

O God save England, may the dawn come soon
When over the unploughed ocean we see the folding star,
Which shone unruly, fade into the firmament,
And like that Easter flower which grew in Syria
Among the golden tares, and wandered lowly
Along the pathways where astonished strangers
Gazed upon his limbs and would have touched them,
But he was flame already and the burning candles
Were lit beneath his feet to bear him upward:
So like this Easter flower shall England shine.

127

O honour Christ, my children, in his glory,
England and freedom second. O honour these——
And let us give full freedom to our children.
Then the battlemented walls of our dear London
Will shine like diadems in the twilit evening,
And all our songs rejoicing shall be heard
Rising from Westminster. There shall be carillons,
Girls shall walk barefoot, men shall love them,
Their sons shall be the image of their fathers,
Firm-footed, strong and tender to their wives,
And from their slender bodies there shall come
Such prayers for peace as in the tide of Spring
The flowers cry out for mercy in the wind.
Not even Canaan nor any golden mountain
Were like this vision of my native England
When peace falls thick as leaves upon the land. . . .

July 17th . . . ALL day students have been coming in to congratulate me on the Labour Victory. I do not know why they come, for I have never spoken to them about politics, and care absolutely nothing for politics; and yet it is impossible not to be moved by their emotion. For them the Labour Government means the beginning of a new world, India will be freed, the colonies will go under international mandate, there will be socialism throughout the world, and none shall starve. It seems, at this catastrophic point in the history of the world, too much to hope that peace will come by a change of government in England, which is no longer a world power; but what was moving beyond words was their youthful trust in a new Britain.

There must come out of the flames of this war some kind of shining. The eight million dead are already being forgotten, except by the widows and the lamenting mothers and peace may be less precarious now that we can destroy whole cities, abandoning them to the rubble from which they were formed by block-busters. I remember the students who said: "Never in the whole course of this war have we had to face such things as V-weapons." There was another student who said: "I suppose they will forget that Britain stood alone, but I will not forget." There was a third student who said: "Freedom was invented by the English, and this must not be forgotten, even though the British have been conquerors. Let India be free, and we
128

shall know that we shall always have faith in Britain." These things are moving, and the heart warms to them; but what is so painful is that so few among the best Britons come to China, though when they come, they are remembered and grow into legends. So did Bertrand Russell's arrival in Peking introduce a new tolerance to the country, and so did Clarke-Kerr's arrival in bombed Chungking introduce a new faith in Britons. I have no jingoistic belief in Britons as such, and nationalism and the patriotism which is exclusive seem to me the rottenest things ever invented, as filthy as fascism, which has fed itself fat on these evils, and made us fat by the reflected glory of having conquered them. Will the nationalization of the Bank of England save us? There are good things in capitalism, there is the desperate evil of bureaucracy in socialism, there are vices in capitalists that cry out to the heavens. I prefer the faith for which Sacco and Vanzetti died—that all men should walk free on a free earth, and neither capitalism nor socialism give promise of that freedom, most desirable of all things. So I said, and perhaps there is some excuse for it, that though I was profoundly glad that Churchill was no longer in power, I hoped that there would come about a government by the people for the people, and saw no signs of it.

July 18th . . . AN INDIAN student came today to say goodbye. He is returning tomorrow to Benares, where the dust is six inches thick and the blue smoke from the burning *ghats* shines all night. I complained a little, saying that I had brought up nearly a hundred books in Sanscrit to the University, hoping that the Chinese would pay more attention to the arts of their great neighbour, the antipodean rival of the Chinese through all the centuries, yet the Chinese seemed to have no aptitude for understanding India. K., who has come to study Confucius, hoping to make the first translation of the *Analects* into Hindi, said: "They are in love with the West, but India has more to teach them. They will never learn from India, because they have such terrible powers of absorption. In the Han dynasty, Buddhism entered China from India, but Chinese Buddhism was never Indian—they took it over so completely, making it so much their own, that we can hardly recognize the source. They are the greatest eclectics in the world. They will take over the West, and make it their own, and already what they have made of the West is so predominantly Chinese that it is almost unrecognizable."

He is not in the least bitter. He knows that Indian culture will never reach China—there are impassible barriers of the spirit as well as impassible geographical barriers.

"And your own country," I asked, "what will you take from the West?"

"Almost nothing, because we are too impractical to be eclectic. We shall take all and nothing. The West has seeped into China. For us, since we believe so frantically in spiritual things, it will come as a sickness comes—and we shall recover. We know in our hearts that only spiritual values have any meaning, and though we have the greatest respect for western philosophers they do not touch us at our nerve-points. The West will come—has already come—but there will still be wandering mendicants. The rich manufacturers will retire and go penniless on their wanderings, for we know that life is short and there is no satisfaction in building skyscrapers."

I said: "In the West we will make life longer—in fifty years, it will be possible for your grandchildren to live to a hundred."

"But a hundred years is still too short to read all Indian literature," he answered.

He complained gently that he found in Chinese scholars less of the burning compulsive intensity which he found in India. There was dedication to scholarship, but no Chinese believed that he could find the secret truth beyond the veils of meaning; they were wise in their generations; they knew the limits of the possible. But the Indians were born with the instinct of tearing through the veils, and though the secret heart of things was perhaps never reached, they went on remorsefully, compelled by no known compulsion, like the lemmings who were drowned every year in the sea. And they found an inner satisfaction in performing impossible feats of spiritual valour. The Chinese had a conception of the universe which they called the Way of Heaven. He had been surprised to find how analogous it was to the Indian conception of *Rita*, which also means the Way; but in China the Way of Heaven had been too closely allied to the Way of the Emperor, the celebrated *Wang Tao*, and had entered into government to such an extent that kings were able to modify the original ordinances of the prophets. And what then? The Chinese was essentially eclectic, honest, rooted in the soil. The Indians were essentially non-eclectic, dishonest in the sense that they will gamble with spiritual truths—the ancient writings are full of gamblers—and rooted in the heavens and the Himalayas, without attachment to soil. And ultimately the Chinese were *attached,* while the Indians were incurably *detached.* And the

130

West? Neither detached or attached, but floating in an imaginary world of its own creation. He said once: "I know an Indian *sunyasis* who could blow down a skyscraper by breathing lightly on it." And then a little later, just as he was going: "The Indian and the Chinese civilizations are the most secure, because one has its foundation in the heaven and the other has its foundation in earth, but the West is not secure—I dread what will happen. There is no sheet-anchor." I said: "At their best they have a sheet anchor in a man who is half-way between heaven and earth, and lying on a cross." He thought of this very seriously for a while, and then said: "Then perhaps the three civilizations make a perfect whole—but the wind might blow down the cross." I am still not sure what he meant by this.

After he had gone, I remembered a story he had told me which pleased me more than any of the many stories he has told me from Indian mythology. We had been speaking about adoration, and I told him how the great German poet Rilke came at the end of his life, knowing nothing of India, having seen the war and suffered all the inevitable hardships which came to perplex his lonely life, to the conclusion that the world was as it is, and everything within the world must be praised—*dennoch preisen*. He was a little startled, and said that every Indian child was born with the knowledge that such praise was necessary, that praise had been the singular prerogative of all Indians since the days of the *vedas* and that without this effortless and all-embracing sense of the necessity of praise, there would have been no India. And then he went on to tell the story of Vyaghrapada, which means Tiger-foot, a pure youth who was the son of a learned Brahman dwelling beside the Ganges. The son wandered over India in search of something so beautiful that he could praise it with all his heart, and at last he found "the lingam of pure light" in a forest of banyan trees dedicated to Shiva. Near the lingam were lotos-pools and many small flower-bearing shrubs. For days he fell on his face in adoration before the lingam, which was blood-red, beautifully marked and veined, and then it occurred to him that his greatest service in the act of perpetual adoration was to heap flowers on it; but not content with the flowers of the pools, he desired to make daily offerings of the most perfect buds from the highest branches, but though he would start early in the morning the sun's fierce rays withered half of the buds before he could gather them, and in the dark hours of night he could not choose the most perfect buds. Then there came a great despair on him, and he implored Shiva to help him, begging that he might have the hands and feet of a tiger, armed with strong claws, so that he might quickly climb the highest trees and find the most perfect buds for his shrine. Thereafter he was known as the Tiger-footed One, for the desire was granted to him.

July 20th . . . I HAVE been browsing through a book of translations of the *vedas* which the Indian student K. left with me. There are two passages, one from the *Atharvaveda* and the other from the *Krishna Yajurveda,* which seems to have a perfect relevance to these times:

> Peace earth, Peace atmosphere, Peace heavens, Peace waters, Peace herbs, Peace trees, Peace may the All-gods be to me; Peace, Peace through all this Peace. With all this Peace, may we bring to peace whatever here is terrible, is cruel, is sinful. May all that be to us tranquil, benevolent, peaceful.

The other reads:

> O eye-like Sun, blessing the gods and rising each day bright in the east, may we see thee for a hundred autumns, may we live a hundred autumns, may we delight and rejoice for a hundred autumns, may we hear and speak for a hundred autumns, may we be unvanquished for a hundred autumns, may we be able to see this Sun for a long time.

July 21st . . . NEARLY all Chinese houses are surrounded by high walls, and living in them you feel like a blue-bottle continually buzzing at the panes, or else you feel like a prisoner sentenced to eternal banishment. And somehow, though the Chinese have a passion for space and are never happier than when contemplating the vast regions of their land, they are content in their houses where the stone courtyard, the rockeries, the stunted plants in the marble urns give no impression of space at all, but only a kind of mechanical imitation, very artificial, like a dress which preserves them from the nakedness of their land. Sometimes I feel that the Chinese who have wandered over their northern deserts for so many centuries delight in this self-imposed imprisonment, feeling that at last they, the most insecure of people, are secure: they have built these high walls and artificial gardens to protect themselves, and also perhaps their sensibilities have been sharpened to the point where they must take refuge in themselves. There, behind monstrous cliff-like walls, the sounds and smells of the countryside and the market-place disappear, and you walk in perennial quiet.

But this afternoon the quietness was broken by two beggars who came into the courtyard and loudly demanded money. There was nothing complaining about their voices. They stood there in the courtyard stridently demanding money, and refusing to leave; and this has never happened before. There are beggars who sit in the roadway creeping with lice, with festering wounds, hag-ridden by sores that burst open with a pressure of the fingers as you approach, but though the beggars looked weak, they were whole. I gave them some money, though R. objected strongly, saying that they are well organized and would come again and again, but it was impossible to read while they were there, and I noticed for the first time (since in this courtyard everything had seemed muted) that the high walls echoed and reechoed their sharp menacing voices. After they had gone, R. said: "It is even worse than you can imagine, because the beggars' and the thieves' guilds are inseparable; they have seen that you are prepared to give, and now they will watch the house carefully." I thought it nonsense till I went out later in the evening and saw one of the beggars crouched just outside the gate, and there was the second one, surrounded by three or four more, on the opposite side of the road facing us. They were waiting.

July 23rd . . . WHILE we were out, an old woman came to the house, and for a long time she seems to have wandered along the balcony till one of the servants asked her what she was doing, and she replied: "I am seeking the foreign priest." But there is no foreign priest in the house, and when we returned a watch in the bedroom was missing. And now, though I hate them, I have more respect than ever for the beggars who are still crouching by the gates.

July 25th . . . THERE was a famous Chinese scholar so poor that he could not afford oil, and worked by the light coming from his neighbour's room through a pin-hole, reading one letter at a time. Sometimes it seems that all our scholars are like this; and we dread what will happen when one of them dies—we cannot afford coffins. Only very occasionally can we afford a feast; we save up for it like maniacs, forgetting to buy shoes for our children and for ourselves. There is a dreariness in this poverty which defeats us all: the University has managed to borrow enough money to buy a

133

small group of houses, has even designed them and built them. The walls are paper-thin: you can hear the man thinking next door, and it is impossible to work. Or rather, one can work, but rarely give of one's best, because there are only two rooms in these cottages and a small kitchen. There are some professors with five or six children; they exist in these two rooms, but I have never understood how they manage to live.

Last week the wife of one of the professors died: students and friends and professors came together and provided the fantastic sum which will allow her to be buried decently. And what of the rest—the soldiers, the beggars, the peddlars? It is inconceivable that they can raise enough to buy coffins. Yet this week I have seen a funeral that must have cost millions. There was a carved lacquer coffin, there were multitudes of flowers, the place where he died was decorated from the street to the roof with enormous coloured ribbons and paper flowers, and at least five hundred monks took part in the funeral procession. The costliest candles were lit, the mourners did not wear white sackcloth but white silk, and when the funeral procession at last came into view, it was as though a fairground was suddenly displayed before our eyes. It was monstrous, and yet it was perfectly understandable—the cost was defrayed by the local government for a deceased official.

July 26th . . . HE WAS beautifully built, with broad shoulders and a high angular face, and he was almost handsome as he lay there beneath the prison wall, where at night I have often heard screams. He was nearly naked, with three or four young and quite remarkably handsome children, also naked, round his feet. He was begging, and it was impossible to understand why he was begging —perhaps his leg was paralysed, perhaps in spite of his beauty he was dying of tuberculosis and therefore could do no heavy work. He whined, and kept on whining until we had passed out of earshot, and then I asked N., who seemed just as surprised as I was, why he was begging and why the children were so beautiful. "Have you heard of the Indian *sunyasis* who spend their lives wandering in the sun towards the Ganges or the Himalayas? So for us, in our fear of starvation, we have come to the stage where begging seems the only solution."

I rarely see anyone giving money to beggars; sometimes a professor's wife with a tendency to Buddhism will give a beggar a ten dollar note—a sum which is almost worthless, yet ten of them may

134

be able to provide a bowl of rice. But the thing that always puzzles and delights me is that the givers are nearly always children. They stand a little aside. They discuss in whispers how much they will give; and at last, having examined their coins and their rubbed brown notes and compared them with all the luxuries they can bring, they go secretly towards the beggar, almost as though led on invisible strings, and then go hurriedly past, ashamed of the little they have given. But what remains—remains above all things—is the curious passivity, the expressions of meditation on the faces of some of the beggar's children. "They hire them by the day," N. snorts. It may be true, but their *quietness* is desperately enviable.

July 27th . . . I DO not know why they were there: it was not a funeral, there was no coffin, and the children were laughing. They laugh at funerals, but this was a different kind of laughter. And there, in their long dark gowns, in the opening of the shop from which everything had been cleared except the bronze censers and the new taoist scrolls showing the King of Heaven riding on a white horse in the Abode of the Blessed, were the taoist priests with oiled black hair raised into top-knots transfixed by jade hair-pins. They wore the little black folding hats which were common in the T'ang Dynasty, and they carried curved jade batons like the ancient magistrates. One rang a little steel pestle against an iron bowl, another clapped cymbals, a third was kneeling and intoning a chant. Fumes of scent came from the brass braziers, and all round the entrance to the shop were small children gazing idly. One of the priests got up suddenly and began to paste on the walls long slender strips of yellow paper, but the paste was bad and they kept on slipping down, and he was too blind to notice it. The priests looked underfed. (So do the buddhist priests who live by the lake in a dilapidated monastery, but much money passes through their hands.) The chanting went on; it had a curious soporific quality which derived from the fact that the monks were half unconscious as they played, drowsy with sleep or hunger, and every note of the cymbals, every note of the bells and the triangles was exactly the same in tone, so carefully measured are our responses in drowsiness. The fat red candles burned with a brilliant yellow flame, the scents swung out into the road and there was all the reverence in the world in that quiet chanting.

I do not know what had happened, and do not care very much— probably it was a sickness. The shop was old: they were not celebrating, as the Chinese so often celebrate, the opening of a shop by prayers and the firing off of firecrackers. Perhaps there was a dead body hidden behind the screens; and it is odd how in China the only brightly coloured splashes of silk appear at funerals. Marriages are dull things. There is a car with a few green and red streamers, or else a small gilt and beribboned sedan-chair which is musty with age, and carelessly carried. But, thank heaven, there are still ceremonies, there are still the tribesmen coming down from the hills, the girls with their pearl-ornamented head-dresses and slippers made of five hundred different colours of silk, there are festivals like *Ching Ming*, when the children wear willow-garlands round their heads, there is all the joy of a thumping good funeral procession.

July 28th . . . GREAT tides of blue shadows wheel over the city in the evening, and at that moment the gold sparkles from the roofs of the temples and the air is filled with ravening hawks. There are moments at twilight of magical intensity, moments when the yellow is exuded from the high walls, when the lotoses in the lake seem suddenly to acquire a colour they never had before, neither pure blue nor green, a colour compounded of all the disappearing colours of the lake. But you must not go near the temples, or near the walls, or even near the lotoses. Everything appears shabby at close contact; but when twilight softens the air and seems indeed to wash the air with silver, all shabbiness disappears, and you realize once more why you are in China. There is the misty golden glitter of morning, there are the silent brooding shadows of evening, and then China is at its best.

In Szechuan I learnt that there were mornings so golden, so fresh with dew and the singing of birds in the orange fields that the mind reeled—the gorges were cataracts leading to heaven, the mist-blue mountains coming silently out of the clouds were apparitions of consummate tenderness. But in Kunming it is the evenings, when the last rays of the yellow sun are being peeled from high walls, that the city is at its best. Somewhere in the distance soldiers are at their bugles. Every tree is black with hawks, every road is suddenly stilled. There are dark lanes to be avoided: moisture seems to exude from all the walls at twilight, but near the lake or outside the city walls among the farmlands and the high-prowed boats or in some places of the city, where a market place is becoming slowly deserted and the last laggards are on their way home, having closed

136

up the stalls, the sun will brighten for the last time some square of plaster, a brick, a coil of orange-peel, a child crouching, or even a hoof-mark, and at such moments you seem to be present at the beginning of the end of the world.

July 29th, Opium . . . I HAVE taken opium five times, and for some ridiculous reason it has never had the slightest effect—not even a headache. I am hopelessly ashamed of this. There are so many visions which are denied to me, so many colours I have never seen, so many *houris* and *devadasis* and golden mountains and vast landscapes which will always be concealed from me. The man who smokes opium downstairs, lying on a bare wooden board, with the long jade pipe and the oil-flame which seems to be burning in a glass ink-well—does he have visions? I doubt it. He is fat and greasy, and hoards sewing machines—there are perhaps a hundred in the house; and it is impossible to imagine that he has enough imagination to have anything more than the drifting contentment of the opium-smoker. I have seen him at night as I pass through the main gate, his eyes closed, his lips pursed together, his bleary face in no contentment whatsoever, but seems only to be angry. Little clouds of blue smoke come from the pipe, he fidgets with the ivory bowl, he sometimes speaks to himself. Dogs snap in the courtyard. He does not hear them, and when his children start yelling in their perpetual nightmares, he doesn't hear them either. Deafness perhaps, a delightful waving contentment, as of one riding a boat in a calm sea, but not visions. Opium costs a fortune even here; perhaps he spends ten thousand dollars a day for three or four hours of opium dreaming. It might be worth it if there were really visions, if Ezekiel and Revelations could descend in a whiff of pipe-smoke, if one could see—really see—the vision that André Malraux describes in *La Condition Humaine* of the grey lotos pond and the boat drifting through it, the two waves coming from the boat seeming to enclose the whole universe.

July 31st . . . WE HAVE learnt from the war many things; we have learnt that nothing is so tenuous as our hold on life, that the accidental and the corrupt enter everywhere, and though we may be able to defeat corruption in time (that corruption of the spirit which is infinitely worse than fear, because nothing naked is revealed, only a continuous rotting), we may never be able to defeat the accidental. The laws of probability do not apply to war, and

137

war itself is in some curious way outside life, taking no part in life, itself the contrary of life; therefore, unlike Rilke, we cannot praise the murderer, for by praising the murderer we praise something that is already outside life. *There are some things that cannot be praised.* (Death is a part of life, but war is not a part of life, for war is the impact by which life is shivered, the expression on the man's face before the jagged knife descends.)

We shall need more and more a philosophy of life which proclaims that life itself is the ultimate aim; and from life comes the enjoyment of life. We cannot go much further than this except to presume that life entails within itself the enjoyment of the most perfect freedom; for without freedom life approximates to war. War is the enemy: it is not, as Heracleitus (who saw no wars) thought, a part of life, one of the poles between which life swings and oscillates interminably. This then: that there must be an end of war, not because war is terrible for its own sake, but because human courage has at last been eliminated from it, because the nerves can no longer withstand the shock of bombardment, because in future the wars will be much, much longer when they occur than they have ever been in the past. (Our wars are so destructive that, if there is another war, the last ten years of it will be fought out with knives: all industrial resources eliminated, all ships sunk, only the human animal remaining.) Not the survival of the fittest, but of a few scientists, a few tribesmen, a few generals and statesmen, a few children. Because the horror has gone beyond all imaginable experience, *and therefore can no longer be described, but is felt over the whole world,* there remains the hope that there will be no more: the extremes of horror and the extremes of the accidental meeting at this point. *We can no longer calculate in war.* Not the mathematician but the psychologist, not the gun but the winged word, not the deaths but the rotting of the spirit, not the defined but the accidental, not the fear but the dumbness which goes beyond all fear, not the sword (which was human) but the block-buster coming through the clouds (which is neither human nor inhuman, but beyond the range of felt experience, a part of the accidental). The final task: to conquer the accidental, so that the plant may grow without a stone from some neighbouring mountain falling accidentally on the small shoot. The final achievement: having destroyed the accidental, to live in freedom, and to *enjoy* all things, having come to a time when all things without exception may be praised.
138

August 1st . . . But when we came out, no one was waiting for us. The air was very green and pure, the gravemounds were little green hills among the flooded cloud-reflecting fields and there were no dogs barking over buried bones. The storm had swept everything clean, the white pagoda in the distance shone with a ghostly luminousness, and there was no sign of anybody else. Now, late at night, thinking of it, it seems to me that this is the landscape I shall remember, a landscape which has become a part of me, bare and green, stripped almost to the bone, leaving only the faint green paint which you could scratch off with a finger-nail. And then I remember that a little while later someone came across the fields in the light of the setting sun, a girl with a green bodice and a great red skirt, her hair smoothed till it shone silver, with pearl ear-rings, and she wore red shoes with little tongues that rose up over the heels; and walked like a queen. She was not Chinese. She belonged to one of the primitive tribes who live in the mountains, suffer from goitre, burn wood into charcoal and fight tenaciously against the revenue officers. They are unconquered still, and sometimes you will see a girl who has the bearing of the unconquered: so clean, so much a part of landscape, so continually *there*. And at night, thinking of these things, China becomes ever stranger: you think of the faces you see, which are not Chinese, the faces of men who have come down from the Tibetan mountains, from Lichiang and elsewhere; the faces of the Burmese; the boy in the bath-house who has a negro strain in his blood; the students from the north who walk like heroes out of a mediæval tapestry. There is not one China, and China is not even a geographical expression, but always a state of mind. I have lived among Chinese for more than six years, and I know now no more than I knew when I was a child. It is still a country of pagodas, of women who are formed unlike the women of other countries, with slim shoulders, slim waists and small feet whose sound you can recognize so easily on the cobble-stones; a country of poets and wanderers; of drunkards and devils; of immense wealth and intolerable beauty and terrible depravity. And it does not exist, it is not real—I have only to close my eyes in the small bedroom with the night-light burning away the ghosts, and I am again eight years old, and I am again dreaming of marrying the daughter of the Prime Minister of China, or at least of a Duke. And if you say, "It is real enough; there are statistics; there are Chinese Industrial Co-operatives," I can reply easily enough by taking you down a small narrow street, where you can smell opium and where

139

you will see surrounded by children of all ages, a man with matted black hair falling down to his waist, holding a tremendous bronze-shafted spear shaped like a trident, with cabalistic signs woven into his helmet, wearing a patched gown of beaver skins and waving a human thigh-bone in tune with his songs. And if you do not believe this, I can take you to the emerald lake where the camel-back bridge is perfectly reflected in the still green water and sparrows hop on the lotus leaves, and there is a silence like the silence of dreams. And I tell you that China is haunted with her own beauty, which is reckless, as her people are reckless, and at the same time I will tell you that China does not exist, it is something out of a fairy-tale.

August 2nd . . . THE young poet was speaking very gently, in a voice so slow that I could hardly hear him. "Capitalism entered China for the first time as a powerful and deep-seated force in the political economy of the country in 1942. It was a product of the inflation. The merchants, who thieved and rooted their way into positions of power, have taken advantage of the inflation, they have grown rich, and if nothing is done to prevent them, they will retain their power. I am not talking of merchants in the Government—they are few enough—and their power is being whittled away, but you will find them everywhere else. This is why the present political situation cannot continue: the merchants have power over the inflation, and everybody depends on the inflation."

The young lawyer sitting in the corner blew out a cloud of tobacco smoke. "They talk about the degeneracy of China," he said, "but we could save the country easily enough. First, an understanding with the communists (but the communists must understand us), then an absolutely incorruptible income-tax system, with power to sequester all fortunes made illegally. There has never been a time when fortunes could be made so easily. And now it must stop, for every fortune means the death by slow starvation of hundreds of others."

The poet objected to the income-tax bureau. There were not enough people in the country who were incorruptible. "You would have to be a god to avoid the kind of bribery and corruption they would be faced with. I know income-tax inspectors who are paid enormous sums by the merchants."

The lawyer laughed: "Then we shall have to be like gods. There are enough gods in this country, surely. There are students—there

140

are professors—there are soldiers. I tell you, it is easy enough to change the whole spirit of the country. We could change it in a year or two years. The revolution did not take place in 1912. It is taking place now. I prophesy that in three years we shall have made bribery and corruption as dangerous as it is in England. We shall clean the country up, we shall make it so clean that it will be unrecognizable. In one year, two years . . ."

So it goes on, day after day, night after night, the slow-rising tide which will sweep over the country and make it pure. But pure it must be: the foreigners who love China love it less than the Chinese. They are proud of their country, which is so beautiful that it must be left without stain.

August 3rd . . . THE childhood visions of China always return—in colours, in people dying, in the heady winds, in the towering clouds, in the grace of the green-clothed women working in the rice-fields in the rain. But this morning it came with a sudden startling vividness: an old gnarled peasant woman sitting on the kerb with the golden jawbone of a dragon on her knees, and all round her baskets heaped high with flowers. It was the kind of thing one sees in dreams.

J., who flew over the Himalayas last night, complained of the bitter cold, but he said the mountains were gleaming blue-white under moonlight, and the great plains of snow gleamed like shelving white sand.

"There was the shadow of the airplane beneath us, and really it was beautiful. The airplane went in a straight line, but the shadow leaped up the cliffs of the mountains and down again." He paused for a while. "It is so odd. From the beginning China seems to have been geographically set apart from the world. The Gobi desert, the Tien-shan mountains in the north-west, the forests of Burma and then the Himalayas. As though, even now, she was not part of the world, but another planet altogether." He had been running across the airfield, and he was breathing with difficulty, for the air is rare on these heights a mile above sea-level. "But the shadow of the airplane. You ought to have seen that. The shadow didn't give a damn for the mountains. It just went up and down."

August 4th . . . RE-READING yesterday's note: I remembered M. telling me that the Yunnan plain as a geological formation came into existence at the same time as the Alps and the Himalayas were

141

lifted out of the earth, and once or twice during the past ten years the rust-coloured bones of previously unknown dinosaurs have emerged from their matrix of purplish rock under the careful chisels of the archaeologists, and perhaps it is this which gives Yunnan, with its bare blood-red scarps, the impression of being a more ancient land than any I have been to. There are times when some remote archaeological past seems to seep into the present, times when you wander over the fields and feel with a curious sense of certainty that all this has been, will be and will never change, a strange permanence. I did not feel this in Szechuan, though the known history of Szechuan is far older than the known history of Yunnan. Once or twice I have felt it in Cornwall, but never anywhere else. And perhaps it is not strange, but something to be expected, that the tribespeople should seem to belong to another age altogether. As they come down from the mountains, in their brocaded coats, with their jewelled ear-rings and curious peaked caps, they seem to intrude on the drab greyness of the city in the rain. I saw a girl riding in on horseback this evening, she was no more than seven, but with her ear-rings swinging and with the jewels embroidered on her coat, she looked like a princess coming into the captured city.

The more I hear of the Miaos and Lolos, the more excited I become. Last year I translated a whole book of short stories by Shen Ts'ung-wen about the Miaos of Hunan. He loves them, and he is himself part Miao, but he dare not return to them: he prefers to write of them as he remembers them in childhood, afraid that all the glory will have vanished if he sees them again in mature years. And yet there is no reason why he should be afraid: you have only to see them here, riding down from the mountains, walking gracefully and swiftly through the city, to know that their lives are full of legends. And surely they have more legends than the Chinese, for they have lost their inheritance.

August 5th . . . . THE strain of being a professor in war-time China. I have known professors who have suffered a kind of madness, a sudden blackout, a terrible dark hopelessness resulting from eight years of war. There are moments when the bare mud-floored cowsheds on the campus where we teach fill me with an ungovernable horror, and I want to tear them down, for they seem to cry out: "This is a degradation so great that only the Chinese would accept it." And seeing the black limousines passing with the wives of gen-

142

erals on their way to mahjong parties, the horror returns. But afterwards I know that it is best to accept them as they are, and surely there is something symbolical in this great University fashioned out of a few mud huts on a levelled graveyard, within a stone's throw of the place where the last Emperor of the Mings was garotted and tortured to death. For with the death of the last Emperor of the Mings the old China died, and from this burial mound the new China will be born.

August 6th . . . I AM sick to death of hearing that China is an embryo power. She is a power in being. Though her soldiers starve still, though her armies are out-generalled, though we look down into the abyss of a civil war, she is a great and enduring power. It is not necessary to listen to her politicians to know how great she can be: it is enough to read her poetry and look at the map. I do not know how often there have been wars in China, or how often the wars will return, but I know that no country so sincerely desires peace. And with what terrible earnestness the students talk of avoiding the civil war.

C. has been helping me to compile an anthology of Chinese poetry from the beginning to the present time. I had asked him to translate the poems of Li Ho, the "ghostly poet" of the T'ang dynasty. He is almost unknown abroad, but in those last days of the T'ang dynasty he was one of the poets who brought new life into a dying technique. I like particularly C.'s version of "The Song of the Arrowhead":

An arrowhead mingled with black ash, brown powdered bones and
  red stains:
Tipped with ancient blood, which is cold and resembles green
  flowers:
The white feathers and the shaft have grown rotten in the rains,
And there is only the triangular arrowhead like a wolf's tooth.

I have wandered over the plain with my two ponies:
To the east of the travelling post, along stony ricefields, among
  weed-ridden hills:
The long wind blew; the day was short; the stars few and solitary.
The damp clouds flapped in the night air like black flags.

The hungry ghosts to the left and the lean spirits to the right cried
  aloud.

143

I poured out a flask of wine, I dedicated and roasted a sheep.
The insects were at rest; the wild geese made piteous sounds; the
    red reeds glowed.
The wind tossed the will-o'-the-wisps to bid the parting guest fare-
    well.

Once, years ago, I found this arrowhead, and my eyes melted with
    tears.
The triangular red head had once pierced human flesh.
In the south village east of the city I met a boy on horseback
Who begged me to buy bamboo to furnish a shaft for this arrow-
    head.

August 7th . . . I HAVE been amusing myself all day translating *The Book of Odes*, where all that is finest in Chinese poetry reaches a kind of perfection which I know in no other poetry. There is an intensity in this early poetry which defies analysis, a freshness which is like morning light and a sense of gracefulness and piety which comes strangely on our sophisticated senses. Sometimes I have the feeling that this is the only real poetry, and that everything that has been written since then is only a variation on the same themes. What is curious is the tremendous and I think conscious use of sexual symbols. The white ponies, the white towers, the rocks and the muddy streams are the necessary implements of their imagination, the prerequisites of all poetry which demands from life the symbols of the purest forms of life. Poetry in *The Book of Odes* is stripped to the skin: it is not stripped to the bone. There is a nakedness about it which is purely sensuous: no hardness, nor any luxuriance, only the rhythmical statement so keenly expressed that it seems to hurl itself from the printed page and assume the form of singing. It is not folk poetry, but the poetry of enchanted experience. And always against the background of the Earthly Paradise. You can see those paintings of the Earthly Paradise in nearly every book of Chinese paintings: a few russet-coloured mountains, a few clouds, a temple in the background, and in the foreground there are the lovers walking sedately along enchanted pathways overlooking a river where children are playing and old men are drinking. In a corner an old man in blue robes is playing on his pipe, and somewhere in the remote distance there is always a white horse or a white heron. It is the landscape of the earliest Gobelins tapestries: quiet, suffused with the light of a sun which

144

casts no shadows, and strangely familiar. There is one love-poem particularly which pleased me, and I include it here because I am not satisfied with Waley's version:

> Pure is the white pony,
> Feeding on the young shoots in my stackyard.
> Keep him hobbled, keep him bridled.
> Let him stay through all mornings.
> So may my lover
> Here take his ease.
>
> Pure is the white pony,
> Feeding on the bean-sprouts in my stackyard.
> Keep him hobbled, keep him bridled.
> Let him stay through all evenings.
> So may my lover
> Here have his peace.
>
> Pure is the white pony
> Who comes to me swiftly,
> Like a duke, like a marquis.
> Let us enjoy ourselves utterly.
> Let us prolong our love-making,
> Let us take our ease.
>
> Pure is the white pony
> Who lies in the empty valley
> With a bundle of fresh hay.
> He is like a piece of jade;
> But do not be as rare as gold or jade.
> Do not go from my heart.

August 8th . . . THE amazing spiritual grace of Chinese students. . . .

It is worth repeating that until recently China lived in an age of magic and ceremonial, and is now entering the age of steel. It is an astonishing and perhaps terrifying picture—the sudden emergence of mechanical civilization in a province where there are still head-hunters, where the latest aeroplanes fly directly over the heads of the tribesmen, and where the tribesmen themselves are becoming skilled mechanics. There is the immense airfield, and only a little way away there are the Taoist temples high up on the red cliffs. There is a legend that any fish which is able to leap up to the

145

Dragon Cliff Gate on the rocks will become a Dragon, and surely something like this is happening now—millions upon millions of fishes are becoming Dragons.

August 9th . . . The great wounded hawk came slowly out of the skies and settled on the roof of the American Consulate. It was grey and blue, with enormous stretched wings and a great hooked golden beak. And then the ravens and the crows came out of their nests in the silver eucalyptus trees, and they perched there, watching the hawk, waiting for it to die. But the hawk remained still, the fine head buried in the shoulders, the feathers unmoving in the strong sunlight, heavy and weary with its coming death.

It was a magnificent hawk—magnificent in the spread of its limp grey feathers, magnificent in its silence and seclusion, its uninterrupted contemplation of itself, utterly careless of the presence of the ravens. There they were—twenty or thirty of them—cawing loudly, hopping along the roof-tree, strutting as though they owned the beautiful green-tiled roof, and they craned their short ugly necks and puffed out their black chests and waited pitilessly for the moment when the dying hawk would be too weak to attack them. And when the hawk made a faint flapping movement of wings, as though weary of sunlight and the incessant screaming chatter of the ravens, utterly weary, they noticed the weariness and stiffened, and I knew they would only wait a little while longer. They knew the hawk was alive: they knew it was sick and dying: they knew its strength was slowly ebbing away. And so they watched, preening themselves, standing against the sunlight, sharpening their evil black beaks and filling the air with their screams.

And then it came—a single desperately slow movement by the hawk, but it was a sign of weakened strength, of an attempt to fly which had failed; and so they came down, flying one after another, screaming, clapping their wings, pecking at the wounded hawk, pecking at the head and the eyes and the soft places among the feathers, flying low, terribly low, so that their black feathers touched the beautiful blue feathers of the hawk, and they were so ungainly that even in flight they seemed to be hopping in the air. And still the hawk remained silent amid all their screaming, silent but twitching, flinging its little gold head round and then quickly burying it again, enclosed within itself, intolerably still and tranquil now that they were passing over it. The hawk was still, clamped to

146

the roof, trying to penetrate deep in the roof, with the small proud gold head buried in the feathers. And then the ravens were silent. They seemed to be afraid. They hardly dared to scream. The sunlight turned the blue feathers gold, and we could see it quivering, tense, waiting for the shock on exposed nerves, edging silently and quietly towards the edge of the roof, so that it could fly away more easily, and already certain of death.

It went on for nearly half an hour. There were long breathless intervals when nothing happened: the ravens strutting on the roof, the hawk weakening, and sometimes, as though at a given signal, the sudden screaming and pecking, the black wings opening like fans. Three times they attacked, not bravely, but fearfully, always in groups, digging their beaks deep among the feathers, so that the hawk moved with frightful spasmodic movements, and was as suddenly still again, quietly contemplating its fate.

And then at last, having gathered all its strength and edged over to the very precipice of the roof, it slowly unfolded its wings and flapped away like a slow-moving sheet of gold in the sunlight. The ravens held a long parliament. They chattered excitedly, they pointed their beaks in the direction of the hawk, and they began to fly after it shrilly and evilly, knowing that in the neighbouring grove of eucalyptus trees other ravens were waiting for them. And soon, in the distance, the whole tree was black with death.

At Maymyo also, that gaunt red-breasted eagle who perched on the milestone and seemed to be counting the steps of the sun . . .

August 10th . . . I WAS working at night, and there was a tremendous roar of spluttering fire-crackers outside, and M. said: "Some poor fool getting married." But the fire-crackers went on and on, and the smell came over the high wall of the house—an astringent smell like ammonia and rotten wood. But it was the end of the war.

It was raining, but nobody cared. The streets were filled with people shouting, singing "*Ting Hao*" at the top of their voices, the wet red flags of the Republic hung from the houses, the jeep headlights swayed across the narrow streets and fell—now on a child cowering in the rain, now on an old scholar who was busily trying to mend his umbrella, now on two lovers in one of the dank alleyways, and it seemed perfectly right that the silver gleam of the headlights should pick out these three people sheltering from the rain. Children were crying. The fire-crackers were exploding in all

147

directions. People threw them down from upper windows, and from door-ways: they were scattered from jeeps, and always after the explosions there was a dull thud of feet as people tried to avoid them. And then we huddled through the dark streets in a jeep to the British Military Mission. The young lieutenant said: "I told the Colonel the bloody war was over. I kicked at his door. I said, 'The bloody war's over,' but he only grunted and snored like a pig."

And then the ride home with the radio we had got from the Mission, and someone throwing a string of crackers into the jeep which exploded all round us, blinding us, and the rain shining on the flooded river, and the people still milling and singing and shouting *"Ting Hao"* and not quite sure why they were shouting, and the older shopkeepers looking sorrowfully from their door-ways, knowing that the Army would go away and they would be ruined, and the young still throwing crackers and sobbing, and the rain falling steadily like a warning. And late at night, waiting for the news to come through and thinking of the long trek home to the coast . . .

August 14th . . . THE salt carts came racing along the Burma Road in the perfect sunshine. They are small and squat, with two rubber-tyred wheels and a square flat board resting on them, and usually there are two small Tibetan ponies with bright yellow flags standing up from their collars. The sun-bronzed rider stands barefoot and bare-chested with the reins in his hand on the very edge of the cart which is piled with crags of white salt, and all the time he is singing and shouting and racing the other carts, entirely unconscious of the great eight-wheeled lorries which drive past him. They are all peasant boys, and they look bronzed and happy, the sweat running off their faces and their hair blowing in the wind. As they come racing up the road, three or four abreast, you have a sudden vision of Achilles riding across the plains of Troy in the days before the atomic bomb.

August 15th, Under the Shadow of the Atomic Bomb . . . It SEEMS now that the end of the war is not important, and certainly it is less important than the discovery which has given us the means to end the world. And surely we are unprepared for these things, utterly unprepared: we are unprepared for the end of the war, and infinitely less prepared for this invention, which alters everything

148

without exception—our relation to the world, our relation to each other, the value of literature, the values we have set on our own lives and on those who are dear to us. And at the time when we most need to think clearly and sincerely, we find ourselves at the end of a war in which all our passions have been aroused, when in fact it is impossible to think at all.

But this much is certain: from now on we are dedicated to peace. The world is smaller than ever, and every grain of dust has power to destroy us. A whole cycle of civilizations ended with the invention of gunpowder, and perhaps we shall date the new civilizations that arise (if they ever arise) from the morning of August 5th, 1945, when the American airmen set out to bomb Hiroshima. And now more than ever we must live in peace—we must be humble—we must go to the Pueblo Indians, to the Balinese, and perhaps to the Chinese philosophers in order to learn how to live in peace. And we must go humbly, not as the proud inheritors of western civilization, but as supplicants: for we have given ourselves power to destroy ourselves, and it is from others that we must learn to live.

From now on every book, every temple, everything we create with our hands and our hearts is in mortal danger. And with what heartfelt relief, with what rejoicing we should welcome this fatal knife, which has brought us once more to the garden of Eden, where the flaming angels stand guard at the gates.

August 16th . . . READ with horror Bryussov's *Republic of the Southern Cross*. I read it years ago, without understanding its implications, in the same way that I read Wells' earlier stories. But this book, written in 1919 and describing a kingdom in the Antarctic in which there is a purely mechanical and totalitarian civilization, where the people are treated like sheep and everyone is in some way less than a cog in the state machine, seems now to have caught up with the times. It is immensely real, and important. This prophylactic civilization in the Antarctic, where all the desires and all the vices of the people are carefully regulated by the dictator, where the cities are covered over with immense vaults and where the people live in an artificial electrically-controlled world, this world is so close to us that we can almost breathe the atmosphere which reigns in these vaulted cities—a smell of deodorants, formaline and crumbling biscuits. And how well Bryussov insists on the validity of the strange mania of contradiction—*mania contradic-*

149

tens—which suddenly and inexplicably captures the dispossessed people of the Republic, and there is one passage which reads surprisingly like contemporary history:

> It must be added that on the twenty-first of July the mob took the City Hall by storm, and the defenders were all either killed or scattered. The body of Deville has not yet been found, and there is no reliable evidence available as to what took place in the City after the twenty-first. It must be conjectured that anarchy had reached its limits. Hordes of madmen and drunkards danced wildly about bonfires. With songs, with incoherent outcries, with idiotic laughter, mingled the cries of those who had lost the power to express in words their own delirious dreams; mingled with these were the moans of the dying. Dancing gave way to fighting—for a cask of wine, for a woman, or simply for no reason at all, in a fit of madness brought on by the emotion of *contradiction*. There was nowhere to flee. . . .

August 17th . . . PAUL VALÉRY died a few days ago. I have no idea on what day, and the day is not important. What is important is that he is dead. In an address which he delivered to the French Academy in January 1941, when France was at the time of its greatest suffering, he said: "In a period when the world thinks and meditates less and less, when civilization seems to reduce itself from day to day to nothing more than the memories and traces we preserve of its many-sided richness and its free and exuberant intellectual production; while miseries, anxieties and constraints of every kind suppress and discourage the undertakings of the mind—in such a period Bergson seems already to belong to a bygone age, and his name to be the last great name in the history of the European intelligence." And surely this is still more true of Valéry himself.

I knew him very slightly, and had only one talk with him, though I would see him often walking through the Jardin du Luxembourg or in the Shakespeare Bookshop in the Rue d'Odéon. I was studying the manuscripts of Evariste Galois in the library of the Bibliothèque Mazarin. It was the winter of 1931, the Seine covered with fog, the Quai Voltaire exactly as it was fifty years before, and I remember how the mist came through the windows of the library, though the windows were tightly closed; and how the statue of

Voltaire, seated and naked, shone down at us. I was tired of reading the closely-written mathematical manuscripts, and begged the librarian to allow me to take down Valéry's poems. The librarian smiled grimly, pointed out that though I had indeed authorization to read the manuscripts, the books in the library of the academicians were not for students; and then the little man in the brown lounge suit, who resembled the Rabbit in *Alice in Wonderland*, turned to the librarian and said: "Eh, voilà!—pourquoi pas?" and the Rabbit himself went to the shelves and produced three books— *Charmes* and the *Ebauche d'une Serpente* was another; I have forgotten the third. He asked me why I read his poems, and I answered lamely enough that I considered that they were the greatest ever produced in France. He smiled as grimly as the librarian: "I am Monsieur Valéry." I said that I had recognized him. He turned to the manuscripts on the green beige table and said, with extraordinary simplicity, "You are studying Evariste Galois—*certainement un de nos plus grands poètes.*" I was immensely pleased, for this mathematician who died before he was twenty and who produced only two lines of poetry, was indeed among the greatest. And then Valéry disappeared through the fog of winter.

August 18th . . . THE war is over. They say it is over, but so far there is no sign of it. Kunming is the same, the streets are the same, the shopkeepers are still cheating, there is continual rain, the price of foodstuffs has gone up, the dollar rate has sunk suddenly and inexplicably to a quarter of what it was last week, the censorship is still imposed, the soldiers still look hungry, and it is all foul and miserable until you think of the University, the scholars, the painters and the poets and the writers who seem to live in another world: a world of infinite gentleness and compassion, and so little power.

J. is trying to leave for Peking immediately. Last night I walked with him through the dark streets to the airport. A rat scuttled across the road, a girl screamed, the green and red tail-lights of an aeroplane broke through the overcast sky, and suddenly—it was four o'clock in the morning—the great white pillar of a searchlight sprang up from one of the airfields and all over the city there was a white flower of winter frost reflected from the clouds.

It was amazing then how the city sprang into life, the dust and dirt peeled away, the darkness evaporated. Under this thin coating of ice everything looked supernatural. Caught in this winter glare, the city seemed made of frozen glass. Nothing moved. There were no more screams. In this dazzling whiteness, the city took on the shape of a Chinese palace in a fairy-tale. And then the searchlight went out, withdrawn into the earth, sucked out of the clouds, and nothing remained but the black damp walls towering above us.

There, in the early morning, the beggars slept limply under sodden mats, motionless, heaped upon one another like logs. All the way down to the centre of the city there were these beggars, cowering in door-ways, young boys and old men, their skins not brown or white, but the colour of brown paper which has been soaked in mud. We stepped over them carefully, and came out at last into the main street, which was silent and deserted, and then, O God, suddenly the sun came through, the beggars awoke and rubbed their eyes, a mist rose, the creek was jade-green and the birds began to sing from the boughs of the plum-trees.

August 22nd . . . "TERRIBLE things are abroad," L. was saying, and we nodded our heads and said we knew perfectly well that the rich were always corrupt. "No, I am speaking of depravity—sexual depravity. We are so sophisticated that the simple animal passions no longer amuse us. There are so many tricks, so many perversions, there are so many opportunities, so much self-abasement that the country is being weakened. We cannot afford the puritanical outlook of the New Life Movement, but we can afford even less this continual drain on our physical resources. I could take you to bath-houses where small rooms are set aside, not for the ordinary perversions—God knows there are perversions which are ordinary enough—but for the most complex and singular perversions imaginable."

I have known that for some time he has been sketching out a book on the Chinese character. There were chapters on the Chinese family system, which he damned wholesale, chapters on Chinese business morality, which he regarded even in these times of cut-throat competition as being as healthy as anywhere in the world, there were innumerable notes and observations which he would weave into a collected whole, but he was always coming back to the perversions of the great cities. There was so much poverty, but poverty did not explain everything. There were the perversions of Peking which are more civilized and perhaps even more dangerous than the rabbit-warren perversions of Shanghai; and the Japanese had deliberately encouraged them to weaken the people. "A nation

152

cannot endure with its sex tarnished. I am not talking about the fishing-boys or the soldiers—it is the same all over the world, and does not last. But the careful cold-blooded elaboration of perversion, which we have learned partly from the Japanese, partly from the Ch'ing Dynasty, partly—and perhaps most of all—from our own inexhaustible delight in sophistication, this is worse."

August 28th . . . FROM the Street of the Snail-skin down to the Street of the Flowery Mountain the three American soldiers came lurching through the night, followed by the most delighted horde of snot-nosed children I have ever seen. They were no more than happily drunk. They took off their hats, they bowed, they made incredible speeches, they clapped their hands, they leaned languorously on one another, and then after a few moments they would tire of the happy, screaming children and pretend to be chasing them. A pretty girl passed. They bowed very ceremoniously. A beggar looked at them wonderingly until they removed all the banknotes from their pockets and threw them in the air; then the beggar was lost in the mêlée of screaming children.

And so they went on, right down to the heart of the city, singing and dancing a little and pausing outside the shops to bow their acknowledgments to the customers, holding up the traffic and sometimes bawling at the top of their voices. "Disgusting," said the American colonel. Liu Lien was there, beaming and stuttering with excitement. "Please tell me, colonel, how can they be disgusting when they make the hearts of the children glad?" And all night he has been talking about this new American invasion of China which is far, far more important than the Flying Fortresses overhead.

September 1st, Obiter Dicta . . . I DO not know why one should do anything except for the sweet hell's delight of doing it. The sun shines for sweet hell's delight, or if you prefer it, because it must, as a lion must wear its red mane or a cock its red comb; the moon shines for the same reason, and just as absurdly. For sweet hell's delight things are born, for sweet hell's delight Christ was crucified.

I would prefer a religion which brought "sweet hell's delight" into things; I would prefer to see people flinging themselves about for no particular reason except that they delighted in flinging themselves about. There is "sweet hell's delight" in Pantagruel, in

153

Chuang-chou, and I suspect that the girl who was sacrificed in the sacred pool of Chichen-Itza flung herself down with the same delight as Tse-yu who, asked whether he feared death, replied: "Good Heavens, why should I fear? Very soon I shall be decomposed. My left shoulder will become a cock and will herald the morning sun. My right shoulder wil become a cross-bow and I shall be able to get duck. My buttocks will become wheels, and with my soul for a horse I shall be able to ride in my own chariot." For the sake of sweet hell's delight, one should be conscious of death—the Taoists were supremely conscious of death, but for them it was a source of strength—and surely no generation of men have seen death so close to them as our own?

I should like to see the flowering of "sweet hell's delight." I do not mean that there should be a religion of doing what one pleases: the spectacle is too frightening. But I do mean that at certain times of the year, all the accumulated restraints of civilization should be put off and people should do things, not because it pleases them to do things (nothing could be more dull), but with the supreme aim of dedicating oneself to sweet hell's delight. One should do the most amazing, the most impossible, the most delightful things simply as an expression of life; for since a flower does the most amazing, the most delightful and the most impossible things, it is extraordinary that men should do them so rarely. The Pueblo Indians, the Balinese, the Chinese peasants all have their rituals which are designed, I suspect, for the purpose of encouraging the little shoots of life to flower prodigiously according to the seasons. There is somewhere or other a vague god to whom the offerings are made, but the god was long ago forgotten and the rituals are now performed for no other reason than that life, the most precious thing on the planet, should be vindicated. And life has no reason—only "sweet hell's delight."

I confess I prefer it like this. I like the Indian conception of the whole universe dancing the dance of Shiva, who is creator and destroyer. I like those odd and febrile passages in the *Vedas* where the whole universe is conceived as a galloping horse, the mountains its droppings, the seas its piss, the mane is the sun and the stars and we are all rumbling things in its belly: there are passages in the *Upanishads* which light up the world with a bright and momentary flame, till we remember that we live in a world where men live in cells and taxes have to be paid and children have to be fed with little bits of paper printed by the national banks. At the begin-

154

ning of civilizations there is nearly always a time when everything is conceived *sub specie flammae.* You will find it in the *Vedas,* you will find it in the earliest Chinese poetry and in the portrait of Achilles in the *Iliad,*—a great shining, as though the whole earth was bathed in the light of fire and men were seeing the flames for the first time. And are we not flames, and do not flames fling themselves about outrageously, consuming themselves, delighting in consuming themselves, restless and unstable and assuming incorruptible and never-ending shapes? I suspect sometimes that we are all unconsciously modelling ourselves upon the dullest things in creation—tape-worms and amoebae. Nationalism—this little bit of world is mine. But is it? It would be better to be like gypsies, to dress as we please, to sleep where and with whom we please, to fly over the Andes, to take ship to the Antarctic, to splash ourselves in the muddy waters of the Ganges and spend a year in a lamasery in Thibet, and ride races on Thibetan ponies, and smoke opium, and roar down the Yangtse gorges, and stick flowers in our hair, and—then, then, when it is all over and we have had our fling and done the most outrageous flame-like things, there will always be some Chinese philosopher with a wart on his nose, wearing a little back pearl-buttoned cap and strolling about in an untidy tobacco-spotted gown to amuse us with the consolations of old age. We must have both worlds—the world of Shiva and the world of the Chinese poets; and having these, there is no reason why we should pay any attention to our own world.

In the last of all his books Bergson stated that "the universe is a machine for the making of gods." I suspect that it was, but it is now running down. In the idiotic philosophies of the West we premiss the existence of gods more handsome and more delightful than any that have been imagined elsewhere; thereupon, bound by a fatal urge towards self-destruction, we crucify them or nail them to rocks or they commit incest and are punished for it, or murder their mothers and are punished for it. The fates occupy an excessive place in the West—they are unthinkable to the Chinese, and only barely conceivable to the Indians. Our minds are cluttered up with Medusaes, who will turn us to stone if we look on their brightness. The angels at the gates had swords which have cut us off from the garden; so, too, if we enter the gates of a Chinese temple, we see the Four Heavenly Kings (*sze ta tien yu*) who are equipped with menacing swords and fierce aspects, but the swords are of *papier-maché* and they have the fierceness only of children who pretend they are strong; and we can enter the garden, where the chrysanthemums are blossoming and the camellias are whiter than snow against the indigo-blue of the sky. Here in these gardens there are no trees of good and evil, only a few stunted pines and perhaps a magnolia-tree which has shrivelled with age and bears the inscription that it was planted more than a thousand years ago in the T'ang Dynasty. We have taken the angels at the gates too seriously. It may even be permissible to believe that they do not exist.

We have bombed Nagasaki and Hiroshima. It may be a crime—I cannot judge, but I am sure that this bombing is only one more aspect of our fatal preoccupation with death. It is an old story that the Chinese invented gun-powder only in order to amuse themselves with fire-crackers, to find some thousands of years later that the English were shelling their coasts with the same powder. The Chinese still amuse themselves with gun-powder, and it will not be long before they can amuse themselves with atomic bombs; but I would suggest that they will employ the atomic bomb reverently and sensibly for the making of lakes and altering the shapes of disreputable looking mountains. I suspect that we are taking science too seriously: the first thoughts of the atomic experts should be to find what delight we can take in it. When we are tired of rockets, we may amuse ourselves by seeing what can be done with different coloured explosions. Certainly nothing out of this war has been so beautiful as the coloured photographs of tracer bullets taken from aeroplanes. If we are to fling ourselves about and take sweet hell's delight in life, we shall have to start soon, before the deadly seriousness of the scientists has deadened us for ever.

I insist: the world was made for sweet hell's delight, and there is no other purpose than that we should take delight in it. One should approach the gods of life without restraint, saying like Tung Feng Su: "I am twenty-two years old. I am nine foot three inches in height. My eyes are like swinging pearls, my teeth like a row of cowrie-shells. I am brave like Meng Pen, assiduous like Ch'ing Chi, pure like Pao Shu and as full of devotion as Wei Sheng. I consider myself fit to be the highest officer of the state; and with my life in my hands, I await Your Majesty's reply." And for the sweet hell of the thing, His Majesty will certainly reply.

September 2nd . . . K. IS writing a thesis on modern American literature under my direction. Unfortunately there are almost no books of modern American literature available. There are, of

156

course, heaps of dog-eared armed services editions; there are the complete works of O. Henry and Mark Twain; there are the speeches of Roosevelt and some odd volumes of Santayana and far too much of John Dewey and a little of Allen Tate, and there is the whole of Muriel Rukeyser's amazingly beautiful life of Gibbs; but there is none of her poetry, nothing of R. P. Blackmur, nothing of Katharine Anne Porter, and this is perhaps the worst omission of all. I do not see how he can write at all of modern American literature without mentioning *Flowering Judas,* or *Pale Horse, Pale Rider.* I have tried to explain patiently and as unobtrusively as possible the sources of Hart Crane—his granite indifference, the metallic sound of his prose, the richness of his colouring and the passion of his adoration for Poe and Whitman; I have tried to convey humbly and sincerely that he seems to be the greatest poet of my generation, a man with the eyes of Baudelaire and the self-mockery of Chuang-chou, possessed like Shakespeare with a desperate fear and attraction for the sea; a man whose mind rocketted and blazed during the brief fever of his life more brilliantly than that of any other man of his time; the man who destroyed the waste-land and built a bridge as enduring as the bridge he described; I have said that Crane was trying to make poetry sing again and at the same time he was trying to give verse the quality of a claw which will scratch the skin till blood appears; and all the time K. has listened politely, nodding his head slowly and wisely, without comprehension, without for a moment moving away from his habitual delicate precise calm. I am almost angry. "But don't you see," I complain wearily, "the excitement—the colours—the pure spirit of the man—pumping into America a new life, his own life—attempting to make out of colours and sounds and his memories of the Pueblo dances a new culture, a new feeling, a whole new orientation of the spirit." He is still very calm, but the faintest flicker of enthusiasm begins to show in his eyes. "Yes, I can see now—it is something like our own poetry at the beginning of the T'ang Dynasty."

The world weariness of the Chinese, who have seen everything, is continually surprising me. In China everything has happened, and all that happens again is only a repetition. They have written in every kind of prose imaginable, they have tried all forms of poetry, they have passed through and gone beyond all the arts of civilization till they are left breathless with despair, having no new worlds to conquer. And at the end of this interminable long journey when they, and not we, have come to a waste-land of the spirit, what remains? To begin all over again, to watch silently and with as much comprehension as possible the curious evolutions of the passing ages, where there is so little invention that everything is a reduplication of what has happened before. "But Shakespeare—Hart Crane—surely they haven't happened in China?" "Of course not, but the same emotions can be seen in our poetry, because we too have possessed our Elizabethan age, and we too——" The opportunity has come. "At least you haven't possessed a Brooklyn Bridge?" He smiles delightfully. "Yes, but we called it the Great Wall of China—it crumbled after a time, and we don't look at it as a Great Wall any longer. You know, these things crumble. They always do. I try to write modern Chinese poetry, but it's probably best to write about peach-blossoms—they come again each spring and they don't crumble. You see, we have gone through it all." His eyes smile like a benevolent fish through the enormous lenses of his spectacles, and once more we return to modern American literature and Hart Crane, who is as old as the ages.

September 4th . . . His feet were bare, full of stone bruises, and the toe-nails were bleeding, and he came up the long dusty road past the University like any one of those ghosts of soldiers returning along the Burma Road who have been tormenting us simply by their terrible presence. He had the thin little red cross sewn to his padded blue coat which has been bleached to the lightest cerulean blue by the sun, and a face like a brown skull. God knows how many miles he has travelled! He has probably had malignant malaria; he has slept in ditches with the thinnest of army blankets; he has been press-ganged from his farm; he has been to hospital; the army has now forgotten him, and in a few days he will die and no one will care very much, for his letters never reached home and perhaps he has forgotten that he ever had a home.

His home now is a little cave in the clay by the side of the banked road. He has put up some shreds of matting to protect him from the rain, he has a ragged paper umbrella and a straw hat, he has made a fire—there are smears of black ashes, and something that may be a kettle; there are some more shreds of bamboo matting on which he probably sleeps; there is nothing else. It is almost a grave. And he is monstrously thin and dying, his eyes sunk so deep in the sockets that he seems already to be retreating from the world which has used him so hardly. It was all unnecessary. He could have stayed on his farm, he could have grown tall and possessed a family and
158

seen the rice grow, but he will not raise a family and he will never see the rice grow again. I try to think of how he looks at the world from the vantage point of his cave. He has long since passed through disillusion and despair. He knows, as we do not know, that there comes a time when the sun fades from the sky, when all this monstrous business of trying to feed oneself in a sparse world is a terrible weight on the spirit, when there is nothing but cold moonlight and fields. He hates being watched. When you die, it is best to die alone and invisible. Then very carefully he squats in the shelter of his cave, collects a few sticks together, lights a fire and warms his hands, though the sun is shining outside.

I remember the way the flames glowed on his face and the way he thrust out his bony hands and the smile as he warmed himself: the last comfort of all men is a flame. I remember how he sank wearily back on his heels with his shoulders against the clay, and the delightful idiot smile of contentment as he rubbed his hands together, I remember the small leaping flame. And I know that he will not be there tomorrow, they will have found his body and thrown it in a ditch; but tomorrow, and the day after that, and the day after that, and perhaps for ever, there will come from Burma these sallow-cheeked boys with gaping wounds and faces like skulls who will see the city of Kunming and not dare to penetrate through the gates.

Death haunts the north gate. There are these grey-green burial mounds right up to the first range of hills. The university campus is only a small square stamped and flattened out of these mounds, which have sometimes fallen in. Here and there are a few pillars, commemorating people whose names have long since vanished; the crows perch on them, and sharpen their beaks on the plinths, and ponies wander among them, and not far from here an Emperor was murdered and almost in the same place executions take place today, and there are the skulls of horses and dogs and men in the open graves.

September 5th . . . Thinking of how I grew—always in the sun—the first time I felt conscious of the sheer intoxicating beauty of being alive was in a South African garden where tremendous red peonies were glowing in the sun—the first time I was acutely conscious of literature was reading Katharine Mansfield in the sunlight overlooking False Bay. Always the sun. The awful feeling of being cut off at dusk, the rope tightening round the throat, the

159

snake gliding out of the oleander trees and my father beating at it frantically with a golf-stick. Insisting on a night-light. Screwing my knuckles into my eyes at night until at last there were bright colours, spinning and whirling, but at least they were colours. And then when I had t.b. in Chungking almost crazily worshipping the sun, the glitter of dust, the cascading rice-fields, the heart-breaking glory of the sunlight flooding everything, everything without exception, so that even the shadows were bathed in sunlight.

The fear of moonless nights, like the fear of dogs, this and the still more intimidating fear of starless nights, when there was blackness entirely: walking alone somewhere: the sudden clatter of a stone: a bark: a leaf waving across my face: the blackness shaping itself into horrors like Pushkin's vision of the *nyedoti-chomka*—an animal which possessed only a mouth and two slits for the nose. The never-endingness of the dark, in which you could fall for ever, flapping your hands and coat-tails like wings, but even if you could guide your flight, it wouldn't matter, there was no sense of direction, you were still falling, and if you turned left it was the same as turning right, or turning upside down. Hardly being able to breathe for fear—not of the dark or of the monsters which might come out of the dark, but for the absence of the sun, in exactly the same way that the lover can hardly breathe for the absence of the beloved.

My earliest memories are dimly-lit nights in England, coal-fires burning, but earlier than the earliest memories I seem to remember great sheets of yellow wheat-fields and burning corn and a Greek-blue sky, and then the blue crenellated walls of a fortress on a hill against a lowering sky. This may be the castle of the Polignacs, where they say my mother's family comes from, near Le Puy, but it may not be; but what is certain is that somewhere there is the burning corn and a blue fortress standing out against a darkening sky.

I am dubious of ancestral memories: I cannot remember ever having been born before: I can remember only a few inconsequent details of my childhood, but my wife swears blindly that she can remember perfectly an incident which happened when she was less than three weeks old, and perhaps if one can remember things so early, there are people who can remember what happened in the womb, and even before one entered the womb. It is not impossible to conceive that memory, like the structure of the bones and cer-
160

tain inherited characteristics, is carried by the little spinning tadpole out of which we are half-formed. Why not? There are greater miracles. But where, and under what conditions, and in what lives, did I see the burning corn and first fear the image of a fortress in the dying sun?

September 9th . . . THIS afternoon I came upon these words from Franz Kafka's notebook: "You do not need to leave your room. Remain sitting at your table and listen. Do not even listen, simply wait. Do not even wait, be quite still and solitary. The world will freely offer itself to you and be unmasked, it has no choice, it will roll in ecstasy at your feet."

What is surprising is that the statement is in no sense European: it is purely and perfectly Chinese, though the Chinese would change the word "table" for "fields," and he would hardly see the world "rolling in ecstasy"—it would be there, in all ecstasy, but not like a pekinese dog at his feet. This waiting, this patience, this knowledge that no moment is lost, this certainty of the final flowering—this is something that one learns instinctively on looking at Chinese paintings. There were painters who would gaze for a whole morning, or perhaps a week, at a single stem of bamboo; and then suddenly and capriciously—for caprice enters into all art—they would find themselves caught up in a spiritual ecstasy, knowing exactly what it was like to be a bamboo leaf brushed by the wind; and imitating the flying shapes of the petals of the bamboos, they would become themselves the bamboos. A few dark lines on brown silk—and between the dark lines and the barren spaces all the quivering joy of the bamboo in the wind!

It would be well sometimes if we imitated them, while we wait earnestly for the flowering of our peace.

September 10th . . . IT OCCURRED to me suddenly that three of the greatest poems ever written were about drowned things. There is Ariel's song in *The Tempest*, there is the lovely *Halfte des Lebens* of Hoelderlin and there is the short poem by Li Po which contains the lines: *The peach-blossom follows the moving water*. Hoelderlin's poem cannot be adequately translated. I have tried many times, but the *movement* of the original is always lost—so fruitful and delicate a thing defies the sea-change to another language:

161

> Full of yellow pears
> And wild roses
> Hangs the land in the lake;
> O noble swans,
> Drunk with kisses,
> Steep your heads
> In holy sobering water.
>
> Alas, where shall I find,
> When winter comes, the flowers,
> And where the sunshine
> And the shadows of the earth?
> The walls stand
> Speechless and cold, in the wind
> Clatter the storm-vanes.

No Chinese would have dared to write those last lines; but all that has gone before, the sudden changes of metaphor and feeling, the sensuous delight in all fading and blossoming things, the mirrored and unmoving swans—surely they have come from a Chinese painting? Here are those rich autumnal colours we see in Yuan Dynasty paintings, and here too there are the scents of spring; for the Chinese see nothing absurd in spring and autumn coming together—Wang Wei once painted a banana tree blossoming in winter snows. But what is so particularly Chinese is the starkness, and at the same time the sensuousness of the statement, the tenderness, the intimations of mortality which is only another kind of eternity, the ripeness in the fall of leaves. You will see it at all times in Chinese poetry—not only in the T'ang Dynasty. In the German the resemblance is still more remarkable: the words are so heavily weighted that they come to possess the astonishing solidity of Chinese ideograms.

But why do these three poems, which are so certainly among the greatest, all describe a submarine universe?

September 13th . . . Dreaming again of peace, I remembered Bergery saying: "When the war ends, there will be such joy that we shall hardly be able to breathe. There will be anthems and processions, and everyone will be wreathed with flowers—such peace as no one has ever dreamed of. And how shall we avoid being consecrated? The mere ending of the war will be a kind of holiness. For the first time relief will become a positive emotion. Perhaps

162

out of our relief, out of the sudden releasing of the spring, we will be able to compose our peace."

I am not sure that I have remembered his exact words, but these are near enough. He would talk about the tremendous spirituality of the Fujiwara epoch in Japan, when Buddhism came in and the country was at peace; of similar periods in India and Persia; of the long peace following the wars of Augustus Caesar; of the *pax Britannica* and the coming *pax Americana;* and of the great flowering of art which occurs in times of settled peace. I think he half imagined that this was the last of all wars. He had no belief in a dialectic of peace and war: the poles did not swing that way, war was never inevitable, the old Heracleitan myth failed before Anaxagoras' "Man is the measure of all things." And for him, too, peace was not the result of a process of evolution so much as a grace from heaven, an undeliberate flowering—you could not explain the great peaceful epochs in history by any rule of thumb or any concatenation of causes. Buddhism may have helped the Japanese in the Fujiwara epoch to enjoy their peace: it did not describe the basis of their peace. War was a monstrosity, a fungoid growth which flourished with the animal spirit of man; but man was naturally peaceful, and a little craven, delighting less in power than the cultivation of his natural animal instincts, which were mostly peaceful. "After the long weariness of war, we shall settle down to look at our toe-nails." And he said once: "In the silence after the bombing, we shall be able to hear ourselves speak and it will be extraordinary to us that we shall be like Paul, continually marvelling. The people of London and Moscow will not let their street-lights go out. Why should they? They will have discovered that light is the source of all being." Bergery may be right, but our peace is as delicate as a flower and from all directions come winds.

There is companionship in war; there is little enough in peace. The front-line soldier knows a companionship which transcends the love between man and woman; and what is necessary in our peace is that the companionship should remain. Neither Bergery nor Liu Lien have talked of companionship; and because in their different ways they were scholars neither have any need of it— their companions are books, paintings, the things they see so directly with their sharpened senses. But the rest of us are in desperate need of it; and once more last night, wondering at the impermanence of this thing we have called peace in the absence of any more suitable name, I thought of the plan we tried to bring

163

into operation early in the 1930's.

It was a very simple plan, though it was expensive. I was working as a shipyard apprentice in Birkenhead. A French cousin had asked me to join him in a camp he was establishing somewhere in the south of France for young apprentices from Paris. I wrote and asked him whether I could bring some of the engineering apprentices from the shipyard—say, three or four, who knew no French, but were sensible people, knew how to play games and were prepared to meet the French apprentices on equal terms. He agreed; and very soon afterwards we were living in a small village on the Drome which was once famous because the Comtesse de Die lived there in the time of the troubadours. It was a heavenly month; there were mountains to be climbed; there was the great bubbling blue sheet of the river, and the air was heady, and the white tents in the fields and the bronzed youths swimming naked in the shallow river, the sounds of singing at night and sometimes an accordion playing: the companionship of youth springing up in the touch of bodies and minds: all these things, and the curious impression that it was all permanent—they had come here to stay. Afterwards they said they had never enjoyed themselves so much: they had rattled away in broken French and broken English, but they had enjoyed everything there. They enjoyed the sun, they enjoyed the sharpness of the impact with the young French boys, and they kept on corresponding with them long afterwards. Then there was a financial crash, and the plans for the next year went awry—we were going to invite a hundred German and a hundred English apprentices to the south of France. But it came to nothing.

I regretted this more than I regretted most things in those early and fatal thirties. There seemed some hope of peace in a scheme which would allow young workmen to travel abroad and stay for a while in camps with boys of their own age. At least, if there was war, they would take less delight in lobbing hand-grenades at each other and twisting each others' guts with bayonets; they would know that the others were so little different from themselves, and they would learn in time that political differences are rarely caused by some empirical political necessity, but are manufactured by men. There might even come a time when war would be impossible, since so many young boys were not in a position to fight: they would be enjoying themselves in another country. There might even come a time when war would be prevented for the simple reason that the boys who would take part in it would im-

164

mediately become hostages in some other country. There was hope in this companionship for other reasons—there would be more inter-marriages, if the numbers of travelling workmen were large enough we might at least have to consider an international language, since broken French and broken English become wearisome in time. There was hope that out of this meeting cultures would flower—the greatest periods in the world's art have always been those when cultures met. The T'ang Dynasty did not derive its greatness from treacherous wars; it was great because there was peace under the Emperor T'ai Tsung, and because he encouraged the Mahometans and the Buddhists and the Christians to settle in his capitals: because trade was flourishing: because a Persian enameller would find himself speaking to a Copt, or an Arab trader would exchange carpets from Mekka with a Turkic tribesman from Bokhara: because a great painter called Godoshi met an Indian monk who possessed a Buddha carved in the Gupta period three hundred years before; because a great poet called Li Po once overheard the songs of some tribesmen near the Thibetan border and learned to write a more vigorous and more sensual verse.

Bergson's universe was "a machine for producing gods"; I would prefer to regard this earth as a machine for producing great art and as much companionship as anyone should ever want. We have cultural exchange—professors are whisked from obscure Universities in China to fellowships in Harvard and Yale; it is a good beginning, but I look forward to a time when a young shepherd in Greece will, if it so pleases him and if he should take delight in it, decide to live for six months with the shepherds in the New England states and see with his own eyes another world: he will not return poorer for the experience. But above all, I would like to see this done on a scale which would embrace all men and women of the earth: let them go where they please: instead of performing dreary years of military service, let them be bundled off on ships to the farthest corners of the earth; let them all be travellers. The world is so beautiful that they will miss nothing by leaving their own lands; they may even add to the beauty of the world; they will certainly return wiser. More and more I suspect that if we are to have peace, the old Father-myth of the dictatorships must give way to the *kameradschaft* of the young. There is companionship in war, but let us so arrange things that there is a greater companionship in peace.

September 14th . . . HE WAS well-built, and he had a face like cool veined marble, the pallor of some northern Chinese. His lips were as red as fresh meat and his eyes were glowing, soft and golden; and he was as handsome a young animal as you would care to meet.

We were drinking tea in a pavilion in the lake near the Garrison Headquarters, and I said something about the shape of the whirling tea-leaves in the boiling tea reminding me of some Chinese paintings of fishes and crabs and birds; and he nodded, and said "Yes, the Chinese painters quite often studied tea-leaves, but there was something better—the shadows of flying birds in a cage." And then I began to wonder where this amazing art of calligraphy began. Did it really arise from the scratchings on tortoise-shell oracle bones after they have been burnt in a fire, and split into curious shapes, or did it arise when the first wanderers over the northern desert, deciding that the time had come to write down their thoughts, saw the shadows of birds on the sand?

The Chinese brush-stroke is full of life; the grey or black line has deepening shadows. Looking at Chinese calligraphy, you feel the emotions of the artist who may have written a thousand years, or two thousand years ago—they are still preserved in stone copies of the calligraphy of the Han dynasty. You feel the point where he exerted pressure, where he twisted his wrist a little, where he plunged recklessly into the unknown. This is not shadow-play— this is the art of life expressed in all its simplicities. And then we watched, for nothing could be simpler, not the sparrow hopping on the lotos leaves but the shadows thrown by the sparrow's wings, and it was impossible not to agree with him that the shadows seemed a concentration of the young bird's life, more amazingly complex and supple than the bird itself.

It became ridiculous. A fat general sauntered out of the Garrison Headquarters—that delightful plump shadow caricatured him, swung round him, played with him unmercifully; it rolled plumply along, taking a sharp turn here, a twist there, becoming nothing one moment and swelling out at the next; and it was impossible not to believe that his calligraphy was like this. Then a girl came past, and though she was beautiful and swung her hips delightfully and showed a clean pair of legs, how outrageously the shadow caricatured her! She pranced a little, all the little buds were swelling out, and the shadow slithered along, bobbed up and down, the curves were monstrously enlarged, the black scissors of her legs

166

were continually snipping; but no one would ever have been able to invent an art of calligraphy after watching her shadow. A beggar slouched along the path under the unflowering peach-trees—his calligraphy was a mountainous shambles; it was not until a child came running with her hoop and her skirts flying that we entered calligraphy again. It must have been a little while later, when the sun was going down, that my friend got excited again and screamed: "My God, look at that elephant!" There was—I had never seen it before—an enormous shaggy blue elephant with flapping ears like dishcloths soaked in water, which had come up from Burma with the Chinese army, lumbering among the peach-trees and the small gilt pavilions; but he was not looking at the elephant, he was looking at the shadow of the elephant's trunk on the grass. "It's not first-rate calligraphy," he said solemnly, "but do look at the shadow—you can feel the life in the trunk, and I like the way it swings. I don't think anyone has ever done it before, but it might be worth trying 'elephant's trunk calligraphy.'"

September 16th . . . THE war is over, I told myself, coming through the dusty streets, where a few beggars were whining, a few snot-nosed children were playing with a dead rat, whose soft grey belly was slashed with the most vivid and most beautiful red, but is it over? Are people happier? Where are the processions and the anthems which Bergery spoke about? Where are the girls with flowers in their hair? Where are the singers? Where are the hymns of thanksgiving?

I doubt very much whether anything has changed in Kunming. The fireworks fizzled out on the night of the murder. The same beggars haunt the streets, the same starving soldiers come up the Burma Road, the same merchants ride in their black limousines, there is the same heart-rending corruption, the same misery, the same unease. The streets are a little dirtier and shabbier than when the Americans were here in full force; the Banks are a little more flourishing; there are more canned goods on the market than ever. A merchant told me this morning: "Well, this is the beginning of the end—we made a pack of money while the war lasted, but now we are ruined." I hope he is ruined. We pay for these things too much in sweat and weariness to care very much about the fate of the Chinese merchants.

There were shoddy enough things during the war in this lovely land. There were officers who kept back the food of their soldiers,

167

there were the hoarding merchants who stored up immense reserves of rice, waiting for the day when want was so great that men would desire it at any price, forgetting that in this country rice is only another name for blood; there were officials who looked on; there were screams of torture from the police stations; there were bodies in ditches; there were soldiers dying on the roads. Kunming will live for a little while longer on its inflated paper currency, but soon the merchants and the bankers will have to look elsewhere—they will follow the whores to the coast. The whores have gone already. I went down the Chin Pi Lu this evening, and only one little brazen tart came out of the shadows, lifting her skirt and saying: "One push—how much?"

I confess there are things in this country I would prefer not to look at. There are terrible diseases: some of them spiritual diseases—and this is worse. There has always been this starvation in China, but is there any reason why it should continue? The land is rich enough, God knows. The people have the richest cultural heritage of the world. There are all the graces and refinements of life imaginable, and yet the art of government is forgotten, and the family still remains—that hard-bitten symbol of the desire to keep everything within the narrow precincts of a single house. So corruption mounts up, since the family grows bigger and more exacting as wealth increases; Seventh Cousin must have his job, in spite of the fact that he is incompetent and has learned a few vices from abroad—he must have his girls, his cigarettes, his cinemas, his opium-pipe, his nights in the dancing-halls. We'll put him in the Bank. Excellent. A vice-presidency? No, not good enough for that; we'll give him a stool, and as long as he puts in an appearance for a few hours in the morning, we'll give him a fat monthly pay-cheque, for after all, is he not in the family? And so it goes on, the vicious and ever-expanding circles of nepotism, which seems to affect all business, all government in this desperately beautiful land.

Up to the battle of Nanking, there was the most tremendous enthusiasm for the war and for the government—a spiritual fire swept over the country, China would arise, the real revolution would be formed on the comradeship of war; men starved and walked threadbare the whole length of China and cheered themselves with the thought of their sufferings, for out of their sufferings and the dead bodies in the Yangtse they thought they would make a new kingdom of their own. But you cannot make kingdoms out of sufferings. There comes a time when sufferings become so long-drawn that the body cries out for opiates, and the opiates were all there—a fortune, a job in the government, a sinecure somewhere. You could squeeze in if you tried hard enough, and if you were merciless enough. The Japanese were a long way away. It didn't matter much, and you could salve your soul on Monday mornings by bowing three times to the portrait of Dr. Sun Yat-sen, who said: "The Revolution is not yet accomplished." The Revolution could wait for another day. It was raining, they were utterly miserable, they were cut off from the outside world, life was short and the things you wanted most were still coming in from Shanghai, but at exorbitant prices. It's pretty rotten for the soldiers, they said, but we have got to make hay while the sun shines.

Of course history repeats itself. During these last four years we have lived through the T'ang Dynasty, and we can even recognize the portraits of the conspirators. An Lu-shan rebelled again in the north, the Nan-chao came in from the south-west—it is not exactly the same, but we could see Yang Kwei-fei, the consort of the Emperor Ming Huang (but she was not hanged at Ma Wei); we can see the Prime Minister Yang Kuo-chung, who was the cousin of Yang Kwei-fei, devoted to gambling and wine, devoted to his cousins and the great fortune he acquired until that day in the winter of 756 when the soldiers fell upon him and gnawed his flesh. And yet something of the splendour of the T'ang Dynasty was lacking—the sufferings were too long drawn out and the criminals were never punished, and there were no cheap goods coming in from Shanghai while the disconsolate emperor Ming Huang was roaming about Szechuan. There were the scholars and the poets and the peasants, there were the broad-faced soldiers and the peasant-girls —and these had not changed. They were starving still. Must they starve to the end of time?

September 17th . . . Liu Lien was sick in bed, lying under the heavy silk embroidered quilt—the bed too big for him, so that his little brown face seemed lost in it.

"The trouble is that we haven't won the war," he said. "The Americans won it for us—or rather a few German, French, Scandinavian, British and American scientists with all the wealth of America behind them. The wealth of America! The old Portuguese and Spanish kings thought it lay in the gold of the Indies and in China; they said there was wealth beyond the vision of men to imagine; but there is no wealth in the Indies now and China is poor.

169

Wealth lay in a virgin land—they might have known it; and now there is only Russia left which is virgin." He was digressing, but he came back a moment later: "We haven't won the war—the Americans won it with the Manhattan Project, but the Chinese will kick the Japanese in the shins and puff out their chests, yet they know, and we know, that we have done nothing to deserve the end of the war. The tactics were wrong from the beginning—it is always dangerous to take flight to Szechuan. And now we dare hardly face the Japanese for shame of our imaginary conquest." He paused and sipped the mulberry-coloured water on the table. "This is what I thought a moment ago," he went on, "but all conquests are imaginary, so there is perhaps little harm in it. We destroy nothing by destroying. The Japanese are beaten to their knees, but never has any nation been so terribly beaten as the Chinese. We learned our weaknesses—pray God we may profit by them."

He was feverish—it is the month of fevers, the rains are coming to an end, but the air is still wet and the rains at least sweep the garbage away; he tried to get up in the bed but I begged him to keep quiet. Through the bamboo-curtained window we could see the swallows spinning among the leaves, yet the room was curiously silent: the shaggy dog asleep on the floor, the curtains rustling so faintly that their rustling only awakened the silence.

I began to tell him how every time I see soldiers now I bridle. Anachronisms, meaningless now that we wage war with invisible weapons, a little tiresome in that they still remained with all their privileges, bearing weapons—rifles slung over shoulders, detestable little green hand-grenades swinging from their belts—all the nonsense of uniforms and salutes and the hint of death all round them. "I see them every morning," I complained, "outside my window—drilling, marching, running round in circles, scaling mountains—the mountains are perhaps ten feet high and the officer wields a white baton and orders them to charge up the mountain at the peril of their lives. What are they training for? Civil war? I doubt whether we will fight national wars with soldiers any more. It's all so damnedly absurd—why can't they go back to their farms?"

He sighed: "There is civil war in China now, isn't there?"

"Yes."

"How long do you think it will last?" he asked.

"Just a few months—until the Americans crack down on them. It's too monstrous—it is so shameful to fight a civil war after the

170

conclusion of this war. Really civil war is unimaginable—too great a shame."

"Yes," he said, "it's too great a shame, it's unimaginable, but it exists—the merchants have made their money and they want to hold their power, and the soldiers want something to do—the officers don't want to feel useless. Oh, this pride. You are quite right, of course. They have no feeling of shame. The military profession is an honourable profession—or rather, it would be honourable if it did not deal with murder. An American soldier came to say good-bye to me. He was going home. He said he was sick of the war— every time he sees a man he is unconsciously looking for ways to murder him: a jab in the groin, an elbow round his neck, some way of killing him—you did it automatically, just as when you were travelling you were unconsciously seeking all the time some place to hide in. He said he wanted to go home and get back to a farm. 'That's where I belong. Never been on a farm before, but I know that's the only place left for me.' And he said: 'Have a girl and some kids and get away from it all.' It's easier to kill than to get a girl. It's so much easier to throw a hand-grenade than to care for children and watch after them. We need women in the government now—by God we need women now. We need people who can smack the faces of the soldiers and tell them they belong to a dishonourable trade, even though their trade is sometimes necessary. There is no difference between a soldier and a hangman—a hangman is necessary, and so is a soldier, but there is no honour in it, though there is bravery. We can learn from women and children —see how terribly children recoil from death, yet we are hardened to it."

A little while later he said: "I realized after Roosevelt's death that I had been thinking for years of a great white Father. There was Stalin, Churchill, de Gaulle, Chiang Kai-shek and Roosevelt. They were the great white fathers, but we don't need them any more. They are dangerous. There comes even a time when they are poisonous. We need no Moses who will lead us to the promised land, for historically Moses never achieves his mission—he remains, as you remember, on the plains of Raphidim. We must learn to be self-reliant and alone, and above all we must learn to be brothers."

I was going to say that I had been thinking along these lines, but I could see no *Bruderschaft* arising on the ruins of this war; we were too penetrated with obedience and discipline; there was too little imaginative life, too little understanding of whatever lives we might obtain if we struggled hard enough. I said: "Let the great white father go hang, but what is there left? The father has his place in the world, though it was perhaps one of the greatest advantages to Chinese civilization that Confucius never had a father; it left a gap somewhere which was never filled even by Confucius' reverence for fatherhood. That immense father of Confucius, who could lift a portcullis with his fist and smash a man's face with a single blow, died when Confucius was three: if he had lived longer, it might have been more terrible." He nodded at first, and I could almost see his brain moiling. "No," he said, "it would have been better if Confucius' father had lived. He was over seventy when Confucius knew him. Think if he had lasted another ten years—Confucius would have seen him shrivelling into old age, senile and gasping. All Chinese history might have been changed. We need to know that the great white fathers are mortal—and remember that Confucius had no brothers. He had seven sisters! We tried to build a civilization on a man's reverence for a father he had hardly ever seen, and on his liking for his sisters, and now you in the West are doing the same. There must be no criticism of Stalin, Roosevelt, Chiang Kai-shek or Churchill. Why not? Fathers are mortal. We did not respect the kings so much in ancient times—there was no propaganda to make us respect them. Then why this desire for reverencing the great white fathers? Are we all adolescents or children? To have self-respect, to have brothers, and to be alone——" It was getting dark. Against the doctor's orders he began to light a pipe and I saw the brown walnut-face glowing above the coloured quilts. "I've told my children they must argue with me if I tell them I have reasons for doing things, so they argue and we waste a lot of time, but the important thing is that they are often right and I am wrong far more often than I expect. It's good for them. They won't have this damned instinct of obedience."

The dinner was brought in, and I was allowed to have a glass of his mulberry-coloured medicine, which turned out to be wine. There were huge pillows—Chinese pillows are sometimes as huge as those you see on Hungarian bridal beds—and he half lifted himself from the bed, stroked his untidy beard and gazed out of the windows, for the bamboo curtains had been lifted and he could gaze out across the darkening garden, full of bamboos and convolvulus. There were a few stars, though the moon was down. At the end of the garden some soldiers were playing shuttlecock in

172

the light coming from an open window. It was clear that he wanted to go on with the argument, but I wondered whether he was well enough—and besides, it was no longer an argument, we agreed with each other too often, so that it was difficult sometimes to sharpen our minds on differences.

"Let us go a little further," he said after a while. "Let us destroy the father. Was Christ a father? No, but he had a profound reverence for the Father in Heaven, and this reverence was perfectly appropriate to his own place and time, but it is no longer appropriate now. Was Buddha a father? Yes, he had a son called Rahula, which means a 'hindrance' or 'obstacle.' He took no delight in fatherhood, or in being called 'father'—I remember that somewhere he ordered that no one should call him by this name, which the Christian priests so delight in. *Bhikkhu*, the name for a buddhist monk, means 'fighter,' for Buddha said: 'We fight, O Bhikkhus, therefore we are called fighters,' and among themselves they called themselves 'brethren.' The communists, of course, have taken the word 'comrade' over, and the Quakers call each other 'brothers' or 'friends'—at least we have that much to learn from them. Like the wandering monks on the plains of India, we must learn to be brothers. *Kameradschaft*—it is the only thing left."

When I left the house the soldiers were still playing, stripped to the waist; they were laughing and the shuttlecock was flying, and I admired how they would kick it up with their heels and how the arms, which are not used in the game, would assume the most delightful postures; and then, all the way home, I thought I could delight in soldiers if they were stripped naked like the dead soldiers by the Liuyang river, or if they were half-stripped or if they were disguised, but I hated still with an ungovernable hatred those uniforms spangled with medals and decorated with gold rings, the wide-flaring cavalry breeches of officers who never rode on horseback except during reviews; and when the inevitable prostitute leapt out of the shadows in her tight-fitting red dress, I remember I thought at first it was an officer in uniform—so gaudy she was, and so death-dealing. And I thought, because I was tired and sometimes the mind rocks into indecency out of sheer weariness: "The officers have their revolvers, and she has something which is not very different—there is death in those little black holes, and it is better to avoid both, and have a world where there are no such obvious symbols of death. Let us put an end to prostitutes and soldiers and the great white fathers who have never led us to the

173

promised land; and let us all be like St. Francis among our brothers and sisters."

September 23rd, Ezra Pound . . . WE WERE talking about translations from Chinese, and the hideous difficulties that arise in transferring a language of clear-cut ideograms into the alphabetical monstrosities we have in the West. I have been attempting to make an anthology of Chinese poetry from the beginning to the present time, and with the help of the Chinese scholars here we shall probably succeed in giving for the first time a bird's-eye view of the whole of that immense landscape. But troubles arise from all sides —a Chinese character never means exactly the same as an English word. Its associations, its music, its colour, its sound, its place in a sentence, the peculiar effect of shadowing, by which one word throws its accent and shape on another, all these are different; and beyond all these differences is the essential difference between the two cultures—English and Chinese. We do not think as they do, our values are different, our feeling for life and for the forms of life, the things that are demanded of us and the things that we demand of others—none of these are the same. The differences are becoming smaller now, as the Chinese drift away from their own culture and enter our own, but there remain even now wide gaps of feeling and sensibility: we are almost like people from different planets.

Then how to get over this? One certain way is to ask Chinese scholars to do the translations themselves, and I have done this wherever possible; but they complain that their knowledge of English is inadequate, I am asked to revise, and I am in desperate fear lest the least alteration will change something of the original, so that sometimes it is best to leave them as they are with their slight faults of English, but with the certain knowledge that no foreign translator could translate as well. Foreign translations of Chinese poetry are full of mistakes. Even the translations of great sinologues like Arthur Waley have errors. Florence Ayscough's versions of Tu Fu, which she composed with Amy Lowell and with the assistance of a Chinese scholar, are sometimes incredibly muddle-headed. There is a translation of some of *The Three Hundred Poems of the T'ang Dynasty* by a curator of the British Museum which according to a Chinese scholar I know is almost childish in their simple-minded delight in making errors. But is this true? They have made mistakes certainly, because it is impossible for a western mind to realize all the associations implied in the Chinese. They have done

174

their best. Too often they were not poets, and possessed little enough feeling for poetry, delighting only in the *chinoiserie* which sometimes appears even in Chinese verse. Their best was sometimes very good indeed. There is Waley's translation of *The Book of Songs* and there are the translations of Tu Fu and Li Po by the Marquis Hervey de St. Denis, but there is little else. There were the idiotic pullulations of retired consuls and ambassadors, who should never have been allowed near Chinese poetry; there was Giles turning the bright sunlight of the earliest odes into murky Victorian rhymed verse; there were others whom one dare hardly mention for wonder that they could so misinterpret so much greatness.

I have been plagued with this business of translation for a long time, and this afternoon I discussed it for the thousandth time with Liu Lien, who is helping me to translate these poems. "There are two things which I demand of a translator," he said. "The first is scholarship and the second is a sense of poetry. There are a great number of foreign sinologues of the first rank—Waley, Pelliot, perhaps a hundred others—but there are almost none of them who can penetrate into the spirit of poetry. Waley does sometimes, but not always; in any case he has chosen for the greater part of his translations the least poetical of our great poets, Po Chu-i. He is an excellent scholar, he is even at times an excellent poet, but how rarely!" A little later he said: "The real trouble is that scholars are so rarely poets. Scholarship demands qualities which are absent from the poets. But there is one very great American poet, who knew as far as I know no Chinese at all, yet he is by far the best of all the translators of Chinese poetry. He made mistakes, but at least he gave the sense and the fiery spirit of the original. He writes cleanly, as we wrote cleanly. I believe they are going to shoot him, because like many poets he lost his bearings in the war and found himself flirting with Mussolini—a great pity, he had no business to be there, but he was a poet and one of our greatest poets, Wang Wei, once found himself in the same perilous situation."

He went to the shelves and took down a small green-covered book.

"I suppose you know Ezra Pound?"

"Yes."

"Have you read *Cathay*? I assure you the West has produced nothing greater in interpretations of Chinese. Oh, there are mistakes. I want to take him by the scruff of the neck, I want to ask him where he got those fantastic notes of Ernest Fenollosa and the

175

decipherings of the Professors Mori and Ariga. Who the devil are the Professors Mori and Ariga? It doesn't matter, probably; he has had someone to write out from a Japanse translation another translation into Italian—it's like one of our famous translations from Tolstoy which are made in Chinese on the basis of a Japanese translation of the German translation of the Russian—but somehow Pound has performed the magic ceremonial, he has said the appropriate abracadabras, he has breathed life into the little wax image and not stuck pins into it like so many of the other translators. Take, for it is worth taking, Li Po's little academy piece, which was once a very great poem indeed but had so many imitators that we have almost forgotten how it was ever great:

> *The jewelled steps are already white with dew,*
> *It is so late that the dew soaks my gauze stockings,*
> *And I let down the crystal curtain*
> *And watch the moon through the clear autumn.*

Let us begin from the beginning. The first line reads literally: A white dew grows on the jade staircase. The beauty of the phrase comes from the word *sheng*—grows. The dew is like a flower. He has left that out. He has said 'gauze' when it might be more accurate to say 'silk' and there is nothing at all about stockings—it should be shoes. He says 'I let down the crystal curtain,' but there is nothing about 'I'—no great matter, for his 'I' is impersonal enough. There are at least five mistakes, but none of them are of any importance, but how magnificently he conveys the spirit of the original! It is not great poetry in English, but reading it in English I feel that he has conveyed the Chinese with the most perfect precision. Precision. Take the poem which he entitles wrongly *The City of Choan:*

> *The phoenix are at play on their terrace,*
> *The phoenix are gone, the river flows on alone.*
> *Flowers and grass*
> *Cover over the dark path*
> > *where lay the dynastic house of the Go.*
> *The bright cloths and bright caps of Shin*
> *Are now the base of old hills.*
>
> *The Three Mountains fall through the far heavens,*
> *The isle of White Heron*

> *splits the two streams apart.*
> *Now the high clouds cover the sun*
> *And I cannot see Choan afar*
> *And I am sad.*

Oh, I want to tear my hair out at the thought of the mistakes he makes, they are such little mistakes, they are not terribly important, but why is it that he could not spend three or five years in China and really render our poems into English? The Three Mountains do not fall through the far heaven. What exactly happens is that half of the three mountains stretches into the blue sky—the other half is covered in mist. There is, I am afraid, nothing at all about the 'bright caps' and the 'bright clothes.' High clouds do not cover the sun—floating clouds shade the sun. 'Far' is a blemish, but how perfect at this place and in this rhythm is the word 'splits' and how perfect is the short last line which exactly mirrors the short last line of the original. There are seven words in each line, but there is a pause after the fourth syllable and he has conveyed that pause. He has conveyed the freshness of the original. We can see the landscape seen by Li Po. We feel the freshness and the immediacy of the vision. I assure you Pound's translations of Chinese give me more pleasure (and considerably more annoyance) than all the other translations put together."

September 26th . . . WHY, when, where and how I shall leave China, I do not know; but I am beginning to suspect that it will be soon. The rumours—they are surely more substantial than rumours—of the civil war sicken me. That there should be civil war at such a time and under such desperate conditions as we are living in terrifies me. Liu Lien talks of his shame, the students and the more daring professors (for not all professors are daring) openly proclaim their horror. Who is responsible—the Kuomintang or the Communists? There are rumours that Mr. Chiang is quietly preparing with American support for a five-year war against the Communists. China has not covered herself in glory in this war, but that she should follow the path of the Gadarene swine is sickening beyond words.

September 27th . . . K. CAME, very mouse-like, wearing a loose blue gown, not very clean. He looked as though he had not slept, and he was unshaved. He said he had to go away, one of his

177

friends was in prison and somehow he would have to get enough money to feed him. I asked: why?—don't they feed prisoners? He shook his head. His friend was a democrat who sometimes bitterly assailed the dictatorial policies of the Kuomintang. Well, they had arrested him in some remote country village, where he was unknown, where no law has ever penetrated since the end of the Ch'ing Dynasty, where the village magistrate wielded absolute power. Probably the boy had been followed by the secret police, and there he was—a stone cell, a few village louts with Mausers to guard him, and he would have to pay for his food, otherwise they would forget about him. He had managed to smuggle a letter out, God knows how, and he wanted fabulous sums of money for his bare existence, he wanted someone to invoke *habeas corpus* and he wanted to have a fair trial. "Will he get them?" "No—he will get the money, some of it, as much as I can raise—we'll try to bribe the guards or the village magistrate, and see what happens. It's difficult. If you offer too much, they'll keep him there and torture him so that we shall offer more. They know all the tricks—they have had three thousand years of this miserable village dictatorship with some illiterate fool acting as magistrate, possessing powers of life and death over the young boys, and sometimes over the young girls. The village magistrate is god, first because he is the magistrate and secondly because he is the recruiting agent. He can send boys to the front. He can be bribed not to send them. I wish we could have some village government—all power to the farmers and the farm-labourers, not this damned illiterate dictatorship."

It would take him probably a week to get to the village; he had written a letter—it might get through, or it might make things worse, he didn't know. There were blue rings round his eyes and a kind of hopelessness, for he would do everything to save his friend and friendship between these boys goes deeper than it does in the west—the unbreakable bond is not broken even in death. I gave him some money. He looked shabby and sick as he went out into the stone courtyard under the poinsettias, but when we came out into the sunlight he braced up. "I'll get him out somehow," he said. "One shouldn't be allowed to die on that stone floor simply for being a democrat."

It must have been a coincidence, for that same evening another boy came and sat on the edge of the bed, the chairs and tables so littered up with books that there was no other place for him. We
178

talked desultorily about Chinese poetry, for he has written many good poems and sometimes even in English he writes with a startling sense of our imagery. And then suddenly, when it was getting dark and the books were beginning to be swallowed up in the shadows, their presence no longer so dangerous, he showed me a poem of four lines which he said his brother had written. They were terrible lines. They could only have been written by somebody in mortal fear and terrible longing for death, so cold and knife-like they were. I remember reading in some Paris newspaper the lines written by a boy on the night before he was guillotined for murdering his sweet-heart, and I told my friend how similar they were: the same poignancy which went beyond the limits of all human feeling. You will see the same thing, too, in some of the last poems of the German poet Friedrich Hoelderlin, and sometimes it occurs in Shakespeare; and once or twice it breaks through the gold and silver-greens of the T'ang poets, the wet red open mouth of the beast.

We talked then for a little while about poetry and how sometimes it will seize upon the ultimate blood-red things of the universe: when the stars crack: when loneliness becomes a skull: the poet describing simply how the abyss yawns. The boy smiled wearily. He was not handsome, but he had a high northern forehead, and his mother had come from the tribes; he was unstable, like all those who have the mixed blood of south and north, but he possessed quite extraordinary intelligence. And just as we were leaving, he said quietly: "The poem was written by my brother on the night before his execution at Hankow. They executed him as a communist, but he wasn't a communist."

September 28th . . . THIS evening, while the flooded field outside my window was jet-black, reflecting the stars, a jeep came ploughing through the mud and slime, throwing all the stars into confusion; but what was most singular was that the headlights were like the Milky Way, and I didn't know whether I was looking down at the lake or at the stars. And then very slowly, as the great black star-shot waves lapped away, the headlamps went out, and the stars were still there, rocking on the waves. . . .

September 29th . . . J. SAID this evening that he wished he had abandoned literature years ago and studied economics. I asked him why. "The world's in a mess, we'll have to get the money into

179

the hands of the people who need it. No, I am not talking about professors—it doesn't matter very much about the professors. I heard a little while ago about a farm-boy in a village who invented a new kind of silk-loom. He took his invention everywhere, someone even introduced him to the manager of a bank in Kunming, but they wouldn't look at his invention, and yet with a little capital it might have helped the village to get out of its misery." He went on to talk about silk-worms and mulberry-trees. "There was a time when the walls of Kunming were covered with mulberry-trees, and there were mulberries in every village. The silk of Yunnan was not famous, but people took pride in it, and the girls would wander among the trees and it was like rice—a settled basis of living, with its own ritual, its own delicate chemistry giving life an added richness; and the walls of Kunming looked good, and you would always see the mulberries at the entrance of every village."

"What happened to the trees?" I asked.

"Oh, the soldiers cut them down for firewood."

October 1st . . . Lecturing on Elizabethan poetry and seeing everywhere the same kind of feverish excitement as I see in T'ang poetry. I have noticed that in all the great periods of literature clothes are described at great length—in the *Iliad,* in the *Mabinogian,* in *The Tale of Genji,* in Shakespeare who is so full of images of gold silk and silver thread—perhaps because he spent so many years with Mountjoy, who was the court-dressmaker. Why this insistence on clothes, this delight in adorning oneself like a peacock? We see the court maidens of the T'ang Dynasty with kingfishers' feathers plastered along their cheeks, wearing brightly coloured silk gowns whose sleeves reach to their feet, and we are not so very far from those maidens of thirteenth century Wales, or the Medicis. Those descriptions in the *Song of Roland,* pages upon pages of complex arrangements of clothes in *The Dream of the Red Chamber,* and there are perhaps forty poems altogether in the Chinese *Book of Songs* which contain some detail of the clothes men wore in those days which must be nearly three thousand years ago, a blue collar here, a green skirt there, till the whole landscape of colours suddenly appears.

I came across at random in the *Song of Roland:* "The helmets shone with stones set in gold, and the shields also, and the blue-edged coats of mail." There is nothing like this in the Bible except in *Ezekiel* and *Revelations*—the Hebrews had no eyes until they
180

were drunk with visions. They did not see things with the immediacy and freshness of the Greeks and the Chinese, they were cursed with emotions which arose from contemplation of a heavenly and uncoloured landscape, in which no peach-blossoms flowered. The Hebrews left the garden behind them, the Greeks lived perpetually within the garden, continually nourishing their senses, the Chinese saw the garden a little ahead of them—you could reach it in a day's walk, it was behind the blue mountains.

And thinking of our own drab discoloured blue gowns, or the terrible pipe-rack western clothes we wear, the ruined walls of the city, the decay of calligraphy, the smoke discolouring the sky from the factory chimneys, it would seem that we are not living in one of those glorious epochs of history in which men took delight in pure colours and adorned themselves, believing that they were kings.

October 2nd . . . YESTERDAY the American soldiers were kept in barracks; there are rumours that Chinese soldiers have been attacking the hostels. A few jeeps go round the city bristling with guns, and wherever an American soldier appears he has a tommy-gun at his belt or a rifle slung over his shoulder. And yet there seems to be no reason for it. It seems impossible to imagine that the local Yunnanese forces could attack the Americans. Banditry? Yes, the country still has bandits, but will bandits attack the Americans? I doubt it.

We live on the edge of an earthquake. The stay of the Americans in Kunming has had one curious result—as they pull out, thousands of Chinese will find themselves without jobs. The better and luckier ones will probably follow the Americans to the coast; the others, accustomed to high wages, will be foot-loose in this city where you cannot live unless you are paid in millions. A municipal officer told me there have been more murders since the end of the war than at any time in human memory. Life is cheaper now. God knows how many jeeps, how many tommy-guns have been stolen from the American depots—a colonel told me that eighty-nine jeeps disappeared in a single year. Everyone knows who has them, they even know where they are, but the new possessors are so highly placed that they are beyond the judgement of the courts; and the judges can be bribed, so it would be useless to bring them to court.

A nasty story. A GI found a Chinese trying to steal the chain-guard of his jeep. "So I socked him on the cheek and smashed his

181

jaw and kicked him a bit, but Christ Almighty, it's better than sending him to the Chinese police—they'd have killed him. And they don't try the water treatment either."

October 3rd . . . A GREY dusk—one of those evenings when time stands still, smoke rises so slowly from the cooking fires, and suddenly and for no reason at all everything is quiet. The birds, even the birds were silent, the shops seemed to lean backwards into the grey mist, there was no creaking sound of axle staves from the little salt-carts driving down to the quay. And then suddenly a child in a red dress came running down the street, setting the whole earth alight.

I find more and more that I like wandering through the streets at night, and best of all are those nights when the electric light goes out, the fumbling acetylene flares are lit and the huge shadows lounge at street corners. I am so accustomed to electric light that I have almost forgotten the beauty of candlelight, and I hunger sometimes for those moments in Chungking when, stepping off the ferryboat at midnight, I would be greeted by a small boy with a bamboo flare which turned the rocks red. In this light the boy's skin was like the fruit of some tropical plant, running with juice. It was dark and cold, and there was often frost on the ground; the steps quarried out of the rock were treacherous; above us were harsh slopes, invisible houses clinging to the dark. But those bamboo flares gave more light than our sickly pellets of electricity. It brought out the texture of skin and rock and mud; there were leaping shadows from these brushes of fire. Electricity stands still. In electric light we are apt to regard the world as safe and unchanging; but I prefer the dangers of the bamboo or pinewood flares, when a rock will suddenly leap out at you, when the steps will suddenly seem to be running with blood, when monstrous darknesses appear, and there are bears and tigers in those leaping flames.

And so tonight, coming down the street where the sweet smell of opium drowsed from the open doors, I recaptured once more those moments in Chungking. The electric light had been turned off—perhaps that was the reason for the mysterious silence. I had gone out to buy a newspaper; and then coming through a dark street near the walls, which have always frightened me, for darkness always seems to be more intense beneath those thirty-foot high slopes

182

of mud, an old man came plodding along with a bamboo flare which sent his shadow rocketting over those immense black sloping walls. A moment later, when the lights came on again and from every house there came idiotic white unchanging squares of electricity, the old man was almost swallowed up in the brightness. But what was delightful beyond words was that he tried frantically to blow out the bamboo flare, and swung it around and dashed it against the wall of a house, but it wouldn't go out, and a moment later the electricity went out again and he looked as proud as Lucifer as he went down the street, carrying shoulder-high that blazing bamboo flame.

I am angry when the electricity goes out while I am working. I can't afford the snow-white American candles; there are only the little three-inch high Chinese candles made of pig's fat, which burn weakly and sputter with a small orange and blue flame. Some of them have no wicks, some melt in three minutes, some suffer from varicose veins. It should not be difficult to make good candles, but at least these wretched candles are better than the sulphurous green glare of rapeseed oil or the cheap acetylene cans which explode in your face. Best to rise with the sun and sleep at sunset— but how, when there are so many books around me and so many million Chinese poems still to be read?

October 4th, Civil War . . . It will take some time to see this day in its proper perspective. It might even be better to leave it out—I can no longer trust myself to speak calmly of bloodshed. I have such a horror of violence now that I can hardly bear the sight of soldiers, and now they are everywhere. They are swarming all over the city with their V armbands, their sleepy faces, their trigger-hungry fingers, their idiotic blank obedient faces.

This morning I was awakened by the sound of fire-crackers. I thought they were fire-crackers. It was a lovely day, blue sky, small puffs of blue cloud. Something was wrong, and I must have realized unconsciously that they were not fire-crackers, and there was no subdued murmur of people and lorries and funeral processions in the streets—that murmur which comes through the high walls of my courtyard and gives a faint quivering life to everything. Then the fire-crackers stopped, then they went on again. One of my windows looks out over an immense field, and at the end of the field there is the Burma Road. There was no traffic on the road. A few soldiers in the field were busily digging a grave.

I have said before that I do not like soldiers; and so I try not to look out of the window in the early morning when they do their idiotic exercises. I prefer this field later in the morning, when the mist has lifted and the ponies are rolling in the grass and small boys play tag and the shopgirls slip away from their counters and saunter beside the muddy pool; or when for some reason which I have never attempted to discover some women come with bales of blue cloth and slowly unroll them and let them dry in the sun. But now there were only the soldiers with their short-handled picks digging a grave in the sun.

The machine-gun was brought out later. A very beautiful machine-gun, nicely oiled and glinting, with three little legs and a nasty snout pointing in the direction of the great west gate. You can see the gate from here with its scalloped flaring roof above the trees, the small machine-gun and the great gate in the distance. The soldiers lay down behind the machine-gun. They were waiting for something to happen, but nothing happened, there were no more fireworks. I went out into the street, and there was another very beautiful machine-gun at the corner, though for some reason it was hooded with white sackcloth. There was dead silence. There were some soldiers huddled in the doorways. They looked tired, and they carried sub-machine-guns, and the street was empty except for the soldiers.

I went back and asked the *amah* whether there was enough food in the house—it might last for a few days, and we seemed to be in the line of fire. There was almost no food, but she did not complain of this. She said bitterly: "If it's civil war, then the peddlars will starve." I asked why. "They can only just live on their earnings, and they must get about in the streets." She spoke very simply: she had seen many civil wars. It was absurd to stay in the house, and so I took a young student who is also staying here and we went in search of an officer. The fire-crackers had begun again, but they were a long way away, and there was a sudden crackling of a mortar, but that was nearer. We ducked into shelter. Seeing us, the broad-faced soldiers were smiling and rubbing their hands.

I asked them what they were doing. Fifth Army. They had been there since two o'clock in the morning. Much fighting? They didn't know. Could we go into the city? No, they had their orders, no one
184

was to pass, no one at all. And if we did pass? They were very sorry, but they would have to shoot. And then someone came running up to say that an officer was expected soon, and perhaps we would be allowed to go into the city under escort.

The streets looked so curiously bare. A shutter would open, a face would appear, very drawn and tense, and then the shutter would be closed again. There was no traffic from the East Gate in spite of the fact that it was one of the main arteries into the city. It was this silence that hurt most, and the shutters opening, and the presence of those soldiers with their rolled grey-blue blankets, their pistols, their hand-grenades, rifles and trenching tools, just waiting there in the doorways. By now we had counted three jeeps moving along the Burma Road. The soldiers looked very tired. They said there had been fighting at the North Gate, and more fighting still at the Great East Gate.

And then it began to grow clear: the city was under some kind of siege. . . .

It will be difficult to catch up with this diary. Things are moving so very fast, and it is all so very mysterious. There is a siege. This much is certain. The Governor is still in the great ochre coloured palace overlooking the lake, and the soldiers of the Fifth Army are all round the lake firing at the palace with machine-guns, and there is a Mitchell bomber circling over the palace. American aeroplanes are still landing on the airstrip and taking off again, there are no American soldiers on the streets, but in all the alleyways and in all the shop doorways there are the drab-clothed trigger-hungry soldiers of the Fifth Army. But I must try to begin from the beginning.

We waited for about half an hour till the escort arrived, two young Hunanese with red cheeks and with four green hand-grenades hanging from their belts. I gathered that they did not relish the idea of taking us to the Little East Gate: there were snipers somewhere, and there were crackling sounds coming from inside the city. There is a wide road which leads down to the quays with shops on each side of the road, and for some reason we did not walk along the pavement but marched down the centre of the road, and I remember I kept on looking up at the windows for snipers. It was like Changsha; the shutters closed, the people inside pretending not to exist, the dead silence and the echoes of our

185

shoes on the cobble-stones. "It's all over now," the Hunanese boy said, laughing nervously, but just as he spoke there was the sound of firing inside the city.

There were a few people on the streets, and we thought it might be true that the war was over. There were these young soldiers from Hunan and Honan at all the street corners, armed with hand-grenades, Mausers and rifles; and all wore a white bandage with a badly-printed V in red on their arms. We noticed they were looking towards the end of the long street; they looked sullen and determined; but there was no firing. We walked up the street past the stone pill-boxes; and then we noticed that the machine-guns were pointed directly towards the centre of the city. What was surprising was that when we came to the end of the street there was another pill-box filled with young Yunnanese soldiers wearing French helmets, and their machine-guns were pointed towards the gate we had come from.

We knew then that the resistance was continuing; that the Fifth Army was a Nationalist army sent to demand the surrender of the Yunnanese guards who remained: though there cannot be many, since most of the Yunnanese armies are in Indo-China. We tried to get round the lake, but they refused to let us pass. It was odd to be stopped everywhere in this bright autumn sunshine, odd to see the silhouettes of soldiers on the rising banks beside the lake, and odder still to hear the crackle of Bren guns directed at the Governor's palace.

Later in the afternoon we managed to get to the North Gate by taking shelter along the city wall. There were soldiers everywhere, small groups of people heatedly discussing what had happened; once, there were bloodstains. The Hunanese boys are trigger-happy, but pasted on the walls are notices saying that if they kill a foreigner, they and their whole families will be wiped out by military order—so, for the moment at least we are safe.

There is a curfew. They said it was at nine, but apparently it was at six, for when we came through the streets in the dusk we were stopped. We went on a little while later. On the Street of the Forest of Learning a mortar exploded just as we reached the house of the President of the University; and then there was rifle fire down the whole length of the street. It looked like those photographs of St. Petersburg taken in 1917—the grey dusk, the people staggering to shelter, the way men hug the walls when there is street-fighting. Heaven knows where the firing came from—probably from the

186

drum-tower of the gate. And then all night there were sounds of firing, not occasionally, but continuously, sometimes so close that we heard the bullets nipping through the trees.

October 5th . . . Some students have been slightly wounded by stray bullets. There seems to have been a short heavy engagement in the hills behind the University. Fourteen mortars were thrown at the North Gate yesterday morning. This is not comic-opera: there is too much fear, and there has been fighting all night along the Street of the Forest of Learning, and along the Street of the Flowery Mountain. J. said he counted eleven bodies early this morning. I asked him what the devil he was doing counting them. "There is a daylight truce," he said. "There is only firing at night—and that's better. You can throw off a hell of a number of rounds without hitting anything." But a child was wounded seriously inside the Great East Gate this morning.

There are rumours that Lu Shen-tzu, the second son of the Governor Yung Lun, is coming from Chaotung, about two hundred miles to the north-west, to relieve the city. But the Yunnanese troops in the province are miserably small, though well-disciplined. There is only one regiment of gendarmerie, one brigade of field artillery and one or two regiments of soldiers. It seems improbable that they will be able to hold out.

October 6th . . . In the still bright air the sound of rifle shots like the dull patter of cricket-bats at the nets: no smoke, nor any explosions, but at night they whine and roar and crackle among the trees. What is odd is that the streets look so normal during the day. There are the soldiers with the arm-bands, which had a great blood-red W today—those who did not change them soon enough were shot out of hand, so that the Fifth Army lost apparently over eighty soldiers this morning.

Last night we again mistook the time of the curfew: everyone was so certain that it was nine o'clock. So we wandered down by the wall in the pitch darkness, and when we came to the Little East Gate someone lunged out of the shadows and said "Put your hands up," and searched my pockets. He was tired and trigger-happy and carried a sub-machine-gun. It was not pleasant, and it became worse later when we were told that we could pass unhindered out of the Little East Gate and found ourselves stopped by shadows at every turn, the road deserted and seeming in the faint light so

187

broad that we were lost in it. We walked down the centre of the road, afraid they would shoot at shadows creeping along the wall.

October 7th . . . I WALKED all over the north part of the city, and found tanks in the great field outside the North Gate. The tanks have machine-guns mounted on the roof, and some small guns which are shelling the Governor's palace over the walls. There are bullet-marks on the British Consulate, there are wires on the ground all leading to Heilungtang where General Tu Li-ming has his headquarters and from where he is operating against the Governor, who is still preparing to hold out in his palace. Shops are open all day, but at the first faint approach of dusk, everything is shuttered, for the soldiers of the Fifth Army are ordered to shoot anything that moves after curfew. What is odd is that this is perhaps the last of the Chinese wars against the barbarians, for the Governor of Yunnan is a tribesman; if the Fifth Army succeed in taking over the province, it will also be the first time that any central government has possessed complete power here; for this province has always possessed, even under the Ch'ing Dynasty, a kind of autonomy.

October 8th . . . I HAVE been to the American Red Cross, where L. tells me that in the long courtyard outside the Military Hospital, perhaps a quarter of a million bullets have been fired without anyone being hurt: they have been firing backwards and forwards between the street and the hospital for three nights, and only the statue of the former Governor has been chipped. Yet hundreds have been killed, and according to all reports I have read, prisoners are executed without mercy.

October 9th . . . T. V. SOONG has arrived, and the Governor Lung Yun has surrendered and emplaned for Chungking. The war is over, but is it over? The Yunnanese have fled to the hills or gone into disguise. Lu Shen-tzu's forces never reached the city: they were decimated some forty miles away, and it was apparently when Lung Yun heard of the fate of the relief column that he decided to surrender. He might have fought it out from the palace indefinitely, or at least until the bombers came, but he can have had little hope of being successful. If it is over, I shall remember the hollow tock-tock of bullet-echoes among the gravemounds, the long dreary
188

nights returning home, seeing shadows and being stopped every-where; I shall remember the bloodstains and the chips of plaster and a green lake ringed round with Bren guns while the nationalist soldiers fired at a castle on a yellow hill.

October 15th, History . . . I HAVE been thinking of the history that may some day be written of our civil war. It may not be a long history, perhaps only a few paragraphs will be wrong. Because we were professors, we collected the rumours and some of the facts, but most of the rumours turned out later to be inventions and hardly any of us have any idea of the facts: yet we were there, we were shot at, we saw the dead, we read the press releases, we were completely neutral in the sense that we took no part in the fighting and could not conceive any great advantages in either side winning—we were passengers here and would soon return to Peking.

Mercifully, the Chinese have never envisaged any philosophies of history. For them it is simply a serious account of things that happened in the past, many of them unrelated to each other, a series of rather lugubrious and sometimes delightful anecdotes. Things happen, they say; there is perhaps cause and effect; there are good men and bad men; most curiously, there are men of goodness. But the ancient histories, though they hint at goodness, are no more than anecdotes, some of them evidently spiteful, some ill-conceived, all coloured by the emotions of the writer.

And so the Chinese will record to the end of time such odd and unnecessary things as that Yuan Te-hsiu went for whole days without eating during times of famine, solacing himself on his flute; that Mi Fei called a curiously shaped rock "his brother"; that Mao Ch'iang, the concubine of the Prince of Yueh, was so beautiful that when fishes saw her they dived deep in the water, birds soared high in the air and the deer scurried away to the woods; that Tao Hung-ching, the hermit of Hua-yang, lived in a three-storied tower, himself in the top story, while his visitors lodged on the ground floor and his disciples below him; and that Chen Tsun loved his guests so much that to keep them with him he threw the linch-pins of their carriages into his well. I confess I prefer it this way. History as cause and effect, as the rise and decline of social movements, of prevailing necessities and leaps to freedom—I think I can half-understand them, but I understand better those histories which are

189

concerned with the curious evolutions of men. We are inclined to despise anecdotes; and this may be partly because we live in urban societies and no longer amuse ourselves by telling stories to each other. The novelist remains the only historian: we shall never know or guess what happened during the invasion of Russia in 1812, but we are more certainly closer to the conspirators on both sides when we read *War and Peace* than when we read the history-books.

October 25th, A Chinese Hand . . . THE post-office was horribly dirty. There was a little tin of rice-paste attached to a string, and everyone was dipping his fingers in it to stick the stamps on the envelopes. We were crowded and huddled there, a sweating-hot mass of silent humanity, and the little window through which we peered had a shutter which threatened to bang down at any moment, for the people inside were hard-pressed. I hated it. I hated the soldiers dressed in ragged cotton-lined uniforms who were all crowding so urgently, so preposterously urgently, against the window; they were suffocating the girl by my side; they had probably already killed the baby who was wrapped in a red silk shawl on her back; they were evil-smelling, drab and unhealthy, and I didn't want to look at them. And then suddenly, on the little counter made foetid with traces of rice-paste, I saw the hand. It was so perfect that you wanted to take a knife, cut it off and keep it for ever. The fingers were finely tapered, delicate and intense, quivering with life, dark brown, shining a little and though they were quivering, they were in repose. It was like a little brown sleek animal sitting there: somewhere in its shadow there were eyes, and there was a heart beating in the palms, and perhaps—why not?—it had lungs, sexual organs, mouth and nostrils. And so it remained there, almost a small brown animal curled up and waiting patiently for the moment when food would be dropped in its mouth, so delicate and fragile a thing that you wanted to stroke it, or even put it in a cage. There were faint blue veins and curious whorled knuckles: the silky brown fingers were longer than any I have ever seen. And then I looked up and saw the snot-nosed, ragged-mouthed soldier, with the clipped hair and the eczema and the unshaved beard, as uncouth and horrible a spectacle as any in the army; and yet it is not in the least puzzling that this lice-infested descendant of coolies and princes should have been the owner of these hands, for nearly all Chinese hands seem to possess this delicacy and intensity, this quivering life of their own.

190

October 27th, Deus absconditus . . . THE fear of Pascal and of the saints—is at last realized. But it may be that the God, who has escaped, may yet return not through our fear of destruction, but because our shuddering on the edge of the abyss may call forth the mediator. The world is not wicked: there is no Sodom and Gomorrah to be destroyed. We have climbed Mount Moriah, we have taken the fire in our hands, and a knife, and we are still waiting for the angel to call out from heaven, Here I am. And it may be, though it is perhaps necessary to look for it very carefully, that we shall open our eyes and see a ram caught up in a thicket which can be sacrificed instead.

I confess that though I fear the atomic bomb, I delight in it. There must be something to be said for a machine that turns whole cities to powder. I have seen bodies on a battlefield which looked, in the visionary whiteness of evening, so young and clean in their nakedness, for they had been stripped by the peasants, like young gods sleeping; but their beauty was disquietening, an error, only a temporary heightening of the human dignity they must once have possessed and were so soon to be dispossessed of. Usually the crumbling remains of war are not pleasing: the human agony is only too evidently stated in the twisted wires, the gutted and continually bleeding horses, the blood-soaked clothes and the unholy attitudes of the dead, whose open eyes among the grass are treacherously imploring, since there is no one who can answer their requests. It is better that we should become powder than that we should become gobs of disused flesh. Now that we know that Prometheus has come into his own, that the fire he stole from Heaven and concealed in a fennel-stalk has power to turn his Caucasian rock into powder, we need a new legend. Dust to dust: ashes to ashes: it was usually a lie, for we turn into mud and worms. But the new paradise of coloured dust in which we shall all soon be floating (unless we disband our armies and have an international government at once) is at least more bearable. The Chinese buddhists call the world "the red dust," and it may be that they were prophesying, though they can hardly have expected that we should make the transition so painlessly. Meanwhile where is the ram caught in a thicket by his horns?

October 28th . . . HE WAS probably a survivor of the Yunnanese guards who fought against the Fifth Army, but it was impossible to think of this as he was brought out of the Great West

191

Gate on his way to the burial mounds. He was tall and wore military uniform; his hands were tied behind his back with a ridiculously thin piece of string which trailed behind him, caught up in the hands of a young soldier who carried a rifle on his shoulder. There were three other soldiers similarly armed, and there was also an officer with a long black coat which dragged at his heels. It was evident that he was being led out to die; his face was desperately grey, without life, already remote from the world, the eyes unseeing and the lips set in a broken quivering line. And he walked on, very fast, as though to make up for lost time, leading this procession on the end of a string, going down an old alleyway where there is an empty shrine to the forgotten gods of the place: and it was impossible to believe that he was not leading them, for he walked in front of them and possessed the utterly passionless and exhausted expression of a man who has seen everything and knows everything, and is therefore appointed to be a leader of men. Five minutes later he knelt on the ground and the top of his head was blown off, and now at night the crows are screaming over him and the dogs are drinking his blood.

November 3rd . . . WE WERE speaking of the desperate poverty which remains in China, that poverty which explains everything, for it explains why the rich desire so desperately to be richer, it explains murder, it explains the dying soldiers coming up the Burma Road to die. And not so much fear of poverty as fear of starvation. When you are travelling, everyone tries to bring with him enough food for a life-time. The buses from Kunming to the south are crowded with Yunnan hams, tinned foods, a pig's head here and some tripe there—everyone is secretly afraid of dying of hunger in this country where so many have died of hunger. J. told me that last week he was waiting for a bus in Kweiyang. There were some mongrel dogs playing in the road, and the bus came and ran over two of them. "And then the beggars leaped out of nowhere and we saw them tearing the dogs apart and eating them alive." A little later he said: "The Chinese do not share our fear of the atomic bomb. They have lived so close to insecurity all their lives that our new-found insecurity is almost strange to them."

November 4th . . . NOTES for a sermon on the atomic bomb. No man may deliver his brother, nor make agreement unto God
192

for him. The crisis of the spirit: whenever power is given into our hands, whenever power is so great that we are compelled by a kind of gravitational attraction to imitate the *recklessness* of the bomb. It is not inconceivable that whole civilizations may become reckless, not through fear but because we unconsciously imitate the manifestations of power, as the poets a few years ago imitated the rhythms of the petrol engine. The new jet-propelled world which has finally abandoned all sense of rhythm. Power becomes silent and invisible, and in this respect like the sun at night. But how to live in this new lunar landscape?

Rilke lamented during the last war that the world had come into the hands of men and left the hands of God. The ultimate fever: when it leaves the hands even of men, and becomes purely fortuitous, whole civilizations at the mercy of a madman. Ghenghiz Khan redivivus, but leaving no trace, no history behind him—the end of history as we have known it, and the end of man as we have known him, and of all love. After writing *Green Jade,* Shen Ts'eng-wen wrote in his autobiography: "Though all men perish from the earth, I have left in this book evidence of how men loved." This above all—that there should be the evidence whatever happens, the evidences which are supplied by great art. The greatest task: to hollow out remote mountains and bury in them, as the Egyptians buried their kings, the greatness we have inherited, so that if by some chance some of us survive we can create a civilization on the basis of what is good in ours. And asking, as always, the heroes—Beethoven and others—what they would do, and knowing only too well that they would ask us to preserve, not their memory, but the works they have accomplished.

I have realized recently more profoundly than before the desperate straits of all art, remembering the lurking fear in Epstein's face in 1939 when it seemed likely, and even possible, that bombs would either destroy his work or his bronzes would be melted down into bombs. What is left to us, as a kind of correlative to the powers we have created (and which we cannot control), is to make art so powerful that it will survive even the greatest shocks. To draw in gigantic patterns in the most enduring metals, to create like the Assyrians, who were also conscious of tremendous and unforgiveable powers, on so huge a scale that they could outwit their own deaths. To find the still centre beyond the whirling circumferences—but one must first pass through the circumference. And will those things which are most delicate, books and music

193

and paintings, survive in the caves we shall have to make for them? Of the greatest things we are most careless, but in the history of civilization it is war that always destroys most—the poems of Sappho survived until the Crusaders burnt them. And to beware also, in preserving our treasures, of the puritanical bonfires of Savonarola, and the more dreadful, because still more puritanical bonfires of the last Emperor of the Liang Dynasty who, when at last forced to abdicate, heaped together 200,000 books and pictures, and setting fire to them exclaimed: "The culture of the Liang Dynasty perishes with me," and to remember that something very similar happened at the end of the Nazi dynasty in Germany.

November 5th . . . I LIKE Franz Kafka's apothegm in *The Great Wall of China:*

> Leopards break into the temple and drink the sacrificial chalices dry; this occurs repeatedly, again and again; finally it can be reckoned upon beforehand and becomes a part of the ceremony.

It is just conceivable, but not entirely probable, that the atomic bomb may "become part of the ceremony."

November 6th . . . IT MAY be that I am growing older and more cynical, but I am becoming more and more puzzled by the foreigners who come to China. Why do they come? To exorcise a childhood dream (which is perhaps excusable, though it will never be exorcised), or because servants are cheaper here (which is no longer true), or because they are moved to rescue the heathen (but the heathen are so often more civilized than they are). I remember a professor of English from some remote University in England who mumbled love lyrics so passionlessly that half the audience wanted to scream and the other half wanted to vomit, and then came back at night to our senior common room in a deserted and rat-infested theatre and told dirty stories to Chinese professors who knew better ones, but would not care to tell them; and I remember how this desiccated professor pecked and fiddled with Pound's translation of Propertius, saying that it was full of mistakes, he had checked all of them and it was beyond doubt the most miserable fabrication ever invented, and it was useless to tell him that Pound's translation was among the greatest things in our literature. "But my dear fellow, the man was a traitor—I
194

hope they shoot him." I hope they shoot the professor for murdering the English love-lyrics, and I am sure Pound was the most ineffectual of all traitors. (Li Po was a murderer, Marlowe a whoremongerer and blasphemer, Raleigh a cut-throat, Shelley a seducer, Rimbaud an opium-smuggler, Villon a gangster, Hart Crane a pervert, but who cares?)

There were others. There was the fat lady and the thin man in the Red Cross who gave parties and sighed for Peking and cared not a damn for the miseries of the people he was sent here to heal; there was the insufferably patronizing and distinguished professor who read out to the assembled faculty a letter he had received from his child aged seven in proof of the sympathy which his country possessed for China, while the watch-chain trembled on his fat waistcoat and the professors wilted into themselves; the colonels who pawed at girl-students; the generals followed by their hordes of Shanghai mistresses; the ambassadors who knew only that they were ambassadors and obeyed their wives; the first-secretaries who delighted in nothing more than drinking distinguished scholars under the table; the plug-uglies; the millionaires. But there were good and great men too who came to China when she was cut off from the world—Willkie and Fairbanks, Dodds and Hughes, Needham and Clark-Kerr and Eliseeff, and a host of others; and at times of greatest stress, when one felt that all that was worst in the west was crawling into China, there was always the memory of Eggleston. O God, God, God, why must China so often be the place of the remittance-man?

November 7th . . . NOT well. The worrying thing is that when the body drops, the spirit drops too. The world cannot possibly be as bad as I painted it this afternoon—going down the street where the mud is a slimy three-inch thick black jelly for fifty yards, though the sun was shining, and the jelly remains forever, because the sanitation in this city is almost non-existent. I do not know how people survive among these unrunning drains, squelching cesspools, dead rats, dead bodies everywhere. Because I have a headache, and probably typhus, it seems worse: the dead rat gnawed by the dogs assumes elephantine proportions—it would have been a dead rat yesterday, and rather beautiful, but today it is a mountainous suppuration of diseased and running flesh. A headache is a magnifying-glass. Must one always be at the mercy of the knife-edge balance of the brain-cells?

And then the night-mare, the professor turning into a rat with wet red lips mouthing something about Propertius. Exorcised the demon at 3 A.M. by writing out the whole of Pound's wonderful translation of "O nox mihi candida":

Me, happy night, night full of brightness;
Oh couch made happy by my long delectations;
How many words talked out with abundant candles;
Struggles when the lights were taken away;
Now with bared breasts she wrestles against me,
              Tunic spread in delay;
And she then opening my eyelids fallen in sleep,
Her lips upon them; and it was her mouth saying: Sluggard!

But the couch is not made happy by long delectations, and the red-faced rat will probably return.

November 8th . . . SICK.

November 9th . . . SICK.

November 10th . . . SICK.

November 11th . . . HEADACHE. Lying in bed, drinking water. The headache quite remarkable: little green wedges trying to split the skull open. If I could see them, it would make no difference. Sometimes they get bigger, and then they are like piston hammers. I am absolutely determined to regard this as a clinical experiment. The pain doesn't matter—too drowsy with fever— but the headache does matter.

November 12th . . . GREEN wedges all night, but they turned to gold this morning, and worse still they became sharper. They are like arrowheads, and probably poisoned. The fever got worse, but the fever is infinitely less important than the green hammers. The idiotic thing is that it is completely impossible to think. The world is muffled and muzzled. I have been reading, but the words don't sink in; if I didn't read, the hammers would be louder, and I would start screaming. If I screamed, I could drown the sound of the hammers. Imagining conversations with R. "Poor darling, you've probably got a brain-lesion." But though there are conversations with R., I remember nothing of them.
196

November 14th . . . I SUPPOSE it is a brain-lesion, and that's
the end, and it doesn't matter. There are no consolations—this I
knew before. The poinsettia tree when I stumbled out onto the
balcony was a consolation, but not for long. Best to worship in
spite of everything, and not care too much whether the poems are
printed—that hurts most. Dust hath closed Helen's eye. If I live,
to work for peace, beauty and learning in that order.

November 20th . . . CONVALESCENCE is also a fever, but so
much quieter. Almost impossible to imagine that I have ever been
happier. Lying in bed and looking at the sunlight on the great
twisted eucalyptus tree in the garden, and the hawks wheeling;
even when they shoot the anti-typhus serum into my arm, even
the great snaky green faeces after constipation, even the sudden
screams at night echoing along interminable corridors, the pure
physical sensation of just being alive. Everything is *received*.

Illness is a kind of blessing. The motor was wound up, and it
would have gone on at the same terrific pace and burnt itself out.
The real trouble was that I had not the faintest idea what typhus
was like, did not suspect that it began with that shattering sickening headache, and in any case too drowsy to know what was happening. The temperature mounts up, but you are completely unconscious of having a high temperature—the human body can
live only within such narrow ranges of temperature. R. says the
doctor came and said: "You'll have to rush him to hospital—it
looks very serious." But it never looked serious to the patient. He
was too weak and drowsy to care and he was mechanically immune from fear—something happens that blots out fear, there is
none of the sterilized excitement I remember with tuberculosis,
when you do fear, fear terribly, simply because life becomes so
amazingly beautiful. (The lungs rather than the heart are the
source of life: the biologists say that life began at the sea's margin
—the waves of air beating against the lungs' shore.) And then, too,
mercifully and for some reason which must spring from the same
causes as sleep, absolutely no sense of the passing of time. The
days were continuous, not broken up by hours and minutes—the
sun wheeling round, not pausing at nightfall, the sense of the most
perfect and delicate continuity.

There was the eucalyptus tree and the changing shadows on the
wall and for some reason which I shall probably never discover, a
girl skiing in Norway and moving tremendously fast down the

197

snowplains and the Malay girl who was dark and walked very slowly in a gold head-dress. What surprises me now is that they were somehow interchangeable, and must have come from the same source. No desire for them, only delight in watching them; and being able to summon them at any time I pleased, just as the branches of the tree could assume any shape I pleased—a horseman on the topmost bough, a grinning old taoist monk somewhere below. And it was so easy to colour those shadows on the walls with small villages, boys playing leap-frog, old mountains.

On the night after reaching hospital, I thought it was over and didn't care; I might not have thought it was over if they hadn't carried me on a stretcher. That was the worst, and the small white-washed bedroom looked so shuttered; and soaking with fever that night. But in the morning the sun came through the window, the leaves of the eucalyptus tree were jade, and some birds hopped on the windowsill—it was as simple as that. And then slowly, in little spurts, the strength coming back, though the food was appalling, and the sensation that something in the air around was flooding my body: not healing: simply this incessant quiet *receiving*.

Convalescence is the best. The little spurts become more numerous, and for some reason they feel terribly like the liquefaction of blood—the solid core melting. Sun-bathing is dangerous. The clouds come so very suddenly, and then it becomes bitterly cold for a few minutes until the clouds pass away. I do not know how these thin clouds can suck so much heat from the sky, but they do. And going to bed early and waking early, things I shall never do unless mercifully I become ill again.

November 23rd . . . A LETTER from Bohumil Janda from Prague. Exactly like the appearance of a ghost, for I have long ago been forced to wipe my memories of people in Europe off the map. Unbearable to think that my friends were in prison camps, and yet knowing perfectly well they were there and being unable to do anything. It is the custom now to regard the horrors as unbelievable, but they were only too believable; nothing is easier than to imagine these horrors. The mind does not break down before them, at a certain point it even acquiesces to them, as sometimes the brain will acquiesce to a nightmare and allow it to go on. Worst was the breaking of human flesh and dignity: the dead soldier, unless he is unrecognizable, looks calm, but the expressions of agony on the faces of the tortured are not the faces of men but

198

of animals: so Picasso in *Guernica* seems to have modelled his martyrs on dead dogs and horses.

But the indescribable joy of receiving a letter from a ghost—this must be remembered.

November 25th . . . WELL enough to get up and give a party. The electric light went out again, and I was pleased in spite of the impossible cost of candles. There were two young poets and a philologist, their faces ruddy in candlelight, sitting below the Chinese painting of Tien Kuan, which they detested; it is a bad painting, but there is so much crimson, so much jade-green and gold that I shall never part with it; and against this background, with the smoking candleflames drawing the health onto the surface of their faces, they looked bronzed and much younger. Liu Lien came later with a small bunch of flowers, but the candlelight withered them away—I must try to find out why flowers lose their colours in candlelight, while everything else grows richer. The texture and sheen of his blue silk patterned gown was perfect. And then, afterwards in another room, interminable discussions on politics. R's story of the cook in a Peking house who absented himself each night and uncoupled some Japanese railway lines, which the Japanese always replaced in the morning. Liu Lien said: "If only the Chinese could employ their skill in destruction to purposes of reconstruction, but we are the greatest destroyers in the world: there is probably no other race so efficient at sapping the spirit of its enemies. The Japanese possessed mechanical skill, but they possessed almost nothing at all of our sophistication. So young, and we are so old." He has a real pity for the Japanese, whom he regards as children; and at the same time he has the greatest reverence for some Japanese scholars. "I hope they are protected—so many of them understand us, and they are the only race that does." I asked him how this squared with his former statement that the Japanese were young and the Chinese old. He smiled and answered: "My grandson understands me better than my wife."

The hair-raising stories of corruption and the activities of the secret police cannot all be untrue. "Surely," said Liu Lien, "the people should have power to investigate the private fortunes of the members of the Government. We know the private fortunes of the Communist leaders—probably five dollars each." He has never been so bitter, and he is especially bitter against some of the pro-

199

fessors who applaud the Kuomintang Party, saying that it is the duty of the scholars at all times to refrain from political action. I objected: "To say nothing may be treason." "No," he answered. "To say nothing at such a time and place is to applaud the good and condemn the evil." And again later: "The scholars must be above politics at this time. The people may invite them into the government, but at least, when we are showing ourselves so inept, they should remain pure. I am ashamed that in this victory, which we have done nothing to deserve, we are both feudal and fascist— nothing has changed." I objected again: "The Chinese do deserve this victory." "Yes," he answered, "the Chinese people do deserve this victory, but no party deserves this victory, no millionaire deserves this victory, no official deserves this victory. The peasants, yes, but not the officials." He is not well. He spoke so bitterly sometimes, and with such passion, that I was half afraid; yet there is never any contempt in his voice, he speaks quietly and sometimes puts in French words, or simply bows his head, and at such moments in the candlelight he was more eloquent than ever.

At nine o'clock we heard a burst of gunfire from the direction of the University. I said: "It is probably someone throwing crackers," though I was almost certain that it was small arms fire. Liu Lien said: "How long have you been in China? Four years, and you do not know the sound of gunfire?" There were a few more bursts later. I was pretty sure they were gunfire by this time, and it seemed puzzling till the poet said that there were hundreds of Yunnanese troops in the mountains. "They are living on the land," he said. "They dare not come into the city—they will be executed. The worst of it is that the new government has photographs and details about every member of the Yunnanese forces, and it may be years before the last man is exterminated." Liu Lien said: "We are manufacturing bandits because we show men no mercy," and told a terrible story of having seen about a hundred bound Yunnanese soldiers taken out of the North Gate to die. "I didn't care a fig for the Yunnanese Government—it was as corrupt as the others, but I do care for these boys, there was no reason why they should die. Some of them were tribesmen. They were loyal to Lung Yun, because Lung Yun was a tribesman himself, but their loyalty was not a crime." And just as he was going he said: "A student has told me that he has overheard General Ho, the new commander of the Garrison Headquarters, saying that nothing would please him
200

more than that I should suffer an accident. Well, let them do their worst. If they kill young boys for no reason at all, boys who are not dangerous, because they are the wealth and strength of our country, there is no reason why they should not also kill the scholars, who have no wealth and little enough strength to offer." He said this sadly, without vainglory.

The electric light was still off when they left, and I led them to the corner of the street with three candles in a candelabra, and remember the light on Liu Lien's gown. He refused to take a rickshaw, though there were a few rickshaws about; and now I do not know whether he will ever reach home.

November 26th . . . THE *sounds of firing last night came from soldiers of the Fifth Army shooting over the heads of the students.* This does not make sense. It is intolerable and unbelievable that the students should be fired on in this way by the orders of the Garrison Commander and with the intention—the very clear intention—of terrorizing the students in the greatest University of China. Have they gone mad?

I am writing this in bed, because I caught a cold when I went out into the street last night and I have not yet recovered from typhus. I cursed this weakness all morning; I could not go out. No one knows what will happen next. There are rumours that the great clash between the militarists and the civilians will come at any moment—have the militarists decided to liquidate the University? It looks very much like it.

Later in the afternoon some students came, and two professors. They are aghast at what has happened, and yet they are perfectly unafraid, they know they have no weapons against the militarists, they know that they are completely at the mercy of the militarists, and if the militarists liquidate the University, it may be months before the outside world ever hears of it. What was strange was that they spoke very quietly about the events last night, and so very simply. This happened, they said; someone has evidently gone mad, but madness is epidemic in this country—we are still fighting the Communists—haven't they the sense to realize that we must have peace?—above everything else, peace, a breathing-space, a few hours and days and months of rest, the country so terribly weary and all except the very few are so terribly poor. Peace—peace—it was only when they mentioned this beloved word that they raised their voices a little.

201

During the last month I have been too ill to understand what was happening, and I was so sick of the thought of the civil war that I paid little attention to it, hoping it would pass; but it has not passed; it is still here, and the students are tormented by the thought that they have responsibilities towards their country. There was very little they could do, but they could call a mass meeting: the sounds of firing last night were directed at the mass-meeting they had called in the Lienta campus. The student spoke very quietly, in a hushed voice, exactly as though he was describing a murder, though no one has been murdered. "It was a perfectly orderly meeting," he said. "We had asked four professors to address us on the subject of the civil war, and we invited the students of the middle schools to listen. It was a dark cold night, and the campus was lit by electric lights from inside the school-buildings. There is a plinth just in front of the library, and it was from there that the professors spoke. They had a microphone, so that all the students could listen to them—there were perhaps three thousand students altogether sitting on the grass round the stone plinth, perhaps more, I don't know, it was impossible to count them because it was so dark. We had very carefully chosen the professors who would speak to us—two were members of the Kuomintang, one belonged to the Democratic League and the fourth was independent. Not one of the professors was a Communist: all of them were famous and responsible people, who would weigh their words carefully.

"It was dark. The first speaker, Dr. Chen Tuan-shen, spoke in a very low voice, saying that the time was ripe for a coalition government. He said it was the greatest mistake, the greatest imaginable mistake, for China at this time to embark on a civil war, the danger of the civil war extending over the whole length and breadth of China was so great, the effects on the life and economy of the nation so unpredictable, the losses in man-power and natural wealth so terrible, that every effort must be made to stop this war at once—a war which could only bring shame on China. He spoke like this for half an hour; it was about seven o'clock; and then the first shots were heard coming from the gravemounds behind the University. No one was frightened. A few shots could be explained. A soldier playing the fool, or an execution—though an execution would be unlikely at night. Dr. Chen Tuan-shen is a member of the Kuomintang Party and a member of the People's Political Council—it was inconceivable that anyone would dare
202

to interrupt his speech by firing. And then a little while later it came again, closer this time, and lower; what was strange was that the firing now seemed to be deliberately punctuating those passages in his speech where he attacked the government for making no efforts towards peace with the Communists. Whenever he mentioned the coalition government there was firing. And then gradually the firing died down, and we thought perhaps that someone was playing the fool and the meeting would be allowed to carry on without further interruption.

"And it did carry on without further interruption for some time. Dr. Chen finished his speech, and he was followed by Dr. Wu Chi-yuan, who is a right-wing member of the Kuomintang. No shots were fired during his speech. It must have been about eight o'clock when Dr. Fei Shao-tung, who is an internationally-known sociologist, mounted the platform and began in a voice so low that we could hardly hear him. He began by saying: 'I have been wondering why I should come to speak to you in the darkness tonight, but above everything else I want peace ——' At the word 'peace' firing began again. This time there was no doubt that the firing was intentional. They were firing from beyond the walls of the University, and we could see the bullets streaking above us, and sometimes they clattered against the slate-roof of the library—they were coming lower and lower, and we ducked our heads. The electric lights went out, and the microphone became dead. Dr. Fei then raised his voice and said: 'I beg you to have no fear—I must raise my voice above the sound of the bullets.' We clapped when he said this, and then the firing became louder than ever, somewhere in the darkness a trench mortar went off, and the machine-guns opened out at full burst. But he went on. They were firing only a few inches above his head, but he went on. Sometimes there would be a little wave of fear among the students, but we realized we were trapped, we could not move, we had to keep our heads down, if we stood up we would probably be shot, and Dr. Fei kept on speaking, in spite of the fact that his microphone was dead and sometimes we could hardly hear what he was saying. A loudspeaker from somewhere outside ordered in the name of the provincial government an immediate cessation of the meeting—this, in spite of the fact that free speech and free assembly were solemnly granted to the nation some weeks before. We paid no attention to the loud-speaker. Someone found an acetylene lamp, and the meeting continued.

203

"Then an extraordinary thing happened. Out of the darkness there suddenly emerged a man wearing dark glasses and a blue gown escorted by thirty or forty young men. He came up to the rostrum and shouted: 'I am just an ordinary man—a *lao pai hsing* —and I have heard that this University is the home of democracy in China, and I want to speak to you.' There was some discussion about whether he should be heard—he looked so much like a secret service agent, and it was curious that when he appeared there were no more sounds of firing. It was decided to let him speak for ten minutes. He mounted the rostrum and delivered a savage attack on the Communists whom he described as bandits and cut-throats. He said that China had fought the Japanese for eight years; now we must have a united country; and the way to have a united country was to destroy utterly the bandits and cut-throats in our midst—in his opinion, as a common man, it was nonsense to call this a civil war—it was simply an attempt by a legally constituted government to put an end to a few scattered bandits who were of no importance whatsoever. He finished his statement, came off the rostrum and was immediately set upon by the thirty or forty people who had accompanied him, all crying: 'Beat him! Beat him!'

"This was really extraordinary! His own aides were beating him, pretending in the darkness to be students, and the students had to rescue him. For a few moments the place was in an uproar, for the students now saw perfectly well what was happening and knew that at any moment the firing would begin again, but this time lower. A few students took the man who called himself Mr. Wang to the main gates of the University and left him there; and they were careful not to hurt him. And one by one the others who had accompanied him went out.

"That's all. There was one more speaker—Dr. Pan Pa-kwei, of the Democratic League. There was another wave of shooting, and though he spoke for some time, about nine o'clock it was decided to abandon the meeting. The continual bursts of machine-gun fire and mortars was getting on our nerves; it was coming from all directions, and no one knew when the angle of fire would be lowered—we could hear the bullets whistling over our heads. In any case, the main purpose of the meeting had been accomplished. We had heard what they had to say, and we were in general agreement that the civil war must come to an end, and we had decided to telegraph to the Generalissimo and to Mr. Mao Tse-tung urging them to put a stop to the civil war for the sake of the nation. Then we slowly went out through the great gates, only to find that a machine-gun was directed against us in the road and the gates of the city were shut.

"That was perhaps the worst moment, because the thirty or forty men who accompanied Mr. Wang were waiting for us in the street and trying to create trouble. Only a very few students had torches. It was dark, there was no moon, and there were soldiers all along the road leading down from the North Gate. We could see them in the darkness, we knew they had been firing at us and there was nothing we could do. They told us the city gates were closed—no one knew why—and many of us were compelled to stay outside the walls all through the bitterly cold night. There were hundreds of girl-students, and we were desperately afraid of what might happen to them if they stayed out among all those soldiers. Some of us managed to get through a small gate. A professor in Yunnan University was knifed on his way home—not a deep wound, but still he was knifed, and he was probably only saved from death by the fact that it was so dark that the man who wanted to kill him could not see him. And in any case he was a perfectly innocent and respectable professor, who had taken no part in the meeting, and was probably mistaken for someone else."

This is the story: it seems perfectly incredible, but it happened. It may be happening in every University and high school in China. This is the greatest University in the country, a huge complex comprising Peking, Tsinghua and Nankai Universities, and free speech is at the mercy of soldiers and no one knows what will happen next.

November 27th, The Strike . . . THE students came out on strike this afternoon. I am not surprised, though I told K. this evening when he came to tell me that he could no longer attend my classes that I was dubious about the validity of a strike, since every moment of study was necessary. "What else can we do? You say we cannot afford to waste one moment from our studies when China needs us so much, but how else can we protest?"

The local newspapers announced that shooting occurred outside the North Gate "because a group of bandits were known to be in the vicinity." K. says: "They insulted us by firing over our heads and by trying to intimidate us, and now they insult us by calling us bandits."

205

November 28th . . . THE strike continues in spite of the pleas of the professors, who have told the students again and again that their studies are so important to the nation that not a moment must be lost. The students are very respectful, but they say that the name of the University has been maligned by the local government, that intelligence has been wantonly assailed, that it is impossible to stop the strike until they have received the apologies of the local government; and K. tells me that some students are determined to keep on strike till the civil war is brought to an end.

He told me, looking very pale and serious, that (1) the city is honeycombed with secret police who have only just been brought into the city, (2) he hopes all the Universities and schools in China will support the strike, and believes that they will, (3) the strictest censorship has been imposed, the censorship office has been enlarged, but there remains one way—he will not tell me what way—by which messages can be taken to the outside world, and (4) the students are taking advantage of the strike to educate the people in democracy, sending small groups into remote villages, putting posters on the walls in favour of free speech, free assembly and *habeas corpus,* making speeches in the city and editing their own newspaper. There is a strike fund, and they have received gifts of paper and even of food from sympathetic merchants. The strike has attracted the attention of the military governor who is determined to suppress it. K. says that they have received orders from Chungking to suppress it at whatever the cost, because there is the danger that it will spread to all the other cities of China. I am dubious about this, but I am still in bed—I am not allowed out, and it is impossible to visualize what is happening. Apparently the streets are crowded with young students from the high schools and even from the middle schools busily scratching in chalk on the walls slogans like: "Down with dictatorship," "End the civil war," "Ask the American troops to leave China," or just simply: "Democracy" and "Freedom." He says: "There was a boy of about twelve years old. He chalked out the two characters for 'Democracy' and the secret police came and clubbed him on the head." He believes this, though he admits he has not seen it. He says: "They are deliberately attempting to intimidate us. We go round quietly putting up posters, and if they left us alone, everything would be all right—but they have daggers and knives and revolvers and even hand-grenades." Another student told me that girl-students have been beaten up and taken to prison. A procla-
206

mation has been issued by Lienta, three other Universities and twenty-seven middle schools saying that the aims of the strike are:

1. The war must be stopped at once: we demand eternal peace.
2. No foreign intervention in the civil war.
3. There must be complete assurances of freedom of assembly, freedom of speech, freedom of the press.

In the same proclamation they have called upon the local government to:

1. Assume the responsibility for shooting over the heads of the students on the evening of November 25th.
2. Cancel the order prohibiting all meetings without the sanction of the Military Governor given on November 25th.
3. Assure the safety of students from illegal arrest.
4. Demand from the *Central News* an apology for their stupid criticisms, and they are asked to apologize to the students who attended the meeting.

It appears that the *Central News* made some remarks about the communist character of the meeting, and said that a certain Mr. Wang attempted to make a speech but was shouted down and man-handled by the students, thus proving that the University was not the bulwark of democracy that some students claimed it to be. The final words of the proclamation read: "For the sake of peace, for the sake of democracy, for the sake of the Three Principles of the People we demand now the freedom which the government has promised us! Let every man's conscience be the final judge—neither with your money nor with your strength support the civil war!" There have been more efforts by the faculty to make the students return to work: so far their efforts have failed.

December 1st, Murder of the Students . . . FOUR students are dead.

I do not know their names, and perhaps their names do not matter. They were young, and they committed no crime; they were killed by hand-grenades; not one of them died outright—they lingered for a few hours, but by six o'clock this evening they were all dead.

It is difficult to understand what happened—there are so many conflicting rumours, and there may be many things we shall never understand. I shall try to describe this thing simply, as it has been

207

told to me; but I can hardly see what I am writing. It is necessary that this thing should be told, because it affects all the schools and all the Universities in the world. Students have died like this in Germany and Japan; I did not expect that they would die like this in China. There have been far greater crimes in history: millions upon millions of people have been murdered in cold blood in recent years: but this has happened in China where scholarship is so deeply respected that until recently only scholars were given posts in the government. There has occurred today an incident of such small importance to the world that hardly anyone outside Kunming will ever hear of it. It was so small a thing, so indescribably small a thing, that a quarter of an hour after it happened the passers-by could see no sign of it—the splinters of the hand-grenade thrown into a college courtyard had been removed, the bloodstains had been washed away, the bodies had been taken to hospital, and the whole incident disappeared into thin air. But in the long history of Chinese education there can have been few so terrifying.

Many things happened this morning. Between eleven and twelve o'clock three Universities—the Sino-French University, Yunnan University and Lienta—were attacked. The Engineering College at the centre of the city was also attacked, but no details of the attack have come through except that some thugs beat up a professor who was experimenting with a galvanometer and accused him of communicating to Yenan with the galvanometer, which they smashed with their fists. There may be more dead in the city: there are certainly about twenty wounded, some of them seriously. The attacks appear to have been careful and concerted, and this time the thugs were armed.

First, all the furniture in the Sino-French University was smashed; then an effort was made to break through the gates of Yunnan University which is only a few hundred yards away. They succeeded in breaking through the gates, but they did not succeed in entering the University, which must be reached by steep flights of steps, and therefore can be defended. They then went along the long road which leads to the Great West Gate—a road which is known as the Street of the Forest of Learning. They entered a middle school and smashed up the furniture there. They went out through the Great West Gate and stormed the Teachers' Training College, and when they had finished storming the col-
208

lege three students were dying from the splinters of a hand-grenade two of them had thrown. One was a girl. At about the same time, between two and three hundred soldiers came down the road past the University of Lienta. They marched up and down outside the campus, and one of them was about to throw a hand-grenade, when one of the professors interfered; the hand-grenade was thrown wild, and instead of killing the hundreds of students inside the campus, killed a young music teacher who had come to have a haircut at the University.

"They had clubs and sticks and stones in their pockets, and some had hand-grenades," S. told me. "I was there—we could see them coming, and we knew what they were coming for. They tore down the notices on the walls—notices in praise of democracy—and they began to try to get into the University by forcing the gates. One or two did get in, and we held them prisoner. The battle went on for nearly two hours, and we never knew if reinforcements were coming up, and we never knew how long the battle would last. Three times they attacked the gates, and each time an officer blew his whistle—it was all so military. And then, when we were taking the wounded to hospital, the soldiers were still there with clubs and carrying-poles, and sometimes they robbed the people who were carrying the wounded to hospital; and what was worse than anything was that they frightened the doctors and nurses away from the hospital, so that there was no one who could care for the wounded."

He does not know how long it will last, or whether it will ever end. Is this the climax, or just the beginning? He has the long narrow face of a northerner, and he came into my room while I was in bed, saying: "They've started killing! Now we know where we are!" And now in the University library, late at night, some of the dead are lying on camp-beds, and candles are burning, and young students are crying, and they will remain awake all night. "We're going to guard the University. We'll have guards at the gate with baseball clubs, and we'll examine everyone who enters. They've killed a girl and three boys—do they expect they can do that with impunity? This afternoon General Kuan Lin-seng, the Garrison Commander, came along in his car and spoke to us. We were completely silent. He said he would punish the criminals, but who were the criminals? Gangs of soldiers are marching through the city assaulting all the schools and all the people in

209

the schools—does he think he can do that with impunity?" He was livid with rage and excitement, and kept mixing up Chinese and English.

December 2nd . . . IT WOULD hardly be possible to imagine a more beautiful day: the campus flooded with young people in blue gowns, the sky blue, the blue flag flying at half mast. The library has changed beyond recognition. Where there were tables and stools and catalogues there is nothing: they have been swept away, and in their place there are only the two camp-beds, the two dead boys covered up to the chest with blankets, their heads bandaged and their faces like wax. There are heaped flowers on the blankets and a terrible sullen silence reigns over the library, which has never looked so bare.

Coffins have arrived. The doors of the library are flanked with those immense red-wood coffins, and already on the campus there are evergreen arches bearing the four characters for "Freedom" and "Democracy"—nothing more.

Later . . . THE ceremony this afternoon was frightening, and perhaps most frightening because it was simple. There were no longer the tremendous blue skies of the morning: mist, grey mist, and scurrying clouds came from over the burial mounds, and there was a wind like a knife. I have never known a day so full of foreboding. The students came, not only from the University but from all the middle schools around, and they stayed there, singing songs or mostly silent: while the preparations were made.

The four dead lay on the camp-beds in the library. The girl looked incredibly beautiful, all hint of sorrow and pain had disappeared. There were oranges and flowers on the blankets. There were young students cleaning up the wounds and bandaging the heads of the dead; and all so quietly and with such desperate earnestness, as though almost they were accustomed to these things. The girl students from the middle schools sang songs with a heartbreaking slow mournfulness, songs which never seemed to end; and meanwhile it grew colder. The coffins were laid beneath the evergreen arches: the coffins were red and gaping like wounds. Till perhaps four o'clock the bodies remained in the library, so we waited outside in an endless monotony of expectancy, the air growing colder every moment. All the students wore small black oblongs on their arms or on their coats. There were rumours that

210

even the encoffining ceremony would be considered by the local authorities as an assembly which must be broken up; but though we half expected the soldiers, none came. There was the mother of Li Liu-lien, one of the students who has been killed; there were students who had known the dead and whose lips were quivering. Inside the library the air was thick with blood and death, but on the campus there was only this waiting expectancy.

And then they came out, one by one, the camp-beds with the bodies lying on them carried by young stretcher-bearers with white lint bandaged over their nostrils. They came very slowly. There was whimpering, but only once was there screaming, and that was when the boy's mother recognized him at the moment when he was being lifted into the coffin; and she ran wildly across the campus towards him. Her screaming turned us all into ice, but the ice grew harder when we noticed the wet red stains on the camp-bed so thick that it was as though all the blood had been drained out of him, and gleaming in the faint light. Quilts were first thrown carefully into the coffins; the bodies were laid in them. And then there was singing, and firecrackers exploded, and the sky grew greyer.

December 3rd . . . THE dead were Pan Yen, a girl student of the Teachers' Training College attached to Lienta, Yu Tsai, a young music-teacher at the Nanching Normal School, a boy from the Teachers' Training College and another from an engineering school. The students say now that they are determined to take the coffins through the city; they are determined to be avenged; they are determined that there shall be democracy and freedom in this country. "You have the right to free assembly," General Kuan Lin-seng is reported to have said, "and I have the right to shoot." These may not be his exact words, but something very similar has been said, and these murders have been committed. The students are heart-broken, and hardly care what happens to them.

I have been reading the student proclamations: "We have no weapons but the righteousness of our cause." "The civil war must end—we have eight years of war to recover from." "We are drifting into fascism, into the rule of the mob, into the rule of the secret police with hand-grenades." "Men of good will all over the world, help us to end the civil war, help us to have democracy and freedom."

We have been to see the Garrison Commander in the hope that

211

we can find some solution to the affair: he has promised to see us tomorrow. Meanwhile there are rumours that two—some say, three—have been arrested for the murder and will be immediately put on trial by the military authorities; but if, as the students say, it was the military who condoned and even effected these crimes, there is not much hope that we shall find anything from the trial.

December 4th . . . THIS morning, between 10:30 and 1 o'clock, an American professor and myself have been to see General Kuan Lin-seng, the garrison commander, in the desperate hope that some method may be found to get the secret police off the streets during the funeral procession. I think we have failed. He has told us nothing that we did not know before, but there are places where he has clarified the issue and once he admitted brutally, and in a kind of terror for the consequences, that he possessed no power.

The interview took place in a small room upstairs, with a blue tablecloth and a few wooden chairs. There were scrolls on the wall and little tables for the tea-glasses: he sat at the end of the long table facing the door opening on the courtyard. The garrison commander has a bull-dog face, heavy eyebrows, a thickset squat man with large hands which he placed on the tablecloth. When his adjutants came in, he told them gruffly: "Go away—can't you see I am talking with foreigners?" He has met Americans in south-west Yunnan, and it is necessary to insist that he treated us with the greatest respect.

He began by opening the *Central Daily News* and pointing to an article by his chief-of-staff which appeared in this morning's edition. This in itself was not surprising, but he insisted that the account given by his chief-of-staff contained the whole truth of the events which led up to the tragedy, and seemed in some way so dependent upon the chief-of-staff's views that it was impossible to resist the fear that the chief-of-staff may have known far more of the truth of the situation than the garrison-commander himself. General Kuan Lin-seng said: "I will speak from the heart—the whole truth," and said he was glad we had come so that foreigners might learn the truth rather than the garbled versions which have apparently already appeared abroad. He said he had the greatest respect for the students, he had been a student at Whampoa Academy himself, he would never allow his soldiers to commit any crimes against the students and he had done everything in his
212

power to prevent the murders, but at that moment his voice dropped and he seemed confused. He then went on to describe the events leading up to the murders. He said—we had not heard this, for we had not read the newspaper—that Yenan broadcast at 6:30 on the night of November 23rd the statement that the University would come out on strike and that a University strike committee had already been formed. He was extremely bitter against the Communists, and said that everyone knew there were Communists in the University; at this point K. interrupted him and asked how many. "Not many, but they are very powerful and have weapons. We have learned this from our own agents inside the University." He then accused some of the professors of being behind the movement and several times mentioned Dr. Chen Tuan-shen, saying once that Dr. Chen was a Communist in Kuomintang clothing, a statement that was surprising, for this distinguished economist was a friend of ex-Vice-President Wallace, a member of the People's Political Council and had often represented China abroad. And then he went on to say in the most matter of fact voice that something like a revolution had been imminent, and only by great good fortune had disaster been avoided. *"We knew that after the meeting there would be processions through the city, public buildings would be attacked and foreigners would be assaulted."* This was surprising, and the statement became more surprising a few minutes later when he added to the first statement: "They wanted the cover of a dark night for their evil deeds." We were asked to believe that the students were intending to use hidden stores of ammunition; they would burn the public buildings: they would create disorder everywhere.

What was strange was that in spite of his knowledge he had taken no measures to prevent these disorders apart from sending ten or fifteen plain-clothes men to attend the meeting. He insisted that the shooting was against bandits, and not at the students. The students had stated that they heard the bullets whining over their heads. General Kuan laughed a little, and said: "I have been a soldier long enough to know that you cannot hear bullets whining over your head—they make no sound at all." This did not, of course, explain the explosion of the mortars, and I have heard bullets whining over my head in Spain, though they may have been small shells. "When I heard that there was firing against bandits in the neighborhood of the University, I ordered my soldiers to

213

withdraw." "Where were you?" "Here."

It was at this point that General Kuan spoke of the disorders among the students. They were Communists, they were armed and they were disorderly. A certain Mr. Wang had entered the meeting and asked for the privilege of speaking to the students. After some delay he was allowed to speak, but afterwards he was beaten up by the students—this was shocking, for it proved that the University was not a democratic body. The son of his chief-of-staff had been beaten at the same time. One of us, I have forgotten which, thereupon asked General Kuan whether the man who had attended the meeting could be traced, since the students had published their belief that he was a secret agent sent either by General Kuan himself or by the Kuomintang Chairman Li Chung-huang. General Kuan dismissed the matter briefly by saying that it would be too difficult to find him. But a moment later he said that the firing the students heard came from blank shots fired by a student called Ho Chung in an effort to create disorder; and it was not possible to ask him how, in a crowd of perhaps 4,000 students, his secret agents had recognized a solitary student in the darkness. We were not there to probe his story, even though the story appeared at all times incredible: we were there to discover whether something could be done to prevent further murders.

A little while later he went on to say how frightened he had been at the thought of the disorders following the meeting—he had referred to this already, but the full horror of the event was so disturbing that he repeated: "They wanted it to be dark, so that they could use fire and hand-grenades." There was nothing we could say. The thought of the University students proclaiming a revolution from Kunming was not one which we could accept: the night was bitterly cold, and by all accounts the meeting was perfectly orderly. General Kuan said bitterly: "On the 26th November, the day following the deaths of the students, the students posted up on the walls of the city proclamations against the civil war and asking for a coalition government, and various other things—the withdrawal of Hurley and Wedemeyer, freedom of speech and freedom of assembly. These proclamations were an incitement to the people——"

K. said: "I understand that freedom of speech and freedom of assembly have already been granted by the central government."

214

"This is true, but we were faced with terrible responsibilities, and it was necessary for us to act in order to safeguard the peace. Remember, we knew from our agents that the students were armed. We knew that they were asking the factories to come out on strike, asking the farmers not to pay taxes, asking the other schools to come out on strike. They were disturbing the social order. Anyone who criticized their proclamations and speeches was immediately set upon and beaten. The headmasters of some middle schools asked me to send soldiers to protect their schools. I have not dared to send them. It might create disorder. Even officers have been beaten by the students. There are pamphlets actually insulting the Generalissimo. The students set upon one officer and beat him with stones, but the good students still want to return to their classes, and they have organized an anti-strike committee to help young people to return to their classes."

About the attack on Lienta he said:

"Three hundred officer cadets were simply marching to barracks down the road outside the University. They were unarmed —even their barracks are unarmed. A hand-grenade was thrown out of the school, over the wall, and it was thrown by somebody who didn't know how to throw it—the pin wasn't pulled out. One of the cadets picked it up, but was prevented from throwing it back into the school by an officer." This was all: no mention was made of the young school-teacher who had been killed.

It seemed that the General had no desire to discuss immediately the attack on the Teachers' Training College, for at this point he referred to the trial which had taken place on the previous day. He said sadly that he had invited the students to send representatives, but the students refused; he had also sent invitations to Dr. Yeh Chih-sing and Professor Tsa Liang-tsao, but neither of them had attended, and the two jurists were present from the University on their own responsibility. He said bitterly: "Dr. Yeh and Professor Tsa must have known they would be found in the wrong. There was much evidence to prove that the hand-grenade was thrown from inside the University, and they were afraid to face the evidence." We said that the students claimed that the soldiers passed up and down outside the University, deliberately provoking the students with insults and striking down the posters on the walls outside. "This is a mistake—they simply passed down the road, and the students flung mud at them, and stones, and one of them threw a hand-grenade. Why should these soldiers

215

say that the soldiers threw a hand-grenade? If I wanted to attack the students, would I use only one hand-grenade?"

It was getting late. A servant came and brought more tea, visitors were being dismissed peremptorily and the General was getting into his stride. The introduction was over, and soon we should come to the main incident of that tragic day, but before he came to that, the General said: "You must believe that we have never had the slightest intention of hurting the students—all this has happened because there are dissident elements in the University who have nothing to lose by the deaths of some of the students."

He explained the murders very briefly. It was true that some officers had taken part in the scramble outside the Teachers' Training College on the previous day, November 30th. It was true that some of them returned the following day for revenge. It was true that the men who were arrested and put up for trial were ex-soldiers, but it was a long time since they were dismissed from the Army and at the time they were wearing plain clothes. He said that the men who threw the hand-grenades had been arrested and already condemned—they had received the hand-grenades from a certain Mr. Chiang Kai whom the police were now searching for. And this was all—he could throw no more light on the murders, but asked us to read the official report of the trial and to pay particular attention to the statement written by his chief-of-staff.

He then went on to explain that after the murders he had done everything possible to safeguard the place; he had himself gone to the University. "The students welcomed and surrounded me, and asked me questions and I promised that the students who behaved need fear no more occurrences of this kind, and I said that the criminals would be punished according to law. I did not sleep that night. I was in constant conference with my advisers. I addressed the school authorities and told them that it was not a student strike, but an effort to create as much bloodshed as possible. I went to the University again the next morning, but this time the students did not treat me as well as before: it was evident that dissident elements had aroused them against me: the day before they greeted me with their hearts, but now they were ordered to attack me": and then he went on to attack the students for allowing the dead bodies to remain unburied—"This is being done deliberately by the students: they leave the bodies there,
216

with the evil smell, and this is done just to inflame the students."
This last statement was incorrect, for I had seen the bodies being
nailed into the coffins.

I said: "Did you know that the murder of the girl took place
under particularly revolting circumstances—she was wounded by
hand-grenades, then knifed or bayoneted in the stomach and
breasts, and then jumped upon."

"No, I didn't know this," he answered, but did not seem very
shocked.

All this had been introductory to the main purpose, which was
to devise some method by which the murders (for it was impossible to believe that they were not deliberate murders) should
be stopped. We had no power. We were not delegated by the
University, and the delegates sent by the University had failed
to find him three days before; the students refused to see him, or
to send messages to him, believing that he was the murderer. We
were not convinced that he was the murderer. He was a soldier,
and he said repeatedly that he would never allow his soldiers to
attack students: in this he was convincing, or nearly convincing.
He hated Communists furiously, and it was curious that he should
pointedly have stated that one of the crimes committed by the
students was that they insulted the Generalissimo. They had not
insulted the Generalissimo: they had called for an end to the civil
war which the Generalissimo was pursuing. They were not loyal,
as he was loyal, to the Generalissimo, and I believe that in his
eyes this was their greatest crime—he had not fired on the students, but he had allowed his soldiers to be used by others, by
Kuomintang Chairman Li Chung-huang or by the agents of General Tai Li, the head of the secret police. The more we spoke to
him, the more innocent he appeared; but there were moments
when the innocence was almost too childlike to be credible. We
asked him whether, if the students held the funeral procession,
he would personally protect them.

He said: "If they hold a procession, tragic things may happen,
but I guarantee that my secret agents and my soldiers will not be
on the streets. The soldiers would be afraid to go near a procession of this kind."

"Are there any other secret police?"

"Yes—the secret police of the former Governor Li Chung-
huang. They are not under my control."

This was sufficiently startling, since he was the direct military

217

representative of Chungking. There are rumours (which I am inclined to believe) that General Kuan and Chairman Li Chung-huang are not on good terms. There is a story that on the day before the murders General Kuan had promised one of the professors that soldiers would take no part in the attacks on the students, but at some time during the afternoon Mr. Li called on the general and pointed out that they possessed instructions to put down the strike by force, and it was necessary to use soldiers. It looked very likely that General Kuan had allowed himself to be involved in the affair, for though he is reported to have said: "I refuse to be a murderer" to Mr. Li, he had condoned the use of his own military forces in the attack on November 25th, and may even have condoned the murder of the students as long as the responsibility did not lie directly in his hands.

He said: "I am in contact with Chungking continually. I inform the Generalissimo about these matters three times a day, and receive his orders. He has said that everything must be settled peacefully."

"This means that the responsibility and blame are all yours?"

He looked hurt and miserable, banged his fist on the table and almost shouted: "Yes, no one understands the terrible position I am in. All the blame falls on me." Shortly after this outburst he said: "I am out-numbered. There are others as well as me. For my part I will do everything I can to prevent further disturbance, but——"

The implications were growing clearer. There were others behind the scenes, more powerful. Who were they? There was the Governor Lu Han, who was installed in office on the day of the murder, a general who had only recently returned from Indo-China, a man who was known to share some of the liberal views of his half-brother, General Yung Lun, who had been recalled to Chungking as a result of the civil war. General Lu Han was in a delicate situation, and it was difficult to believe that he wanted to see bloodshed with all its unavoidable and unpredictable consequences so early during his tenure of office. There was Chairman Li Chung-huang, who retained the office of municipal affairs and wielded enormous powers by reason of his connection with the Party. There may have been others.

But if General Kuan Lin-seng was, as he said, out-numbered, there remained some hope that a person of high ministerial rank could be brought down from Chungking, a man with such power

218

that he could order the secret police off the streets and allow the procession to move unhindered. T. V. Soong had flown down when Lung Yun was removed. Why could not some responsible Minister be invited down? The matter was serious, and involved public feeling in America and England, where sooner or later men would be aghast that soldiers had thrown hand-grenades at students for no other reason than that they disagreed with the government's desire for a civil war.

I asked whether I could fly up to Chungking on a Chinese army plane: I knew Dr. Sun Fo, the son of Dr. Sun Yat-sen, and Marshal Feng Yu-hsiang, and thought I could induce them to use influence in the highest quarters to send down an emissary with complete powers. "But they are not powerful," he objected. "They are not powerful enough." He looked frightened. We discussed the possibility at some length, but it seemed that only the Generalissimo had power to settle the matter, and since it was only too certain that the Generalissimo had been misinformed, it was too late to ask him to send down someone with plenipotentiary powers to overrule any decisions which might be made by the Governor, the former Governor or the dark shadow, whoever he was and whoever he represented, who might order the throwing of the next bomb. General Kuan had almost acquiesced to this solution, when the telephone bell rang: when he returned, he said: "It is impossible—I am the representative of Chungking. This cannot be done."

By this time I was feeling feverish and exhausted. There seemed to be nothing, nothing at all, that could be done; and there was no assurance that the secret police could be removed from the streets, for though we believed, or half believed that General Kuan was in mortal terror of further incidents, there remained the former Governor and the invisible presence of perhaps some other power. He asked us to convey to the students a request that he should be told when the procession would take place and offered to provide a guard of honour. And then we went out into the blazing sunshine, across the lake towards the arched stone gate leading to the city. His green car followed us, and he jumped out and begged my companions not to reveal anything he had said.

December 5th . . . YESTERDAY some members of the Yunnan People's Political Council came to pay their respects to the dead.

219

Today, outside the North Gate, the Great West Gate and the Little West Gate I noticed crossed timbers woven with barbed wire. J. says: "The soldiers have been given orders to prevent the procession from entering the city by closing the gates." K. told me this evening that it was accounted bad luck to allow bodies to enter the gates—it brought misfortune to the city; this may be true, but it happens occasionally, and the students are so determined on the procession that I doubt whether they can be prevented. They do not care if they are killed, as long as the civil war comes to an end and constitutional government can be brought into force. I have been down to the library again. There is no longer the great grief of Sunday; the students look hard and more responsible than ever. One student said: "The professors have taught us to be democratic, then why are they not behind us?" I try to explain that the funeral procession through the streets of Kunming is interpreted by some as deliberate provocation. "But what else can we do? So silently to bury them in the campus? We cannot return to our studies until the murderers are punished, and we know who the murderers are." I am beginning to doubt whether they do know—there are darker forces than they imagine in this land. He said: "Dr. Fu Ssu-nien, the acting Chancellor of Peking University, has asked us to return to our studies and to put the matter in his hands. He promises us that the murders will be avenged, but can we be sure that he will avenge them? Is he powerful enough? He is utterly sincere, but we can hardly trust anybody except ourselves."

I have been to see Liu Lien. He is so shocked by the murders that he can hardly speak, stutters abominably and says over and over again: "Why did they kill students? Why didn't they kill us?" He said: "There are some professors who put it down to the illiterate soldiers—this is being unfair to the illiterate soldiers." And then again, just before I left: "Out of this grief, there may come life. Even in our corrupt government there are members from the three Universities comprising Lienta. If the students can demonstrate the strength of the human intelligence they may yet save China."

I do not know what to think of these events: the mind is numbed continually by the possibility of more murders.

December 7th . . . It is useless to go on rumours, and there are so many. I can understand why the students are wild with horror and determined to take the coffins through the city; and they hardly care what happens to them. The Garrison Commander has insisted that there must be no more meetings, the local press is still gagged, there is absolutely no evidence that a factual report of the murders has reached Chungking.

I am so sick to death of all this bloodshed. At any moment the students may take the coffins through the streets, and there is nothing on earth that will prevent an *agent-provocateur* from throwing another grenade. I have been to see the strike committee. I have begged them to postpone the procession for at least a few more days, and they listen very politely, but they say the students are determined. This is the greatest University in China: if they do not assert their rights for freedom now, no other University in China will achieve them. They have their martyrs still.

There is a curious sullen temper among them. They are still half-dazed with shock. There are still blood-red posters on the wall openly attacking General Kuan Lin-seng and Chairman Li Chung-huang of a deliberate murder. There are student guards at the gates of all the Universities with baseball bats in their hands, there are notices on every wall shouting out for freedom of assembly, for freedom of publication, for *habeas corpus*, for a coalition government, for democracy; there is still a strike; there is still the feeling that we are on the edge of the abyss. A minor official has come down from the Ministry of Education, but he has no power over the local garrison command or the provincial government. There are rumours, which may be true, that General Kuan is prepared to hand in his resignation. Fu Ssu-nien, the Chancellor of Peking University, has arrived. He saw General Kuan three days ago and said bluntly: "I was your friend up to this moment, but now you are no longer my friend—these students are like my own children to me," and walked out in a towering hatred for this military despotism, for though General Kuan may not be responsible for the murders, he is responsible for peace and order and could probably have prevented them.

Worse than anything else is the statement I have heard from one of the professors that on the day after the strike, Chairman Li Chung-huang invited the headmasters of middle-schools and the President of Yunnan University to a tea-party, at which General Kuan was present. Chairman Li is reported to have said that he was determined to break the strike, and there were exactly three methods by which it could be broken. First, it could be

221

broken by organizing some students into an anti-strike committee which would be given the support of the provincial government. Secondly, it could be broken by using thugs to break up demonstrations. Thirdly, it could be broken by armed force. He did not use the word "thugs." He used the words "Plain clothes police," but the difference is of little account. Then why were Chen Chi-ta and Chen Yun-lu arrested? Were they armed thugs, paid by the provincial government to throw the grenades? Chiang Kai has not yet been found. Is Chiang Kai only another name for someone in the provincial government? Who possesses hand-grenades in this city? It is true that some have been stolen from the American armed forces, but it would be considerably easier to obtain them from General Kuan himself. General Kuan said the students were armed. There is no evidence that they were. He said that there were communists in the University, but he has produced no evidence of the existence of any. I have asked one of the students whether he believes the rumours that the murders were ordered from Chungking "as an example to others." "No, but there is nothing to prove the opposite. There is a tremendous struggle going on, in which we are pawns. The Kuomintang wants to maintain its dictatorship and fight the civil war. We were the first to object, and they want to know how strong we are. They do not realize that we are desperately weak, but all the stronger for our weakness. We are the greatest University in China, we represent the only intellectual force in the country which is respected abroad, and we are determined to do everything in our power to prevent the war. We might conceivably have done nothing if the military had been so foolish as to shoot over our heads. We were enraged; and we were determined to shout for political democracy and a coalition government, and it didn't matter to us that the Communists were shouting for the same thing. So we came on strike. There were probably orders from Chungking saying that the provincial government had complete power to prevent the strike—in time all the schools in the country would come out on our side. So they used their complete power. I don't think they intended to kill us, but we were killed. Some idiot in the provincial government thought he would make a show of force, and it must have been someone very high up—but no one knows who it was, though there is mounting evidence that it was Chairman Li Chung-huang himself. He has killed students before. Like all criminals, he can only follow the tracks over which he has gone

222

before. He detests and fears the rising intelligence of the schools, which will put an end to the corruption in the Kuomintang Party in time. We worship Sun Yat-sen, but he died poor. How many of the leading officials in the Kuomintang Party are poor? Not many, and Chairman Li is among the richest of all."

I do not know how much credence to put to this story, but I have an increasing suspicion that the murders were committed only indirectly by the two ex-soldiers who are under arrest and who are going to be shot tomorrow.

December 8th . . . FOR some odd reason I carried the *Analects* of Confucius around with me during the Civil War. They are hardly more than anecdotes; no one knows how many of the recorded statements were really made by Confucius; there must be some truth in the story that some passages were forged for political reasons, or because it was thought afterwards that Confucius would have said something of the sort, or because a legend had grown up and it was necessary to give substance to the legend. There are few things so delightful as these *obiter dicta*. Here there are no Socratic arguments. Confucius has all Dr. Johnson's delight in apothegm; and since the disciples listen industriously and are only too pleased to receive the master's advice, we can almost see them craning their necks and solemnly bowing at the words which hit their hearts. There is a great deal of nonsense in the *Analects*. I am sometimes wearied beyond endurance by the Chinese delight in anecdotage. It does not seem to me necessary that we should know Confucius's habits in detail, how he would walk before the Emperor, how he arranged his sleeping quarters. "We are the greatest gossips in the world," Liu Lien said once; and reading Confucius and the *Spring and Autumn Annals* I am half prepared to believe him.

But this morning I came upon this from the *Analects*:

> The Master said, Be of unwavering good faith, love learning, if you are thrown back on the defensive be ready to die for the good way. Avoid those countries where dangerous courses are pursued; avoid those also where the people rebel; but show yourselves openly when the good way prevails under Heaven. When there is no good way, the scholar must seek solitude. And if it should happen that the good way prevails in the land, then it is a disgrace for the scholar to live

223

in poverty and obscurity. But when the good way does not prevail over the land, how disgraceful it is to receive honour and riches!

December 9th . . . I WAS very moved when H. asked whether I would like to read the biographies of the four people who were killed. I did not want to read them—there were times when it was better to imagine martyrs living anonymous lives. They seemed, when they were lying on the camp-beds in the library, so very much like other students, a little frail and thin and not very well fed. In death they had reached a stature which no other students had reached, and what did it matter that they had lived like all the rest of us such obscure lives?

I said something to this effect to H., who was almost angry. He said bitterly: "If they had wanted to kill the best, they have succeeded. A girl from one of the oldest families in China, a young music teacher passionately in love with music, the only son of a poor peasant and a boy who was so representative that no one can say more of him than that he liked sports and worked hard. Is it fate? If you threw a hand-grenade at random among the students on the campus, would you find you had killed such good people? All four of them were poor. Not one was a radical. I have spoken to people who knew them, and they always say: 'It is better if they had killed us—we are not so good.'"

When he was gone, he still seemed to be in my room, the young Honanese with the hair falling across his forehead. He looked ill and pale. I doubt whether he has slept much or eaten much since the murder; and there was so much decision on his young face that I am beginning to have greater hope for China. The miracle may happen. The pressure of the schools may prevent the two governments from carrying out the civil war, for even now the scholars of China wield invisible powers. The Master said: "It may be that one has to give one's life in order to achieve goodness." He has translated for me the biographies of the dead students.

PAN YEN

She was born twenty-eight years ago in the small feudal city of Suichow. She belonged to an old family that had been declining for some time, yet it still retained a position of importance. She was brought up according to the old-fashioned custom of her family, and so for seventeen years she passed her life inside the house. At that time modern thoughts were beginning to fill people's minds, and Pan Yen recognized the deep importance of being well educated in order to achieve a responsible position in society. She was determined to be educated, but coming from such a family it was almost impossible for her to enter school. She was learning her lessons privately from her cousin, and in the winter of 1934, as a result of her hard work, she entered a junior middle school. I must point out that for a girl to enter a middle school after never having studied in a primary school was no easy thing. She requested her parents for permission to join the school, and in the end she succeeded. Meanwhile she employed all her influence to allow other girls from her family to enter school. So, with her help, I too was allowed to join the school the next year.

She finished the three year course of junior high in two and a half years; then she took the entrance examination for the Girls' Normal School. It was very unfortunate that war swept over the country before she could enter the school. She was not the kind of person who would willingly submit to fate and remain enslaved at home; and so, being deprived of her chance to study, she entered the army.

One cold night in winter I came across her at a railway station. She had joined the Eleventh Army. Fully equipped, she stood there waiting for the train to go to Suichow, where a battle was about to take place. Except for the journey from Suichow to Su in Anhuei, she went on foot all the way from Su to Huangch'uan in Honan, passing through Hankow and Ichang, fighting against sickness and disease as well as the enemy, always going by night. She had joined the army, and she was determined to be always the last to retreat. She was undaunted by danger, and found comfort in it.

In the winter of 1938 she arrived at Ichang with no other belongings but the thin uniform she was wearing. I do not know what happened to her during that winter. The next time I heard of her she had joined a girl's middle school, but she stayed there only a year—not because she did not want to study, but because she wanted to study too much, and this was not a school where studying could be done profitably.

She arrived in Chungking in the winter of 1940. She entered school, but in the end months of poverty and misfortune made her give up. Then for four years she kept on struggling, and at last she gained her aim and joined the Teachers' Training College. Once again she could study—but now she has gone. She has gone before us all.

HSUN CHI-CHUNG

He was a boy of only seventeen, a student of Kunghua Technical School, and strongly built, fond of sport and writing. He had considerable ability at these things, and was very good-natured and liked by his teachers and schoolmates.

His parents were deeply grieved by the loss of their son, yet they plainly understand the significance of their loss. His elder brother, also a student, heard of the death of the boy while he was making speeches in the street. He rushed to the side of his dead brother and swore to take vengeance on the murderers.

His death indeed was glorious. When the Teachers' Training College was being attacked, and the students there were outnumbered, they were forced to retreat to the Technical College and summon aid. He at once gathered some of his schoolmates together, and with a large club in his hand led the party against the thugs. The shrapnel from the grenade pierced his skull; he died four hours later in hospital.

LI LIU-LIEN

Li Liu-lien was eighteen years old, a native of Chekiang. I met him first in 1942 in the Provincial Sichung Middle School in Sikong Province. He was studying in the school because his father had some business there. He was well-known for being an assiduous student.

Some time later he left Sichung and wandered over the country with his father. He was born in Shantung. Since the beginning of the war, he was always travelling from place to place, yet he remained an innocent boy. He entered the Teachers' Training College of Lienta in 1945; it was there that we met again. We lived in the same room, studied together and played together. He only lived for his studies, and had almost no feeling for politics.

The shooting on the night of November 25th aroused his deepest anguish. He spent all his time working with the strike committee. About noon, on December 1st, sixty or seventy armed ruffians broke into the Teachers' Training College. The students all took refuge in the adjoining Kunghua Technical School by forcing their way through the windows. They were provoked by the sight of the ruffians wantonly destroying the school furniture. Five or six students immediately rushed to prevent them. Li Liu-lien was among them. After the hand-grenade exploded, he fell at the gate, all covered with blood. He was carried to hospital by the other students, but he died on the way.

YU TSAI

He was so gentle, so kind-hearted and so quiet, yet his body was sturdy. I met him for the first time three months ago at Nanching Middle School. He was fond of weeping, but never for his own sake. Once he wept for a whole night after talking with a friend who had given up all hope. He did not behave like this out of cowardice, but because he loved men.

He was born into a wealthy family in Shanghai—a family without warmth or liveliness. When the war broke out, he left his home and went to Chungking with a small sum of money which he secured by selling the only thing he possessed—a bicycle. On his way he took part in all kinds of warwork, being especially attached to the work which concerned refugee-children. In Chungking he joined the army, for a while he was conductor of a ferry. He refused to receive any money from home, but provided money for his friends when they were badly in need.

Six months before he died, he returned from India. His father sent for him to take care of the family property. He refused, and advised his father not to worry about money.

He was twenty-four, and he was born in Hanyuan, in Chekiang. He had graduated from a normal school in Chungking, majoring in music. He was a member of the Kuomintang Party. When he died, he was a music-teacher in Nanching Middle School.

He praised the passionate spirit of Beethoven but deeply regretted the silence of Goethe.

227

December 10th . . . I HAVE been to see Robert Winter. He sits disconsolately on the edge of his bed, wondering, like everyone else, what will happen next. He has kept aloof from the tragedy, but even here, in that remote eyrie perched up above the stage of a warlord's crumbling private theatre, the impact of it has reached him and hurt him. He has spent nearly thirty years in China, but nothing like this has happened before; and at first he was very quiet, not caring to discuss it.

It was very quiet up there. The hawks beat against the tiled roof next door, but you can see the lake through the eucalyptus trees. Where does one go from there? The sleeping beauty is kissed, suddenly awakes, but what does she do then? Probably like the Malays, she runs amok. All the pent-up Confucian rigidity of the Chinese mind disappears, and you hear the coarse laughter of some Taoist priest with an oiled topknot who knows that the rigid ritual is a waste of effort—men die, their deaths more important than the ceremonies which surround their deaths. And the students? Numbed with grief still, but the numbness will pass. Already I have seen that terrible desire for martyrdom which I saw among the Spanish soldiers in Barcelona, when the Germans and the Moors were approaching the gates.

"They want to die," I said. "They believe there is a conspiracy against them, and they are determined on death."

"It is not so very strange," he said. "It has happened before. I do not know whether it is true of the students, but it is true of the Chinese, in the same way that it was true of the Balinese in 1908, when they hurled themselves against the Dutch. You remember how they dressed in their ceremonial robes, with garlands and jewels on their heads, and begged the Dutch soldiers to fire on them. The women were worse than the men. When the soldiers stopped firing out of sheer weariness of so much bloodshed, the women threw handfuls of gold coins as payment for their own deaths; and if the bullets did not come soon enough, they stabbed themselves with their krises, and they were all killed in that shambles of Den Pasar. And I remember reading that the next morning a young headman came to see the Dutch commander and said that he had been away the day before and missed being killed with the others, and asked to be shot. They refused, of course. So he stabbed himself in front of them all."

He paused and began searching for Arthur Waley's *The Way and the Power.* "I don't understand this desire for martyrdom," he

228

went on. "I have never felt it, but I can sympathize with it—it springs from very deep roots in the human consciousness. When a civilization is doomed, as the civilization of the Balinese was doomed by foreign invasion, what else could they do? Salvador de Madariaga says of his own countrymen: 'Nature, allied with reason in the Englishman, bowing to reason in the Frenchman, triumphs here over reason.' It is unreasonable to seek martyrdom —it may even be stupid, but surely it is splendid? Some of the students have never felt their responsibilities so deeply before. Emotion—this terrible emotion of martyrdom—comes in, and they are side-tracked from their purpose, just as the Balinese in a sense were side-tracked from their emotion—their desire was only another form of a desire for life."

I could not always follow this argument: there were overtones which impinged too hardily on the living. Were these quiet grief-stricken students really overcome with a desire for martyrdom when they insisted on holding the funeral procession in spite of the threats of the local government. It was something more complex than martyrdom. There was envy in it—envy for the dead, and there was also pride—pride that out of all the Universities in China they alone had been visited by death; pride that they were the spearhead of scholarship; pride that they more than any others held the destiny of China in their hands. For they were very conscious of this. They desired martyrdom, but they desired also to live. By some miracle, though Lienta was bombed during the war, no students had been killed; but in Fuhtan University in Szechuan a great scholar and three or four students died during a savage bombardment, and I remembered how dearly they held the dead to their hearts. One loves the dead more than the living. They are closer than the living, for though a man is dead and buried underground, he is also everywhere. . . .

I was trying to think in this way when Winter returned from the shelves with *The Way and the Power*, where after describing Chuang Tzu drumming on a bowl and singing after his wife's death, explaining that death is not something unnatural, but something that flows out of life itself, Waley comments: "This attitude towards death, exemplified again and again in Chuang Tzu, is but part of the general attitude towards the universal laws of nature, which is not one merely of resignation or even of acquiescence, but a lyrical, almost ecstatic acceptance which has inspired some of the most moving passages in Taoist literature."

229

And it seemed right and proper, when Winter closed the book, that he should remark: "They are in love with death, because they are in love with life."

December 11th . . . THE Vice-Minister of Education came two days ago, a tall man with buck-teeth, wearing a dark blue patterned gown and a black *makua*. We went to see him last night to see whether he could throw any light on what is happening, but though he has been in conference with the Governor, who is at last formally instated in office, so that we no longer have to depend entirely on the government of Li Chung-huang, he seems to know even less about the affair than we do. He complained that the Communist newspapers in Chungking contained complete reports of the murder, but no other newspapers contained them. "It proves that the Communists are behind it," he said. But does it? Doesn't it prove rather that no other newspapers will print it?

He has seen the Generalissimo, who said: "Something is wrong —very wrong. I give you complete powers to settle the matter." The Vice-Minister insists that he has plenipotentiary powers, but do these powers extend over the local military or even the local Kuomintang office? Kuan Lin-seng has been recalled; a new general has taken his place. The Vice-Minister said: "Our attitude towards the matter is very cold—cold." We asked him what he meant by this, for surely the seriousness of the attacks was realized in Chungking, but he evaded the issue by saying that he was sent down only to find facts. What was strange was his continual denial about the censorship. Theoretically free speech and free assembly had been granted by the government, but he insisted that the local government had over-riding powers. "So the provincial government can over-ride the central government when it pleases?" But to this he only answered: "There are conditions in China which cannot be compared with conditions abroad." He admitted that it was likely that the provincial government had used its over-riding powers to prevent messages being sent out, but the messages had come out all the same—the news was printed in Chungking, Chengtu and Shanghai, and very probably it has already reached America and Hongkong. "But the important thing is to keep cold—keep cold."

It seemed odd. We were very cold indeed: impossible to tell whether he has power, or has been sent only on a fact-finding
230

commission. He seemed not to understand the seriousness of the situation which tolerated these murders, and said: "General Kuan Lin-seng talks too much—he is a good soldier, but not a good diplomat." But we do not need diplomats, and General Kuan did at least speak openly according of the things he knew; though he seemed to know less than anyone else.

"The funeral procession may be held by the students," K. said. "Is there any way in which bloodshed can be avoided?" and he spoke for a while on the terrible effect further bloodshed would have in foreign academic circles. "Such things have happened in Nazi Germany—inconceivable that they should be allowed to happen in China." The thrust hit home. The Vice-Minister began to growl about the enemies of China. "They try to hit us with everything they have—there are enemies everywhere," and since he evidently included us among the enemies, this seemed the strangest of all. He had spent the first night of his arrival with a general connected with the garrison command: there had been objections: he thought tonight it might be possible to stay in a bank. And so we left him, two hours later in the deserted courtyard, a tall man who seemed not to know which way the world was going, who possessed power of a kind and yet hesitated to use it, afraid of his responsibilities, afraid of the deaths of the students, the only man connected with the Universities who had access to the highest quarters; and it seemed impossible to believe that he would be able to add anything or take anything from a situation which had grown above our heads and enclosed us all.

December 12th . . . It is a time of rumours, of strange whispered threats, of still stranger silences. The students and the provincial government are fighting a war of nerves. The censorship is stronger than ever; three hundred more censors have suddenly been enrolled. On the surface everything is quiet, the students are no longer molested, they even make speeches in the centre of the city calling for an end to the civil war. Yet you are conscious all the while that there is terror in the silence, though the silence in the University library where all the coffins are is deeper.

December 13th . . . *THE true knight must have broad shoulders and a stout heart, for his burden is heavy and he has a long journey to go. For Goodness is the burden he has taken upon himself. Only with death does this journey end: then must we not*

231

grant that he has far to go. CONFUCIUS.

And surely the students are doing no more than echoing these words when they announced so courageously in their proclamations: *Death we are not afraid of, for we are assisting a new China to come to birth.*

December 19th . . . THE weight of this murder is like lead. We forget it for a while, but the memory of it returns, obliterating the memories of other murders. Even now Liu Lien is grief-stricken. He speaks so humbly of the students that one almost forgets his own goodness. There, in the tangled garden, where the convolvulus were dying, he leaned on his stick and spoke about the students he has known in the past. "They are still among the most complex animals in creation. I remember the time when every student wore long silk gowns and carried a fan and even the boys wore jade bracelets—less than twenty years ago. They played football in those days so delicately that it was like watching a slow-motion film. They have grown taller and sturdier; they have cut themselves adrift from the past, and because they are even now saturated in Confucian doctrines they are still drifting. We could combine Buddhism, Taoism and Confucianism—it made the whole man. But mechanistic opportunism as well——" At that moment a boy student and a girl passed through the garden arm in arm. "What will save them is that no one in China is more than four generations removed from a farmer. In spite of the three curious religions which have formed their ancestors for two thousand years at least, they will always be practical."

December 24th . . . THE strike goes on, the faculty meetings go on, there have been interviews between the Student Council and Governor Lu Han, there has been a message from the Generalissimo calling upon the students to return to their classes, but no one knows whether the students will return.

The campus was flooded with sunshine and has never looked lovelier. There can be no campus like this. The mud-huts shone this morning like honey in the sun, and the small green lakes among the vegetable gardens were thick with duckweed; but it is not the campus which is beautiful—what is beautiful beyond all words at this moment is still the library which stands like a great crumbling cowshed beyond the small lakes. The archway of evergreens has been removed, and there are no longer any

232

guards at the University gates with baseball bats to prevent the entrance of *agents-provocateurs*. There is the immense cowshed, and the girls in blue gowns from the middle schools who are making their way there. Inside the library there must be at least two thousand funeral scrolls hanging from the rafters, some on white silk, some on paper, and many of them composed with great heavy black brush-strokes; and you wander through this forest of scrolls until you come to the four black coffins covered with the red and blue national flag, and on the way you pass the altar where the enlarged photographs of the dead students gaze down at you. There is Yu Tsai looking a little like a young prince, with a small mouth and dreaming eyes; there is Pan Yen who gazes out of her frame, more mature than the two youngsters beside her, already a woman, with such stores of character and forthrightness on her gentle face that one would have thought her worth preserving for the future of China; there is Li Liu-lien who looks for all the world like a young footballer; there is Hsun Chi-chung who looks almost like a child. Before the photographs red candles are smoking; oranges and apples and bottles of wine are heaped on the white table-cloth; there are joss-sticks burning in urns and wreathes of evergreens. And then you walk on for a little space, and suddenly on the walls you come across small photographs of Pan Yen: there are photographs of her in military uniform, photographs of her playing with children, at picnics, climbing mountains, the inevitable posed photographs of her in a long student's gown, and then there are the other photographs showing her body being placed in a great iron cauldron with the head still showing and the fires burning; and you remember that this happened only two or three hundred yards away, and that the air you breathe contains more of her than you can guess. And somehow it is not terrible—it is as you expect it to be—and those photographs which were taken from her purse contain her whole life, you can understand everything, and she is young China still in all the glory of her young womanhood. So you go slowly round the library, where the funeral scrolls swing gently in the wind and the blue gowns move silently among them, here in the library where there is no longer the musty smell of books: there is only the scent of flowers and of blood. For there on a table against the wall are the clothes they wore when they died, and a camp-bed with a great oval rust-red stain on it. They were put here deliberately: the students were probably wrong to have done

233

this, for the middle-school children come and gaze at them and even touch them, as others touch holy relics, and go away afraid, realizing that they wear the same kind of clothes and simply by realizing this, they come into so close a contact with the dead that they are like people who have seen visions.

There is no place in China so hallowed as this University library, and there is no greater quietness anywhere else.

December 30th . . . I WROTE this poem for Pan Yen last night. It is not finished, and may never be finished.

THE MARTYR

She lived in storm and stress,
Yet quietly she wore
Youth like a shining dress,
As though her nothingness
Would let her pass through life
And take what comes, before
The tempest rose like a knife
And cut her from this war.
They come, the falling leaves:
Earth weighs upon her breast.
Still in the night she grieves.
No farmer has such rest:
Would God that there were more
To turn so straight a furrow,
And I who grieve in peace
Turned, turned into such sorrow,
Must take this candle soon
And lift it to her face
To see from her grey eyes
What light will shine tomorrow.

O eyes that burn and bleed,
Gold now, and broken head,
And silent too she is
With childish wistfulness,
Turn now and shine that we
Caught in these deadly toils
Can count our hidden souls——

Make bread, drink wine with me.
Let death take from you now
No thought of life laid low
But dream of utter snow——
Make now this grace and peace,
O child in the shining dress!

God knows from where they come
Who fought your beauty there.
The lean mole has his home
Far from the sunlit air.
They have their creeping trade.
Who threw the hand-grenade?
I know, but shall not say:
Here in this time and place
I seek a mystery,
For secrets must be held
And shielded must they be
Who live like the falling leaf,
So tender and so swift,
Boys, girls, all these shall fall
Unless we save their soul
And utter bitter truth
With red wide-open mouth.

"Democracy is a name,
Freedom is filled with lies,"
They said, but to their shame
The bitter mouth replies:
"The heart is filled with grief,
The broken head that bleeds,
The fruit they laid beneath
Her breast when she was dead,
All these cry out at night
With leaden eyes like fires.
The youth in the shining dress
Must live, lest nothingness
Descend descending years."

O hear her voice which sings
Upon this night of pain:

"Though they denied our youth,
We died; we come again;
We fought, but not with arms,
We made our purpose plain
And thought not of the storms,
The bitter fall of rain,
The bitter fall of blood.
These things we understood:
Democracy is a truth,
Freedom is filled with flowers——
We died, and the coming hours
Are now forever ours.

We draw a deeper breath.
We are not afraid of death.
We speak through darkness now
But soon our eyes will break,
Though tempest fills the air,
With light, and the burning wake
Will scorch this yellow land
Now broken everywhere,
Till it shines white as snow.
My dress I leave behind:
My body shines like sand.
The sun shall flower indeed
Upon my broken head
And you shall see the flames,
Democracy's bright names——
O joy among the dead!" . . .

1946

January 1st . . . WE BREAK our bread and sleep and wander
in the sun, and those are the three best things—and all these we
do to perfection in Kunming. If we must add a fourth, there is
scholarship; and if there is fifth, there is love-making; and the
sixth is adoring the perfection of this lake a mile above the sea.

So I wrote when I first came to Kunming, but all of it has
changed. In those days, with a kind of grim selfishness, we could
forget the war, content to live in this cleansing air, to study and to
breathe. But things changed so deeply, there is so much terror
abroad, and life is held so cheaply, that we are beginning to look
at this mountain valley with something of the attitudes of soldiers caught up in a citadel and determined not to surrender,
though they starve. We have lost faith completely in Chungking.
We had little enough faith, but now it has gone completely. We
have not much more faith in Yenan, though we admire much of
their program for agrarian reform. What is important is that
until October there was freedom in Kunming. No man was killed
for uttering "dangerous thoughts." The prisons were nearly empty.
There were no armed thugs on the streets. There were desperate
ventures—no one knows how many guns, how many jeeps and
how much ammunition have been stolen from the Americans, but
none of these took on the scale of a relentless civil war. There was
a time when I first came here when Lienta was among the most
glorious things in China; it is glorious still, but something is lacking among the professors, their spirits have been tried too hardly,
their suffering has reached breaking-point and it is no longer true

237

that Lienta is "the last bulwark of freedom in China." The last bulwark has fallen. The students have not changed; they are as determined as ever that the principles of democracy should survive, but with the exception of a handful of professors, the faculty has thrown in its hand. The students will be forced back to work, are already forced back to work, and the faculty has promised that the murderers will be brought to justice; but everyone knows that the promise is worthless, and the faculty has no power. We must go on from here, but the way seems darker than ever now.

January 2nd . . . I MET Liu Lien walking gravely through the gardens near the lake. There are goldfish and small temples, and places where you can drink tea under bamboo shelters, and great hawks wheeling overhead. His newspaper has been suspended indefinitely; he will be arrested the moment it appears, if it appears illegally. He has been from one printing-press to another, always trailed; he said: "It's the most idiotic thing of all —to know that you are being trailed. It gives you the most damnable impression of your own self-importance." He laughed. "We haven't deserved this—the students haven't deserved it—they will still fight, but somehow they have got into their heads that they must fight in the ancient Chinese way—dramatically, as one fights for lost causes. But these causes are not lost. They say they are going to take the coffins through the city whatever the cost; a hundred thousand children believe this, but it would be better if we had just one good man in the government, or one bad man less." With bent back, walking slowly, he disappeared among the silver trees.

January 4th . . . I SHOULD like to set in order, carefully and consistently, in their own atmosphere and in their proper clothes those things which have most moved me in China, seeing them at a time when the wars are nearly over. How generous was China to the eye that had been trained in Malaya only to distinguish the heaviest and most elementary colours! All Malaya was a flame-of-the-forest tree seen against a liquid gold sky. It was too rich, the glory so great that it was always incommunicable even to oneself. And then this other glory, quieter, more desperately earnest, of shadows and calligraphy—gold cliffs lost in the mist, the boy crouching by the river bank and one colour after another spilling over his shoulders and thighs, and even the wicker basket by
238

his side brimming with the suffused reflected colours of the earth. The world is made of coloured stones. Imagine any stone of any shape, and then colour it, or let it alone in the sun—we need no more than this; at most we need a handful of these stones.

Where is the end? One must watch colours unceasingly, because colour is a greater enchantment than music. In music we drown, but colours are ourselves floating to the surface, the most living of all things because we see the living movement of the sun in all that is around. And see how delicately we live—with six inches of soil we plant our rice, and with a millimetre of reflected light, that millimetre which clings to everything, we see the world around us. And then too, this afternoon, thinking how all colours are pointed towards the sun.

January 5th . . . THE nakedness of China. Not only the ragged beggar whose clothes are broken, but the hills which are also unclothed, and the women who seem to have assumed deliberately the garment which is most revealing. The nakedness, and the elaborate decoration, so elaborate that you know that it is no more than decoration, the barrenness of a Chinese courtyard made more barren still by the gold ornaments of the roof and the gold-studded doors. So it is in my garden, day after day, the poinsettias shedding their pale red light over one quarter of the yard and the rest seems to be nothing more than pebbles thrown haphazard on a seashore. They say that the Chinese lived in tents once, but I have known nothing which confirms the statement; but of one thing I am sure, and that is that they have lived for a long space of time on the sea or facing vast rivers. And perhaps in the end this is why they have so much in common with the English, who like their fields best when they have waves like the sea, and are coloured deep green. What is delightful about this theory is that it fits in so perfectly with what J. was saying yesterday: that the Chinese remained for thousands of years on the banks of the Yellow River, and they worshipped the river and gave it the name of the Yellow Emperor.

January 7th . . . THIS was not the place we had hoped to come to, because we had lost our way, and the dust was getting into our shoes, and there was nowhere to rest. I remember I was frightened because we might have to walk all night, and I feared the yapping of the dogs more than the bandits in the villages,

239

and besides, all the comforting things of evening—the smell of woodsmoke, the colours of the fields, the sense of being surrounded by friendly people—all these die away at night. Nothing is so unfriendly as a Chinese night when there is no moon. Night the enemy, and the houses all shuttered, and you couldn't see the pathway, and we were utterly tired of crossing fields, and sometimes L. would stop and say he heard the sound of a pheasant or a barking deer, and I heard nothing, the night enclosing us both so that we were doubly afraid.

There is a shuttered horror at night in China, and I remember that Tu Fu complained about it, and God knows in his wanderings he must have seen these landscapes under a black moon, the dogs like avenging and invisible furies and all the houses darkened so that they look like unfriendly stones. The Chinese are callous—it is better to admit it—they say they must be callous to survive, but the night is more callous still, and we couldn't go on much further. I suppose a rise in the ground hid us from Kunming, but the most extraordinary thing was that there was a heavy mist, and we were not conscious of it, and only knew of it afterwards. And then, quite suddenly, we came to a small village near the gates, where there were dim lights and the smell of dogs and children were playing. Those last moments before we reached the village were almost as terrible as the night last year when we were coming home after curfew and someone with a submachine-gun pushed it into my stomach and told me to put my hands up; the night was as calculated and bestial as that.

And then the sudden recovery, the sense that the world was safe, because there was the smell of woodsmoke and sleepy children were playing, and there were rapeseed oil-lamps, and money in our pockets to pay for food—sweetened eggs in milk, juicy figs which are called "dragons' eyes" and whole loaves of unleavened bread. And afterwards, coming to Kunming at last, seeing the gate opening like a great white horn leading to the world of dreams.

January 10th . . . I AM continually amazed by the ambiguity of the novel, the sudden changes and evolutions of the matter, the inevitable lack of any central eye which can look upon the scene wholly. The eye and the sensibility are continually changing, and there is no unchanging lever between myself and the novel I am writing. Archimedes could support the whole world with a single

240

lever, but the world I am trying to support in the novel is buttressed with eight or nine different levers, of different lengths and different colours, simply because there are eight or nine characters, and I must see it all through their eyes or fail completely. And so there is not one novel, but at least eight novels, eight ways of looking at life, eight characters to be presented to the sunlight, to be given lungs and breath and flesh and bones and appetites and emotions.

I can see no escape from it: there must be these levers, there cannot be a central lever. I seem to remember from applied mathematics that all forces afflicting an organism can be resolved into a single force. It is not true of the novel. In *A Bear Coughs at the North Pole* a single event—the bombing of Chungking on May 3rd, 1939—is seen by nine people, and yet there is a sense by which all these nine people become one person, because they see the same thing. They are at odds with one another. There is conflict between them, and the most unimportant things in their relationships are made to have superlative importance; and this is deliberate, and at the same time it arises from the nature of the novel, and also from the nature of the Chinese climate and the Chinese scene. A bear coughs at the North Pole, a flower fades in Burma, a girl wanders down to a river, and each of these things can be shown to have widening circles of significance, and there is no end whatsoever to the immeasurable growth of the smallest things. This is the theme of the novel, but also there is another theme, half hidden in the angry shadows which play over the whole novel, the theme of adoration against all our growing despairs. And though the form of the novel still seems to me to be insufficient, because it is not strict enough, I know no other form which can so prodigiously reflect our own civilization. I suspect that the diary as a literary form may come into greater favour, for though it lacks form it gives arrangement and shadow to the naked impressions of life seen daily. In the diary there is the single lever, the personal eye which never leaves the subject; in the novel there are so many subjects that the eye must be always wandering, taking details here and there, imposing them within the arbitrary scheme of the novelist's invention. Richardson's novels were letters—two diaries confronting one another, and both written in a form which possessed at least some kind of balance, like mirrors perpetually reflecting one another and perpetually still, because every question is answered. But for the novelists of our day no questions are answered, and we must simply state the things as we see them, in their nakedness, beauty and ferocity.

January 12th . . . I HEARD today, looking over the lake in full afternoon, when all the trees were swinging in a gale, a single line of music which has haunted me for more than eighteen years, and will, I believe, haunt me forever. There are months when I never hear it, I think I once forgot it for a whole year, but like the phrase of Vinteuil it continually recurs. Buried somewhere among the coral reefs of my mind is a musician who plays unbidden this thirteenth century phrase of a *Jubilate* first sung in France—or is it unbidden? I suspect it comes only when an authentic joy of landscape is seen through eyes made joyful by that other landscape inside the mind.

February 1st . . . WHAT is Taoism? One hears so much, and one knows that it is characteristically Chinese, and we can learn much by studying those ancient fragmentary texts written more than two thousand years ago. There is a strange sense of irresponsibility in the Chinese, a sense which derives perhaps more from the continual hungers of the people than something intrinsic in their character. They are the world's anarchists, who know that responsibility is often ridiculous and obedience is a shallow simplicity, for they know only too well that laws are man-made and are used by judges to incriminate others. There is no law in China. *Habeas corpus* goes regularly on the statute book; the imprisonments and the arrests and the political assassinations continue. But this evening I came upon my friend, Dr. Lin Tung-chi's description of the Taoist, which is so important that I shall write it down here:

"Taoism may be defined as romantic individualism. It is the natural and necessary counterpart to the complacent and yielding gregariousness of Confucianism. Come what may, the first prompting of a Taoist is to "debunk," so much folly and bad taste does he see in this all too human world.

"One can best describe the workings of this mentality in terms of a curve.

"It begins with an ascending movement, whereby the discharging energy of debunking is directed outward to the external world until it reaches a point where the fire of debunk-

242

ing turns into a white flame of defiance. It is the moment most supercharged with possibility of action, the juncture at which a Chinese intellectual may most readily turn into a revolutionary if ever his defying mood finds its way to combine with the popular discontent of the age.

"A typical Taoist nature does not, however, become a revolutionary as a rule. He does not actually mix with the populace. A proud artist, he stands alone, contemplating no comrades. He, predestinedly, sees a war of one against all and one against everything. And a more exalted and tense frame of mind cannot be imagined.

"Yet there is no vent. Totally unable to view the impending battle in terms of practical interests and concrete issues, he is at a loss as to where and to whom to deal his blows. The intensity of his charged feeling, thus blocked, soon recoils upon itself. A mental crisis develops when an involuntary repression compresses the rising temper, which, foundering at this tremulous height, quickly turns into a state of Dionysian drunkenness. The Taoist revolt at this stage takes on the character of emotional self-abandonment. He gives himself up to himself. He no longer defies, he simply disregards. A sort of ecstasy takes place, in which the half-conscious bitterness and the half-felt rapture combine to produce a vent peculiarly Taoist—the devastating laugh of the intoxicated. But this blessed stage cannot last long. A mental numbness born of helpless desperation is foredoomed to come to a *dénouement*—the beginning of the descending curve.

"As the effects of intoxication clear away, the last possibility of action disappears. He cannot but question now the worth of it all. 'Why excitement and fury?' asks the erstwhile rebel. And he begins to debunk *himself*. With a chuckle he drops the gauntlet and retires into the mountains. The boisterous rebel becomes the saintly recluse. After the tempest the serene sunset."

I do not know any description of the Chinese mind so honest as this. It says much that has been on my mind for many years, and though not all Chinese are implicated, there is a Taoist irresponsibility in all of them to some smaller or greater extent. There is a sense in which the whole of the Confucian ritual was simply an effort to *invent* order and stability where there was

243

none before. Starvation and wars have worked so much havoc in China that it would be folly to minimize the irresponsibility and detachment of so many Chinese. The world goes on—it is their world—but so great are the forces arraigned against them that they realized in the past how little they could do. Could the small man in a gown, who wanders beneath the craggy mountains in the paintings, do anything to change the world he sees? And now, when the power of change has come into the hands of their young engineers, can we expect the officials, brought up on an earlier code, to understand them? China is divided. It must be that the division will be healed, but until the last officials have been swept away and the engineers take their place, I see no hope that it will come about. And this is the importance of the Communists in China, those mildly revolutionary agrarian reformers—they have cast away for ever the ritual and the verdicts of the Chou Dynasty philosophers, and have none of the obsessions of the Generalissimo. In China, as elsewhere, we have nothing to lose if we begin from the beginning. History is meaningless now that atomic bombs can sweep us all away. What is needed is the new blood of the west; and this will come, and we in our turn are the only ones who will benefit by the ancient detachment of the Chinese. But from now on, in this long and hazardous process of healing which is the only essential task of the generations immediately ahead of us, we must learn that it is safer to make a clean sweep of the past and begin again.

The more I think of this world with its suppurating and increasing wounds, the more I believe that we need the patience and incisiveness of doctors. The wounds are there. What are needed are swabs, ointment, a long and peaceful convalescence. And just as a doctor needs to know the complete history of the patient, so we need to know all that has happened in the minds of countries in the past. But once the wound has healed, or is healing, the mind of the patient is no longer so important, for he will begin his life again like a man new-born. I like the statement of Lieh Tzu: "The joy of travelling lies in its purposelessness. Others travel to see what they want to see, but I travel simply to see the whole earth perpetually changing. Travels, travels, none can see my travels." Though I like it, I know that it is wrong-headed. We must know where we are going. We cannot afford this detachment and irresponsibility, even in our private lives; and nations can afford it still less. The Chinese puzzle is like a game of
244

chess, with every player able to see only a single move ahead; he has long ago forgotten why he is playing, and he is so absorbed in the game that he does not see what is happening to the room where he is playing. The irresponsibility of the Chinese government knows no end. The game of playing one against the other is played for its own sake, and no one knows the end of it all.

When I came to China, I was concerned that the values of the Kuomintang should be maintained. Now I no longer believe they are worth maintaining under their present form. Sun Yat-sen was admirable, but he has left a dangerous legacy; and the greatest of all his mistakes was the order in which he announced his three principles—democracy came second, livelihood of the people last. First he wanted nationalism, the unification of the land under a single government. I agree that this is necessary, but to place it first, and to pay no consideration at all to the second and third of the requisites, to allow them to be drowned in the obsolete clamour for nationalism, which has already been obtained without struggling for it, because it was given readily by the Americans and the British—all this shows the weakness of his vision. Then, too, his five-power control of the government deliberately weakens the legislature and gives the executive at all times overriding powers—this is something which cannot be reconciled with democracy. And livelihood—the most sacred of all the three principles—is hopelessly forgotten, because the members of the government have acquired too great a wealth to care for the fortunes of the people.

I know nothing in all recent history in China quite so disturbing as a statement in the Generalissimo's *China Destiny*. The antiquated and obsolete forces which drive the present government become clear in the pages of this remarkable and intolerant book. He says: "The various political parties each revere one particular foreign country and worship one particular theory, forming groups of their own, proud before their countrymen but submissive towards foreigners. Since the theories of the various countries are forever changing, therefore the theory of each of these groups has to change unceasingly in accord with foreign changes. As to the struggle between Liberalism and Communism, it is merely a reflection of the opposition between Anglo-American thought and the thought of the Russians. Such theories are not only unsuitable for the national life and the people's livelihood of China and opposed to her original culture, but they reveal that

245

their promoters have forgotten that they are Chinese and have lost their learned respect for China and fail to apply their learning to the Chinese situation."

I can think of nothing so brutal as this statement which demands of the Chinese that their ancient systems and virtues should be resuscitated from the Chou Dynasty of nearly three thousand years ago. There is a new China, profoundly and unalterably influenced by the West. The Generalissimo knows no more of the west than the smallest Chinese peasant, though he uses its methods in his secret police, in his bombing planes and his war factories. The limited, obsolescent mind of a second-class private in the Japanese Army is as dangerous for China as the detachment and the irresponsibility of the Taoists. There must come an end some time. It is better that it come soon, otherwise all will be lost and the war will go on forever.

I had hopes when I came to China just after the Pacific War broke out, but the hopes grow smaller. China is awake. It is not wholly bad that the war should be fought between the feudal landlords and those who insist on agrarian reforms; it is a sign of the awakening; the struggle has purpose and direction, and somehow a synthesis will be formed. But must we go on forever in this grimly irresponsible mood, with inflated currency and vast fortunes being made from the sufferings of others? There may come a time rather sooner than we expect when those who do not serve the people will be swept from power. If that time comes it will not be because "various political parties" reflect the differences between Moscow and Washington; it will be because China has accepted what is common to Moscow and Washington—the sense of efficiency, the refusal to believe in legends, the values which are placed on human lives and the belief that the world can be made safer by hard work. And still, and for many years to come, though her eyes are wide open and for the first time the Chinese lion is awake, there is no profound belief that the simplicities of western civilization can be moulded to the Chinese pattern. On the highest levels of the Kuomintang there is the most profound ignorance. The books of Chen Li-fu and Chen Kuo-fu—the first on the nature of life and the second on education—are shallow, perhaps the shallowest documents that have appeared from high government officials in China. The Generalissimo's *China's Destiny* reveals an uneducated mind. Must China suffer indefinitely from the pervasive ignorance of its rulers?

246

China is awake. Of this there can be no doubt at all. But what a complex awakening! After so many years of slumber, intoxicatedly dreaming of the Celestial Empire, she wakes to find herself at war, her face covered with blood and her eyes still unaccustomed to the light. Time is the only cure. Gradually the old dreams will be forgotten, the old rituals and chronicles will pass from the consciousness of men, and in the place of the old slumbering lion there will be the newborn youth in his glory.

February 5th . . . THE almost German obedience of the Japanese. J. told me today a story which is well-known in China of a certain Captain Hagekawa who was captured by the Chinese at the battle of Shanghai in 1932. After being imprisoned, he was at last released and made his way to the Japanese Consulate, where he was informed that he was officially dead, and his ashes had been removed to Tokyo. Captain Hagekawa loved his young wife, and was determined to live. All this he explained to the Consul-General, who replied: "Your ashes have been taken to Tokyo and the clothes in which you died have been buried in your coffin a little way outside Shanghai. I suggest that you go to your grave." Captain Hagekawa listened politely, bowed towards the portrait of the Emperor and immediately went to his grave, where he shot himself, in order, as the Chinese say, "to rejoin his clothes."

February 14th . . . "I HATE this place," he said. "I hate it more than any place I know. I hate the sights and the sounds of it, and the police in black and the young fat-bottomed soldiers with the little green hand-grenades hanging from their belts, and the lake, and the vile smell of flowers which is like dead bodies, and the poverty, and the way we kowtow to the Americans, because we are starving, and the way the Americans will support the central government, however bad it is, and the way it is all becoming clear now—there is peace, but it won't last long, and on both sides they will fight, and the peasants won't care, they only want peace, and they are not prepared to die for Mao Tse-tung or the Generalissimo. It's all such a mess. We deserve it, probably. I'm not whining, but we can't go on like this—we must have peace. We go to the Central Government and say we want peace, and they say we must have 'unification' and 'nationalization' and

247

'democracy' and 'livelihood.' My God, what we really want is peace, the first of the principles of the nation. The others don't count. Do you understand that? They don't count."

He went on a little later: "Put it all in. Put the smell of the dead soldiers who come up the Burma Road, put in the four students and how the blood was so thick that there was a red jelly on the stretcher, and the fat-arsed generals, and the little boys they kiss, and the lack of sanitation in Kunming, where after all there have been Americans and the authorities should know better. Put in the political murders and the other murders—the men who have lost their jobs when the Americans left, and had no other job except murder. Put in the continual thieving of American guns and jeeps and ammunition, so that they could have their civil war. Put in the gangsters and the secret societies, and the way we are running to ruin, because we have no principles—not even the three principles of the people. We recite every Monday morning, bowing before the photograph of the perpetual President of the Republic, the will which was written by the greatest traitor of all, a will which says 'The Revolution is not yet finished,' and do you think any of the government officials who bow are revolutionaries in any sense whatsoever? Do realize that it is dangerous even to paint the Chinese scenery, it is dangerous to say anything at all which will make people think we are charming—we are not charming, we are suffering from a disease, we are the most dislocated people on the face of the earth. The people who have done most harm to us are the missionaries and others who come to us with kind intentions—how brave we are, how courageous and self-sacrificing and noble under our rags, how cultured even the dirtiest snot-nosed peasant is, and then those tremendous collections of money they have made for the starving Chinese! Oh better a thousand times that not one penny was ever collected, because then we should have to solve our own problems, and we should never be forced to rely on the assistance of others. It has become a disease. We pretend we are what they think we are, and we do this with the utmost subtlety, as a child does exactly the same thing in his relations to his parents. Tell them to let us alone. Tell them we want no more missionaries, no more foreign assistance, no more Christian charity—if we continue to have these things, we shall lose our self-reliance completely. There is only one thing from abroad that is necessary to China—modern science. Give us this, and then forget about us completely, and let us work it out for ourselves."

248

The man who said this, as we walked round the lake this afternoon, was Wen Yi-tuo, the man whom I believe to be the greatest poet and scholar in China.

February 20th, The General . . . I MET him first at a party last year, a small man, with a white moustache and beady eyes, who said he was working with the American Intelligence and indeed was often seen in the company of the American naval officers who are the intelligence advisers to the government. He was a man who had taken part in the old civil wars, had possessed a command and had shifted unaccountably from one side to the other. He had been at West Point, and he would say openly that they gave him a good grade because he was Chinese, and though he had worked hard he had not deserved the grade. And sometimes he would tell you that the present hush-hush job would soon be over, he would be given a command again and he looked forward to nothing better than the life of the camp. I asked him who he would fight against. "Oh well, against the Communists, I suppose, but you don't think I'll fight against the Communists—they are Chinese. No, what I'll do," and here his voice lowered to a whisper, "what I'll do is to hold my troops in reserve, I won't attack the Communists, I've got close relations with important members of the government and I'll be able to bring a liberal attitude to bear. Maybe, I'll be able to solve the whole problem if I have a command and use my political influence."

He was not impressive, and I met him very rarely, once at a party at which the President of the University was invited and everyone played mahjong. I did not play, but he came downstairs into the cold tomb-like antichamber of a house near the railway station and insisted that I should learn the rudiments of the game. "It's part of the tactics. A Chinese general will invite his opposing general to a game of mahjong. He will learn more from the way he plays the game than from anything else." But the game was so complicated and it was impossible to learn what was on his mind from the way he played.

He said he had connections with the War Ministry, and what did I think of such-and-such a professor? I said that I knew nothing, but he was probably starving—a safe enough reply, since they were nearly all starving. And then he mentioned other names, the names of liberals and opponents of the present government, the names which were most respected by scholars abroad, and I could

249

see him watching closely, the small beady eyes exactly like those of a small rat hiding in the darkness of his rat-hole. "I'd like to help the professors. I've got a lot of money tucked away, and I could get more from my political associates. Tell me how I could help them." I told him. I explained there were a hundred books which needed writing, but there was no time to write them—the professors were starving and had to take jobs in primary and secondary schools to make ends meet.

"Well, tell me where we ought to begin."

"We could begin with a history of China written by Chinese scholars. It would help the west to understand China, and these professors write perfect English. We could begin there."

"And can you tell me their names?"

"I could discuss it and let you know. . . ."

He became very friendly. He clapped me on the shoulder and held my hand.

"It's nice of you. You have come to help China. Yes, I respect you. Come and have dinner with me on Friday. I want to help the professors, you understand. I'm only a soldier, a mercenary, as they say, but I have been to West Point."

I learned something about him in the intervening days. He had changed sides so often during the civil wars that men had lost count of his broken allegiances. He was famous for gun-running, and there was considerable evidence that he had traded in opium. He was an agent of the Chinese Gestapo as well as being an agent of the American intelligence; he had a pretty and well-born wife in Peking, whom he had not seen for fifteen years, not daring to come into her presence. Why had he wanted to help the University? It was true that at one time he had been an eurythmics teacher in the University, but eurythmics are hardly criminal, and the University had very little interest in eurythmics, for shortly afterwards he disappeared—a war-lord was coming close to Peking, or perhaps there were more guns to be unloaded in a barren creek of Formosa.

He was perfect civility when I went to see him last night. He had changed his civilian clothes for an embroidered blue gown, and over the sherry we exchanged the inevitable civilities. A room had been set aside for us. He told stories of his life in America, told them extremely well and there was I know not what nostalgia in his voice for the youth he had spent abroad. "You know," he said, "Chinese politics is a dirty game—the dirtiest of all games. I want
250

to go into it and clean it up." It sounded delightful, even though incredible. "I know Ho Ying-chin well. Why, he was once one of my subordinates. We are even related to one another. An extraordinarily gifted man, or he would be if he had gone in for anything else except war-mongering. The Generalissimo detests him. They made him war-minister because he was dangerous anywhere else. As war-minister he would be directly under the Generalissimo's thumb, and do you think the Generalissimo has ever forgotten that Ho Ying-chin was prepared to bomb Sian when the Generalissimo was imprisoned there by the Young Marshal? No, we must clean it up. We must use some of our professors. I have a complete respect for the professors. It's shameful that they should be starving. If there is any way in which I can help them . . ."

I said: "They want help badly, but I can't even beg them to do anything unless we know the source of the money. I'm a foreigner. They won't take assistance from me or through me. But if the money was purely for purposes of scholarship, and for nothing else, they would take it, I think."

He said: "All money is tainted," and sighed, and lifted up the small porcelain cup of *hsiao-hsing* wine. And then a little later he said: "Please introduce me to some of the most liberal, the most honest. It would give me a great deal of pleasure to give them money."

I said nothing more on this subject, and the conversation became desultory. I wanted to watch him. He was an extraordinary man. If only half of what I had learnt of him and his associates was true, it was worth while watching him closely. He liked talking about West Point. He liked drawing his hand down his smooth face, and he liked pouring out wine, not only because the effortless gesture was perfect but because he knew he had beautiful hands. Long after the dinner was over, we were still talking. He talked about his house in Suchow, which was unharmed. There was wine from the early days of the Ch'ing Dynasty buried in the cellars; and looking very straight at me and putting his hand on my knee, he said: "I would enjoy it immensely if you could come and stay with me in Suchow. I have the best pornographic library in the whole of China. And not only my pornographic library, but the little figurines—they are the best too—and surely you have heard of my paintings. No one can compare with my collection. Ho Ying-chin tried to buy them off me, but I refused, and I suppose that is why he refuses to give me a command."

February 23rd . . . SUDDENLY out of the mist and heat over the lake this afternoon, we came upon the prow of a sunken boat, and K. was at once in ecstacies, saying that the way the green tendrils curved over the prow was one of the most beautiful things he had ever seen; and the ripe brown swollen colour of the wood—this too pleased him—it was a colour, he explained, that you see sometimes in deserted and sunken rafters, and it did not belong to this world. I could not follow him when he was discussing these diseased colours, but when he went on to describe the reeds lapping against the boat, their colours as fresh as spring flowers, he began to use a language which was communicable: "They have been doing this perhaps for a hundred years—the boat looks very old—and do you see how the leaves and the boat have formed a perfect equation. They exist for one another, they subtly explore one another, they form a continuing pattern, as all old things juxtaposed together form in the end a continuing pattern, and this is what makes it so beautiful. Think of the scratches on bones which formed the basis of Chinese handwriting. The bones alone are nothing, but the scratches or the places where marks appear when they are burnt—this is what gives them character and art. So it is with the boat. By itself, it is only a crumbling thing, and with these weeds softly waving over it and making faint incisions in it, it becomes real, it has purpose and direction, and the purpose is art."

He went on: "Have you been to the Gold Temple? It is not gold, but made of brass and the brass has turned black with golden lights in it. But how much more beautiful it is now than when there were those brass panels on a hilltop shining in the sun. I think this is one of the things we feel so deeply that it has become a part of ourselves. We are conscious, no one more than the Chinese, that time makes things more beautiful. So even now we reverence old people instinctively, and have a desperate desire to cherish our old civilization, though in fact it is hardly to be compared in age with the civilization of Egypt." And once later, very softly, he said: "We call landscape painting 'mountains and rivers.' The mountains stand firm, and the rivers are eternally moving. When the rivers frighten us, because they are so evidently telling us that all things pass away, we look to the mountains for composure."

February 27th, Conversation between two students . . . "WHAT is the best thing that the Americans ever brought to China?" "The Declaration of Independence." "And what is the worst?"

252

"That no one ever defined sufficiently what is meant by government *for* the people and *by* the people."

March 1st . . . DURING all these years I have enjoyed most of all teaching Shakespeare, roaring out the verses of the last plays till at last I think the flint has struck bone and ignited within their skulls. The last three acts of *Pericles*, the whole of *Lear, Antony and Cleopatra* and *Romeo and Juliet*, the sonnets, *The Phoenix and the Turtle* and above all *The Tempest* have made those days memorable. The long summery afternoons, the black widows in the sky, the lazy green pool where the soldiers bathe not far from the class-room, the Chinese flag fluttering lazily outside the library, and then Shakespeare's voice leaping from the page. "Did you not name a tempest a birth and a death?" "Behold Divinenesse no older than a Boy." "I dedicate myself to your sweet pleasure." "Though the seas threaten they are mercifull." "It is the stars, the stars above us governe our conditions." These plays, and our English lyrics, and the best music, Palestrina, Mozart and Beethoven, surely these are the things that must be taught together with our engineering, naval architecture and calculus and theory of fluxions. We cannot go to the East without these, the music and the poems. They are our passports; and when our mechanics and sciences fail, and the orientals become weary of them, there will be these other things by which we will earn their forgiveness.

March 6th . . . HE WAS talking quietly about the revolution of Asia and yet there was enormous determination in his voice. He is a Chinese from Siam, very sparse, sallow-skinned, with eyes as fine as the eyes of Malays.

"And so it comes to this: when the war is over, and soon even the scattered little remnants of the war will be over—the wars that are being fought in Indo-China, Java and in some places of Burma —when this is all finished, the West will find itself at a loss to understand the transformation. Up to this moment, you have understood us well enough. You have known something of our suffering, something of the economic problems which occur when an ancient feudalism is confronted with modern industry, but has it ever occurred to you that henceforward you will find us far more difficult to understand? You can understand us now because we are weak. Our weakness reveals, but what if we become strong, what if there is no weakness, what if we have our own stock-exchanges, what if

253

we refuse to allow our labour to be exploited except for our own purposes?"

I said something to the effect that even this was known to the people of the West, who at least possessed enough imagination to realize that Asia was in a state of revolution, and that this revolution was probably the greatest single event in the world's history —Asia coming to her feet, obeying the injunction of the Japanese, Asia for the Asiatics, Asia in command of her own finances and her own trade, her own engineering, her own schools. I said: "We have counted on that. We know the way the wind is blowing. Independence, economic security. It's the same story. We went through it in the fourteenth century. Now you'll go through it with all the advantages of not being in the fourteenth century, but in the twentieth."

He looked thoughtful.

"Is it an advantage?" he said. "You may think it is, but we have no traditions. What shall we put in the place of religion? There will be a gap somewhere, a vacuum, and there's nothing to fill it yet. I think I can see what is going to happen—our loyalty will be towards Asia. Asia as a whole. Asia—not against the West, but simply Asia. Our brethren in India and Java and Sumatra and the Malay peninsula and in a thousand other places. We can jump very easily from independence to a state of federation. We shall acquire our independence simply in order to throw it away—the greater loyalty will be towards all the countries of the east. I can see this happening in my lifetime. Loose, but extremely close-knit federations. We shall have a Parliament of the Asias, and with this Parliament—I imagine it will be meeting continually—we shall rule ourselves. We shall discover Asia for ourselves, and having discovered it, I doubt whether we shall have much time to think of the West. There's no Yellow Peril. There is just Asia for the Asiatics, and the West for the Westerners and Russia for the Russians—the world split up into three. I think that's how we'll have to regard the world of the future."

What was delightful, even though disturbing, was his insistence that the picture was already coming into being. There would be soon enough a loose federation of the smaller states in the Far East—Siam, Burma, Indo-China. Who would be the leader of the federation? Perhaps, after all, it would not be India, and certainly China was in too desperate case to have any leadership over other nations. "Do you know," he said quietly, "it seems to me very

254

possible that the most important of all the states in the Far East may become Indonesia. There are no communal problems there; no political problems which cannot be easily solved; no deep-seated legacy of hatred against the West, though there is hatred here and there. Think of the virgin wealth of Sumatra! Think of the ease with which the revolutionary movement has come to the fore! I am a Chinese from Siam, but it seems to me that the leadership will come from nearer the Equator, and it will not be leadership as we have known it in the past. Simply because within ten years the Indonesians may have a higher standard of education and production than any other country in the Far East—even more than the Philippines—we may see the Indonesians leading the way. And I am bitterly ashamed of this. Here in China we carry on our fratricidal wars, forgetting that if we had peace the whole of Asia might be looking to us for advice."

March 9th . . . WE SHALL never understand China unless we understand Taoism. In this alone China has learnt nothing from India. Even Confucianism has curious relics of Taoism—the search for the way differs among the Confucianists and Taoists, but often their roads overlap! There are passages of Mencius and Confucius which could not have been written without some knowledge of the principles of the Taoists, or perhaps (and this is more likely) both stem from the same root.

I suppose it was inevitable that one should use the word "root," which comes so often into the literature of the Taoists. "The gate of the dark emptiness is the root of Heaven and Earth." "Everything blooms, then returns to its root which is quietness." "The return," "the root," "the entrance of the mysterious female," "the quiet valley"—these were their obsessions: the root, the unmoving cause of things. Arthur Waley has detected in the earliest fragments of Taoism the influence of India, and particularly of the concept of *samadhi*. It is difficult to understand how in these early times there can have been communication between these two countries. I cannot remember anything like this obsession for the "root," the sources from which all things flow, in Indian literature. It is wholly Chinese, and I am not sure that even now it does not tell us much about the Chinese mind, which has no concern on how things behave, but has every concern for origins. The first question one Chinese asks of another is: "Where have you come from?" He is not concerned, as we are, as to where you are going.

The future does not disturb them as it disturbs us. They are men who look to their childhood and their youth, knowing that they were happiest then; the old men in their paintings have the innocence of children.

It is all dying now. There will be nothing Chinese left soon; the last great scholars belong to our time—after them there will probably be none who can afford the time to study the voluminous papers of the past, the mountains of state documents still unexplored. The best Chinese are those who have found an equation with the West. But what happens afterwards? The West will come in like a flood the moment the first tractors arrive.

Wen Yi-tuo, who is the greatest of our Chinese scholars, believes that the long history of the Chinese race, as a race in itself, is finished. The West has come to stay, with all its intangible and far-reaching modifications of the Chinese character. One begins to wonder what will remain of the Chinese character? There may be only a primitive strength, the unyielding resolution which has supported so many Chinese in this time of war. The drum-beat has come back at last to Chinese poetry. Speaking of a new poet, Wen Yi-tuo wrote: "Here is no sound of lutes, no half-notes, no delicate arpeggios. Each sentence is carved, simply and powerfully. Those short steady sentences move with the sound of drums, they penetrate into the ears and beat with the sound of heartbeats. You may say that it is not poetry, but if you do, it is because your ears are habituated to lute-strings and have become too delicate." So it is, I think, with all the new music that is coming out of China. But what is so strange and so beautiful is that this scholar is himself one of the last who will explore critically the documents that have been handed down from the remote Chinese past; he reveres them; his whole life is dedicated to their interpretation; and because he sees the new China, and is in love with vigour, he has no remorse at the thought that it may all disappear.

March 15th . . . QUITE suddenly and almost without any explanation the atmosphere of Vienna came into the classroom this afternoon. I suppose it was a trick of light, a momentary thickening of the shadows or the appearance of some unfamiliar colour which brought me back to those days in March, now eight years ago; and I think it was because the sun shining on the wooden desks was blood-red and I remembered the blood-red flags in
256

the Ringstrasse the day after Hitler announced the invasion of Austria.

Eight years, during which red has been the dominant colour. That was the worst of it. The unfurling of the blood-red flag with the swastika, the sudden spasm of red outside the Westbahnhof, the terror in the hearts of the people struggling to board the train, knowing that Hitler had arrived but seeing in the evidence of the sudden unfurling of the flag a proof more positive than if he had stood menacingly before them. The worst was not the murder but the terror, the terror which came at any moment, which was deliberate and at the same time unconscious, because it came not only from men but from the atmosphere around us. You could not breathe in that atmosphere. You choked. If a storm-trooper came along and spat at a girl's face, you would make an effort, you would bridle, you would almost throw yourself at the storm-trooper, but in fact you would do nothing. I remember wandering through a station-yard when the swastika was unfurled. Across puffs of steam and smoke we saw the people trying to board the train. Darkness swallowed them, and sometimes S.S. men leapt onto the runningboard, and the shouts from the engines were exactly like the shouts in the inner city. "*Sieg Heil, Sieg Heil, Sieg Heil . . .*" The tom-toms were beating in the station-yard.

So it went on for days, the terror growing closer, the despair growing increasingly visible; and you would notice the despair even on the faces of those who supported Hitler. The soldiers came into the Ringstrasse with flowers in their helmets. They smiled broadly, they did not look in the least like S.S. men, they were young peasants who had no idea what they were doing or how soon they would be dead.

Then it comes back: Schuschnigg's voice over the radio saying that the Germans had manufactured all the evidence which made the invasion necessary from A to Z, every single scrap of it was invented, and then when the quiet speech was almost at an end, the words: "*I take leave of the Austrian people with a German word and a wish that springs from the heart: 'May God protect Austria.'*" The words were not ignoble, yet the man himself had never shown any depth of feeling for the people—he was as remote from his people as Franco or Salazar. And those last days in Vienna when the streets were still crowded and the hysterical cries of "*Sieg Heil!*" were still being repeated, but the blood-red

257

flags from the windows of the Mariahilferstrasse looked tawdry beyond words, and then the pale-faced boy shouting: *"Hitler ist hier!"* and then for the first time we saw mass conversion, in an atmosphere of relief and hysteria, taking place before our eyes . . .

March 17th . . . WE HAD almost forgotten the four bodies of the students lying in the library of the University. Gradually, imperceptibly, we had become accustomed to our library as a mausoleum. The dead were there, in the lacquered red coffins, amid the forest of scrolls, but a new and much smaller library had been formed behind the main library, and so we allowed them to stay there in peace. For weeks past peasants have been coming to the University on pilgrimage. They came from all the villages around, they wandered among the scrolls, they watched the nuns chanting and the candles gleaming on the altar, and sometimes they bowed, but more often they simply gazed at the immense portraits of the youngsters who were killed. I believe this is what the students liked—the simplicity of these peasants who came in their coarse blue cloth, shambling and quietly reverential, not so much paying tribute as coming to see the place where democracy had been fought for, and where students had been killed.

For some months now a stone tomb has been in process of being built near the foreign languages department. At first there were only heavy cubes of glistening white stone, the masons continually chipping them into shape, so that it was dangerous to pass by them for the flying splinters. Now at last it is ready. There is a great stone wall, six or seven feet high, steps leading up to it, an avenue of saplings, stone railings, and at some future time there will be a stone carving behind it. The University will leave for the north, but the tomb will remain. And they have done it well, very simply, with only the names of the students engraved in the stone and the date of their death.

Late last night they chose today to march through the whole city with the coffins.

I have rarely seen anything so moving as this long procession which seemed to comprise all the students of Kunming. There were school-children, there were boys and girls from the technical schools and there were representatives from all the Universities, with banners and muffled drums. The police had disappeared from the streets. The procession started out from the University

258

early in the morning. The whole procession must have been at least two miles long, and it went very slowly, the banners were slit, so that they wouldn't flutter in the wind, and the drums sometimes gave place to muffled trumpets, and there was a tremendous gravity on the faces of the students.

Now, hearing the muffled drums, the tinkling of small bells and the soft deliberate padding of their shoes on the ground, seeing still in the mind's eye the banners with the portraits of the four dead students, I remember odd details here and there. A white flower was a sign of the mourners, and under the blazing sky there was the sea of calm faces and the sea of white flowers. I saw a schoolboy wearing a white flower, and when the procession came past, his father, wearing a mottled blue gown, noticed the boy's white flower for the first time, seized it and crushed it underfoot; and the small boy's hands were jerking uncontrollably. Every two hundred yards tables were set out, with oranges and bottles of wine and incense sticks; and at these tables the processions would pause, the incense sticks were waved over the coffins, but the bottles of wine, the oranges and all the other fruits remained on the tables. I did not take part in the procession. I saw it only towards the end, when it was coming out of the Small East Gate, and already they were weary, and the coffins were no longer being carried by the students, but were hoisted on small carts with rubber tires. The bloodsoaked clothes were carried on rickshaws. Hundreds of the long scrolls which have hung for three months in the University library were being held by the students, but the wind had torn them to ribbons by the time I saw them. And always the sound of the muffled drums and the tinkling of bells.

They started out at seven this morning; it was five when they returned to the campus, more weary than they expected to be. They told me that they were never frightened: one obtained an extraordinary sense of security—the same illusory sense of security which accompanies an army on the march.

I went into the library, the immense tiled library under which we have all worked for so many years; there was nothing now except a great emptiness, the floorboards dirty and here and there were mountains of torn and littered scrolls. Once they had been like a forest—these long, carefully inscribed scrolls hanging down from the ceiling, so close to one another that it was difficult to move among them. Now gradually and slowly the students were surging into the campus, very silent, the weariness showing on

259

their faces, the last sunlight falling on the green mounds. It was a long time before the ceremony began. The crowd stood round the white grave with its enormous black holes carved out of it, and one by one the coffins were brought up the steps and laid beside the grave. Not all the coffins possessed relics of the dead. One possessed only the books and some of the clothes of a girl student, for her body had been burnt not far from here; and this is according to an immemorial Chinese custom which decrees that the things nearest to a dead man may be conserved in his tomb. Unlike the Greeks the Chinese have no reverence for empty tombs.

Wine was sprinkled on the steps, and red incense sticks were waved by a professor, and already the sun was going down and it was beginning to be cold. Bells rang, a song was sung, and then three professors climbed the steps and made short speeches, saying that the students had not died in vain, though afterwards we might think they had died in vain, and freedom and democracy were things worth fighting for. The professors were Wen Yi-tuo, Chen Tuan-sen and Wu Han. They spoke very simply; there was no rhetoric, and only Wen Yi-tuo seemed to be desperately conscious of the importance of this moment in the history of China. Then the names of the students were called out, as though we half expected them to answer from among those present; and then the relatives of the dead students, and some of those who had been close to them, came up the steps and walked round the coffins. Then lime was brought, and the coffins were lowered with ropes, and it grew darker. Acetylene lamps began to shine, and we began to see that the coffins had entirely disappeared into the ten foot holes, and then there was the sodden sound of the lime trickling and later falling heavily on the lacquered wood. It was over now. The workmen would cover the four red coffins with cement, and there would be marble facing, and meanwhile the dusk was growing stronger and we could hardly see one another. Afterwards, I remember in the streets outside the University, how grey the shadows were as we drove home in little carts.

It is over, but we have no certainty that this will not happen again; we are at the mercy of men with hand-grenades, and until the students find out those who are responsible we shall have no peace. We shall be haunted by this evening and the grey shadows. Not far from here, under nameless graves, lie two Kuomintang ex-officers who have been put on trial and executed for these murders; but they were not responsible. The search for the murderers must begin again.

March 18th . . . IN HUNAN they are selling their children, there is almost no food, men are living on grass roots. The responsibility lies where? It is easy enough to say that it lies on the warmongers and the inefficiency of the transport system, and certainly it does lie heavily on the government which appears to be increasingly detached from the people. But K. said this evening something so frightening and true that I have been disturbed ever since. "In the old days when there were floods, the men who were sent to safeguard the lives of the people were those who were known to have high standards of morality. The Emperor Yu became Emperor only because he was known to be good. The stories of the old Emperors are well-known. When the floods came, or when there were ravages in the country, they dedicated themselves to their task; they never visited their wives; they took no care for themselves. Nowadays, when the floods come, we open a subscription and collect money and think that by doing this our consciences can be absolved, and even when some wretched official runs away with the money, we still think our consciences are absolved. The ravages that come over China are more terrible than the ravages of atomic bombs."

March 20th . . . WE STILL dream of the day when the long pilgrimage will be over and we can return to Peking. The books are being packed. There is even a provisional date for our departure—May 4th. But how shall we go? The railway to Mengtzu has been broken by the Japanese. We have discovered that we shall have to walk for seven days through malaria infested country before we can reach the Indo-Chinese railway. We cannot all fly to Peking. If we go by truck, at least a tenth of them will overturn on the roads, and heaven knows how many students and professors will never arrive. Safest is probably to walk across the whole breadth of China.

But the worst is over. The long exile of these three Chinese Universities from Peking is nearly over. We pretend we are "working as usual," but how can you work when nearly all the books are no longer available, and when every time we cross the campus we see it as it will be next year—abandoned and forgotten, with its stone tombs and its fifty cattlesheds in which we have taught for so long.

March 22nd . . . THEY were crushing rice. The heavy beam hung above them, and then it would be let loose, the wooden hammer fell into the ground and the rice was pounded into small square cakes. They sang as they worked, and they wore their coloured trousers, which are all patches of bright reds and greens, and the sun came through the overhanging trees, and near the lake there were great blocks of white stone like ice.

Impossible to imagine they could be happier. In the hard sunlight, their faces red, chanting as the beam swung, the voices exploding at the moment when the hammer hit the rice, they seemed, as so many things seem in this clear-cut atmosphere, hardly to be people; they had stepped out of a painting. There was a warmth in their bodies which is not like the seething warmth of the marketplace. Sturdy, with huge shoulders, they sang with all their attention concentrated on the small cake of rice which was gradually growing whiter.

It must have been some special kind of rice, or perhaps some special cake which is only eaten when it is pounded till it is as hard as rock. They were oblivious of everything else, and in the sunshine they had assumed the simplicity of the white cake of rice in the same way that the poet Blake, gazing at wood, would find himself becoming the wood. They were *sunyasis*, devoted to the act of concentration, and at the same time they were lords of the earth and all it contains.

March 23rd . . . HE WAS looking slighter than ever, hardly more than bone and a few shreds of skin beneath the faded blue gown. He had come from hospital, there were blue bruises over his eyes, he was still weak with typhus and he was laughing his head off. It was a long and complicated story, which he told hesitantly at first and then in spate.

"I was ill, and of course it meant living in a crowded hospital ward, on camp-beds, and there was hardly any food, and the doctors were bad—sometimes dangerous. We were not wealthy enough to deserve their attention. We lay there, dying more of hunger than anything else. One of the people in the hospital, in the bed next to mine, was an old man, the most miserable of old

262

men, brown-faced like a beggar, repulsive to look at, who wore a white cloth coat and white pyjamas, and sometimes he would get up and carefully look through the bundle he carried with him—and we noticed that there was a silk gown, and perfectly preserved white underwear. We thought he was a little mad. If you are old in China, you must be a little mad. We would watch him and pass comments on him, and he seemed to be dying, and we wondered what would happen to the bundle when he died. Then he died, and the nurse took away the little bundle and everything went on as before. And then an extraordinary thing happened—they began to come into the ward and offer us private rooms, and they brought in good food and swept the floors. We thought we were dreaming. The doctor came and spoke to us very gently, saying he had done his best for us, and we were recovering now, and we would get better treatment in future. But why? No one dared ask him. Great yellow bowls of white rice arrived, and there were flowers in our small rooms, and the doctor came in again, very red-faced and apologetic, to say that our treatment in the past had been scandalous and would never occur again, and begged us almost on his knees to forgive him. And so we pretended to forgive him and wondered what would happen.

"It was some days before we were able to put all the details together. The old man was a distant relation of the governor of the province—very distant, perhaps ten cousins removed. He wore a ring which was a family ring, the ring was stolen by one of the hospital attendants when he died, and it came on the market. Now the market for gold is controlled by someone who has very good relations with the governor, and this man noticed the resemblance between the ring the governor carried and the ring worn by the old man in the hospital, and brought it to the attention of the governor; and so they found where it had come from, and the doctors were in desperate fear of an examination by the governor's staff. The old man's coffin was taken to a distant village—a village of tribespeople, for much of the power in this province still remains with the descendants of the tribal princes. But this time he was buried with the ring."

The student laughed: "In the end, of course, there was an examination, not by the governor but by his secretary and his military chief-of-staff. From the hospital's point of view this was much worse than an examination by the governor himself, for the hospital attendant was executed and the doctors were severely
263

warned, and during the examination many of their own rings were stolen by the soldiers."

March 24th . . . My own experience in hospital had been bad; the doctor was good, indeed excellent, but after a while the first nurse left, and another nurse took her place—a frail toothy thing who possessed no talent for nursing, crafty and cynical and never in the place where I wanted her, always chatting and gambling just outside the door or disappearing on mysterious errands. Convalescence was so delightful that I was hardly conscious of her absence; it was her presence that was disturbing, for when everything else seemed beautiful she was a purposeless interruption on the life around me. The gold tree outside the window, the curious sensation that snow was falling through bright sunlight, the dragons and horsemen who appeared in the markings of trees, the shape of a commonplace rice-bowl or the blue porcelain spoons—these were the things that occupied my attention, and I thought of them all this evening when L. told me of how when she was twelve she went to hospital.

"It was the time of the civil wars, and I think the enemy were coming to our town. The family was frightened. I was too ill to be moved, and they had decided to escape. So I was left in the local missionary hospital where the nuns looked after me, and they told me afterwards they had hung huge red cross flags outside the hospital and the Communists had left them in peace. I was very ill, and I remember the sounds of firing and then for a long while the room where I was in the hospital was deserted—the patients had disappeared under the beds, and none of the nuns dared to come to us. I was so sick that I hardly knew what was happening, and I remember all day watching a corner of the grey bedsheet on which, perhaps many years before, a drop of blood had fallen— there was a dark brown stain on a thin cotton blanket.

"That was all. Nothing else. All that day and all the next day I gazed at the brown stain, and the sunlight came through the torn paper-cover window, and there was dead silence except for the rats. And then, I think it was less than a week later, the Communists passed through the village again and disappeared, and my parents returned, and they took me out of the hospital, and I remember how I struggled to keep the blanket. I wanted it. It was the most beautiful thing I knew. I screamed and screamed, and at last they gave me the blanket, and I took it home, and made a

264

doll out of it and three weeks ago I found it again—it was eaten by moths, but there was still the corner with the bloodstain, and I remember wondering how strange it was that for a week or more my life had hung, not on a thread, but on an old stain of blood shining in the sun which had seemed to me the most beautiful thing in the world."

March 25th . . . I WENT with my student J. to a hospital— for some reason all news recently has been news from hospital— and we went to the children's ward, where the plaster was falling from the walls and the floor was covered in dust, though it is true that at the moment when we entered a nurse, in a ragged blue shirt and blue trousers, began to sweep it up. The doctor explained how the inflation was making it impossible to operate the hospital; how drugs now could no longer be bought; how hope had long ago vanished that they would ever be able to keep up with the mass of patients who should go to hospital. "There are things that are beyond us," he complained, the small face made dark with weariness. "We are at the mercy of too many different things and too many different people. We must struggle on." I think he was sincere, but the heart had gone from his work, and it was difficult to think that he had any emotions left, or that he could *care*.

He complained about some soldiers who entered the hospital the previous week. They were young officers, and they brought with them four wounded officers, all unconscious, all heavily bleeding; and very tactfully he had attempted to find out how these wounds were made. They said they were drinking. One of them had obtained a large sum of money, and so they were gambling, and then one of them drew his revolver and soon there was a fight. The young officers came from well-to-do families and gave orders to the whole hospital staff: "If you do not heal them, we will kill you." The doctor shrugged his shoulders. He had done his best for them. The soldiers mounted guard over the hospital; their own four wounded comrades took precedence over everything else. They were uneducated, they were determined and they showed no signs of obeying authority, for they were authority. "Two of them are still here," the doctor said, "and later I'll show you them."

But we had come to see the children, who lay in their unpainted wooden cots, looking up at the sky, for the paper windows were torn and some of the tiles had fallen through the roof. What was

265

amazing was their pale starved incandescent beauty, the whiteness of the thin faces, the bright eyes, the slow tenderness with
which they regarded the world. J. brought them some toys, which
they regarded gravely, almost as I imagine those who are deeply
religious regard holy wafers, and put out their hands for them,
and did not smile. I went into another room where their food was
prepared—it was the bad rice which we used to have among the
professors, greyish in colour, filled with stones, with hardly any
vegetables. One child was receiving milk, but the others received
none unless they were exceptionally weak; and it was not the fault
of the doctor, who hardly expected more than a few of the children to survive. They lay back in the cots and talked quietly to
one another, conserving their energy. The nurse was young, hardly
more than sixteen, and you felt that she was doing her best and
hated the sight of children dying around her, but could do nothing—it was beyond her powers—she took her orders from others,
and received little enough herself.

So we went away, remembering those quiet hungry eyes, to the
place where the officers were lying in beds surrounded by their
guards with Mausers hanging at their waist-bands, with food
brought in from a neighbouring restaurant and clean sheets everywhere. It was the cleanliness of the place that was astonishing,
and the sleekness and beauty of the young nurses; and it was the
oddest thing to see a bottle of whiskey on the table. The doctor
shook his head—one of those nods which could be taken by the
soldiers as assent, and perhaps by others as perturbed dissent.
And then we went out into the busy streets where all was colour
and hunger for life, and you wondered how it was that the people
you saw in the streets had survived. With what strength, what
compassion and what treachery had they fought for their survival,
here where the battle is waged with the keenest edge!

March 30th . . . At night the whole of Cornwall seemed to
flicker into life, the grass was phosphorescent, and as I remember
this most beloved of all counties, the moon is eternally full on
the white rocks and the still whiter pyramids of kaolin. So it was
tonight, the fullness of the sky and the fullness of the earth, and
the lake like parchment. There was nothing eerie at all, even
though the roofs shone with the same green light as they have in
Cornwall after rain, so that it seems sometimes that there are no
roofs, but innumerable small green waterfalls hanging in the air.
266

And this green and parchment white world was full of the noise of youngsters and lovers near the lake. I thought of Versailles, and of how the buildings there seemed to be made for the ripeness of an afternoon in late summer; and of Paris, which is grey-white and therefore most beautiful in chilly mornings of spring; of autumnal London and wintry Greece, with snow on the Acropolis; and of how all places are made for the appropriate season, and how this lake is best in full moonlight or in the early morning when the mist is rising. The Chinese have planned their architecture to the lay of the earth and the appointment with the seasons, and the sun and the moon. So have we all, but I can think of nothing more magnificent than the half-ruined archway leading to the lake, which glittered this evening like the purest moonbeams.

April 4th . . . HER pure face has like the moon its increases and decreases, its periods of fullness and absences; she is always changing, and some subtle trick of light or dress makes her change always for the better. And this young student, who looks almost Spanish, her cheeks and lips as red as apples, who hurries about with books under her arm and looks after a baby in the intervals of studying philosophy, seems to me in many ways an epitome of the modern Chinese student.

She wrote once in an essay: "I am like a dark glass in a dark room, and the glass is covered with dark cloth. I do not know what is inside." In this she was exactly like all the other students, caught up in the Chinese crisis and hovering between East and West. She belongs, like nearly all Chinese students, to a lost generation which may yet find itself. I say "lost," because they are so convinced that they are lost; but to know that you are lost is the first step to being "found." These students know the odds against them. They know that under present circumstances they can obtain useful employment only if they have friends in the government, that nepotism goes on unchecked, that their resources are small in comparison with the resources of the men who have no love for the things they love. They see the wall round them coming ever closer, and it is only very rarely that they can break through. Where shall we go? What shall we do? What shall we fight for? They know what they want to do, and where they want to go, but simply because this University has the reputation of believing in democracy and a freer system of government, they are made to hesitate—the forces arraigned against them are too great, and though they have not yet lost heart, the time may come when they will be compelled either to silence or to a part in a government which represents none of their ideals.

I think of the girl who looks so Spanish, who reads and sings and teaches in a middle school and attends lectures and tries to bring up her baby and says little, because there is little now that can be said, though she struggles with her books and feels a kind of assurance when she remembers that she has married a mechanical engineer from the University—the hope of China lies perhaps more in her young mechanics than in the others. I think of the young chemist I know, whose dark sensitive face I shall remember always, and he too wonders how he can ever fit into the pattern which is being made by the government. Or the young students of foreign languages, the boy who plays the violin alone to himself among the gravemounds because there is nowhere else to play and whose writing in English shows more signs of promise than that of anyone I have ever known. They come from the territories once occupied by the Japanese. It may be a year before they go back, and before they reach their native villages bureaucrats and time-servers will be there already. The young were not sent to occupy the places recaptured from the Japanese. The old generals, the old time-servers were sent instead. The lists appeared —hundreds upon hundreds of men who had taken part in the prodigious civil wars and whose names were almost forgotten have suddenly come into the limelight again. Youth is cold shouldered and not trusted with responsibilities, yet it is only the young who could make China habitable again.

I think of these things with dread, knowing that the students must batter for a few more years against the walls; but when they break through, what a flood of energy and fine simplicities will be released! What hopes there will be for the country which seems so often eternally at war with itself, the north fighting against the south the same battle which has been fought through China's history, though now the battle is bloodier than ever. We had hoped for a sunburst; we dread the continual thunderstorm. If the battle must be fought, surely it is better that the Chinese should fight it alone. American aid will only exasperate the Chinese on both sides; the Americans will receive no gratitude for their L.S.T.s, their aeroplanes and their donations of grain. Gradually and imperceptibly, as the result of a decaying regime, the

268

Chinese have lost a sense of responsibility, they have lost something of their self-reliance, it is government by dictatorship or by ruse. What is needed is that the great names shall go, and that we shall be left with the smaller and more representative people. I love this country too much to have any faith in its torture chambers, its black-clothed police, its undisciplined soldiers, the air of treachery and treason which surrounds us all. This is not how it should have been. I came to China just after the outbreak of the Pacific War—there were still high hopes—the Generalissimo was still beloved—the government was not yet incapable. But during these last five years they have allowed the inflation to continue, allowed trading with the enemy, allowed power to drift into the hands of those who were least likely to use power profitably, except to themselves; and now we know, better than we knew before, that there will come a time when all that the Kuomintang stands for will be questioned. It was not for this that the northern expedition was formed. Dr. Sun Yat-sen never allowed that the Principle of Livelihood should be forgotten, nor did he regard the period of military tutelage as more than a short term experiment. The threads have become lost, or they have rusted to nothing. The fine frenzy has gone. What is left is only the desire of the people for peace; and in this desire is the greatest hope of the future.

These are the things that batter on the brain while you look at the young girl reading her books beside the small bamboo cradle in the sun.

April 5th . . . HE HAD tales to tell of Viet-Nam which made our hair stand on end. He had come from Indo-China almost alone, he had been left for dead by Chinese bandits on the frontier and when he reached Kunming he went at once to the French hospital. "It was the strangest impression. There was the small French fortress, we lived very quietly, each day was exactly the same as every other day; and then suddenly the Japanese came and asked us to surrender our ammunition within twenty-four hours. We decided to fight. And really it was exactly like a film, the sun very hot, and the small fortress in the forest, and the Japanese sending wave upon wave of men against us, and the Indo-Chinese held aloof—hating both of us, and yet you felt that they were there, somewhere in the forest.

"They were loyal to us sometimes, these Indo-Chinese, but

neither the French nor the Japanese could trust them. They wanted their own liberty and talked mysteriously of an old Chinese scholar called Ho Chi-minh, of whom we had never heard. I was in the customs. I took refuge in the fortress with my wife and child, because we knew what would happen to French citizens caught in the town. I locked the door of my house—there was no time to do anything more than just lock the door, though my wife took a pair of gloves and two dolls for the child. And then we hid in the fortress, and the Japanese breached the walls, and ordered us all to dig trenches, and we knew the trenches were graves. But they did not shoot us because a thunderstorm occurred, and the graves were not ready—some had fallen in. We waited. They gave us something to eat. Shortly after the thunderstorm had cleared, they ordered us all outside the broken wall of the fortress and we saw the Indo-Chinese standing on the cliffs above us. They were silent—and there were hundreds of them. The Japanese did not know what to do. They feared, not that the Indo-Chinese would come to rescue us, but that they would remember the murders and fear for themselves.

"I felt entirely unchanged. That was the extraordinary thing. No emotion, or only the slightest quiver of emotion—it was like those small stirrings of emotion that come with convalescence. The women and children were ordered to watch us. We were barefoot. We stood there, in the wet red clay, the sun burning down on us, and we just waited, and then after a while the Indo-Chinese on the cliffs went away, and we knew that we would soon fill the graves.

"I swear there is a difference between being executed in sunlight and being executed in a cell, or in winter. Dostoievsky went mad after he was blindfolded, but we were not blindfolded. We could see everything so clearly, and though I could not see my wife I knew she was somewhere there. What was strange and odd was that the Japanese were not concerned only with bayoneting us, but they must strike our faces—one man began to piss, and his face was struck, and another man started screaming, and he fell to the ground, and they lifted him up in the air and bayoneted him when he fell, and somehow it seemed unreal, we could hardly believe it and we were relieved when the screams came to an end and he was kicked into the red ditch. And then the captain of the fort, an old grey hard-bitten legionary, seeing that the end was near, began to make a short speech, telling us to have courage

270

and to love France, and they let him speak, and then they cut his head open with a blow from a rifle-butt, and he too fell into the grave, and still there was a long pause, and nothing happened, and the sun fell down on the red grave, and we just waited.

"There was a whole company of Japanese divided into two groups, one immediately behind us and another immediately in front of us, on the other side of the ditch. They had bayonets, hand-grenades, rifles, they even had short clubs. But I swear to God I felt no fear. I knew they were waiting for someone, the general perhaps, or some high official, and then at last—it must have been breakfast time—the general arrived in a jeep, and what was disturbing was that he brought with him a beautiful girl, taller than an average Japanese, probably his Korean mistress, and she wore a long yellow gown and carried some flowers. We waited. He did not expect us to be there. I think he must have thought we were already killed. He was angry, and he walked with angry little prancing steps up to the Japanese commander, and shortly afterwards he walked down our lines and stood facing the place where our captain lay in the ditch, and then he saluted, and ordered the execution.

"It lasted much longer than any of us thought it would last—a sudden screaming scurry of Japanese who began to shoot us from one side of the ditch and bayonet us from the other. I fell into the ditch. I knew I wasn't dead because I could hear the screams all round me, and yet I wasn't screaming, and I felt no pain. And then there were the excited voices of the Japanese, and I knew by the shadows that they were jumping into the grave and bayoneting us. It was ridiculous. It was ridiculous in the first place because the Japanese themselves were in danger of killing each other—they had been firing at each other with us as a thin veil between them. The screams died down and began again, and this time they were much louder and seemed to come from our women, and then for the first time I felt sorry and ashamed.

"I stayed there all day. No one came to cover up the grave, and the worst thing of all was the knowledge that people were moving in the grave near me, moving quietly, alive but pretending to be dead, and sometimes the screams of pain were muffled; and worst of all, for I was conscious of it all the long afternoon, was the sensation of thirst.

"The Japanese were so sure of themselves that when night came they left no guards. Out of about sixty legionaries and twenty

271

officials who had taken refuge in the fort, more than twenty survived. We waited until it was dark, then some of us slipped quietly in the direction of the cliffs, and others remained to look after the wounded. There were no signs of our wives.

"We lived in the cliffs for three weeks. The Indo-Chinese hated us perhaps as much as they hated the Japanese, but they were willing to help us to leave for China. They said that our wives and children were not killed—this we owed to the girl who accompanied the Japanese general. They had been given as concubines to the officers. What was even more surprising was that the children were unharmed, though it is true there were only six children who had taken refuge in the fort. Through the Indo-Chinese we maintained contact with the camp, we even received letters from our wives, and we also received compasses. I was lucky. As inspector of customs, I knew many of the bandits in this area, and I had never pressed them too hard—a reasonable amount of smuggling seemed unavoidable, and once or twice when a smuggler was imprisoned I had helped his family. The smugglers knew all the tracks, and they were prepared to help us escape. It was not easy, even then. There were so many Indo-Chinese who still hated us. Somehow or other the women escaped, and then we began to make our way to China, but the worst thing happened when we reached the frontier—the Chinese bandits came and stole everything we possessed, our rings and most of our clothes, our passports and papers—for the most surprising thing of all was that the Japanese had not taken them from us. The bandits even stole my children's dolls."

April 6th, Chungking . . . For a year, for two years I have told myself that Chungking is pleasant in spring. Why not go? It is two hours by air.

I remembered the stern white cliffs, the flooding river, the caves in the rocks, the hardness of the place, the mud, the filth, the inevitability of corruption in such a soil, I remembered the long winter nights when a yellow mist comes and the loveliness of the Chialing river at dawn—surely there is no other river so beautiful, and it was all I had expected it to be, though sterner and more miserable than ever. Chungking was not unrecognizable, though at moments it seemed to be another town altogether. I had forgotten the scream of the automobiles, the greyness of the shop fronts, the dreary white cohorts of the dead, for here in
272

Kunming—now that I am in Chungking I still feel that I am seeing everything from a window in Kunming—the funerals are brilliantly coloured, the shop fronts are painted yellow and blue and for some reason the automobiles seem quieter.

There can rarely have been a more bumpy passage. We flew low over flooded Kweichow and dropped a parachute with millions of dollars of national currency, apparently so that the flooded farmers should be able to propitiate the dragons of the rain, and as we sank slowly down to sea-level from the 6,000 foot heights of Kunming, you were conscious of another atmosphere. Kunming is heady wine. You feel all the time you are living on top of a mountain. Under the mat-sheds in the small sand-strip at Chungking, you feel you are at the bottom of the sea.

Then the long climb up the steep cliffs, the greyness of the air —all greens and blues washed away, Chungking the colour of granite, the roads muddy, the people wearing black, the motorcars with their following plumes of purple wood-oil exhaust, the sense of treachery in the air, of a city from which the life has slowly crumbled away. This is not the true picture, but this is how it seems tonight. Kunming has colour, the patterns and shapes vibrate with their own integral life, but in Chungking the sun never shines. It shone once. Grandfathers remember the sun, but no one else remembers. And all of it is below the sea.

April 8th . . . THE frail grey sky opened this morning to receive the sun, and you would have sworn that the day would be grey again, but the clouds cleared, the moist burning sun smothered us all, and it is summer already. We sweat in the cheap hotel bedroom. We drink iced lemonade all day, knowing we shall have dysentery; but it is better to die of dysentery than to die of thirst.

Old Marshal Feng Yu-hsiang is better. He looked ill when I last saw him two years ago; now there is ripeness in his cheeks, and he carries himself with greater assurance. He has been dismissed from the Executive Committee of the Kuomintang. Laughing, very pleased with himself, he lifted his cup and said: "I have two more jobs under the government. Today I have drunk a toast to express my delight that one job has been taken from me."

"And when the others are taken from you?"

"Then I shall drink more toasts."

He said: "The murder of the students shocked me profoundly.

This cannot go on. We cannot afford any longer to allow fascism to go unchecked."

He has mellowed with time, and his assurance is bewilderingly evident. One has the impression that he grows stronger with the years, more robust, even more understanding. They say he still wants power. I doubt it. He is sixty-five and power can mean almost nothing to him, and his sympathies are with the powerless. He talked for half an hour of the ship he has asked the Government to give him; it must be a big ship, sufficiently large anyway to allow him to take under his protection the writers and artists of Chungking who want so desperately to go to the coast. "If they stay here," he said, "they will be at the mercy of every little government-paid cut-throat. We must take them down safely. It must be done." Very gently he dropped his huge fist on the table, not banging the table but bringing it down with so much force that it was as though a giant was demonstrating strength.

He told a long story of his native village. In the reign of the Emperor Chien Lung, the Emperor's favourite concubine was dying. All over China imperial emissaries were sent to demand that those with power of healing her should come to the capital. Orders were given to the country magistrates to send the men who seemed most promising. One day a young meat-ball seller called Liu-yeh-yeh was picking his teeth outside the walls of Peking, absent-mindedly looking at the imperial rescript on the walls. He seemed to be reading the rescript, and he was nodding his head from side to side. Militia-men saw him, and asked him whether he could cure the concubine. Liu-yeh-yeh was suddenly struck with nervousness. He could not read, he did not know what was happening, he began to stammer, and the militia-men began to think of the reward that would be theirs if they could find the man who would cure the imperial concubine. He was taken to the palace, and given into the hands of the Emperor's doctors, and at last he was presented to the Emperor, and then he was too nervous to speak, he merely shook his head from side to side. On the afternoon of the same day he was taken into the room where the imperial concubine was lying.

Liu-yeh-yeh only knew that she was ill, and that unless he cured her, his life would be forfeit.

He said: "I must think about this. Give me a room where I can think."

They gave him a room, and they gave him young attendants,

274

and new clothes. He could not think what to do. He meditated. He strode up and down the room, and he knew that his head was in danger, and he thought: "I must think of something." He thought of his feet, and the little balls of dirt between his toes. He ordered the attendants to go away. He collected the dirt from his toes, rolled it all into a large ball, placed it in a cup of hot tea and summoned the attendants. "The medicine is ready," he said, giving them the tea. The tea was taken to the imperial concubine, who drank it. Next morning she was better.

No one was so surprised as Liu-yeh-yeh. More medicine was required. Unfortunately he had no more medicine. He walked into the garden, trying to make his feet dirty. The Emperor sent him a scroll. He could not understand what was happening. He was promised a bride from the imperial family if he could cure the concubine. Guards followed him. Panic-stricken, at a moment when the guards were not watching, he leapt over the wall.

Then all over China there was a hue and cry for Liu-yeh-yeh. The Emperor sent new imperial rescripts in all directions. Large rewards were offered for the mysterious doctor who had so successfully cured the imperial concubine; but the concubine was sinking again. All matters of state were held up. He was rumoured to be going in the direction of Paotingfu. Soldiers were sent after him. They were waving immense embroidered flags and calling on him to stop. He was coming to the river near a village, he saw them creeping up to him and in utter desperation he threw himself into the river and was drowned. The concubine was dying. A report was sent back to the Emperor, who ordered that the body of the magician should receive a state burial and that a large temple should be raised in the Buddhist faith on the bank overlooking the place where the man was drowned. The temple was to be named the Temple of the Magician, but today it is called more properly: "The Temple of the Balls of Dirt which appear between your toes when you have been walking for a long time."

And saying this, Feng Yu-hsiang roared with laughter, the immense face dark with wrinkles and the great plump hands making staggering blows on his knees; and never had he seemed more likeable.

April 9th, The Control Yuan . . . WE SAW him this morning in a house close to Marshal Feng's, a man nearly seventy. He wore an emerald gown, the long white beard like a cloud flying in mid-

275

heavens; the room was bare, the chairs creaking, and yet somehow the room seemed perfectly appropriate. He stood very silently in the middle of the room, bowing and smiling, the face deeply lined. He is the greatest calligraphist in China, writing with tremendous short sweeps which half-destroy the original character of the letter, yet the strength is overwhelming.

We talked of the murder of the students and the decay of law in this country. The smile had frozen on his face. He shook his head from side to side, and once he opened wide his hands and said: "I am ashamed—every day more ashamed. I am the Minister of the Control Yuan, but I have no power."

I said: "Who can we go to so that justice will be done?"

He answered: "You can go to the Generalissimo."

"Will he listen to us?"

There was no reply.

We spoke of calligraphy, and he offered to write some characters for us. He has written on calligraphy, and gave us some of his writings and his recent poems.

He said: "I do what I can that justice should survive, but the Control Yuan has no powers. Dr. Sun Yat-sen desired that it should have powers—yes, the widest possible powers." He suggested that we see Dr. Sun Fo. In theory the Legislative Yuan also has wide powers.

"Then who has power?"

He refused to answer, but when I said: "One man?" he nodded his head.

A little later he said: "The President of the University has sent in his report. It will go through the usual channels."

He said he was over-weighed with grief and terror for the future of the country. As a young man he had fought side by side with Dr. Sun Yat-sen; he was almost the oldest surviving member of the original Kuomintang. He had entered many Ministries, taken part in many wars, made many visits to many parts of China, conferred for many days with Dr. Sun Yat-sen, but there was little to show for it except the tremendous dignity of the man and the worship in which he was held. He said: "I am old—in a few days I shall spend my seventieth birthday. I have seen many things." He shook his head sadly again, for so few of those things except calligraphy and the beauty of the Chinese scene had been pleasant.

276

He said: "I am old, and Feng Yu-hsiang is old. We belong to the same generation, and we are happy together. We are brothers," and I think it was then that for the first time I realized that deep, fervent and unchanging desire of the Chinese to form small bands of brothers among themselves. In China everything is so insecure, and the brothers who are dedicated to each other have greater powers to survive. So the Generalissimo had formed his small band, which wielded great power; there was no power except death which could dissolve that band. Brotherhood of a kind unknown to the West there was; and often it has dangerous roots going beyond all reason.

He came out of the house and stood for a moment at the top of the steps, bowing gracefully, the white beard against the blue sky of his gown, an old man whose memory was failing, who knew that power had been taken from him yet remained upright, and would remain so to death.

April 10th . . . NOTHING surprises me any more in Chungking. I saw a man walking stark naked through the Street of the Seven Stars this morning, and hardly anyone turned to watch him; I saw a mad girl reeling and singing drunken songs, and no one paid attention to her except a few children who followed after her, whispering among themselves; I saw starved dogs fighting over a bone till the blood sprang. But worse than the things one sees are the rumours one hears—of the civil war.

This afternoon, in the rain, I went to see Dr. Sun Fo in his strange circular house overlooking the Chialing river; and on the way I was responsible for the death of a man. I am appalled by what I have done, but I cannot see what I should have done, yet merely by my presence at a certain place and a certain moment of time, the man died, and another has been wounded.

Near Dr. Sun Fo's house a huge army lorry was backing into the hillside. Here the road winds steeply above the Chialing river; maize grows on the slopes, and in the rain the road was slippery. I had passed the lorry. The driver waved and shouted *"ting-hao"* and I remember I turned back and grinned at him, and caught his eye. He was young, with a full round face, a forage cap and his coat was open at the neck. He slipped the gears with one hand, and with the other waved again, and the army lorry began to back against the hill-side, and then there was a sound like a sub-

277

dued sob, the wheels began to race and the lorry overturned and began to bounce, very slowly, down the hillside, with all kinds of things being thrown from it—clothes, boxes, great strips of tent-cloth. It happened as in slow motion, and one moment you would see the wheels and the soft underbelly of the lorry, gleaming black and silky, and the next moment you saw the torn hood; and then a soldier was thrown clear, to crumple in the red mud of the sloping fields, but there was no sign of the boy who had waved to me. I ran down. It took at least ten minutes to make my way down the slope, and one boy was dead, his back broken, and the boy who had been thrown clear was moaning, his face covered with blood. I tried to stop the blood flowing. Five minutes later some officers came down. Ten minutes later I was in Dr. Sun Fo's drawing-room. He had said to friends of mine that he had been puzzled the last time I had seen him, because I wore muddy shorts; now the shorts were more muddy than ever, and blood-stained.

We talked of the death of the students. He said: "What can I do? We have no power. We pass laws, but the government pays no attention to the laws we pass. They invent new laws. They have invented a law relating to the duties to be paid on incoming merchandise. This is a law which the Legislative Yuan has never passed. The government has increased the duty. On what grounds?"

I said: "If there is no law, then there is no nation and there is no revolution. If this kind of anarchy prevails, then everything your father fought for will be lost."

He nodded and said: "We have done our best. We are up against forces over which we have no control. Have you seen the Minister of the Control Yuan?"

"Yes, he suggested I should come to see you. Can anything be done to safeguard the lives of the students?"

He answered: "There are laws on the statute book against murderers. If we could have protection for the law——"

He did not go on. The rain poured outside. Fifty yards away they were taking the body of the soldier up the slope. He talked of a book I had written, and very kindly lent me a copy of his own book. I have been reading it all evening, and do not know which to admire more—the logic of the man, or the passion behind the words. He has grown immeasurably since the war; his
278

hates have grown too, and his loves. He shook his fist this afternoon and said: "Must we be saddled with T. V. Soong? He knows nothing—nothing whatsoever—about banking, and he knows nothing of economics. The whole country depends upon him, he orders our whole economy—and look where we have come to!"

April 11th . . . EATING cherries, I went to Feng Yu-hsiang's house in the country. For miles you go along the motor-road north of Chungking. Here there are no mountains, only great rice-lakes, a sense of desolation, crumbling ruins of mat-shed houses. And then quite suddenly the car stops, guards appear from somewhere, and you find yourself walking in the evening mist along the raised mounds between the fields, the sun sinking, the sky like a wound; there is something ill and cheerless about the Chungking evenings.

I can never associate Feng Yu-hsiang with any ordinary background. Twice as large as most men, he seems to demand vast mountains and immense rivers to be his accompanists through life; and so it was this evening when the rice-lakes seemed to go on forever, and huge shadows of clouds leaped across our paths. Steaming bullocks wound their way slowly through the fields; there was no sound this evening, and no sign of a house.

One should have expected it. The house was in a great gulley hollowed out from the fields, and you reached it by steps carved out of the livid rock. We could see guides coming, with lanterns; and then more guides, and then the lights of the house went on—a giant's palace, not large, but giving in this evening light an impression of immensity. On the rocks beside the path he had ordered his poems to be carved in characters six inches high—he had left his mark on Szechuan which would remain for generations.

I have forgotten how we spent the time; he talked of Chinese characters, and he refused to talk about the condition of the country—he was *en pantoufles*, happy with his brush, with the sense of security which came from the immense overhanging rocks, this hollow dug out of the earth, the sound of a river somewhere, and the rustling of bamboos.

"Do you like it?" he asked.

"Yes, but it's not real—I've always seen you either on top of mountains, or somewhere in the bowels of the earth."

279

I went back by car after supper, but nothing was so good as the long journey across the dark mist-laden fields, and the journey back across the same fields, turned black and silver in the moon.

April 12th . . . STILL in search of murderers, we went to see Dr. Chiang Mon-lin, secretary of the Executive Council. Years ago I had met him in Chungking, and liked him for his courtesy and his gentle devotion to a China which no longer existed. For a while, while I was in Kunming, he was President of Peiping University, which was one of the three associated Universities in Lienta; and I would see him at annual meetings, and sometimes he would pass in his car. For many years he has been head of the Chinese Red Cross. I expected to find him unchanged, helpful, hating murder, but he said nothing that would put our minds at rest.

"I have nothing to do with the Universities now," he said, the voice clipped and dry, the life gone from it. "I'm getting old—I can't do more than one thing at a time."

"Is there any way in which we can safeguard the lives of the students?"

"I can't do anything——"

"But people tell me you can. Can't something be done to get the secret police away from Universities, away from everything—altogether away?"

He said, the voice like a whipleash: "We must have the secret police, otherwise there is no safety for government officials. I might be shot on my way home by car."

I spoke of the danger in which the democratic professors found themselves. They were good men, but the military clique of the Kuomintang had threatened them.

He said: "There are men in Kunming whom I dislike intensely —it is no affair of mine what they do. The Democratic League is the tail of the Communist Party." He smiled: "A large dog wagging a little tail——"

I could hardly believe that in his position he could believe such innocent nonsense.

"They are good men, and they are democrats, and they are in danger——"

He said: "They are not good men, they are not democrats."

It was useless to go on. The telephone bell rang. Someone was telephoning to ask whether dollars could be exchanged at a better
280

rate than seemed appropriate according to government rules. He answered: "I will see what can be done."

April 13th . . . WE KNOW him as the Honourable K. P. S. Menon, which sounds intimidating, but not so intimidating as his title: The Indian Agent-General. But neither the man nor the title should be intimidating, and of him one thing is certain—of all the foreign representatives to China, he is the most beloved. Men loved and admired Eggleston, the Australian Ambassador, in the same way that they love and admire Menon.

We had lunch with him today. His wife wore a scarlet sari and on her forehead there was the red circle; his children were there, in saris also, and there was Wen Yuan-ning, the editor of *Tien Hsia*. The sunlight kept bursting into the large room on the shores of the Chialing river.

Wen Yuan-ning told a story of Mme Kung Hsiang-hsi, the wife of the Prime Minister. He had a great admiration for Mme Kung, who is the richest woman in China. He admired her for her dignity, her strength of mind, her immense interest in the financial dealings of the country; and this was strange, because Mme Kung's fortune has been amassed at the time when the people of China have starved on an unprecedented scale. Most of all he admired her strength of character, and related a story of Mme Kung's visit to Signor Mussolini. "In the Palazzo Vecchia Signor Mussolini lived and worked in an enormous room, his desk two hundred yards away from the bronze doors. The *carbonieri* led you to the doors, opened them and you were left alone to walk across the marble floor with Signor Mussolini glowering at you from his desk, his face becoming larger and larger as you approached. But Mme Kung was made of sterner stuff. She refused to walk across the marble floors. Was she not the wife of Mr. Kung? She stood there and held her ground, and Signor Mussolini was compelled to walk the full two hundred yards towards her. What a triumph for Mme Kung!"

The triumph, however, was short-lived; someone asked who were the people who had observed the scene.

Wen Yuan-ning answered: "Signor Mussolini and Mme Kung."

"It is impossible," a young Chinese answered. "Signor Mussolini is dead, and therefore we can have no verification of the story, and are we expected to believe about Mme Kung a story told by herself?"

281

I shall remember this afternoon for the gracefulness of the saris, Menon's boyish laughter, the sunlight streaming through the window and falling on the gold rings and armbands of the colourful daughters.

April 15th, The Democratic League . . . EVER since I came to China, I have heard rumours of the League, which was founded in 1941. In all the weary days of civil war and murder, the ideals of the League, caught between the cross-fires of the Communists and the Kuomintang, seemed greatest and most likely to succeed, given time and some well-being and great luck. They stood in the centre, isolated, often attacked by both sides, always at the mercy of their poverty; for they possessed no army, and unlike the Kuomintang which could raise money wherever it wished, and under whatsoever conditions it wished, it was poverty-stricken. The League received money in the form of private donations— no other sources were available.

I have known Lo Lung-chi, the spokesman of the Democratic League, for years. Shortly before I went to Kunming, he was dismissed from his post in the University on the Generalissimo's express orders. I have never understood why the University expressed its agreement with the Generalissimo, but Professor Lo Lung-chi was compelled to leave his post. They said he had spoken bitterly about the Generalissimo's policies, as though that was a crime. It is true that Lo Lung-chi is often bitter, but when there is so much bitterness in the country, it seems strange that he should be marked out for a failing that is almost universal in China.

Occasionally I would call and see him in his small rooms in the former Japanese Consulate in Kunming. He worked hard, spoke brilliantly and though he lacks the power of invoking the admiration and adoration which Wen Yi-tuo invokes, his mind works along straight lines, and his honesty is self-evident. Today, when I called to see him at the headquarters of the Democratic League, he was almost unrecognizable: he had matured, and there was more precision than ever in the clear, cold voice.

"We're trying to work out the plan of mediation, and God knows it's difficult enough. We're getting somewhere, I hope. As I see it, the role of the Democratic League is to represent the moderate groups always, and to convince the extremists on both sides that moderation is necessary at this time—especially at this

282

time. We were working all last night on plans. The Kuomintang threatens to occupy a town in Manchuria by force. The Communists refuse to surrender it. I have begged them both to settle the issue in peace—and let there be no occupation in the ordinary sense, let the city be occupied by a Committee which will include one American, one Communist and one member of the Kuomintang. This is reasonable, surely. We have almost convinced them. Later we shall know whether we have succeeded."

We spoke about the student murders. He said: "If only we could form a coalition government, then we would have guarantees that the law would be just. This above all. We must have a sense of law, or perish."

Of General Marshall he said: "There is nothing so exciting as working with him. He has a mind like a clasp-knife. He knows nothing whatsoever about the problems which concern us all—the problems of personalities—but on the subject of peace I have never met a more persuasive advocate. What is certain is that if he fails, no one else will ever succeed. And perhaps he is right—the personalities are not permanent, and the Chinese pay too much attention to them, and see even this terrible war in terms of the prestige of generals. General Marshall should at least be able to teach the Chinese militarists that their personalities have no weight against the suffering the civil war produces. He should know—he is the greatest general of them all."

Later I met Carson Chang, who is the head of the National Socialist Party—a party which has nothing whatsoever to do with fascism. He lives in a house near the Generalissimo's, surrounded by woods, the furniture unbelievably Victorian, and English, so that it is almost impossible to believe that you are in China. There are ebony elephants on the mantel-piece, antimacassars, ormolu clocks; and outside the bow windows children were playing tennis. Even Carson Chang himself, in his brown business suit, looks like an Englishman of Victorian times, pudgy, smiling, with a great forehead and an old-fashioned not hesitant manner. As leader of the Socialists, he has probably more power than any other leader within the Democratic League.

He said: "What we are witnessing is the birth not of a new China, but a very old China indeed. We are struggling slowly, and not always successfully, to make people realize that they have responsibilities. Our members are students, university professors, school-teachers, technicians. We simply do not know how many

283

members there are in the Democratic League, but of one thing we are sure—we represent a large body of moderate opinion. We have worked closely on the boards which have been brought into being in an effort towards mediation. We stand for certain very simple principles, and the most simple of all—*habeas corpus*."

It was odd how the Victorian seemed to grow visibly in stature and power.

He went on: "We have our representatives in various towns, and as you know they are constantly being attacked and threatened. We know the names of the people who threaten them, but we can do nothing—they are in positions of power. But at least we are struggling, we know that in the end the difficulties may be insuperable, but someone will have to take the moderate path —we cannot simply watch China being torn between two extremes. Outside China, they know very little about us. We are supposed to be an infinitesimal party, without power or influence. Partly true. But we do represent great untapped forces, for the Chinese are naturally moderate and this new passion for extremism will pass. Meanwhile we need all the help we can get, and we hope to have constitutional government—then, and then only can the moderates exert their power."

April 18th, General Marshall . . . HE ARRIVED back to China two days ago, and word came yesterday that he would see me. We live in the baking heat of full summer, the roads glaring white, dust everywhere, the subdued roar of the city breaking on exposed nerves; but in T. V. Soong's house near Liang L'u Ko everything was quiet, the roar of the city could not be heard, and General Marshall in stern khaki uniform looked as though he had lived all his life in cool weather.

He was taller than I expected, the chin firmer, the eyes clearer; and when he walked across the room there was an amazing elegance in his movement. The fans whirled above his head, and the immense painting of a tiger behind him accumulated in the dusky shadows a menacing power of revolt and terror; and this was as it should be. After the blinding heat and sunlight outside there was something dreamlike in this room which seemed immense, full of whirling shadows and tiger-heads.

I cannot remember everything he said, but I remember a few odd phrases thrown out at random, the odd strength in the voice, the absence of all gestures. This is not strictly true, for during the

284

course of the conversation he made one gesture so overwhelming that I was amazed, and wondered no longer at the thought that gestures have power. Suddenly, and it seemed for no reason at all, looking above my head, he flung out his arm horizontally, the fingers following the line of the arm. The strength of the gesture, for no apparent reason, directed at no visible enemy, the way the head shot up and the eyes gleamed—all these were confusing; and then I heard the scurry of feet, and saw a small Chinese general scuttling away from the door, where presumably he had been listening. The general was Yu Ta-wei, Minister of Munitions. With a gesture so perfect that it assumed immediate obedience, General Marshall had thrown him out of the room.

We talked of the secret police, the murder of the students, the intolerable abuses of power by the militarists; and though he said little, he nodded, and sometimes the sharp edge of the words, crisp as steel wedges, surprised and delighted me. It is impossible to convey the menace and cautious hate which appeared to exist behind his use of the words "the circle round the Generalissimo," the sibilants of "circle" swinging across the room like iron shafts. He said: "We are doing our best under the most trying circumstances. I have not given up hope." I asked him whether there was any possibility of introducing into China a legislature independent of the judiciary. He smiled wanly, and seemed to be wondering whether American justice was the appropriate model for China, and passed on to the affairs of students, saying: "I think all the time of the young. What I am trying to do concerns less the political leaders of this country than the young people of China." He said again: "I think of the young all the time—all the time. I work for them."

I cannot explain the nervousness that overcame me. I was tongue-tied, baffled by the extraordinary pattern of this room—the tiger on the wall seeming at every moment to bear down on the general, the symbolism too perfect to be credible. I know a man who has been through many battles, but he never heard his knees shaking together until he was decorated by Marshall. I asked him why. "I don't know," he answered. "One gets the most damnable impression that he knows everything. It's like that. It's not hero-worship. The man isn't a hero—I don't think he's done any actual fighting, but one gets so appalled by the thought of the responsibilities he has accepted. They were so great, and he was so successful."

Now, when I think of Marshall, I shall always remember the painted and terrible tiger on the wall, with great exploding eyeballs and bared fangs, and his own gentleness, and how the tiger and the general met on a hot day in Szechuan in the house of the richest and most unscrupulous banker in China, and the general who disappeared as though he was a bullet shot from an invisible rifle, and somehow the pattern becomes one and what is certain is that if Marshall cannot succeed in bringing the contestants together, anyone else will fail.

Later . . . I CANNOT think of any greater contrast than that between General Marshall and Dr. Wellington Koo, the Chinese Ambassador to the Court of St. James, whom I saw immediately after leaving T. V. Soong's house. Marshall is simple, direct, without political convictions, stern with the justice of those who have commanded wars. Dr. Wellington Koo is complex, his thoughts weave into entangled and intangible shapes; his political convictions are deep-centred, and because he is a diplomat he must think of advantages rather than abstract justice, and toy with conundrums all his life. Inevitably, thinking of him, one thinks of a spider's web glistening with dew and waving in the wind. He speaks English excellently and precisely, and it was possible to admire him and at the same time to realize that he was the diplomat of all diplomats, and the wiliest of all Chinese, who have some experience of wiles.

His hair was white, the face very thin, the lips pursed into a small button, and I have never seen anyone who so much resembled the early portraits of Henry VIII. The half-shuttered lids expressed continual weary surprise at the malice of the world. He had been a diplomat all his life. He believed rightly that diplomacy still has its place in human intercourse, and he said he regretted that foreign ministers now thumped the table and spoke outright for home consumption rather than copy the old pattern, which was to speak quietly, decorating all subjects with politeness, all infringements of law with diplomatic terms.

"Something has gone," he said, "and may not return. In the old days we could make some kind of compromise. It is not difficult to thump tables." He brought his fist down on his open palm. "You see, I can do it as well as the next man, but why do it? It will get head-lines, but I am not sure that the acquisition of head-lines is worth while. If you want peaceful settlements, then the old

286

mediæval policy was still the best—we spoke quietly, hardly above whispers, and tried to get a compromise which inevitably made you lose face—but you didn't lose so much face as you do now, when you thump tables."

He was surprised by the Soviet-Chinese agreement, and put it down, as so many others have put it down, to the political and diplomatic inexperience of Mr. T. V. Soong. He was surprised that diplomats had not been called in to mediate in the Chinese civil war—surely, here, if anywhere, there were reasons for the use of settled diplomatic terms. There were rumours that he would be appointed foreign minister. Were they true? "You know, I'm not terribly popular now," he said, and the shuttered eyes opened wide, and he looked down at his long fingers and stroked his moustache. He gave the impression of a species of animal which hardly exists any longer: a man who is superbly civilized. And I suppose it was for this reason that I dared not ask him the question which had been uppermost in my mind. I had been told by quarters very close to the Chinese Foreign Minister that Dr. Koo had recently joined the dreaded C.C. clique. Was it true? Impossible to ask such a question, for at such a time it would have seemed to be in repulsive bad taste, worse than the thumping of diplomatic tables, worse than head-lines.

April 20th . . . THE ponies struggled up the slopes bringing blocks of salt towards the high hills where, as evening falls, a multitude of telegraph poles gives the impression of gallows. Evening is the worst in Chungking. Then vapours come from the earth, mist swirls, and though the poverty-stricken bamboo huts huddle into shadow, and the sores and diseases on people's faces no longer show, the solemnity breeds a kind of remorse: in the evening your conscience strikes—why should these things be allowed? There is the same poverty as when I came here first. A few new streets have been built, you no longer need to climb 321 steps to reach the ferry-steamer, for they have introduced a funicular railway; and you no longer fear Japanese bombs. At night, too, you are conscious of the secret police, and even today, though I have only spent half an hour in the streets, I have seen gangs of conscripts roped together, walking silently through the dusk.

Tonight the sun set like an eye closing, so softly that we were hardly aware of the coming of darkness, passing from one darkness to another. I have been wandering round the streets, where

287

so much of my life has passed. It is better not to count one's life in years, but in towns—the number of the towns, and how they changed you, and what they gave you, and how the people lived. Of Chungking we know that people lived more intensely and more terribly than elsewhere, ringed by enemies, with expanding rings of enemies in their midst. The river will flow for ever and always the white-sailed sampans will come down the Yangtse, and always there will be the jade-cutters and the coolies drawing pails of water up steep stone steps and always these people will own this land, though for some years more the wealth of the land will be taken from them. One walks through these streets in a state of blessedness. Candles gleam inside houses. Red lacquer ancestral altars shine under the hanging red pepper-pods. The young girl takes the door from its hinges, lays it gently on the earth outside the hut and sleeps, the light from the ancestral candles burning on her cheeks.

I shall go back to Kunming, and then fly to Pekin. I shall never again set foot on Chungking, and this is for the best. It is presumptuous to bless a city. It is presumptuous to believe that roots torn out will ever grow again. Yet how can one leave Chungking without blessing it, and how can one believe that the roots are wholly torn? Something of all those of us who stayed there will remain. And so one blesses it, knowing that it does not need our blessing, knowing too that it will survive all our hopes, our fears, our ideologies and torments. The way was grotesquely hard, and so it will remain, but it was the way they chose for themselves: to live under clouds in winter, and under the intensest heat of the summer sun, children of extremes, and wise because they knew life and death at their sharpest points. But when I think of this city again, I shall not imagine it, as once I did, as a great ship about to cast anchor and swinging eastward towards the sun. I shall think of it as a rock, greater than all other rocks, greater than the Himalayas, because there has soaked into it from so many millions of suffering people the strength of their hearts.

April 29th, Kunming . . . THE sun was strong, the rice-fields gleamed in their moon-shapes, the whole earth flowered in the sun. Chungking's heat has gone; we enter a more temperate land, where flowers grow all the year round, and the earth is soft, and there is less suffering.

The hot glare of the sun remains. I noticed it first when I went

288

to the campus, where the softness of the mud-walls contrasted with the hard gleam of the sky. Southwest Associated University is coming to the last stage of its life. We shall leave the mud-huts forever on a day chosen to avoid any demonstrations by the students, because it was on May 4th, 1919 that they rose in protest against the Versailles Treaty. We leave in spring-time, and this is as we wanted it to be: so that we can leave in good heart.

The students talk of going by lorries, knowing perfectly well that there are dangerous roads and perhaps five per cent will die on the way. The roads of China are littered with dead and broken machines. The skies are equally unsafe, particularly in Yunnan, where the wind currents are dangerous. Some speak of going by rail, but all the bridges into French Indo-China are broken. The journey will be hazardous, but all hazards are worth while as long as they can reach Pekin.

April 30th . . . I HAVE been to see Professor Wen Yi-tuo. He is in good shape, his face very red with sunburn, no longer drawn with typhus-pallor. Because he led the students down from Pekin, he is looking eagerly to leading them back again. "But they want me to attend the People's Political Conference in August in Nanking, so I shall go, and then if there are any students left here——" Some student interrupted at that moment. He said only: "You must do what your conscience dictates," and then the student left. Soldiers were bathing in the pool, and the red-winged dragonflies were already spinning across the universities' small lakes.

He said: "The students have done wonders here. They have gone the hard road, and they have accepted hardness. Do you know, people offer me the most extraordinary temptations to leave China. The University of California wants me to go in the summer to America. Why? I didn't think anyone knew of my existence. But I shall have to stay."

He spoke about his hopes in the Democratic League.

"We must use whatever pressure we can employ continually on both sides to avert this disaster of all disasters—the civil war. I am proud that the students of this University were the first to realize the danger. And no danger could be greater, for no one can win, and the Chinese people will lose."

I told him of the strange conversation with Chiang Mon-lin, secretary of the Executive Council and former president of

289

Peiping University.

"Well, if they want to believe we are the tail of the Communist Party, that is their affair. They make up their beliefs as they go along. Myself, I believe we are the tail of the Chinese people, and we'll keep on waggling."

We went across the Wen Lin-kai. I said I was going to fly to Pekin immediately.

"Then your dreams will come true?"

"Yes—part of the dream."

"What's the other part?"

"Oh, peace in China—a hundred things, but peace most of all." He held my hand.

"We must pray for peace, there *must* be peace. The rest doesn't matter." Then he grinned and said: "I am writing a poem again. I shall dedicate it to you—a very satirical poem about China, and the way so many people squabble over her." Some peasants were passing. "Do you think they want war? There is only one fair generalization about China—we are pacific people—continually at war."

I watched him for a long while as he went down the narrow lane, the long blue gown scurrying in the wind. I have more faith in him than in any man in China. There is no limit to the abilities of this quiet scholar. Nothing pleases me so much as the thought that in Pekin we can work together on a new translation of the old Chinese philosopher Chuang Tzu.

May 2nd . . . I HAVE been to see Liu Lien, who will stay here for the rest of his life; the hot, sandy summers and the freezing cold winters of Pekin are not for him. He strokes his beard and looks out across the garden, and looks lost, and sad. Though he did not teach in the University, he was a part of it.

"They were the best years of my life, and the worst," he said. "You see, I had always lived in Pekin. There was corruption in Pekin—the vicious little circle began there, and went on from there until it embraced the whole of China. But this was worse. The police were good in Pekin. They hit you with the flat of their swords; here they torture you, and when they have tortured you sufficiently they take you out on a rope and shoot you beyond the wall. The best is now—the students thinking of the days when they will walk along the wide, smooth streets of Pekin. You must have faith in China; the war will end some day, and what then?

290

Then we shall build a state we can be proud of."

He talked of his health. He would like to see Pekin once more, but perhaps it was best to imagine it, the cypresses, the yellow tiles and the perfection of the architecture. "I'd like to go, but how? With the kind of heart I have, they won't let me go by aeroplane or by lorry, and there's no train from here to Pekin." He talked of trains, and said he wondered sometimes whether it was advisable to have railways all over China—the hinterland would be more than ever drained to serve the coastal ports, and the country would become more rigidly centralized than ever. "Best that each province should have the maximum of independence—the country is too big to be ruled from a capital. Let it be like America, a country of federated states—then there will be peace."

The convolvulus are still flowering in the garden, and the bamboos creak in the wind. He looked older, a little weaker, and much sadder. He will be more lonely than ever now that the University has gone.

May 5th, Flying to Pekin . . . NEVER have I seen a landscape so wild, so rock-hewn—the livid green cliffs of lava spreading north of the Yangtse. We climbed straight into the sky, and when we looked down there was nothing but the desert of high blue hills, sharp-edged, covered with forests, uninhabited; and all this happened almost at the moment when we left Chungking—the unimaginable barrenness of the place. Li Po talks somewhere of the "desperate height of these Szechuan hills." It was true enough of Chungking itself, but here the wildness goes to extremes, you fly over mountains where no one seems ever to have lived, mottled and roughened like an elephant's skin, an immensity of peaks, with sometimes a river gleaming like a fish-scale below. A place of shaggy hair and horror, and the grey sky above, and the earth menacing. Bucket-seats. The aeroplane slipping and sliding down invisible sudden roads. The sensation of *falling towards* Pekin.

Gradually the earth turned yellow. You were conscious of a moment when the green hills folded beneath the earth, became spaced farther apart, were mingled with sand; and yet it is not really yellow, there are green shadows and mysterious mists, and there is green still in the crescent-shaped rice-fields, and gradually the rice-fields disappear, the land becomes less fertile, rock and clay, without trees. No villages—a tenantless land. Professor Chen Ta would say sometimes: "It is nonsense to believe that the popu-

lation of China is four hundred million—so little of this country
is under cultivation, you can travel for hundreds of miles by air
and see no villages at all."

We dream of Pekin, the gold palaces, the blood-red walls, the
bringers of tribute who came once along these hills; but there
are no signs of wealth here, a few square-cut fields and then the
desolation begins again. A great white gash appears. Perhaps it
is the old bed of the Yellow River, which now flows south instead
of north. We have been flying for four hours. The air is already
full of dusk, not menacing green but menacing yellow; and the
aeroplane ploughs through the dust and throws on dust its amazing
shadow. And what is surprising is that through the clouds of dust
you see other clouds, low-lying, and they are the only soft things
travelling over the vast plain; and then, too, above the dust
there shines the blue sky, deeper by far than the molten gold-
blue of Szechuan, an intense silvery white-blue, blinding the
eyes.

And then, five hours after leaving the airport, we come to richer
fields, the sand-haze darkens, there are villages everywhere; the
aeroplane swings low—and you have come to fairyland, a place of
golden bricks and glittering roofs, everything in squares, an immense city ringed by another immense city, the square city in the
centre all gold and the larger city which frames it dark blue; and
the maize ripening to its walls, and blue lakes everywhere. The
intoxication of Pekin! The delight in order, the marble bridges,
the depth and blueness of the lakes, the wide streets with their
freight of swift-moving traffic—gold tiles everywhere.

The aeroplane swung low over the Altar of Heaven: white marble, blue roofs, the perfect circle south of the city where offerings
were made at the winter solstice, and all other things are square
—the golden imperial city is square, the roads run squarely and
the parks and the walls are square. Seen through this summer
haze, Pekin was unreal, as unreal as a spike of maize bursting with
life.

May 7th . . . GRADUALLY over the years one makes one's
peace with a city, but here there is peace at once: not friable,
but perfect. It is better than all our dreaming, all proportions perfect, all colours disarming. Over the gate leading into the imperial
city someone in an access of hero-worship has placed a canvas
picture of the Generalissimo, the face blue, the expression sullen,
292

almost snarling. You pass the great wall with its winged cloud-pillars of victory, the marble bridges and the moats, and it is confusing to see this immense portrait over-riding all things. Not even the Emperor would have dared to place his portrait there; and though this is bad enough, the same face with the same expression looks down from all the other gates.

We wander all day; there are parks, pavilions, smooth asphalt-covered streets, sentries with white Japanese nose-bags, the plump and fertile northern Chinese, the grace of the girls who fill the avenues with their bicycles, the utter sparkle of the sky. I have stood at the centre of the world, and seen all the kingdoms to north and south, standing in the midmost marble circle of the Altar of Heaven, and this was perhaps best of all; coming towards it in heavy noon through a forest of stunted trees. The city seething with life; fairs everywhere, and outside the Legation Quarter so many kimonos, so many Japanese hunting-trophies that they are past counting. For the first time in seven years I have come upon second-hand bookshops. Morrison Street, in the glaring sunlight; the immense marble halls of the Pekin Union Medical College, where the Executive Headquarters are; the gaudy-painted drum-tower to the north of the city; the rocks, the flowers, the weight and singular proportions of the imperial palace, and all these are perfect, and of them we can only speak in whispers. There is no city that can compare with this. Life, with its urgent Chinese flow, passes before the quietness of splendid palaces; and it is all and more than we expected, and we are immeasurably grateful.

For years I have lived in rat-infested hotel bedrooms; now I live in a palace with two hundred rooms, great courtyards, marble lions guarding the doors; and though the palace is falling into ruins, and part of it was burnt, and there are other parts which the Japanese have occupied, this too has a perfection of its own. Sand spills everywhere, but the yellow of the sand seems perfectly appropriate where all that is best is coloured yellow. And then, too, there is a child who is half French and half Chinese who lives with me, who has stayed here in a convent throughout the war and whose presence is like a blessing, so perfectly is she endowed with all that is best in East and West. So one lives here, quietly, living behind high walls, as secretly as one could desire, and you have only to cross the courtyards to come out into the golden city.

293

May 12th . . . AT NIGHT the North Lake glitters in the moonlight, and the old imperial barges float across the smooth surface, and the lovers hide among the cypresses, the dagoba shines ghostly white and everywhere you look there are black flaring roofs which will turn gold tomorrow. The whole of this lake, all the marble bridges, all the hundreds of buildings around it, all the temples once belonged to the Empress Dowager; now they belong to the people who crowd everywhere, quietly, with good manners, enjoying the spectacle which was reserved less than forty years ago only for princess and dignitaries.

The wind blows over the lake, the lotoses turn up their smooth undersides, and there is so much freshness here that one can hardly breathe. There are moats a hundred feet wide brimming over with water-lilies which will ripen in a day or two; already the pink tongues are bursting through. But what is more surprising than anything else is that the elaborate gold carving of the decorated pillars enchants still, never becomes wearisome. You climb the Coal Hill behind the imperial city and see the whole landscape before you, not rigid but spaciously ordered; an empire in a blood-red frame of walls, the wealth overflowing. In this city you move and have your being in a haze of gold splendours; and this is as it should be. Painters are regilding the roofs, men wear the softest silks and fan themselves continually. Prices are rising. Every day a new concrete block-house is set up against the possibility of a Communist incursion; but we cannot take these things seriously, we cannot believe that Pekin will ever change.

In Bali and Barcelona I have known something of this splendour; a sense of continual rejoicing, an accepted way of living, a tradition so secure that none could break through it. There are secret police, garrison troops march through the dust, sometimes you will come upon men marching with ropes bound to their trussed arms. All this is true. The war reaches here; there are more and more block-houses piled up at street-corners—for some mysterious reason there is a block-house with a machine-gun pointed directly at the Pekin Union Medical College, where the Americans, the Kuomintang and the Communists are trying to make a peace—yet the residual glory remains. There is hardly any poverty, for one can grow fat on maize, and maize is still cheap. There are no beggars, few prostitutes, a sense of security remains, and cigarettes are cheap and food is not yet exorbitantly dear. The havoc may come later, but in these early days of summer,
294

wandering alone or with Jacqueline through the city, all tensions seem to be relaxed, and hopes rise like the roofs of these buildings, which twist into the sun.

May 28th . . . AT THE winter solstice the Son of Heaven sacrificed to the Honoured Ones. The great yellow palanquin came through a shuttered snow-bound city, the imperial guards raced forward, the Emperor threw himself down in penitence during the ceremonies to the unawakened sun and the awakened earth and the people who fed from her. A furnace of green porcelain received the offerings; a white calf, rolls of silk, and hymns were sung which descended from the time of Confucius.

I confess that there is no ceremony I would so much like to see performed as this. In those days there was some balance between men and Heaven, and communication flowed down from one to the other. We shall never recapture those days, but at least we have no reason to believe that we have made ourselves better, in our unritualled lives; there may come a time when Pekin will be meaningless, and no one will know that there was an ordered way of life which sprung naturally from the soil. The city has been built according to a priestly code, mapped out in the shape of a god—they will tell you that this part of the city represents a man's head, and that part a man's legs opened wide, and that part the utter extremities of his fingers. Rivers flow underground, and this too may be explained, but nothing explains its beauty so well as that in the days when Pekin was being built, men believed in their own strength. Strength flows from these palace walls, and certainly it is not the strength of feudalism but of human worship and endeavour. Wealth flowed here from all the provinces of China, but these Emperors cannot have been wholly bad who placed their wealth so tenderly and spaciously around them. The springs of religious feeling are beginning to be sealed in China, but as long as the scholars remain to study the ancient poems, we shall know something of the motives that brought this majesty about.

May 30th . . . THE heat suffocating, and yet how we become accustomed to it, we even feel that it is necessary, for in this heat the colours glow more; and how rich are those reds, greens and golds which surround us everywhere. We are willing hostages to the heat, and this evening, while the heat continued, the shattered sky opened and within three minutes the earth was a foot deep in water—and this too seemed appropriate. Lightning flashed over the North Lake, striking the white dagoba, and even then, in those sudden gleams of frigid blue light, you saw the small boats moving across the lake.

June 3rd . . . I SHALL fly soon to Yenan, the Communist capital, where they say it is even hotter. It may be, though I cannot imagine a heat greater than this. Yet it becomes cool in the evening, almost ice-cold. The rain comes again, drowning whole courtyards, but in the morning there is only the freshness of rain-dew and the clearness of the sky. I have been wondering what place in the world most reminded me of Pekin, and at last I have found it—an apple-orchard in the south of France, ripening in the sun.

June 4th . . . How, when and by what stratagems can one tear oneself away from this city? There is more beauty than I thought the world possessed; but it is better not to write of it, best of all simply to enjoy it quietly, and perhaps even better to go away from it, because in absence it will appear even more lovely.

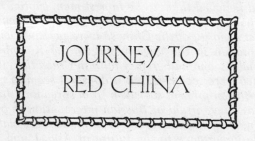

JOURNEY TO
RED CHINA

While I was in China, there were three great centres of resistance—Chungking, Kunming and Yenan. Chungking was the Kuomintang capital, Yenan the Communist capital, Kunming the centre with the largest number of students, the greatest Universities and the greatest concentrations of American power. Inevitably Kunming was compelled to take the middle course, and the general impression seemed to be: "A plague on both your houses —let us have peace, and let the best men take control."

We heard little of Yenan. Very occasionally reports came through. Yenan was a mysterious valley somewhere in the north, unapproachable in time of war, still more unapproachable during the time of undeclared civil war which followed Hiroshima. The Communists knew it as the administrative centre of the Shen-Kan-Ning area—Shen-Kan-Ning standing for the liberated regions of the provinces of Shensi, Kansu and Ninghsia. Other areas with equally strange names existed—there was Chin-Cha-Chi, Chin-Chi-Lu-Yu, Huang Chung and perhaps twenty others. Within these areas the Communists claimed to govern a population nearly as great as the population of America. On the borders of these areas fighting between the Communists and the Japanese or the Kuomintang had been continuous for nearly eight years.

By the kindness of the American air authorities in Pekin I was able to make two flights into Communist territory, one to Yenan and the other to Kalgan. These notes were written late at night or early in the morning after long interviews with the Communists. My main interest was to see what could be done to pre-

297

vent the civil war from spreading. I have attempted no statistical enquiry and no evaluation of the forces at work. I was interested in people, landscapes, the hopes men had, their poetry and universities and dances and songs. I was impressed by the Communists and believed them to be honest men, cautious, not domineering, scholarly and careful in their policies, always conscious that the vast majority of the Chinese were peasants who received no representation in the government of the Kuomintang; they were nationalists, and had greater faith in China than in any other country; they were socialists, but it does not seem to me that any force on earth can prevent socialism from spreading through Asia; they were as much afraid of Russian intervention as of American intervention; they had made an experiment in social reform of incalculable importance to the future of Asia. I saw no signs of Russian weapons, and I saw every indication that they were relying on their own strength. In the quality of their manhood, and in the quality of their faith in the future of China, they showed a greatness which I had rarely seen in government circles in Chungking. They were good men, with firm handshakes, clear eyes and quiet strength, and I hope something of their courage has come through these pages. But for myself I cannot see China in terms of an essentially political struggle—there are other forces besides politics at work, and the last of all our hopes seems to be that the best men of all parties should take control.

June 8th, Journey to Yenan . . . You go down the long road which leads from Pekin to the Western Hills early in the morning. All the way down the road there are stiff, gold wheatfields in the sun, and here and there are marble memorials—stone lions, dragons, turtles. You tell yourself that this is one of the oldest places in the world. The walls of Pekin are crumbling and all over the imperial city grass is growing through the roof-beams and the thrones of the emperors are falling into powder, the brocades are torn and soon there will be nothing left except the ancient court-yards filled with ruins. It is true enough, but in this fresh morning air, with the blue haze on the hills, it doesn't seem important. The whole place is alive with birds and immense square fields and farmcarts and workmen—the air has never been brighter, the colours have never been fresher, and you wonder why you are leaving Pekin to go to an old, abandoned city in northern Shensi.

298

The macadamized road goes straight to the West Field, where there were at least fifty aeroplanes on the ground. They were camouflaged with green and ochre paint to remind you that the war was hardly over, and they were attended by young Americans in shorts who looked amazingly tall and fair, so that you half wondered whether you had strayed from a court-yard in Pekin to another planet altogether. The old traditions in China were dying. There was a new, more vigorous world coming, a world of skyscrapers and aeroplanes and social reforms. There will be more equality, and sooner than most people suspect there will be less corruption. Giant forces were at work, yet no one could see their end. All we could tell with certainty was that inevitably the Chinese would become as western as ourselves, as western as those aeroplanes whose humming in the clear sky as they circled over the air-strip was not unlike the humming of the flutes inserted in the wings of the pigeons in Pekin.

In the plane there was a doctor, a general, a girl in a red print frock, some soldiers. The brown paper bags crackled, the pilot came plunging down the cabin in search of the lavatory and the parachute harnesses began swinging from side to side. Through the pin-hole you saw the gold-red roofs of the summer palace disappearing, and soon you were over blue-tented mountains, wrinkled like an elephant's skin, with deep green shadows and here and there a space where a peasant had carved out on the steep slopes a place to live and farm in. The mountains were poor pasture land. You felt the poverty of the place, and you were shocked by the white sores on the mountains where rivers had once flowed and would flow again in autumn, though no water fell down them now. It was a bleak, hard, desolate unavailing landscape after the rich yellow plain in which Pekin stands; yet it was brilliantly coloured, with every variation of blue and green. Then at last the blue tents gave place to the plains again, the earth changed colour, ochre and brown, and much sooner than you had expected you were among the yellow hump-backed mountains of Shensi. Here was loess, most fertile of earths when watered, but the land looked dry, the villages in the valley looked unbelievably small. I do not know why they make China yellow on the map, for China is all colours. From the air it is lead-green over Chungking, and all the colours of the rainbow over Kunming. Here it was the colour of faded yellow tiles. But where did people live when there was no sign of houses?

After nearly four hours, the aeroplane came streaking low over a plain between yellow hills, driving straight for a tall pagoda. There followed inevitably that most delightful sensation which comes when one wing shoots straight into the sky, and all the yellow hills were above, and the blue sky lay beneath. Above you were houses, not many, perhaps five or six, a river, caves in the mountains, dusty roads, and you saw the long yellow valley with its loess walls. The pagoda streaked past again. The airfield was a green field, and the first thing you noticed when the cabin door was opened was the sweet smell of dust and grass. This was Yenan.

I never discovered where the sweet smell came from. There was mint in it, and parsley, and scented flowers, and clean mountain air. There was no sign of any flowers, only the long low plain between the hills. The air was cleaner even than the air just outside the walls of Pekin, which is cleaner than anything I have known in the south, a soft sweet glowing air which belongs to North China alone. Yet everywhere there was dust.

The valley was the colour of yellow dust; the small huts in the fields, the stone bridges, the shops, the hills which were sometimes covered with scrub, all were yellow when seen from a distance. There were three valleys, radiating from the broken walls of Yenan, which was bombed savagely at intervals between 1939 and 1943, so that almost nothing remained. There were almost no trees, though I found peach-trees later in a court-yard, and there were pear-trees from which they made an excellent wine. There was date-wine, too, but there was only one grove of date-trees in the whole valley. For the rest it was a hard barren land, the river too low at this season to irrigate the fields, but when autumn came the river would flood its banks. It was the last place in the world where you would expect to find the administrative centre of a communist empire.

From the airfield you see nothing—no houses, no caves, only the soft contours of the yellow mountains. You find Yenan on Chinese maps with extreme difficulty. It is not called Yenan, but Fushih, which is an old name now restored; and when you wander through the dusty roads where there are mat-shed shops and ask where you are, they will answer that you are in Tufuchuan, which means according to some the Spring of the Beancurd and to others the Spring of Tu Fu, after the greatest of Chinese poets who wandered disconsolately through these hills.

300

There is a river, but no sampans come down it. Women washed clothes by the river, small children paddled in it and old men clung desperately to the slippery stepping-stones. It was so small a river that you hardly noticed it when you flew over it. What you noticed was the steep loess cliffs, which glowed at all hours of the day but best of all at sunset: they hemmed you in on all sides, and there were moments when they seemed hard and menacing, and other moments when their soft contours were charming. Their colours were always changing. There were depths upon depths of yellow in those hills. It was easy to imagine that men were content to stay there. You would look out for the sunset and the afterglow, and at dawn again they glowed with an entirely different light. At midday, in the dust and the heat-haze, they seemed not to be there at all—they were crumbling, or had already crumbled. Soft earth, so soft that you could dig into it with your finger-nails, but sometimes at the foot of the hills you would come upon massed layers of hard white rock.

The dull blue clothes of the people fitted in perfectly with the land, and the people themselves seemed to belong there, as the Spaniards seem to belong to Spain, the men of Provence belong to southern France and the Welsh to Wales. The land looked old and overworked: occasionally you came upon peasants who looked older even than the land. It was bare enough in summer; in winter, at the time of frost and floods, it would look unendurably barren except for its clear skies. But even so, after wandering round it for a few days, you felt that it was a place to stay in, where you could dig your roots deep and attend quietly to the changing of the seasons.

Later . . . I HAVE come to the end of the world—we are imprisoned by these loess hills, and with the very greatest difficulty can we believe there is any world other than this. It is the oddest impression. You feel that you have come to a place so ancient, more ancient than anything else in China, and its very ancientness makes it impossible to move away from it. It is very much like the surrealist paintings you used to see before the war. And everything is in slow motion—the horsemen ride across the valley and over the river in slow motion, and people walk slowly. They walk slowly in Pekin, because it is a habit there; but here they walk slowly because of the heat. The sky is a deep, ever so deep blue. The starlings chatter in the willows, and there is no breath

301

of air to shake the leaves. Dogs and pigs lie in the shade of stones. There are perhaps sixty thousand people here, but you don't see them—they are hidden in the caves.

Of course it *is* the most ancient place in China. It was among these strange flat-topped yellow hills that the Chinese began their journeys. I am amazed by the curious resemblance of these hills to the temples in Pekin. The temples are supposed to be modelled on tents, but there is no record that the Chinese ever lived in tents. But the hills have the same golden roofs, when the winter wheat is ripe, and the sides are notched and edged to give room for more fields, and it is a little like the flaring roofs in the imperial palace. Unconscious race memory? It may be. You have the oddest impression of a place *which has remain unchanged*. This is what is surprising, because I thought of Yenan as a small walled city—there are no walls, there is no city, everything bombed, except the caves and a few offices, like the bank and the military headquarters. There is an old fortress-like temple on a bluff, and a perfect pagoda. . . .

June 9th, Red Virtue in the Date Garden . . . Chu Teh came along the path through the date-trees, limping a little, wearing a dark blue cotton coat, blue cotton trousers and a blue cap. It was dusk. In this light his face had the colour of old bronze, very dark, and he was smaller than I had expected. He grinned and shook hands, and then you noticed with a shock that he was unlike the early portraits, he had grown much older and you could only recognize him by the boyish smile and the broken nose.

We had come a long way from the clustered huts and caves which is all that can be seen of Yenan. In the dusk the starlings went wild, the caves disappeared, there was only the dark outline of the yellow loess cliffs. The sky was dark, and sometimes you saw a wolf prowling in the distance or a solitary white-turbaned horseman coming along the river bank. They said Chu Teh lived in a date garden. There was no sign of a date garden for miles. And then suddenly, very blue against the sand-coloured hills, you saw the date-trees and a long low earthen wall with two pillars. On each there was inscribed the Chinese characters for "Date Garden." It was the head-quarters of the Commander-in-Chief of all the Communist armies in China.

He looked nearly all his sixty-five years, and he resembled none of the photographs taken by Agnes Smedley and Edgar Snow. He was unshaved; there was no beard, but there were a few faint bristles on his chin. You thought at first he was an old farmer, who had seen many wars and had come at last into this date garden in northern Shensi for a long rest before he died. He gave no impression of power, but he did give an impression of dignity and composure, and a kind of quietness. You noticed telegraph wires among the date-palms, and you wondered what the devil they were doing there, and he said nothing but walked slowly towards a cave in the hills. He had small bright eyes—Edgar Snow says they are large, but they are small nevertheless—and there was something bird-like even in that slow limping walk which led up to a terrace near the caves from where you could look down on the darkening valley. When he took off his cap, you saw that his hair was thinning, but it was still jet-black, and when he smiled he had the teeth of a young boy in the face of an old peasant. He was a good man, a *hao jen,* and you wondered why he kept a few soldiers round the place.

He spoke very quietly and confidently, in a husky voice, and sometimes there was in it I do not know what note of disturbing sombreness, as of a man who knows that date-palms live for ever and all men die young. He was so obviously the good farmer that you were amazed by the legends that had grown up around him. Was it true that he had led the Long March? Was it true that he assisted Ts'ai Ao to dethrone Yuan Shih-kai? Was it true that once in Yunnan he had lived in great state, with concubines and opium-pipes and immense wealth? Was it true that he had directed the Hundred Regiment attack against the Japanese, and countless other attacks? They were all true enough, but it was hard at first to reconcile the old farmer with the legends.

It was growing dark, the moon was rising and there was only a single soldier standing like a shadow against the low wall. The battle of Shihpingchieh had come to an end a week before. It was a bloody, positional engagement which lasted a month before the Communists retreated northward. The Kuomintang official newspapers announced that there had been 100,000 casualties on both sides. It was positional war with a vengeance. In *Red Star Over China* Edgar Snow quoted General Peng Teh-huei: "Static warfare must be avoided. In a lengthy positional war the enemy has every advantage, and in general the chances of partisan success diminish in proportion to the duration of the battle." The Kuomintang were credited with having thirty tanks and ten bombing planes. Up to that time the Communists had never fought positional wars on any large scale. Why did they fight them now?

Chu Teh answered: "Why not? We had to hold up their advance—they were getting swell-headed. They forgot we are a strong army and capable of positional warfare. There were very good strategical reasons why we should hold them up. Shihping-chieh is an important nerve-centre. The enemy did not know we would defend it, did not know our strength, was led blindly into the trap. It lasted a month, and stopped quite a lot of their energy. The casualties were less than the Kuomintang have recorded. We lost 10,000. They lost more."

Of the fate of the prisoners he said: "They killed the prisoners they captured. We did not need to kill the prisoners we captured. There is never any need to kill the prisoners we capture. They are fascists." He said "fascists" with a faint note of bitterness, hiding the real bitterness. The voice became louder and tougher. "They kill and arrest everywhere. They have prisons and secret police everywhere. We must have an end to the secret police and we must have a democratic government. If the Kuomintang had carried out the People's Consultative Council's agreements in February, there would never have been the civil war. There are three agreements—the reform of the government along democratic lines, the reorganization of the armies and the cease-fire agreements. The Kuomintang violated these agreements, rejected democratic reforms and insisted on maintaining its dictatorship on a nationward scale *including our liberated areas*. There was a meeting called to congratulate the success of the People's Political Consultative Council's success. They sent in their hired thugs to attack the great poet Kuo Mo-jo and half a dozen others, including Li Kung-po.* Do you like it? Our Chinese Kuo Mo-jo is like your Bernard Shaw. Do you like it?"

He spoke with energy, but very quietly. It was growing dark. An oil-lamp with a brown paper shade was placed on the table among the cups of tea. A soldier came and threw a thin coat over his shoulders. You could see only the dark face in the glow of the lamp. He went on: "We don't want to fight a civil war, but their troops attack us, they close down all our newspapers in Pekin and

* Li Kung-po was murdered by Kuomintang officers in July 1946. He had previously been attacked at the conclusion of the People's Consultative Conference in February.

304

Shanghai, and they keep on arresting and murdering us and breaking agreements. What else can we do but resist? I say deliberately they are fascists. Under a fascist dictatorship how can we realize peace?"

I said: "Both sides are stiffening, and as far as I can see we are in danger of a civil war that may last ten years."

"If there is no democratic government, it may well last ten years. The Kuomintang must keep their political agreements. If they would set up a democratic government according to the Foreign Ministers Conference, the civil war would end at once. We cannot—we must not have a fascist government ruled by one man and a small party clique. When General Marshall first came to China, there was great hope for democracy, but for some reason America has not supported the decisions of the P.C.C. We want democracy and nothing else. As for the help the Americans have given the Kuomintang, let bygones be bygones—we will not quarrel about the past. The Kuomintang couldn't fight us if they didn't get gasoline for their aeroplanes and troopships for their troops. I cannot understand why America should want to support a dictatorial government. All over the world it is a question of the realization of democracy—and democracy means a coalition government. Democracy doesn't mean secret police, dictatorship, tortures, murders and the disappearance of people everywhere."

He was still speaking quietly, but when he mentioned the secret police his voice rose. He would mention them again and again, so that they were like an accompaniment throughout the long four-hour conversation at night.

I said: "There is an impasse somewhere, and it must be solved."

"How would you solve it?"

"I don't know enough, but I would guess three things are necessary. The whole Chinese army reduced immediately to a token army. For the moment the Chinese army cannot fight against any of its neighbours—America, Britain or Russia. Put it on the frontiers of China, and it cannot fight. Put it inside China—it can only fight Chinese. Would you be prepared to dissolve the Communist army altogether, or make it a small token army?"

He thought for a while, grinned and said: "Yes, if the Kuomintang do the same. I agree that we cannot fight foreign powers, and the army is only good for fighting between ourselves. Why not dissolve the air force and navy—we cannot fight foreign powers with them?"

"There are two other things that seem to me necessary," I went on. "The leaders on both sides should go. A democracy is best run by ordinary people. The leaders have far too much prestige. The prestige of Aristides in ancient Greece was too great—so the people got rid of him. I think it was the same thing with Churchill. It was necessary to get rid of him. The country is too small to bear the weight of its great men. Would you be prepared to go, if the Kuomintang leaders also went?"

He answered quickly: "It is not just a question of deposing some of the leaders. The Communist Party has 1,200,000 members in China. The Kuomintang has a large membership. The leaders are not important, the parties are important."

"There is a very real danger which comes from the tremendous prestige of the leaders on both sides. Would you and Chairman Mao Tse-tung be prepared to go if the leaders on the other side also went?"

"Yes, if there was a real danger, we would be prepared to go."

"Thirdly, there must be free elections, as there are in America and England."

His face lit up.

"I agree entirely, but the government should not be a government which carried out 'false democracy,' and the democratic practices of the Kuomintang are all false."

We had not got very far, because as things were in China none of the three propositions seemed workable. They were probably necessary: it is possible that there was no other solution, but it was improbable that any of these things would be carried out in the near future. China is not like France, which had deposed its greatest leader and cut down its army and had free elections. China was at the mercy of forces over which the people had no control. But it was good to see Chu Teh agreeing with the propositions which had been on my mind for a long time. He rubbed his chin, grinned and drank some tea. It was very strong tea. I could still see only the dark reddish-brown face behind the oil-lamp.

More than anything else now he resembled the old farmer. He was an old man, he had seen many wars and he preferred to live among his date-palms; he was looking out into the distance, the moon had risen over the black cliffs, and the soldier was still standing by the low parapet and the wall.

"Let us go back to what we have been saying," he said. "I agree we must dissolve the army, or at least make it much smaller. But
306

how can we dissolve their secret police? We have no secret police, no torture chambers. We can only get rid of these things with a democratic government. How can we get a democratic government? There are elements in America which are supporting Chiang Kai-shek against the people. I have met General Marshall. He came to Yenan. We trust him, but we do not understand why America is supporting the Kuomintang against us. If for one month America refused to support the Kuomintang armies, there would be an end to the civil war."

I mentioned the violations which had been committed, according to Executive Headquarters, on both sides. He said: "I emphatically deny that there have been violations of the truce on our side."

I was surprised by this, and asked whether there were not sometimes moments when communications between the widespread and decentralized communist areas became difficult. Orders from headquarters were perhaps not always carried out.

"There may be delays of two or three days," he answered, "but there is no difficulty of communication. We have radios."

"What are the possibilities of peace?"

"If we can extend the truce now or later, there may be peace. At some time or other it may be possible to get together and work out a peaceful solution."

It was growing darker and colder, and we went into the cave. There was no furniture, no maps and no pictures except at the very end, where there was a small table and three battered sofas whose springs pushed out through the cloth. The oil-lamp was put on the table. You could see him more clearly now, for the walls were whitewashed and reflected the oil-lamp. He looked older than ever, but he looked stronger. He said:

"We are not an independent government. We are a temporary government, without consuls or any official intercourse with foreign powers. Yet there are 130,000,000 people in the liberated areas. We want international intercourse and we want trade, but we have only three ports, Weihaiwei, Chefoo and Lungho. We would like foreigners to come here, and we guarantee their freedom of movement, and we guarantee freedom to all missionaries. We want trade—international trade. We will not confiscate and we will not break our agreements. . . . In our border areas production is continually increasing."

I asked him to define Chinese communism, for it was evident

307

that communism in China differed from communism elsewhere.

He said: "Chinese communism is democracy plus capital."

I very nearly jumped out of my chair.

"It is quite easy to explain," he went on. "The Chinese communists do use the Marxist theory in their analysis of social, political and economic conditions in China. The conclusions they draw are those which answer the needs of the people. There is not yet any Marxist communist theory in actual practice—it is still in fact largely a capitalist system. In China today we support the capitalist system, because today the communist system of Marx is no more than an ideal. The only prospect of communism lies in the distant future. To be communist now would not be realistic. China today cannot realize such a system. Today, the system which can be carried out and is needed by the people is democracy with the free development of capital. We must develop our capital resources, and increase the wealth of the people, and raise their livelihood, and we can only do this by industrialization and foreign investment. Our program has always been to find out what people want and to satisfy their needs—it was only by doing this that we could be successful against the Japanese. We will not confiscate the wealth of the capitalists, but we will not allow big trusts to be formed. We want democracy, free elections and an end to the feudal rule which the Kuomintang has inherited from the Manchus."

Saying this, he had put on a pair of horn-rimmed spectacles and resembled the old farmer no longer. He was an elderly professor, who spoke quietly and distinctly and a little wearily, as though he knew beforehand that there was so much distrust against Red China abroad that it was impossible to make them realize that communism was no longer the immediate objective in north China.

He went on: "How can we exist without capital? Our standard of living is so low. We must have the means of production to raise the standard of living of the peasants, and we cannot have it without capital. We are not against private capital, and we cannot follow the Russian model." And then, later: "This is not communism —this is the new democracy."

It was growing late, the lamp flickered on the rickety table and he looked more than ever the elderly professor who had returned after an exhausting lecture. A soldier came in and handed him a slip of paper. He glanced at it, and in silence handed it back again, and we were still somewhere at the end of a long low whitewashed tunnel. He talked about the Long March.

"They keep on thinking of us at that time as small guerrilla units," he complained. "We were not small guerrilla units—we were a comparatively large army, and so our activities were different from those of the Russian guerrillas during the war. We were an army continually increasing in numbers, because more and more villagers came to join us. Through the whole journey we relied for our intelligence on the villagers, and they gave us food, transport and supplies. We had little time for training. The training came largely on the field. We had some well-trained officers. Both Peng Teh-huei and I were old Kuomintang officers who went over to the Communists when we realized that the Kuomintang was simply a machine of oppression. During the revolution of 1911 I was a company-commander. When the Yunnanese revolted against Yuan Shih-kai I was already in command of a regiment. I was a member of Dr. Sun Yat-sen's *Tung Men Hui*, a forerunner of the Kuomintang. Afterwards we were always fighting against the war-lords. We were regular soldiers first and partisan leaders afterwards.

"Our tactics developed gradually. Partly they came from our experiences in the regular army, and they came too from books. One book which impressed us largely was a book on the American war of independence. But it was not books or technical knowledge which were most useful—more useful than anything was the creative ability of the masses. We fought for political aims, our tactics depended on political aims. During the Long March we wanted to get to the north-east as quickly as possible, because it was from there that the greatest danger from the Japanese arose, and this was what the people wanted. We had artillery, mountain guns and mortars. We were not really guerrillas—we fought positional wars in Hunan, Kweichow, Szechuan and Kansu. We were a real army then, and we are a real army now."

For years I have been obsessed with the beauty and revelation of character which comes from Chinese calligraphy, and I was glad when he showed me some of his handwriting. It was very much what might be expected, good handwriting, heavy and dark, the characters crowded together, the down-strokes thick and determined, each character over an inch high. There was the beauty of ruggedness and heavy deliberation, and more than anything else of determination. It was his commonplace book. He turned over the pages slowly, the thick local-made paper crackling under thumb and forefinger. On each page there appeared a character so perfectly in keeping with the man that the revelation was complete. Then very slowly he put down the book, which contained heaven knows what secrets of diplomacy and military affairs, and we went out into the garden, past the solitary guard on the parapet, the date-trees and the small gate. There were no signs of the guards. The stars shone, and some low clouds were moving up the valley in the west.

Chu Teh, which means "Red Virtue," has to his achievements a march greater than any accomplished by Ghenghiz Khan. He does not look like the great military leader; he has no ties, no gestures, no dramatic flare. Somehow the photographs had never suggested the heavy reddish-brown colour of the deeply tanned face; they showed neither the smile nor the firmness nor the slow voice. The greatness of the man was not apparent, and he remained the old farmer till very slowly the accumulation of so much patience and quietness and instinctive strength revealed the man in his direct simplicity. This was not Feng Yu-hsiang's simplicity, which is infinitely complex. He was a farmer who had planted his trees, and whatever storms came, he was determined they would grow.

This was not greatness as we are accustomed to measure greatness. He was incapable, I think, of turning on suddenly and capriciously any personal power. He had no mannerisms—he had killed the marionette, or perhaps he was too old, and the marionette no longer possessed any validity. When you are sixty-five and have spent all your life fighting and see no end to the fighting, it would be strange if you continued to think in terms of drama. There was no drama—only a great impatience and sadness. Once he escaped from arrest by throwing a white towel round his waist and shouting: "I am the cook. Why kill me, when I can prepare such good food for you?" Today, he could no longer disguise himself as a cook. He seemed to have no love for power, and the only concession he ever made to his title of commander-in-chief was to wear occasionally a drab purple cloak with a ragged fur collar. You do not grin like a boy unless you have a good conscience. Among the date-palms and in the great silence of the cave-tunnel he gave the impression still of an old peasant who was simply saying the things that were on his mind.

A wolf was prowling on the walls of the garden when we went out; it stood there, shaggy and thin and black against the moon-
310

light, then suddenly jumped away and disappeared in some undergrowth. As the jeep rolled through dust-clouds towards the river, some more wolves appeared, but they too scattered. A cold wind came down the valley, the date garden disappeared, there was only the moonlight, the hills and the darkness of the plains between the black cliffs. Once a candle gleamed in a cave high up the mountainside. When the candle went out, the valley looked lonelier than ever.

June 10th, Temple and Pagoda . . . YENAN is dominated by its pagoda, which has the same colour as the surrounding loess, very tall and slender when seen from a distance and curiously commanding. Against that bright summer air, standing on the chalk-coloured buff, nothing could be more perfect. It is not, like the spires of European cathedrals, an incitement to spiritual things. It is of the earth, earthy, neither too high nor too low, and like the other pagodas you see all over northern China it proclaims a kind of dignity to the mountain, and nothing more; for nearly all pagodas are set on the heights of mountains, to attract your attention, to give you a visible point of support, to make you see the mountain contours more clearly and to show you that men are important in the scheme of things, for the man-made pagoda makes the mountain more beautiful.

They said that the pagoda was first built in the Sung Dynasty. It may be true, but it gives the impression of being considerably older; and it is impossible to imagine a time when there was no pagoda there. It stands on the high buff at the intersection of three valleys, facing the old town whose walls have long ago disappeared, and the new town which has been battered into crumbling fragments of stone, only the broken walls left standing, by the Japanese. For thousands of years there had been merchandise in these valleys. One of the main roads to the capital at Ch'ang-an lay through the south gate of the town. The T'ang Dynasty priests once carved their 10,000 buddhas in the neighbouring caves, and there are rumours that there are other caves, as yet unopened, in the neighbourhood. The pagoda dominates the valley for miles, and even in the distance, when you see it as a mere pinpoint, its place, its commanding presence are perfect. At sunset, when the winter wheat on the uplands glows, the pagoda glows with the same bright red-gold colour. Near Pekin, on the western hills, there are so many pagodas that you are bewildered, and do not

311

know which way to turn. In Yenan there is one pagoda, complete and perfect in its solitude.

But on the opposite side of the river there is a temple which looks, from every angle, like a butcher's shop perched on the bluff. It is not a butcher's shop: the temple has fallen into ruins, and has been rebuilt to accommodate the priests who still remain there, a thing of flat walls and square roofs—the ugliest thing in that delightful valley. Yet once the temple must have been a fortress; ledge upon ledge of stone wall and buttress crane down from the summit. From the valley you can see the old pilgrim paths, the broken gates, the granite steps. Once it was commanding, but it no longer commands anything. And when you have climbed up the mountain you are bewildered by the massive strength of the outside walls, and the crumbling idiocy of what lies inside them—the buddhas which seem to have been designed and painted by a country bumpkin, with the stuffing falling out of them. In comparison with the buddhas in the Cave of the Thousand Buddhas they are monstrous, not only made without feeling or devotion, but with incredible *inexpertise*. It is impossible to imagine them worse, and it is difficult to understand why they have been allowed to remain. As they stand there in disorderly rows in low rooms that resemble cattle-sheds or morgues, some already fallen to the ground, others still spilling the straw stuffing, you feel that buddhism which has demonstrated its perfect attainments in a cave less than a mile away, has here reached the nirvana of idiocy. They are not buddhas, nor are they animals, nor are they men. They are the crumbling relics of something so outworn that they have lost all meaning. It was delightful to find, written in chalk on the wall above one of these disgusting creatures, the inscription: "O God of Heaven, since the aeroplanes are coming, why don't you run away?" One wished heartily that they had rushed away as fast as their straw-filled legs would carry them.

Someone had told me that in the main hall of the temple there was a perfect buddha in porcelain. It was true that there was a porcelain buddha, and for some reason this fat Laughing Buddha in white glazed stone, with red ribbons tied round its neck, and offerings of fruit placed all round it, had become the main object of worship. The priest was anxious that no one should touch it, though he was perfectly prepared to allow you to touch anything else in the room. He said the buddha was very old and possessed magical qualities. Which was odd, for it could not have been more

312

than forty years old and was almost certainly made in Manchester.

But as though to compensate for all this inanity there stood, in a dark corner of the room, an earth-god of bronze with an archaic smile. It might almost have been a Greek Apollo, so quiet and dignified, with the folds of the long gown carefully spaced, and the face giving signs of not yet being awakened, though it would awaken soon. It was odd to find it there, and one wondered how old it was, for certainly no one for many hundreds of years had made things in northern Shensi of such overwhelming beauty and simplicity. We took it into the sunlight and watched the rusted bronze absorbing the light, and then placed it gently in the dark corners of the temple.

There were other things in those weed-grown gardens. There was an enormous rusted bell which dated from the Ming Dynasty and which had been used until recently as an air-raid warning; there were stone monoliths with incredibly dexterous carving of inscriptions celebrating the virtues of long-dead emperors. From these gardens, overlooking low walls, you saw the three valleys, the chequered plains and the crumbling forts on all the hilltops. The sun was setting. The winter wheat was ripening, and somewhere in the distance a soldier was riding through a cloud of yellow dust to headquarters. When the dust settled, you noticed that the saddlecloth was arterial red—the only splash of colour among these mountains and valleys of soft yellows and softer greens.

Later . . . THE soldier came walking up the hill with a grey pack over his shoulders, his blue cotton uniform stained bright yellow with dust. He had a round red face, the colour of a red pippin, and he wore the uniform of the Communist Army, which is exactly the same as the uniform of all the other soldiers in China —the same blue and white enamel badge on his cap, which signifies the white sun in the blue sky, the same cut of the coat, the same puttees—but on one arm there was a small white square with the legend: 18 G A. The old Eighth Route Army has been transformed into the Eighteenth Group Army. He was about eighteen, and he walked up the hill looking in no way different from the soldiers in the south except that he looked better fed.

We watched him as he left the road, where the dogs were sleeping and the horses were plunging against the rock to avoid the only motor-car that had passed that day. He went down to the river, took off his wheat-straw sandals and bathed his feet. Then

313

he waded through the river and climbed up the bank towards one of the caves in the hills, and for a long while we heard him singing. And for days afterwards you remembered the clear smile and the sound of the voice coming across the darkening valley.

June 11th, The Dance in the Peach Orchard . . . THE *yangko* dance has an old history. It may be as old as historical China. There are songs in the *Book of Odes* which may have been danced to these simple steps and simple drum-beats. Usually the dance was performed at the time of transplanting, and again at harvest, and at wedding festivals, wherever there were great feasts and ceremonies.

It cannot have changed very much through the centuries, but it was changing now. The dance remained, but the Communists were inventing a new kind of dance—the *yangko* was played at the beginning and the end, but in between there were short plays. These plays were occasionally acted separately and had grown up with the tremendous new interest in drama. Now the Communists were using the *yangko* dance and the play in a deliberate effort to change the old village customs. There were plays against witchcraft, illiteracy and bad habits; there were plays designed to show the necessity of increasing production, co-operatives, medical work in villages and sanitation. In the old *yangko* the leader held an open umbrella and was followed by long dancing lanes of boys and girls, heavily painted, in gaudy dresses. They raced from one court-yard to another, sang songs, danced to the sounds of a pig-skin drum, and perhaps to fifes. The love dances were the best. In these the two lanes of boys and girls danced facing each other, swaying their bodies provocatively, clapping their palms on their knees, bending forwards or leaping backwards, while the clown buffooned and the audience beat time to the drums. Sometimes fireworks were let off. The dance differed slightly from village to village, but in essentials it was simply a slow dance—three steps forward and one back—which became more and more furious as the dance progressed. There were different interweaving patterns of the dance, and sometimes there were competitions between the villages. Also, the musical accompaniment could be changed at leisure, and from time to time new songs were invented. Essentially, it was a robust dance for the young which may have had its origin in a fertility cult, a complex interweaving of two lanes of youngsters till finally they appeared once more, lips parted,
314

sweat streaming from them, in two formal lines. The drums were played loudly and with abandon with the bare knuckles or a small weighted stick; and it was the thumping of the drums which gave the theme of these simple dances.

When the Communists came to northern Shensi in 1933, they watched the dances but did nothing to change them. They might never have changed them if there had been no war against Japan. In 1939 they began to realize that the dance could serve as the introduction and the finale of a new kind of propaganda, which would reach all the villages in the areas over which they ruled; for the villagers were known to have an extraordinary fondness for these dances, which they cultivated on every possible occasion. They began tentatively by replacing the leader with an umbrella (who may have represented the Emperor) by a farmer carrying farming implements. They allowed the love-dances to continue, but they insisted that there were other things as important, and they replaced the clown with a Japanese or a traitor. The first of the new *yangko* dances were deliberately designed to increase production, and the first of all was called: "Brother and Sister Cultivating the Virgin Land." It was a clever title, for "brother and sister" in Chinese folk-song have the significance of "lover and beloved," and increased production had never been so urgent.

The new play introduced between the old dances was purely experimental. It was to be performed in the open air, by a small group selected from the dancers, and it had to be written with extreme simplicity so that it could be followed easily by all the villagers. There was no tradition. They took what they could from the west, and they improvised on the basis of the symbolic traditions of the Chinese stage. A farmer could suggest the presence of mountains by standing on his toes and shading his eyes; the crackle of machine-gun fire could be expressed by cymbals; animals were simply men wearing masks; but since the actors in the play wore their ordinary blue cotton costumes, how could you distinguish between them? You could, of course, make them announce to the audience that they were tax-collectors, government officials, farmers, labour heroes or people fleeing from the Japanese. It was not difficult, but it was a waste of time, and the traditional Chinese stage, by using deliberate artifices of gesture and symbolic costumes, had long ago got over this difficulty. But they never found a satisfactory solution.

In the peach orchard near the small house where Mao Tse-tung lives, the *yangko* dance was played. The setting was perfected, and because it had rained recently, the peach-leaves gave off a heavy scent. The audience formed a circle round the dancers. On one side there were western violins playing together with Chinese violins, on the other sides there were cymbals and flutes. The dancers came rushing in, tall Shensi boys with white knee-breeches, brightly coloured waistbands and green shirts, with their heads in coloured kerchiefs. They danced amazingly well, beating both sides of the drums and singing at the same time a song of welcome, which changed later into a song in praise of democracy and peace. The drum-beats became louder, the beat more insistent, and they were followed by boys and girls with heavily rouged faces who began to weave within the magic circle of the garden incredibly complex patterns to the tune of the fifes, the violins, the cymbals and the drums. You could recognize the ancient pattern of the love-dance, though the words had changed, for they formed two lines which came together and parted, and raced and clapped hands and in general followed the pattern of the ancient steps of the dance; and though the songs had been changed, the imitation of the emotions of love remained. And then very suddenly, in a final roar of drum-beats, they departed and their places were taken by the protagonists of the interlude.

There were two interludes. The first was a comic movement in the drive against illiteracy, showing how a small farmer sends a letter from the town to his old father, saying that the price of beans had gone up. The old man could not read. He asked help from another farmer, and was told that the price of peas had gone up. He knows that if he leaves his fields near harvest-time he is in danger of losing his crops, but the price has gone up so much and he is so avaricious that he decides to set out with his peas. He goes to the town. He cannot find his son, and he discovers that the price of peas has not gone up at all. Cursing, he returns to the farm and discovers that his son has forestalled him, his crops are ruined, his daughter-in-law, who can read, is insulting him and life is no longer worth living. Some of this is spoken, but most of it is song. The audience is roaring with laughter—the old man is near tears, and even towards the end argues bitterly against book-learning. "You can't make children by book-learning, you can't raise crops by book-learning, it's all a waste of time." He dances round the ring in an agony of remorse, shaking his head, nervously lighting his long silver pipe, for ever bewildered by the magic
316

power of the words he has misunderstood, until in the end, with the blissful smile of the initiated, he promises faithfully to learn to read.

It was a morality, and absurdly simple, but it was evidently effective. It was not a theoretical incident; it was an incident that had happened very often, and it was played dramatically and effectively by actors who knew how to imitate the finest gestures of the peasants. They spoke in the local dialect, there were purely local jokes and though doors were opened according to the same gestures which take place on the Chinese stage and a twelve-hour journey on foot from the village to the town was accomplished in two minutes, it was clear that the audience could identify itself with the actors.

The second play was shorter and concerned two soldiers returning to headquarters with some pigs they had bought at market. The pigs were imaginary pigs, but the gestures of the soldiers as they pummelled the pigs with sticks along the dusty roads gave a curious air of reality to the scene. They rested, and suddenly discovered that they had one pig too many. They were nonplussed at first. Impossible to explain the presence of the pig. They argued. Probably the pig had joined them of its own free will. Perhaps it was lost, and they were doing it a service by bringing it to headquarters. They were also doing the soldiers a service. They decided to proceed on the journey with the additional imaginary pig, but when they reached headquarters questions began to be asked, and worse still one of the soldiers had lost his passport. The moral of the play was evidently that soldiers should not take pigs that do not belong to them, and should be very careful about their passports. According to the kind of lives which soldiers live all over China, the moral seemed well worth insisting upon.

And then the dancers came in again, the interlude was over and the pure dance, hardly modified at all, took the place of insistent propaganda. Once again there was the beat of the drums, the heavily painted faces, the swirl of skirts and waist-bands, and the clear voices of the singers. The thumping of their feet on the earth, the small clouds of dust, the tremendous force of the drums—they were things that you remembered for long afterwards, because they seemed so appropriate to these thickset sturdy people. There was nothing professional in their dancing; they danced with a kind of natural abandon, and because they liked dancing, and because they were young. So had they danced in the time of Con-

317

fucius, and so too would they dance when all our present quarrels are over.

June 12th, The Communist General . . . HE was Vice-Commander-in-Chief of the Border Armies, not tall, though he gave the impression of height, but dark and swarthy, and like nearly everyone else in Yenan he grinned like a boy. He had been ill of a stomach complaint for a long time, but looked healthy and even vigorous, and he wore the usual wheat-straw sandals and faded blue cotton coat without insignia. He walked heavily and determinedly; his hands were fine and covered with innumerable dark wrinkles, and sometimes when he spoke the eyes seemed to fill with pain. He was General Peng Teh-huei. He had been fighting since he was eighteen.

The military leaders in the Border Areas belong to no special type, but among them you notice very soon two dominant trends —those who resemble peasants, though sometimes they were never peasants, like Chu Teh, and those who resemble scholars, like Mao Tse-tung and Chou En-Lai, though they are scholars who have never taught or studied for any length of time. Peng Teh-huei resembled a thickset peasant even to the heavy curve of the shoulders and the dark sunburned hands. He did not seem, like Chu Teh, to be completely at ease in the world; nor was he nervous. He was a man who had hated and fought passionately, but with a clear brain, with little education but immense driving force. He had led one of the four armies which composed the Long March, and now, as he spoke of those days which were already disappearing into legend, there was an odd sadness in his voice. The old voice came from the youngish face. So perhaps had Napoleon's generals spoken in the years before Waterloo, remembering the victories in Italy and the Nile.

He spoke about the past for more than three hours, delighting in his reminiscences.

"If you go back a long way, you can see how it all began. You have to go back to the time when Sun Yat-sen was still alive, and the Whampao Academy was being born, and from Canton there was being planned the long march to the north against the warlords. It was 1923. Under Sun Yat-sen there was peace between the Communists and the Kuomintang, and in Whampoa Academy itself there were important Communist leaders like Chou En-lai, Lin Po-chu and Li Fu-chun.

318

"Sun Yat-sen had proclaimed that only a people's army could fight the war-lords in the north, and in fact it was a people's army which began the march from Canton. During the first stages of the march, until the army reached Wuhan, there was complete co-ordination between the Communists and the Kuomintang. The march had three main purposes: to resist foreign imperialism, particularly the Japanese, to wipe out the war-lords and create a democratic government. But when we reached Wuhan, it became clear that the right wing of the Kuomintang was not prepared to resist foreign imperialism, was indeed prepared to make overtures with them. On April 12th, 1927, there was the Kuomintang *coup d'état.*

"The Great Revolution failed. There was a reign of terror, and hundreds of men like Tung Yen-ta, the leader of the Third Party, were arrested and later killed. The Kuomintang, instead of collaborating with the revolutionary forces, co-operated with the feudal forces in order to overthrow the revolutionary movement.

"There followed the Nanchang uprising, organized by General Yeh Ting and supported by Mme Sun Yat-sen and many other liberal elements. General Chu Teh, at that time, was only a regimental commander in Yeh Ting's armies. No one had ever heard of him till then. The uprising failed. The armies marched out of Nanchang against Kwangtung and were defeated in Tungchiang near Meihsien. Of the survivors Chu Teh led a bare thousand men through Kiangsi into Hunan.

"As I say it now, it is not very exciting—names of battles, places, marches. But they *were* exciting, though the old revolutionaries have gradually forgotten them. The battles all become one. But at this stage there occurred battles which are remembered by us, for suddenly Mao Tse-tung comes on the scene.

"In 1927 Mao Tse-tung was organizing peasant self-defence corps in Hunan. At first they had no weapons—only sharp sticks, spears, bayonets. Later they were to capture rifles from the Hunan provincial troops. Mao Tse-tung was moving around the area of Tingchiang in eastern Hunan, and then he came south to Chingkansan, an extraordinary range of mountains, not very accessible, which produces two or three good crops a year and where you can live in some kind of isolation. Mao mobilized the peasants and redistributed the land. Chu Teh came up from the south and joined him. He had begun with hardly a thousand soldiers, and by now he had hardly more than 2,000. Out of these 2,000 and the peasants on Chingkansan two regiments were formed—the 28th under Chu Teh, and the 31st under Mao. I have forgotten why these regiments were given these numbers. Perhaps there was no reason, or they wanted the enemy to think they had many regiments. It was the first time Mao Tse-tung had met Chu Teh, and it was the beginning of the formidable combination which was to be known later as Chu-Mao.

"So there were two regiments defending the mountain, and several guerrilla units armed with old spears and swords and whatever else they could lay their hands on. It was the winter of 1927. The Hunan provincial troops and the Kiangsi troops were sent against them, and there were even Yunnanese forces under Chu Peh-teh. It was the first of the annihilation campaigns. I wasn't there, but Lin Piao was there. Lin Piao, who comes from Hupeh, was a battalion commander of the 28th regiment under Chu Teh. He was unknown then. They were to hear about him later.

"We did not stay on the mountain. When we had broken their attacks, we attacked. We destroyed five regiments under Chu Peh-teh at a place called Yunghsin on the eastern borders of Kiangsi, and captured 7,000 rifles. This was the beginning of our military strength. Afterwards, in the spring of 1928, Chu Teh led his troops to southern Hunan, taking the main forces away from the mountain stronghold. Chingkansan was left now weaker than ever—there were only guerrillas and untrained troops to defend the mountain. The Kiangsi and Hunanese troops heard that the mountain was undefended. They brought between 20,000 and 30,000 troops against the mountain, against Mao Tse-tung and perhaps 400 well-trained guerrillas. This was all he had, but he was well-entrenched, the peasants on the plains would work for him, and they managed to break up the enemy's supply lines.

"Remember that in those days there were no aeroplanes, no railways, no tanks, no trucks. The defenders knew the terrain and concealed the grain, and it was not impossible for them to put to flight armies vastly superior to theirs by sudden, devastating attacks. We had an excellent intelligence system, and besides Mao Tse-tung, whose military training came from the field, there were regular officers like Chang Tse-ching, who was later killed in action. At the battle of Wangyangchieh Mao Tse-tung and his guerrillas routed an army of 20,000 men. The victory partly belonged to Chang Tse-ching, who was regimental commander at the time,

320

but it was Mao who organized the peasants and constructed a vast intelligence system and directed the campaign. The mountain was still in our hands. We waited for another annihilation campaign, for we had no strength at this time to attack.

"I say 'we' did this, but I was not there. I knew very little about what was happening until the third of the annihilation campaigns, in the winter of 1928. At this time Mao Tse-tung and Chu Teh left the mountain and went to Fukien and southern Kiangsi to organize the peasants. I was left in charge of the defences of Chingkansan.

"In July 1928 I had organized an uprising in Pingchiang in north-eastern Hunan. I heard about the defence of Chingkansan, and after the uprising failed, I led about a thousand men to join the mountain soldiers. By this time our forces had grown. I had a thousand men, and the peasants were flocking to the mountain, so that we had between 4,000 and 5,000 men altogether, with a considerable number of bayonets and rifles. But we were still weak in numbers compared with the enemy. They said publicly they had 60,000 well-trained and well-equipped troops. They may have had about 45,000. At that time Chu and Mao were somewhere in western Fukien. The enemy had good leaders. Their officers were all regular Kuomintang officers. They had three armies, with Chu Peh-teh in command of the Third Army. But we defeated them, first in hundreds of skirmishes and later in battle. It was the first time the Kuomintang used radios: we did not even have telephones. Nevertheless we drove them away. Actually we never had radios at all until after the battle of Changsha in 1930. Even if we had had radios, we would not have known how to use them.

"We occupied Changsha for ten days in 1930. It started with the anniversary meeting at Pingchiang the year after the uprising. Ho Chien's troops arrived, but we routed them about six *li* away, and then decided to follow them. We had nothing to lose, and they were very frightened. Changsha was defended by five regiments—a total strength of about 30,000. To attack Changsha with our 10,000 was technically impossible—the city was difficult to attack and favours the defender—but our morale was high, and we were bitterly determined to show the war-lords that peasants can muster enough force to get through. We got through. We fought a nasty engagement on the Nanling river fifteen *li* from Changsha and attacked with bayonet charges, since our main weapons were

321

bayonets. It was costly. We had between 2,000 and 3,000 casualties. There was fighting along the approaches to Changsha the whole day and part of the night, and even when we had entered the city, there was still fighting going on outside. It was a hard war, and in ten days Ho Chien was bringing so large a force against us that we evacuated.

"We had started from small beginnings. We were still small. In the Nanchang uprising we were still smaller. After the defeat in Kwangtung, there was left only Chu Teh's troops numbering about a thousand and Mao Tse-tung's peasant guerrillas armed with spears and homemade bayonets—and there was the uprising I directed at Pingchiang. Now we had large resources in equipment, and we were beginning to think we were a real army. We withdrew from Changsha to southern Kiangsi. The enemy began to launch another annihilation campaign under the direct orders of Chiang Kai-shek. We defeated them, we captured their signal officers and began to learn how to use radio. We were 10,000 when we captured Changsha. Now we were at least 17,000, for our losses were more than made up by farmers and workers who joined the army.

"The uprising at Pingchiang was an entirely independent peasant uprising. I did not join the Communist Party till March 1928. I had no real military training, though I studied for a while in the Hunan Military College. Military schools are useful for giving you technical knowledge, but you learn more on the field, and battles are largely fought with morale—it was hatred of imperialism and warlordism that drove us on. The oppressing powers are always more powerful in military equipment, but they lack the morale of the oppressed. The American War of Independence lasted eight years. We modelled ourselves on the Americans, and were prepared to consider ourselves lucky if we could win in twenty years.

"We have never had any time to collect a history of our wars. I am giving you what I remember, and I cannot recollect all the details. In the Long March I was commander of the Third Group Army. We started from Kiangsi with 70,000 men, and when we reached northern Shensi there were no more than 10,000. Mostly they died from natural causes. In western Szechuan the air was so thin that we could hardly breathe, and in the grasslands there were almost no villages and no people, and it was all a kind of desert and we often starved. Best of all the battles was the crossing of the Wu river in Kweichow. We were surrounded. We had already crossed the river, but the enemy lay on both sides of us. We drove back again across the river, and put half the enemy to flight, and then drove against those who were on the south bank. The Kuomintang forces were led by a good general, Wu Chi-wei —he had won many victories in the past, but we destroyed his army.

"The river was about 400 metres wide. There were five regiments of Kuomintang troops entrenched on the bank, and all the ferry-boats had been taken over to the opposite side. We silenced their guns with our own mortars and machine-guns, then one man swam across the river and brought a single boat back to our shore. We sent the boat back under heavy fire with twenty men in it— backwards and forwards until we had established a bridgehead of 300 soldiers. They knew we had landed, but in the dark they could not tell how many we were. Then we captured their ferry-boats, and put all the men we could spare into them, and routed them."

He could not remember all the details which had taken place in the famous crossing of the Tatu Bridge:

"It's a long time ago, and I cannot remember all of it. There were so many rivers—the Gold Sand river, the Hsiang river, the Wu and the Yangtse. I remember the bridge was about 140 metres wide, with six or seven iron chains placed about thirty centimetres apart. It was a shaky bridge at all times, and the current was too strong for us to cross by rafts or pontoons. So the soldiers crossed one by one, hanging down from the bridge, hand over hand, their only weapons hand-grenades and pistols, for a rifle would be useless. The current was terribly fast. The bridge was a hundred metres above the level of the water. I cannot remember very much, but I remember the people falling into the water, and there was nothing we could do to help them."

We had lunch then. He ate little except milk and porridge; he still suffered from stomach ulcers—part of the legacy of the Long March. He talked about the recent changes of tactics in the Communist Army.

"We have been fighting guerrilla wars for twenty years, but we have also been fighting positional wars. The Kuomintang still regards us as partisans and guerrillas, but the battle of Shihpingchieh should have taught them better. We have American equipment now—captured from the Kuomintang.

"We cannot be defeated, but it is probably true that we cannot

323

win. We cannot be defeated because we have the support of the people, who are the source of our soldiers, our supplies and our intelligence. They can harass the enemy and keep all intelligence away from the enemy. Then we have another thing which they have not got—the close co-ordination between the officers and the soldiers, and their determination for self-sacrifice. Lastly, we allow our commanding officers tremendous flexibility in command.

"There were times in the past when we had heavy equipment, or captured it from the Japanese, and then we had to destroy it, because we could not use it. Sometimes the same thing happens now. What is the use of having a tank when you have no gasoline, no spare parts, no repair shops? We burn it, because the enemy would use it against us if they recaptured it. We have done the same with heavy guns. So, in general, we avoid positional war because our troops are not so well equipped as theirs and often we find ourselves numerically inferior. We have no constant source of supplies, as they have. At the very beginning of the battle of Shihpingchieh we had only one regiment in the town, reinforcements did not arrive till twenty days later. The Kuomintang had American equipment, but their morale was low; and so we fought them without any great difficulty and held up their advance for a month. We can do this whenever we like. We are an army now, and because we are fighting for democracy, we have never been tougher or more determined."

June 13th, Mao Tse-tung's Head . . . I was beginning to think that it would never be possible to see Mao Tse-tung. They said he was busy, the threat of civil war hung more menacingly than ever on China, and he was working through the night on papers and despatches. You reminded yourself that Yenan was the administrative centre for a population of over a hundred millions: on those clear summer mornings, when the air was bright and deathly still, it did not look like it, but it was nevertheless true. The destiny of China was being decided in Nanking and Yenan, the small yellow back-water which had been forgotten by the world.

Mao had flashed past in an overladen jeep on the day I arrived. He looked strong and well in his blue cotton clothes, the face dark-tanned by the sun, and I noticed that he had large hands which clutched the side of the jeep as it went through pot-holes of yellow dust. They shrugged their shoulders and said: "You probably

324

won't see him again."

Meanwhile there were other people one could see, and in the intervals there was Mao's book, *The Coalition Government*, to read. It was a curiously impressive book, written in a dryly humorous style, without bitterness. It was very long, and they said the whole book had been delivered as a speech in a single day—nearly 200 pages of it. There were moments when you came face to face with the man, moments of quietly passionate fervour, without rhetoric. He did not grow larger as you read the book, but he grew more human. You began to see how his mind worked.

"Our starting-point," he wrote, "is to serve the Chinese people earnestly and wholeheartedly, and never to be severed from the people; to set out always from the point of view of serving the people's interests, not serving the interests of a small group or oneself: and to give equal responsibility to the people and the guiding organization. Experience during the last twenty years has taught us that all tasks, policies and methods that were correct corresponded to the demands of the people at that definite time and place, and all that were incorrect were separate from the people's will."

Or again:

"Our comrades must not think that what is unintelligible to us is also unintelligible to the masses. Very often the masses stride ahead of us, and want urgently to advance forward, while our comrades do not act as leaders of the broad masses, but on the contrary reflect the opinion of some backward interests. Every comrade should be taught to comprehend that the highest criterion of all our statements and activities is whether they correspond to the highest interest of the broadest masses, and whether they are supported by the broadest masses. Every comrade should be taught to comprehend that as long as we rely on the people, firmly believing in the infinite creative power of the people, then we may be able to overcome all difficulties, no matter how serious they are, and no enemy will be able to overwhelm us, but will be overwhelmed by us."

And then finally, in the only note of passionate protest in the book, which is also a note of passionate faith:

"They must understand that no matter how tortuous the path may be, the independence and liberation of the Chinese people will be realized and the time for it is already at hand. The great aspirations of countless martyrs during the last 100 years must be fulfilled by our generation. Whoever desires to prevent these

325

aspirations from being translated into fact, that man will fail."

Meanwhile the undeclared war was going on. Chungking and Yenan radios were bitterly assailing one another. We sat over the radios and wondered which particular incident would later be taken by historians as the beginning of the war. It was neither peace nor war—only a ragged nervous interval, while we held our breaths and prayed that the final incident would never take place.

Three days after my arrival I went to a play based on an incident from *All Men are Brothers.* In front of me in the audience was Mao Tse-tung. It was not difficult to recognize him; he had long blue-black hair, fine cheek-bones and an immense sweeping forehead. He was enjoying himself completely. No one came in to bring telegrams concerning the civil war. At one moment when the feudal landlord was abusing the captain-general of the peasants, he became lost in a horrible fit of giggles, turned to his companion and seemed to be in danger of sliding under his seat.

The play was splendid and exceedingly simple. You knew that the captain-general of the peasant armies would inevitably capture the fortress of the white-faced feudal chief, and that the feudal lord and all his sons would be scattered to the winds. You knew, or you thought you knew, that virtue would be rewarded; and it was only a question of waiting four and a half hours before the good received their rewards. But four and a half hours, looking at the stage whose setting was a gigantic square of bright blue cloth seen under arc-lamps, is a long time. It became increasingly necessary not to be blinded and to seek some kind of rest by looking at Mao Tse-tung's head.

It was a good head, and unusually expressive. The shoulders looked powerful, and perhaps because he is a Hunanese he made no effort to hide his emotions. I have seen photographs of a man's back that are more revealing than his face. It might be possible— the clanging of the instruments and the high-pitched voices and the fantastic richness of the colours of the stage were becoming intolerable at times—it might be possible, I told myself, to learn something about him just by considering the head.

Other reflections occurred to me. The play was a morality, as primitive in its calculated simplicity as *Everyman.* It was also very relevant to the times, for there was no doubt in the minds of anyone in the audience that the captain-general of the peasant forces represented Mao Tse-tung and the white-faced old man with the long grey beard represented the Generalissimo. But chiefly it was

326

a morality, and like all good moralities there was represented for you the whole world: not only peasants and soldiers and chariot-driving generals, but cooks and servants and gatemen and officials. They were all there, and though they wore fantastically embroidered clothes, they were recognizedly the same all over the world. It was a play describing the passions of the people and virtue triumphant. The heroes wore the finest silk, the finest dragon-painted gowns; the evil wore ugly red and black masks which gave them the appearance of tigers. It was Shakespearian and impenitently romantic; and seeing Mao giggling almost to sickness it was possible to come to one conclusion about him—he remained the romantic, in spite of the hard-headed deliberate speeches which are so organized and biting that they read like the works of Mr. Sidney Webb.

It was an opinion that was to grow with time. I was glad I had seen him first at the play. I knew that he was Hunanese, I knew that he wrote first-rate poetry and I had suspected for a long time that he had deliberately or undeliberately modelled himself on the old Chinese heroes, believing that democracy and socialism and perhaps communism—though there was little enough evidence in his speeches that he was a Communist according to any existing pattern—were things that demanded heroes; could be fought for with heroism; were the deliberate and essential aims of heroism in the twentieth-century world. Impenitently romantic. It seemed possible. Or if not the impenitent romantic, then the impenitent dreamer who had already peopled the world of his imagination with innumerable Chinese peasants who no longer feared their feudal lords.

Meanwhile the Chinese play went on. The scene would change instantaneously: a girl would come to the front of the stage, open an imaginary door with a twist of her fingers and at once you were in the house. A moment later you have gone through three courtyards and have reached the garden; you know you have reached the garden because someone takes up a perfectly imaginary flower from the boards. Then instantaneously a carriage is waiting: there are two yellow flags with a cart-wheel drawn in black on each. The captain-general appears, lifts his baton and steps into the chariot; you know he has entered the chariot because he lifts his right leg generously and the two men carrying the flags walk by his side. You know he is certain of victory by the extravagant song he makes through his black beard.

327

The captains come in with their nodding plumes, their crowns of emeralds, their robes of flowing jade and red-gold, with their wives and ministers. The handsome youth whom you last saw in a gown of ruby enters now in a white gown embroidered with yellow racing dragons. With every scene there is a change in costume for the leading actors, so that you fail to notice that the background is simply a sky-blue sheet which burns the eyes—other things burn the eyes more effectively. The music is like an incantation; it keeps you awake, but it sends you half-asleep, an exceedingly repetitive music which possesses neither harmony nor melody nor any melodic theme. By this time you have forgotten that you have been gazing entranced at the stage for over three hours. There are no pauses, no *entr'actes*. You are assailed by rich colours, by the blare of trumpets, by the roar of the audience which has by now completely identified itself with the actors. You begin to look again at the back of Mao Tse-tung's head, or some of the other heads in the front row.

There was Chu Teh; there was Lin Po-chu, the chairman of the government of the border region which extends round Yenan, who looked like the manager of a bank; there was Tung Pi-wu, Communist delegate to Chungking, who resembled a professor; there was vice-chairman Li Ting-ming, an old landlord who sucked continually at a silver-stemmed pipe and wore a blue cotton cap rakishly in spite of his sixty-seven years; there was General Peng Teh-huei, who had led one of the four armies which comprised the Long March, the only man there who resembled in the least the popular idea of a Communist guerrilla, with his rough laughing brutal peasant face, and his fine hands. There was Mme Mao Tse-tung who was (though no one will believe it) more beautiful than Mme Chiang Kai-shek. There was Mao Tse-tung, in a well-cut brown Sun Yat-sen uniform, looking up at the actors as he leaned forward, planting his elbows on his knees, grinning continually. And behind them, in vast crowds, were soldiers and girls and peasants and farmers and government leaders and students. In those rare moments when Mao Tse-tung was not about to fall from his seat, you noticed that he put his palms together in the attitude of someone praying and his face was grave. You wondered where you had seen it all before. Then you remembered that the boy at his first party had changed instantly to the vicar in the parish hall who would make a speech in a moment and call on
328

everyone present not to forget their subscriptions for the harvest offerings.

But he made no speeches. When the citadel was attacked at last, when the actors with wooden swords had capered round the stage, when all the feudal landlords lay dead or were supplicating mercy on their knees, when the walls disappeared in the smoke of blinding saltpetre flames and the dead bodies had risen and run into the wings, when the last procession of virtuous peasants and smiling heroes had circled the stage, everyone got up and walked out into the night. I saw only one soldier with a bayonet—the leaders of what is known as Red China were not being guarded very efficiently; or perhaps there was no need to guard them. Mao bowed to several people he knew: he was still the vicar. A moment later he passed me again outside, looking grey and huddled in the darkness as he tried to find his place on the waiting lorry. He bowed, then disappeared. The head-lamps went on from the two jeeps, and then once again the night was blinding with light.

The Guerrilla . . . HE was thin and dark, had a nimble mind and spoke English perfectly, or so nearly perfect that it made no difference. He was born in Palembang in Sumatra, but for nine years he had heard nothing from his parents, and he had studied for a while in Hongkong. I have forgotten what fortunes of war brought him to Yenan. In the early days of the war he had been with the guerrillas in Shantung; now he was in charge of the English broadcasts sent out by Morse from Yenan radio, his quick wits delighting in journalism as much as he delighted in the long night-marches, the ambushes and the intricacies of the war against the Japanese.

"I was everything at once—a school-teacher, and leader of a small group of guerrillas, and a doctor, and five or six other things. Nothing very important. You know, it's like fighting everywhere else—long periods of boredom and waiting, and then you would suddenly find that a Japanese column had been announced. We were badly equipped sometimes. We fought often with nine foot long spears—you get a great deal of pleasure sharpening the edges to a razor thinness. And there was no mercy for you if the Japanese got you—they killed you and got a great deal of fun in killing you.

"It has changed a lot since the time when Edgar Snow wrote *Red Star over China*. There was no tunnel warfare in those days,

329

and we hadn't built up the technique we have now with land-mines. When the Japanese were bringing their blockhouses closer to us—the Chinese peasants were compelled to make the block-houses with the stones from their own walls, so that there are places where the villages have been destroyed and in their place there are only the blockhouses—then sometimes we mined the land all round the blockhouses, and they could move neither in nor out. We had rifles, hand-grenades, land-mines, spears and swords —this was about all. They had mountain artillery. They had can-non. They had their 'nibbling tactics.' The blockhouses were so close to one another that the Japanese could see at least two block-houses on either side of them. It was wasteful, but it was the only thing they could do to keep us in check.

"We had armed propaganda groups. This was about the most exciting thing we had—small bodies of youngsters with Mausers who would go out to make contact with the puppet forces, and if they got into difficulties, they would shoot their way out. But usu-ally they did not get into difficulties. The puppet troops often only needed an excuse not to fight for the Japanese. It was the duty of the propaganda groups to find an excuse. They usually found it. The chief job of the puppet troops was to guard the railways. We left them to guard the railways, but we took away their arms.

"This wasn't the only thing they did. They mobilized the peo-ple's volunteers—the *Ming Ping*—for sudden attacks on block-houses, and they kept up constant communication with the vil-lagers. The Japanese would demand grain. The propaganda troops taught the peasants to sabotage the demands. The grain had to be kept from the Japanese wherever possible. But how? We would teach the peasants to bury it. This worked sometimes, but the Jap-anese began to take hostages and threaten to shoot them unless the hiding-place of the grain was revealed. We would wall up the grain within false walls. We would arrange with the village head to hold out as long as possible, and if the whole village was fined —well, we could pay the fine with captured Japanese money for them. We even taught the women and children to cry and beat themselves and pretend to be starving when the Japanese came in to demand the grain. We had to. For us, preventing the grain fall-ing into Japanese hands was only second in importance to extermi-nating them.

"It was fun while it lasted. Sometimes it was hideous. We were fighting on our own middens, and for our own lives—a decentral-
330

ized warfare, and very personal. They were getting desperately frightened of us by 1942. We mined their lines of communication and dug man-high trenches along the sides of the main communications—you can still see traces of the trenches in Yenan, and sometimes the trenches were amazingly complex things. Trenches would disappear into tunnels. The trenches assumed all shapes— the Japanese could not fire along them. We broke up their roads. They 'nibbled,' but we went underground, and it was worse than mechanized warfare because the hatred was prolonged and went deeper on both sides. We fought to the utmost with incredible patience; they fought with incredible despair.

"We had four kinds of troops. There was the People's Defence Corps, armed with spears and swords, who acted as sentries and spies in the villages. There were the People's Soldiers—*Ming Ping* means literally People's Soldiers—who had guns and hand-grenades and land-mines and were better trained. There were the armed guerrillas and the regular army, which comprised the Eighteenth Group Army (the old *Paluchun* or Eighth Route Army) and the New Fourth Army. Everyone was in the fighting line. It went on for a long time, but the kind of things I remember now are not the days of fighting—I remember walking slowly at night, and how sometimes we would suffer from night-blindness, and how quietly we walked. You had a lot of time to think, and chiefly you would think about the end of the war and getting married. There were soldiers who had not touched a woman for ten years. Discipline was strict. We did not dare to touch the village girls, because we wanted all the peasants on our side. Sometimes there were dances, but they did not often happen, and it was too exciting altogether to take part in a dance with a girl when you had not seen one for months on end."

He would come to my room often, and once I went up the long path cut in the cliff-side to his cave in the editorial section of the newspaper. I have never seen a cave so bare. There was a book-case with less than ten books, there was a table, two stools and behind the book-case a bed. He said he was given no money, and would have no use for it even if it was given to him—everything was provided, food, paper, pencils, clothes. The food was good, but not plentiful. The leaders of the Government got the best food, he received the "medium mess" and the common soldiers and administrators were in the third category. I said it was not very communistic. He answered: "We have to do that. All the food is ade-

331

quate—have you seen a single person looking pale or starved?—
but we agreed long ago that the leaders should have the best.
After all, it happens everywhere else, and the difference between
the three categories is hardly noticeable." I asked what happened
when he got married. If there was no money, how did you celebrate the marriage? He smiled wryly. "It's easy. The Government
will give you another plank to put in the bed, and there will be a
hell of a good feast. The trouble is to find the girl." He looked contented, though he wanted a good book on journalism and as many
books as possible about the modern world in English. In these
high caves overlooking the valley there were long poles with sag-
ging radio aerials; beneath them were small huts where monitors
lived and listened on Japanese radios to the news coming from
all the radio stations of the world. They had spot news, but they
had little informed criticism, few books, only a few handfuls of
magazines. This was in a very real sense the capital of a considerable number of millions of Chinese, they were desperately cut off
from the world, ingrown and curiously content to remain in their
primitive simplicity. They were so accustomed to their caves, their
wooden spinning-wheels—you saw the wooden spinning-wheels
everywhere—and their vision of a democratic landlordless China
that you wondered sometimes how they would behave in vast industrial cities. They had almost no experience of heavy industry
outside Manchuria. "It's different in Kalgan," the guerrilla said.
"That's a biggish city. In Yenan we're ingrown—that's true, but
there they are getting down for the first time to the problems of
industry on a large scale. They've got coal, iron, asbestos, mica.
They've got a lot of machinery left by the Japanese." As we sat
there in the cave, with the shadows playing against the wall, thick
darkness outside, Kalgan looked eminently delightful and respectable. He wetted his lips. "Bathrooms with running water, electric
light, streets which are paved—not just mud-traps like the Yenan
roads in winter. You have a roof over your head, not a moist dripping cave to live in. And the food's better. Do you know what it is
like when you have lived eight years, like some of the people here,
in a village cut off from the world, and suddenly you go into a big
city? I haven't been to a city for more years than I care to remember, but I know what it is like. When you see a comfortable chair
with good springs, you hardly dare to sit in it. A tiled bathroom—
hell, you'd get into the bath and stay in it all day and all night. We
don't like this life, but it's worth living it. I want to get married
332

and I don't want to live all my life in a cave."

He was severely critical of his own broadcasts, which were simple and factual, and not very exciting. They were not intended to be exciting. I read through hundreds of pages of them, type-written on good paper—there is an excellent paper-mill thirty miles from Yenan—and it was odd to notice how scrupulously all the modern headline techniques were avoided. They were grave, and innocent of all ornament. It was good, clear-cut journalism, but it was not the journalism that was going to make America or England excited. In Barcelona the broadcasting station had won its own victories. In the end I came to the conclusion that the Communists in China were nearly the worst propagandists in the world.

It was not their fault. They had neither the electric power, the technicians nor men trained in writing for the outside world. Mao Tse-tung had never been abroad. Chu Teh had studied in France and Germany, but it was long ago, and neither the French nor the Germans were of any use at this crisis. There was an incredible lack of knowledge of foreign psychology, and a very ready belief that this was one of their outstanding faults. In contrast to the Kuomintang, whose members were often returned students from America or England, the Communist leaders were nearly all re-turned students from France or Chinese who had never been abroad. They had good reason to be bitter against the Americans for sending troops northward in L.S.T.s, for offering military advice to the National Government against the Communists and for the continual lend-lease of materials which could be used to fight the civil war, but the editorials which appeared in the two Yenan newspapers had a bitterness which was purely Chinese and incomprehensible to the Americans or the British. Unfortunately for the Communists, these editorials were later translated by Embassy translators. They were circulated and sometimes reprinted. They were not necessarily factual, and they did nothing to heal raw wounds, and sometimes they gave the impression of a desperate vindictiveness which was foreign to all the Communist leaders I met, who knew perfectly well that vindictiveness led nowhere. Yet both sides were committed to a war of nerves, played up the real and imaginary crimes of their opponents *ad nauseam* and declared that they alone possessed the true faith in their screaming editorials. In all this the English Morse-broadcasts were innocent, but I would have enjoyed reading them more if they were written

333

with more fire and excitement. The guerrilla shook his head. "We're still learning. It's taken us a hell of a long time to get this far. And there's one thing worth remembering when you say we are ingrown—which is true—and this is that we have placed all our attention and put all our energies into educating the villages of China. Until they are educated, until every villager in China can read and write and realize his own strength in a democratic community, other things can wait. The important thing is that the villagers should be told what they are fighting for. We have no quarrel with the American people, but they are so far advanced industrially that they can learn nothing from us, and probably they can teach us very little; our problems are our own, and our isolation is a measure of our efforts to grapple with the problems of the villagers. We'll carry on like that. We're rotten propagandists to the outside world, but we're pretty good in China. We've given the peasants a new dignity and honesty, and—oh hell—there are four hundred million of them, more than the whole populations of America, Britain and Soviet Russia combined."

I confess I preferred it this way. It was honest, and it was independent; they were standing on their own feet, not begging for arms and lend-lease supplies. The Kuomintang was pinning its hopes on an industrial recovery which would owe a great deal to America. They had every reason for this. The Communists were pinning their hopes on the farmers and peasants, and they had every reason for this. The tragedy lay in the fact that they so often thought themselves exclusive when they were mutually dependent on each other. American know-how, a rise in the standard of living of the peasants, the three principles of Dr. Sun Yat-sen and the new democracy of Mao Tse-tung—these were the essentials of the new China. China had everything to learn from Russia and everything to learn from America. Then why fight, and delay the process of learning and the rebuilding of the country? Why the violations of the truce on both sides? Why the L.S.T.s piled with American equipment and Chinese crack troops from Burma? Why the screaming and misleading editorials on both sides? Only a few weeks before *Ta Kung Pao* had stated: "The corpses starved to death strew the roads. People eat grass roots and tree-bark. Troops are sucking the blood of the villagers. . . . If ambitious persons insist on more adventures, we shall all perish." Yenan was not entirely guiltless, but you got the impression that she was considerably more conscious of a responsibility towards the peasants

334

than the Kuomintang. Chu Teh had said: "Let bygones be by-gones, and let's start afresh." The guerrilla had hope. He, too, wanted bygones to be bygones. I asked him how it would end. "It doesn't look as though it will ever end. There will be negotia-tions, and when the negotiations fail or even before the negotia-tions fail, there will be trials of strength. Neither side can defeat the other. There will be more negotiations and more trials of strength, and it may go on for ever and ruin the country completely. That's what I think sometimes. But more often I think it will all end suddenly—the nightmare will collapse—and we will go for-ward with the coalition government."

June 14th, Faces . . . ALL were sunburnt, for there is little shade in these valleys except in the caves and most men spent their lives in the fields. Mostly they were northern faces, deeply lined, with square foreheads and handsome features, but some-times and more often than you expected you saw the aquiline features of descendants of the Turkic tribes that came down from the north; they were darker, and often the men were taller.

For years the valley of Yenan lay on the frontier. Tribesmen came down from the north and intermarried with the original stock, and from Sian in the south people fled northward. As in Vienna and Okinawa and in all those places where there have been mixtures of widely differing stocks, those who survive seem often the handsomest, and these people of Yenan were handsome and sturdy above the average. I never saw a girl who was not delight-ful to look at. On old Chinese tapestries and paintings of the T'ang Dynasty you will come across girls and women with pear-shaped faces. I had thought this kind of beauty had vanished till I came here and saw a girl walking along a road, who resembled one of the pear-faced goddesses on the tapestries. They say there are hundreds of them in this region, but they seem to be growing rarer. They are called *gua-nien-tzu,* and may be descended from the court beauties who once decorated Sian, when it was known as Ch'ang-an, the capital of the Empire. I never saw a man with one of these faces, but I saw at least four girls. And one wonders how they can survive when there is so much foreign blood, and always new waves of people are coming to these valleys.

Once I saw a man riding furiously on horseback, and noticed that the horse was one of those heavy-cruppered horses which ap-pear in T'ang Dynasty memorials, a descendant of one of the

335

horses which a famous T'ang Emperor captured in Ferghana; as he rode through the dust, he resembled a prince, the face very red and heavily bearded, the saddle-cloth bright blue and embroidered with Persian roses, and he wore bright yellow sleeves and a red cape fell from his shoulders. When he had disappeared at last, you could have sworn it was someone you had seen in a dream.

Down from the hills come the peasants to their markets and co-operatives. They come in thin-wheeled carts, the wheels studded with brass, carts which are exactly the same as those you find modelled in clay in Han Dynasty tombs. These people are unusually well-built, and you wonder where you have seen them before. In Szechuan they are thinner and have tighter lips. In Kunming they have Burmese blood and higher cheek-bones. The Hunanese are more sombre, unless they smile. And then you remember the old carvings of the Liang Dynasty, the princes in flowing robes, the ministrants and the priests, and you remember that Shensi was always the cradle of China and these men are survivors of the earliest beginnings.

Landscape . . . THE heat was terrible. It was the kind of landscape that van Gogh would have liked to paint—the dust rose like flames. And yet life went on, a small peasant cart with immense wheels went down to the river, the few mat-shed shops were still open and people walked slowly down the street, kicking up bright yellow fans of dust.

That morning a Kuomintang aeroplane had flown high over Yenan. We went out to watch it, puzzled by its presence. What could it find? Only a baking hot valley with dust-clouds rolling. If they dropped bombs, it would only make a few more dust-clouds. There was nothing at all in Yenan except the river, which was growing shallower each day, a few ponies which shrank into the walls of the cliffs and a few peasants. Yet they kept on sending these aeroplanes, and it was always puzzling.

And sometimes the earth seemed dead, without life, with nothing growing, a lost country which no explorer would ever find. Chu Yuan wrote a story of the Peach-blossom Fountain. He described a country which he reached through a cleft in the mountain near a spring where peach-trees were growing; beyond the mountain he came upon a race of people with flaxen hair who had escaped from the empire in the Tsin Dynasty, and knew

336

nothing of the coming of the Hans. They tended their fields and wore their hair in loops, and they were content to live as they were. There were peach-trees in Yenan, and it was not impossible to believe that you had come into this undiscovered country. The people looked contented. There was millet and wheat enough for everyone, and a little rice. Men dug out of the friable soil a hard living. They ploughed the slopes, every mountain was crowned with its plain of ripening wheat, but they had not yet reclaimed the desert—dams, hydraulic power, electricity would make the earth fertile.

Though the air was clear and delightfully transparent, the sun scorched everything within sight, and you did not feel the full force of the sun till you went out into the fields. The caves were cool. The fields were furnaces during those midsummer days, and the hot whirling dust got under your eyelids and made the mouth sore. Glaringly, the sultry indigo-blue sky made havoc of the shimmering landscape, which sometimes seemed to melt as all things melt when seen through the fumes rising from boiling lead. There were days when the heat was like a million flaming spears: yet the evenings were cold. They said it was bitter in winter, and I could well believe it.

There was so little shade. All that remained after the bombing of the old city were the walls and the gates. At noonday men clustered under the wall's shade, or sat in the dark shadows of the gates, motionless, saying nothing, too hot even to move their legs when jeeps and lorries passed through. It was too hot even to fan yourself. The dust rose—when a car passed quickly it would lift a column of dust fifty feet high and half a mile long. There was nothing anyone could do about it except to bathe in the muddy river.

I have forgotten why we went down to the river that day, but I remember the three boys sleeping on the shore. They had bathed and there were still bubbles of water on their skins. There was no shade, but they had spread out their clothes under them and put up sticks near their heads from which hung their immense farmer's straw hats. The hats protected their faces, but their bodies remained in the sun, and what was extraordinary was that their chests were burnt dark brown, but their thighs were white, and then again below the knees the brownness emerged. They were all about sixteen, but they slept soundlessly, in the heavy stupor of heat, not noticing our approach. They were farm-boys, and

337

their arms and hands stretched out on the dust were burnt darker even than their chests. When I think of those heavy summer days, I think of the farm-boys in their heavy slumber, and how difficult it was sometimes to move when the sun was vertically above us. But in the early afternoon life flowed back again into these rich, desolate valleys.

June 15th, Yog . . . WHEN the Americans first came to Yenan in 1944, they had certain disadvantages. They had every intention of helping the Communists to open an effective front, they were determined to do everything in their power to put an end to the military differences between Kuomintang and the Communists, but they were faced with what seemed at first a deliberate apathy on the part of the Communists. The Communists were helpful and polite, but in some things they were adamant: they would not reveal all their military secrets, and they were indifferent to any attempt to seal up the differences between the two parties. Superficially, things went well. There was Colonel David Barrett—this meant something considerable, for he knew the character of the Chinese better than most Americans and he could talk with them in his curious Mandarin Chinese in a way which gave complete confidence. In Washington Colonel Yeaton looked for reports about Red China. Nothing was coming in. Something was wrong, but what was it? It was only when he came out many months later, when the war was coming to its conclusion, that they learned they had been employing as interpreters during the whole stay of the Yenan Observer Group agents of the Kuomintang Secret Service. And the Communists were not pleased by the thought of having official secret agents in their midst.

But the Yenan Observer Group stayed on. It established a meteorological station, medical supplies were rushed in, electric generators were set up, and they provided first-rate radio facilities for the first time in the history of Red China. Michael Lindsay, as radio adviser to the Eighth Route Army, had done his work as well as possible with inadequate equipment, but now there was a real radio station. There were also offices and photographic laboratories, and there was a large mess-hall and recreation room built in memory of a young American called Whittlesey, who was killed by the Japanese. It was rumoured that the Japanese had abandoned a village after a fight and left important documents behind.

338

Whittesley was determined to get the documents. The Communists thought the exploit foolhardy, but consented to send a small team with the young American. Meanwhile the Japanese had returned, and when Whittlesey and his companions entered the village they were cut down. The defences of the Japanese were improved, and later when the Communists made an attempt to recover the bodies, they too were mown down. It had been a nasty affair, with some minor recriminations on both sides, but it ended amicably with both sides respecting the heroism of the other. There was neither the time nor the need for recriminations at any time afterwards.

Over the large compound there floated in June the American flag, but of the large Observer Group, which at one time numbered over forty men, there remained only a single American major. He was the only official representative of a foreign power in Yenan, a Chinese-American, born in Hawaii. It was a lonely life. In the morning he raised the American flag, in the evening it was taken down, reports came by radio from Executive headquarters and these were taken by a Chinese interpreter, translated and sent across the river to General Yang Shan-k'un, the acting Chief of Staff in the Communist Government. And that—officially—was nearly all. Unofficially the American major did considerably more. He gave cinema shows which were attended by members of the Government and he was the most useful man imaginable when cars broke down. He was always fretting about the lack of mechanical sense of the men around him, and always and entirely at the service of anyone who wanted assistance. He had fought his way across the Pacific and after all the excitement he had come at last to the quiet lonely backwater which is the administrative capital of a hundred million Chinese.

He was proud of his job as the only official foreigner there. There were two Russians in Yenan, both doctors, and he was certain that they were no more than doctors. Journalists would come occasionally; sometimes they would stay with him and every ten days an aeroplane would come from Pekin with supplies. It was something like the life on a small Pacific island: you waited impatiently for the aeroplane to come with its reels of film, and there would be an opportunity to talk with the pilots, and perhaps they would bring some fresh fruit—there was hardly any fruit at all in Yenan. Yet he was perfectly self-contained; there was always something that could be done and he was enjoying himself quietly. "The best time is when I put up the American flag in the morning. That's good—I don't know why, but it's good." He was bronzed and well made, and he liked to sit out on the dusty porch in shorts and look across the valley, through the willow-trees, at the ripening mountains. He wanted to bring his wife to study at Yenching, and perhaps in the holidays she could live with him in Yenan. "I don't care how long I stay in Yenan as long as I can bring my wife here. The people are good and—hell—it's fine to be with them." He amused himself sometimes by wondering whether he would dare paint an emblem on the jeeps under his control— the emblem would be a bearded Bolshevik with hand-grenades and pistols bulging from his pocket. "But I don't know. The Americans would hate it, I suppose, and Mao Tse-tung would think I was trying to be funny." And sometimes he was galled because the Communists kept on sending the same purely formal military reports as ever; he wished there was something he could bite his teeth on.

YOG, the Yenan Observer Group, remained. It was good that it should remain in such capable hands but you felt sad that the administrative capital of so great a part of China had only one permanent foreign resident. There was no Kuomintang representative, no British, no Indian. There were no consuls, no trade representatives. There was Chou En-lai in Nanking, there was General Yeh Chien-ying in the Executive Headquarters in Pekin; the representation of the Communists hardly went further than this. The Communists in China were connected with the outer world officially only by an American major and the staffs of two or three generals in the south and the Morse tapper which broadcast for a quarter of an hour a day from Yenan.

It was not of course the whole truth of their representation. They possessed vast and invisible forces. They possessed well-trained, well-equipped and well-indoctrinated armies. When they spoke of democracy and put it into practice they possessed powerful allies in the west. They knew that if they waited long enough, made fewer and fewer mistakes and found the will of the people, not imposing their own will on the people, they would eventually win—not perhaps the power in China, but so great a measure of it that their best efforts and contributions to government would prevail. And it was the oddest thing in the world to discover that in Yenan there was only one American major.

340

The School in the Caves . . . HIGH up on the cliff walls there was all that remained of the Lu Hsun Academy, one of the most famous universities in all China, for the Lu Hsun Academy had marched on foot to Kalgan, a thirty days' journey. We went there on a baking day and just as we left the jeep before the academy gates, the jeep rolled over the cliff-bank and fell twenty feet into a pig-pen. The driver was thrown clear. He was dazed and frightened and confronted with twenty large black pigs which ran screaming in all directions in the pig-pen. The sun was startlingly bright and you saw the boy with oil smeared all over him, waving his hands, while the pigs tried to leap at him. One pig was crushed under the wheel. A peasant came with a three-foot knife, searched for the vein in the neck and dug the knife in up to the hilt.

It was not the perfect beginning to a visit to the University. We were all shaken and a little dazed. Most of Lu Hsun Academy, known as Lu-I, had gone, but part of Yenan University, known as Yenta, remained. The classrooms and dormitories were in caves, the professors lived in caves and the libraries were placed in the best caves of all. There remained in its entirety only the college of administration, and most of the books they had ever had.

Previously the college possessed an extraordinary importance as the only large centre of learning in the Communist areas. Like all the other Chinese Universities, it had suffered atrociously during the war years. Everything was inadequate—books, scientific instruments, even paper. They made crude glass test-tubes in the factory, they hammered out scientific equipment in the local arsenal. But there was a time when Lu-I had been the advance-guard of most of the educational work in the north. The innovations in the *yangko* dance were developed there. Drama had been given special importance, and it was among these caves that the best of the new dramas were written. Best of all these dramas was *The White-haired Lady* which told of the daughter of a tenant-farmer who failed to pay his rent. The landlord took the daughter as his concubine, the farmer died and at last the landlord drove her away. She hid in the mountains, going out only at night to find food in the temples, and gradually, because she never lived in the sunlight, her hair turned white. All over the district there were legends of a white-haired lady whom no one had seen. For twenty years she remained there, until the Red Army came into the neighbourhood, and then she returned. It was

341

not unlike the University I was to see later in Kalgan. The students were well-fed, they wore the same blue cotton clothes as the peasants and their work in the University was deliberately directed towards the final aim of keeping the students afterwards in the closest possible contact with the peasants. The courses were short-term courses—accounting lasted one year, law one and a half years, education two years. Yet you derived the impression that even under these restricted time-limits they had done well. The students were husky. The professors were often professors who had escaped from Kuomintang areas.

The fortunes of the war had brought a strange collection of English books to the library. There was John Buchan's *The Three Hostages* and *Mr. Standfast*, R. W. Seton-Watson's *Munich and the Dictators*, a collected edition of Walt Whitman, four Bibles, H. G. Wells's *The Shape of Things to Come*, the poems of Virgil, Liddell Hart's *The War in Outline*, Madame Chiang's *Messages on War and Peace*, twenty Penguin Shakespeares and William Faulkner's *Absalom Absalom*. On political science I could see only two books by Lenin, Gide's *Political Economy* and Bernard Shaw's *Intelligent Woman's Guide to Socialism*. There were about seventy books in English altogether, and you wondered where the devil they had come from.

The professors received no salary, but were given everything in kind—even to the carton of cigarettes which arrived on their tables on the first of each month. I went into some of the caves where the professors lived: they were as comfortable as anyone else in Yenan, the caves whitewashed and gleaming, the furniture solid and well-varnished. There was an orchestra, a small clinic, a cloth-store where the clothes of the students and the professors were supplied. I asked them whether they preferred to live without salaries. One of the professors answered: "It saves a lot of time if you get all the services free—almost no shopping is needed." I did not see one person who did not look vigorously healthy.

"The best days are over," the president of the University told me. "Once we had all the best professors and the best students. What is left is only a quarter of what there was. If you had come here a year ago, you would have seen the yellow cliffs blue with students, but look at it now." But when you looked up the cliffs, they were still blue with students, and I suppose they will remain there until Yenan once more becomes a forgotten village in northern Shensi.

342

June 16th, Yellow River Cantata . . . THEY would speak about him endlessly, as one of the great geniuses produced in war and who owned all the strength of his genius to the people. His name was Hsu Hsin-hai. He was a Cantonese, and he was not more than forty when he died—it is the fate of nearly all Chinese musicians to die young, before they have produced a quarter of what they might have accomplished. He was a tall man, with a face brown like a nut, and beautiful long hands which played at least twenty instruments. He wrote *The Yellow River Cantata,* which has now been played all over North China, the first piece of serious music employing western instruments to be written by a Chinese.

It was a song dedicated to the Yellow River, and the people who live on her; there was no sadness in the song. The song calls on the men to stem the tide of the river, and to use her, so that they themselves shall flourish; and as you listen to the young voices passionately evoking the strength of the river, and of their land, you are caught up in a vast wave of hope for the future, so earnestly and with such challenging precision do they sing. "I wrote *The Yellow River Cantata* in order to describe the spirit of the old world," wrote the composer, "and at the same time I wanted to convey the spirit of the new. The Yellow River is the source of the five thousand years of Chinese history, and so this river reveals to us the struggle and creation of all these years. We sing this song, as we sing to eternity and freedom." It was inevitable that he should have written the cantata: what was extraordinary was that it should have been possible to write in Yenan, where there were almost no musical instruments and where almost no students were capable of performing the music. He had to begin almost from the beginning, training his singers and accompanists until they could perform the work which he wrote shortly after his arrival in Yenan in 1938, at the height of the blockade.

They said he was a man who worked with infinite method, making out of old sugar-boxes and catgut the violins which produced at least half the fervour of his cantata, where the strings predominate even above the voices. No musician ever worked with greater difficulty, or with greater ease—for he was highly respected, everything he needed was given to him, his students were his slaves. He did not impress you by his appearance until he mounted the conductor's stand. Then they said—they were Chinese, and they sometimes expressed themselves in this way—it was as

343

though flames sprang from his baton, and he could conjure out of the air the centuries of the Yellow River and the people who had lived on her. He was composing his hymn in the old cradle of Chinese civilization. Though he was suffering from tuberculosis, and lived in a damp cave in the mountains, they said he always seemed perfectly content—for the first time in his life he had the students he wanted, enough food to eat and the respect he craved for.

He had lived a hard life. So have a hundred other musicians in China, even the best. There was Nieh Erh, who died of tuberculosis in Japan, after composing *The March of the Volunteers,* a song which is sung by soldiers all over China: probably in the whole world no other song has been sung so often. There was Liu Chi, who wrote a cantata on *The Defence of Madrid,* for there was a time when Yenan and Madrid were close together—he too died young. There was Chiang Hsu and Kuang Shih—all were good, and all died. Hsu Hsin-hai survived longer than most, composed countless songs and two long cantatas, then in 1940 he left Yenan and four years later died of tuberculosis of the lungs at a Moscow hospital.

It is easy enough to understand why he died. His contemporary, Sitson Ma, who knew him in Paris, wrote after his death: "It must have been either in 1928 or 1929 that I met him for the first time —a Cantonese dressed in a ragged coat walking down the *rue de Madrid*. I was coming out of the Paris Institute of Music when I recognized him—it was Hsu Hsin-hai, who had worked on a steamer as a coolie to obtain passage to France. We talked and talked as we walked down the road, and at last we arrived at a shop with a glass-paned door, and there we stopped. Hot vapours steamed through the door. It was a house for baths and manicures. He was the waiter there. . . . The next morning he took me to his attic in a nine-storeyed house. The small room was about the height of a grown man, with a desk close to the bed. Above the desk there was an opening, a bull's eye, a glass window with its face to the sky. When Hsu Hsin-hai practised the violin, he stood on the desk with the upper part of his body stretching outside the window towards the sky, playing his music to God."

He was twenty-five at the time. In 1935 he returned to China and composed his hymns to the people. He was working in Hankow during the early stages of the war against the Japanese, and there he wrote songs for the soldiers. *The Song of Midnight,*
344

The March of Youth, The Song of the Three Thousand Wanderers
—the titles were symptomatic of the times. He went to the front
as a political speaker for the Kuomintang, and then something
happened and he said that the war was being lost from Chungking, and he made his way secretly to the north.

I attended a performance of *The Yellow River Cantata* in Yenan.
It was played with extraordinary skill, but it was not in any sense
a professional performance. The voices were lusty, and the singers
abandoned themselves completely to the music, but they were
not always singing in time. And perhaps it was better that way.
You felt the urgency of these youngsters, and it was not difficult,
seeing those red faces under the glare of the arc-lamps on the
stage, to conjure up the emotions which possessed Hsu Hsin-hai
when he composed the song. There, before you, yellow, immense,
feeding the country and at the same time ravaging the country,
overwhelming with its portents of suffering and fertility, lay the
river.

June 17th, The Dead . . . You do not see any signs of the
dead in Yenan. In all other Chinese towns you see the gravemounds rising north and east of the city, and sometimes on all
sides, and there the dogs play and scabble among the grasses, and
the rooks come, and in the old burial pits for a reason I have never
been able to discover they put dead horses. The burial places are
also the execution grounds, and since sometimes you must wander
on the outskirts of the city to see your friends, or to go to neighbouring villages, you are always in danger of seeing a man with
his arms tied behind his back, kneeling, and by his side a rough
pinewood plank coffin. But in Yenan there are no grave-mounds,
and no dead.

It was strange at first, for you are so accustomed to these mounds
that their absence becomes striking. In other Chinese towns the
dead are the besiegers of the living, waiting outside the walls.
Perhaps, one wondered, people did not die in Shensi. The children in their white caps and blue trousers looked ridiculously
healthy; the old men looked as though they would live for ever.
There were an incredible number of monuments to past emperors,
inscriptions on rock, but there were no dead.

In these soft, friable loess valleys all the earth must be ploughed.
There is no room for the dead. And if the dead are invisible, so
are the people invisible: there are days when you can walk in the

outskirts of Yenan and see almost no one at all—in the heat they are all hidden in the caves. You would see a man working high above you on the mountain, or perhaps a cart would lumber by, but the driver was hidden in the bales of hay. All round Yenan, on those clear hot summer days, there was a curious emptiness. Nothing stirred. No one came out of the military headquarters, and you forgot that inside the mountains men were sitting in shirt-sleeves over telephones, taking down radioed statements from all the stations in the world, giving orders, even in this heat making plans for the future of China. Something of the future was there, hidden in the dark caves.

But the dead were there, and so were the people. You noticed at intervals, at the foot of the mountains, under jutting ledges of rock, in the most barren and uncultivated places, small lead-coloured and pointed plinths. Sometimes they carried a red star, more often they carried nothing except the name of a dead peasant. "Where are the dead?" I asked once. "We forget them," a young soldier answered. "There is no room for them here."

The Boy . . . YENAN was hardly more than a cluster of small villages in a broad valley. They were agricultural villages, and sometimes you sighed for a splash of colour among those baking hot yellows and faint greens. There were few trees; the women wore the same faded blue coats and trousers as the men, and though you noticed the brightness of their faces, there were moments when you wanted to take a paint-brush and put violent reds and purples and magentas on the scene. There were festivals, but they occurred rarely. There were theatres where the actors wore the brightest brocades and painted themselves merrily; there were marriage ceremonies where the bride came on horseback down the streets dressed in ceremonial costume; there were the *yangko* plays where the native genius of these people for violently contrasting colours came into full play; but on those sweltering afternoons you could only look forward to the moment of sunset when the winter wheat on the hill flashed gold.

Yet sometimes there was colour in the Persian saddle-bows, or in the young girl whose apple-red face gleamed above faded blue cotton so brightly that you were startled. You noticed that the yellows and the greens changed colour. A lorry or a motor-car would pass in the distance, throwing up a tower of yellow dust, and in the late afternoons, when the tower reached the sun, it blazed splendidly. Or else you noticed on the cliff-walls a solitary woven blanket in striped reds and purples, and this too would absorb the sunlight till the eye, so long accustomed to yellow and green, grew dazzled in exactly the same way that you are dazzled when, looking at the white walls of a Moorish palace, you see a square blue stone inserted at a place where it relieves all monotony and gives strength and continuity to the place.

One evening, when the sunlight fell on the uplands and the valley was already frozen in greyness, a boy came down the dusty road leading some pigs. The pigs were black once, but now the yellow dust had turned them almost silver. The boy was about fourteen, but tall and well-formed, and you would have said he was older except for the childishness round the mouth. Sometimes he played on a flute, and sometimes he shouted at some girls who were talking to soldiers on a low wall; and when he had passed down the road and thought there was no one there, he began to sing. It was dark in the street, but he had come at that moment into the brazen red light of a forge, and then you noticed that he wore a bright blue cap, torn white trousers and some bands of red silk round the waist as bright as a gash. He was bare-chested and in the light of the forge his boyish chest shone like gold. He had forgotten about the pigs. He leaned negligently on the staff, and continued to sing and play on his flute until someone came to attend the forge. Then he went down the road, and you heard the boy singing and the grunting of the pigs.

June 18th, Chief-of-Staff . . . HE WAS a young Szechuanese, hardly more than thirty, who lived just outside the Army Headquarters, in three tunnels scooped out of a small hillside. He was nearly always bursting with tremendous fits of laughter, and he was often amused by the world which seemed to be full of delightful imbecilities. General Yeh Chien-ying, the former Chief-of-Staff, had gone to Pekin as head of the Communist delegation at the Executive Headquarters; in his place was the Szechuanese, Yang Shan-k'un, who insisted that the rank of acting Chief-of-Staff did not entitle him to be called "general." He wore the usual blue faded cotton cloth, the usual coarse wheat-straw sandals, and I never saw him without his usual grin. There were three things he appeared to like above all others—Mao Tse-tung, his wife and American cigarettes. American cigarettes were his only vice, and he consumed them in monstrous proportions.

347

I saw him many times, and one afternoon, while his children were playing in the court-yard, he told me as much as he could remember of the Sian Incident, which had taken place nearly ten years before. The Sian Incident, however, is not yet out of date. It is important because it introduced radical changes in the program of the Chinese Communist Party, and because it set the tempo for many things that happened later. Yang Shan-k'un was there at the time, and though he was not then a member of the Central Executive Committee, he was well-informed about everything that had happened.

"The Communists had only been in Yenan for just over a year when the Sian Incident took place," he said. "It was a time of extraordinary stress and strain, we were fighting continual guerrilla wars against Kuomintang troops and the Japanese were known to be about to attack. Then, suddenly we heard that Chang Hsueh-liang, the Young Marshal, had captured the Generalissimo. Chang Hsueh-liang took the responsibility for the capture from the beginning, and he *was* the responsible man. At first we heard nothing in Yenan. We were as mystified as everyone else. Some days later we sent a commission of three men at Chang Hsueh-liang's invitation to Sian. These were Chou En-lai, Yeh Chien-ying and one other. In view of the urgency of the times, they were given wide powers, but the Central Executive Committee was to make the final decisions.

"Chou En-lai had many conversations with the Generalissimo. The Generalissimo does not mention them in his book *Fortnight in Sian*, but he does mention in the Chinese edition that at one point he met 'a man he hated.' This was General Chou En-lai. He had the hardest of all tasks, for Chang Hsueh-liang had decided before the capture that it was necessary to kill the Generalissimo, and the Central Executive Committee was determined that he should be kept alive. It was not altruism. We were faced with two alternatives—the Generalissimo or General Ho Ying-chin. Ho Ying-chin had signed the infamous Ho-Umezu agreement, and we regarded him—we had documentary evidence—as pro-Japanese and prepared to surrender to the Japanese. On the other hand we were beginning to learn that the Generalissimo was determined on fighting the Japanese, and if he was killed, power would fall immediately into General Ho's hands. So the Central Executive Committee insisted that the Generalissimo be kept alive. The decision was made here in Yenan. It was unanimous—

348

or rather there was one dissenting vote by Chang Kuo-tao, who later went over to the Kuomintang side! It is odd that the Generalissimo should want to kill us when we have done so much to save his life.

"It was a time when the most extraordinary things were happening. The Tung-pei (North-East) and Hsi-pei (North-West) armies possessed few, if any Communists in them. It is not true that they were honeycombed with Communists. But what was clear was that they were preparing under the leadership of Chang' Hsueh-liang to take independent action—action independent of the Central Government. On November 21st Hu Tsung-nan's army had been defeated by the Reds. It began to look extremely likely that the Generalissimo wanted the armies of Chang Hsueh-liang to be destroyed by us, too. It was more than likely that the real cause why he came up to Sian was not to destroy us, but in the hope that we would destroy the armies of Chang Hsueh-liang, and be left too weak to fight against him for some while. If this was his plan, and we have very good evidence for it, it was remarkably short-sighted; for if we were destroyed, the Japanese would have taken the opportunity to sweep through Shensi and Shansi.

"At these meetings in Sian when the fate of the Generalissimo was being decided, a great change of policy was made. We decided not to attempt to annihilate the Kuomintang. We realized that the immediate danger was the invasion of the Japanese, and we could not afford one ounce of energy in fighting the Kuomintang."

June 19th, The Cave of the Ten Thousand Buddhas . . . . THE waves of honey-coloured suffocating sand came rolling along the road, but inside the printing shops everything was cool. The printing-presses were high up on the cliff-face and you reached them through an ornamented green-tiled gateway. Cut out of the cliffs were inscriptions in praise of Buddha, and near the gateway there was a small wooden board on which was written: *Liberation Daily*. An old temple had become the headquarters of the most important Communist daily in China.

In Pekin, Shanghai and Nanking all Communist newspapers were banned. No newspaper was allowed to print news from Communist sources; in the whole country there were only seven Communist newspapers, and these were produced in the Border Areas. These were the newspapers for general circulation; but every

349

army possessed its own printing press and hundreds of magazines were in circulation. Of all these newspapers the *Liberation Daily* was probably the most influential.

I had not expected to find modern machinery high up in these caves, but least of all had I expected to find caves like these. They were not cut from loess: they were cut from rock, and from every wall there were buddhas gazing down at you. There were the small black printing-presses, some powered by treadle, others by steam, roaring and hammering and clicking, and beside them were the great guardian gods, life-size, with the paint still on them. And in another cave, twenty times vaster, made in the shape of a great square and stacked with ream upon ream of brown paper, were ten thousand buddhas.

It was curious and enchanting, and among them were some of the best buddhas I have ever seen. There were row upon row of small buddhas reaching from the floor to the ceiling, and here and there you saw a much larger buddha of the T'ang Dynasty, almost feminine in its elegance of expression and gesture, reclining or blessing, untouched and unharmed by the centuries. In spite of the reams of paper, it was easy enough to imagine you were in the temple. On some of the buddhas faint colours remained— malachite green, and red and blue. It was annoying to remember that at the greatest period of T'ang Dynasty art the buddhas were all painted, but how well they had survived! The paint had flaked off, but the unchanging stone remained. Mostly, there were the rows of small buddhas, but there were at least eight of these larger carvings, and there may have been more among the stacks of paper, hidden in corners. The printing-presses were the new prayer-wheels, and the new priests were these boys in fading blue cloth who ministered to them.

I have seen in revolutionary Spain a lovely fifteenth-century chapel made into a motor repair-shop, the altar littered with the rusted red entrails of engines. I had hated it at first, until at last, remembering that there was no other house standing in this village near the Ebro, it had seemed less desecration than the accomplishment of a good purpose: a Red Cross flag flew over the church, and this was a repair shop for ambulances. And here too the change seemed necessary and inevitable. The old city had been bombed to rubble. There was no other place where paper could be stored. And the buddhas did not care and were carefully preserved.

350

Among them was at least one which would have melted the mouths of the curators of the world's museums. Buddha lay in a half reclining posture, fingering his stone necklace with one hand and blessing the world with the other. The nose had broken off, but you could still see the chaplet of flowers in the head-dress and the faint Grecian folds of the gown. There were no lights in this store-room except oil-lamps, and when it grew dark, the stone glowed. And perhaps nothing had changed through the centuries, for the first people in the world to use paper were buddhist priests, as Aurel Stein discovered in the Gobi, and more than a thousand years before the Communists came here, there may have been stacks of paper and printing-presses in caves nearby.

It was oddly disturbing to find the buddhas there. I had never seen these carvings in their original sites before. The square temple, with its huge stone altar and smoke-blackened ceiling, the tens of thousands of buddhas lining the walls, enforcing by their sheer repetition a sense of disturbing calm, all these were unexpected in Yenan, and more than ever unexpected in the printing-press.

Mao Tse-tung . . . Photographs are unfaithful and give no impression of the man with the long streaming blue-black hair, the round silver-rimmed spectacles, the fine cheek-bones, the pursed, almost feminine lips and the air of a college professor. Usually, you see him in photographs wearing a cloth cap, and you notice the round peasant face and the small nose and the heavy eyes—but the moment the cap is taken off the peasant disappears. It is true that he hardly ever remains the same for more than a few minutes on end, so that one moment he giggles like a boy, and the next moment the soft voice takes on depth and authority and a quite extraordinary resonance. He is fifty-three and looks thirty. You will see him any day on any campus in England or America.

Partly, of course, it is the fault of the legend. If you remember the Long March, if you remember Edgar Snow's famous story of Mao Tse-tung undoing his trousers and scrabbling for fleas, or taking off his trousers altogether when he entered Lin Piao's cave one sweltering hot day and gazing at a map on the wall, then you will be perfectly satisfied to regard him as part military genius, part peasant leader and part barbarian. Edgar Snow wrote *Red Star over China* nearly ten years ago. Mao has matured and taken

351

on a deeper gravity of manner, but he was obviously never the barbarian. Agnes Smedley describes how she was shocked by his feminity. It is perfectly true that there is a streak of feminity in him, as there is in all Chinese scholars to the extent that their gestures are graceful, they speak in carefully modulated soft voices and sing their poems falsetto. There is something of the same feminity in Chu Teh, whose voice has a tenderness which would resemble weakness in any western general, though no general has been tougher than Chu Teh. Ultimately, a man is what he is without his cap. Remove the cap, and Mao Tse-tung gives all the appearance of a scholar, with all the odd chameleon strengths and weaknesses which come from an intense absorption in scholarship. The course of study he has set himself is the revolution of China.

I watched him carefully for more than three hours in a bare room which was the Yenan equivalent to the Foreign Office drawing-room. He was not at first sight impressive. No flashes of electric energy radiated from him, and for a little while I was not even conscious of his presence. He wore black cotton slippers and a brown woollen Sun Yat-sen uniform. When he shook hands, he lifted his elbow to the height of his shoulder, an odd gesture, which suggested that his hands had been mauled before by foreigners. Yet he did not in the least give the impression of weakness. He had burly shoulders, and his hands were large, like peasant hands. He smiled delightfully, and when he spoke the voice was very low and almost inaudible. He had a high forehead, and his face was bronzed.

It was a party given for three professors who had come down from Pekin; among them there was an old man who had been his teacher many years before. There was Mao Tse-tung, Chu Teh, the American major, the three professors, an interpreter and myself. Mao was very much the host, and though the professors wanted to talk about him, he insisted on talking about Chu Teh. "It was extraordinary. Chu Teh had the courage to go through the grasslands *twice*. It was pretty dangerous to go through it once, but twice——" The legend of the Long March returned; he had no desire to side-track it, and answered the professors' questions gravely. They wanted the whole history of the Long March. The Communists were old men now. The Long March was still the legend around which their lives revolved; they were absorbed by their recollections of those long journeys as others are absorbed by their memories of their youth. He spoke of the grasslands

352

again. "We killed our oxen and horses for meat, and carried them on our few remaining baggage animals, and then in the end we ate the baggage animals and carried the meat ourselves. It was desperately hard, and the best fighters we ever had to face were the aboriginal tribes—the Miaos, the Fans, the Mis and the Huans. We learnt from them more than we learnt from anyone else." And then again, a little later: "We have to thank the Generalissimo for driving us into all those strange places—we would never have seen them if it had not been for the Generalissimo." Someone asked him how they had managed to come through unharmed. He answered: "The vast territories of China and the backwardness of everything." He said later: "There are territories near Sikong where there are so few fishermen that the fish just aren't afraid of people." It was a rambling and desultory dinner-table conversation. The electric light came from the power-plant belonging to the American Observer Group on the other side of the river. It was late tonight. When it came on, it was already deep dusk; and when the light burst over our heads, he giggled again. He looked self-conscious only when the American major began to photograph him with a flash-bulb holder poised in his hand. He ate slowly and carefully, and he would look up for no reason and smile at someone. He was still the college professor. You expected there would be coffee and liqueurs, and perhaps the college servant would come in in a moment with brandy on a silver salver. Then the party came to an end, he accompanied his guests to the door, bowed, and shortly afterwards disappeared to accompany them a little farther down the road.

He had said he would return and talk to me, and I waited alone in the bare room with its portraits of Sun Yat-sen, Chiang Kai-shek, Truman, Stalin and Attlee on the wall. It was so odd to find the portrait of Chiang Kai-shek, and odder still to notice in the corner portraits of Mao Tse-tung and Chu Teh. You saw these portraits occasionally in the government offices, and sometimes in shops and peasant homes, and you wondered why they were there. The interpreter said they had great difficulty finding a portrait of Attlee—no one knew what he looked like, and hardly anyone had heard much about him—but at last they had found one in *Life* and enlarged it. Mao Tse-tung came back. He sat on a stool and put another stool between us; the dinner-things were being cleared away, he was no longer the genial host but a man prepared to talk about the civil war, socialism, China, the heavy things that lay

353

on his mind. He looked grim now. The line of the mouth became hard and determined, the voice deeper, the gestures far more restrained. But I hadn't come to talk about politics—I wanted to find more of his poems and translate them. He grinned again. "They're really very bad—terribly bad. I just write poetry to waste time."

It was useless. Whatever you said about his poetry, he had one final, absolute answer—it was shockingly bad, and he would be ashamed to have it seen. It was nonsense, but the kind of nonsense that gave him pleasure, for he giggled again, knowing only too well that the poetry was good. He had written a poem called *The Snow* which had become famous all over China. "I gave it to my friend, urging him not to let anyone see it, but he published it without my permission."

Then the hardness returned, the romantic disappeared and in its place was the cool brain which wrote *New Democracy* and *The Coalition Government*. They are hard-hammering, with few literary graces, books written in ice-cold composure and with a formidable logic. Calmly, logically, he spoke about the civil war, and there was nothing at all original in what he said, but in the manner of it there was a hidden strength and a quiet purpose. I had said something or other about the failure of the Spanish Republicans during the civil war against the massed artillery of the Germans. He said: "In the first place, Spain is not China. There were only 8,000,000 people fighting against Franco, but the Chinese liberated area numbers a population of 130,000,000. The Spanish Republic fought for three years. We have fought for twenty-one years. But from the very beginning up to now, we have desired peace and we do not want this war to be prolonged."

He went on: "There are some people abroad who are helping the Kuomintang to fight with their offer of ammunition. These supplies should be stopped, and the democratic peoples of other countries should oppose the sending of ammunition to the Kuomintang. There are people abroad who do not want or approve of democracy in this country: these people are acting with the consonance of the reactionaries in China. Let them know that whatever happens, if we are faced with mechanized war, we shall fight on, if necessary with our hands and feet."

I asked him what were the conditions for peace in the civil war. He said: "When there is democracy, the civil war will end. The people who are fighting really do not want to realize democracy at all."

354

He was dubious—or had not read enough—about socialism in England. He thought the socialist government's policy of taking over the heavy industries was partly dictated by the necessity of an export trade. He was glad there were no British soldiers in China, but said that British intervention in Indonesia was "not correct." He liked the phrase "not correct" and used it often. He said: "There are some people abroad who hope to extend the civil war in China—they are doing everything they can to extend the war. But on our side we do not want war, and we look forward to the time when all democratic elements in all countries are united towards the common aim of peace. It is as simple as that." And then again: "We are not afraid of being defeated for we shall not be defeated," and then made a gesture with his hands and feet to explain that they would fight with their hands and feet to the last man. It was the second time he had done this. He talked for a little while about the aims of his small government, saying as Chu Teh had said before that in the civil war neither side could win, it was better to have a coalition government and that China could not afford a civil war either now or at any other time. The voice grew deeper, the scholarly graces vanished, and you noticed for the first time the inflexible temper which lay behind the air of refined scholarship. Like Chu Teh, he was unimpressive at first sight and possessed no tricks of expression at all. But gradually he showed his quiet power. It was then, and only then, that the peasant, the scholar, the politician and the military commander seemed to be fused together. A few moments later he left and walked up to his house. All you saw in the darkness were the stooped shoulders coloured with the blood-red light from a lamp which a soldier held as he walked behind him.

Mao Tse-tung is a complex figure, but it is becoming increasingly necessary that the world should understand him. No other political leader living, and very few in the past, have his formidable reputation for scholarship and for poetry. It is known that he has made a selection of his poems, which has probably been published —information about his poetry is hard to come by, but the selection called *Feng Chien Tze* certainly exists. *Feng Chien Tze* means "wind sand poems," and is probably meant to refer to their fleeting, turbulent character. But the collection, if printed at all, is printed privately. No copies were available in Yenan, and Mao said himself that he wanted his poems to be known neither in China nor abroad, he was annoyed that some had been published

355

and he frowned on all poetry in the old classical tradition, though he wrote it.

I give here the only three poems of his I was able to find. The first and second were written during the Long March and the third was written either just before he went to Chungking in 1945 or shortly afterwards.

I

The sky is high, the clouds are winnowing,
I gaze southwards at the wild geese disappearing over the
*   horizon.*
I count on my fingers—a distance of 20,000 li
I say we are not heroes if we do not reach the Great Wall.

Standing on the highest peak of Six Mountains,
The red flag streaming in the west wind,
Today with a long rope in my hand,
I wonder how soon before we can bind up the monster.

II

None in the Red Army feared the distresses of the Long
*   March.*
We looked lightly on the thousand peaks and the ten thousand
*   rivers,*
The Five Mountains rose and fell like rippling waves,
The Wuliang mountains were no more than small green
*   pebbles.*
Warm were the sheer precipices when Gold Sand river dashed
*   into them,*
Cold were the iron-chained bridges over the Tatu river.
Delighting in the thousand snowy folds of the Min Mountain,
The last pass vanquished, the Three Armies smiled.

III

The Snow

All the scenery of the North
Is enclosed in a thousand li of ice
And ten thousand li of whirling snow.

Behold both sides of the Great Wall——
There is only a vast confusion left.
On the upper and lower reaches of the Yellow River
You can no longer see the flowing water.
The mountains are dancing silver serpents,
The hills on the plains are shining elephants.
I desire to compare my height with the skies.

In clear weather
The earth is so charming,
Like a red-faced girl clothed in white.
Such is the charm of these rivers and mountains,
Calling innumerable heroes to vie with each other in pursuing
        her.
The Emperors Shih Huang and Wu Ti were barely cultured,
The Emperors Tai Tsung and Tai Tsu were lacking in feeling,
Ghenghiz Khan knew only how to bend his bow at the eagles.
These all belong to the past—only today are there men of
        feeling.

The poems are difficult to translate. In the Chinese, for example, "I desire to compare my height with the skies" possesses a note of grandeur, but not of personal grandeur—he is speaking of an aeroplane. The "Three Armies" do not refer to the *four* armies which took part in the Long March, but refer to a technical term, as ancient as the Chou Dynasty, to describe the armies of the Emperor, which he identifies with the Red Army. "The Red Army" itself possesses immense emotional force in Chinese, because one is conscious at first only of their colour, which suggests to a Chinese reader on reading it for the first time, youth and virility. The last poem when published in *Ta Kung Pao* was hailed as a masterly summary of all Chinese history, all landscapes in China—in the shortest number of words he had produced the most complete picture of the Chinese scene. Nearly all the poems he has written, I was told, have a kind of dagger-thrust in the last line. So it is here. The poet builds up slowly the vivid portrait he desires to convey, and crowns it in the last line of all, and this method is something altogether new in Chinese poetry, which knows no climaxes comparable with these.

This is all we could find, but somehow it was satisfying; the pattern remained, and though there were probably many other

357

patterns, it would be difficult to imagine that the essence of the man's poetry changed. You know more about a man when you have read some of his poetry, but you know less when you have read too much of it. He said of his poetry that it was a private game, it was all *ma-ma-hu-hu*—a delightful word meaning anything you care to imagine between "idiotic" and "useless." It was not idiotic or useless, and it was horrible to think the poetry might never be published when it introduced something so new and so long desired. He did not want them published. His calligraphy was magnificently bold and sweeping, his best prose was finer than most. And it was sad to reflect that some of the best poetry now being written in China might well remain in manuscript.

June 20th, Doctor Ma . . . His real name was Dr. George Hatem, but he was known in Yenan as Dr. Ma Hei-teh. He was an American with fine dark hands and heavy eyelids, and you felt immediately that he would do everything in his power to heal the sick. Years ago, returning from Switzerland, where he graduated, to America, he stayed for a while in Shanghai with the intention of studying tropical medicine. And then someone told him about the Communist experiment in Shensi. He was not a Communist. He made his way up through Hongkong and Sian at the time when Edgar Snow was first visiting the Communist areas; and he has stayed on ever since.

He was proud of his hospital which lay on the road to Chu Teh's date garden. He had seen it in the days when Yenan was cut off from the world and entirely forgotten, when everything had to be improvised—drugs, stretchers, surgical instruments, even bandages. There was no X-ray machine in those days. You used cotton gauze boiled in local lye to get the fats out, you made Mayo tables of wooden packing-cases, and you made catgut from local sheep intestines and you tried to make adhesive tape—it was one of the most difficult problems, and never solved satisfactorily—with cotton bandages dipped in tree-sap. Surgical instruments were made in the local arsenal; they looked homespun, and they did not glitter like surgical instruments in well-equipped hospitals, but they were adequate. It wasn't a perfect hospital. The patients were kept in caves on different levels along the cliffs, it was a hard job climbing the cliffs, especially in autumn when the lanes would be ankle-deep in mud, you couldn't control flies and there was far too much dirt. But they had done their best with their home-made

358

steam sterilizers, their home-made drugs and precipitation tests and charts and glass test-tubes, which shone a murky green colour, because they were made in Yenan. There was a time when they only had one microscope, and the hand centrifuge made in the arsenal was hopelessly inadequate for their needs. But they had learned a lot, and above all they had learned how to improvise. Because medicines were withheld by the blockade, many people had died and many would have been healed sooner; but on the whole they had done their best, and they were almost content with what they had done. "We got a tremendous satisfaction out of working with nothing," he said. "I've been to Pekin. There's a doctor there, trained in the Pekin Union Medical College, who won't operate for less than a million dollars." The Chinese doctor who was accompanying us said: "Okay, I've earned ten million dollars today."

It was getting better now. The American Red Cross had sent in 1944 a fine X-ray machine and a great deal of gleaming surgical apparatus, which made the home-made instruments look inconceivably tawdry in comparison. They had done everything imaginable to break the blockade, and at last they had succeeded. It was no longer an important hospital. There were far bigger hospitals in Manchuria and Chahar under Communist administration, but the cave-wards were filled, internes were still being trained and there was still a great deal of work to do.

"It was a difficult time, but we enjoyed it," said Dr. Hatem. "We were faced with the task of building up a scientific tradition in a province which is 4,000 years old. There were witch-doctors with close-fitting black clothes, four-bladed swords and a host of incantations; there were herb-doctors and acupuncturists; there were midwives who did not know the rudiments of human physiology. This is what we were faced with when we first came here.

"The witch-doctors we banned. They were dangerous. We got rid of them by introducing them in *yangko* plays, so that the people laughed at them, and we got them better jobs—gave them farms—anything as long as they would stop harming the people. The herb-doctors, the acupuncturists and the midwives we kept, but we gave them training in the essentials of western medicine. Chinese herb-doctors have done an enormous lot of good. They have medicines against malaria, and they can cure intestinal, abdominal and muscular pains—we don't know how they do it in every case, just as we do not know how the acupuncturist, by

359

putting a silver needle through your flesh, manages to effect the same cures. Acupuncture can cure malaria sometimes. It does work clinically. So we accepted them, taught them how necessary it was to sterilize their instruments, gave them elementary training in anatomy, physiology and asepsis. We hadn't enough western-trained doctors and we had to use what there was.

"From the beginning we never despised Chinese doctors. Their herb-medicines contain an enormous lot of nonsense, but the discovery of ephedrine, which is an adreniline substitute, is due to the fact that the Chinese have been using for centuries a particular herb from which ephedrine is still distilled. That was about 1926. There haven't been many great discoveries in Chinese herb-medicine since, but there is no reason why one should not appear some day. Acupuncture is another matter. We know almost nothing about it, except that it works sometimes.

"From the beginning, too, everything was improvisation. *Sze ch'i tung hsueh*—move your own hands. This was the principle under which we worked, and it was the principle which applied throughout the Border Areas." We were going through the pharmacy in the caves, and he pointed to the bottles on the shelves. "This meant that we made tannic acid and tannic albumen from bark, glucose from local beet sugar and from the salt-wells in the north we made magnesium sulphide, sodium bicarbonate, magnesium sulphate and all the other derivatives from salt. Only it was bitter salt, and not very good. We got merchants to smuggle in a few things in bales of cotton, we made our own woollen blankets and dyed them in our own woollen dyes, we made our own dentist's chairs, we invented our own technique, and though nearly everything was home-made we brought the infant mortality down to a figure which is fantastically low for China—2.8 per cent."

He liked to talk of the witch-doctors, with their swords, whips, rattles and circles of blazing fire which they drew round the patients. All that was strange and dappled in the world delighted him. In one of the caves he found a patient who was thought to be a girl until some curious sexual development occurred, and he became a boy. "How the devil could they tell what has happened?" he laughed. "There are hardly any secondary sexual characteristics among the Chinese. The girls have hardly any breasts, and the boys don't have to shave. Well, we've sewed him up, but the poor devil probably won't be able to do anything with it, even though he's got it." He liked talking about the details of the hospital man-
360

agement, the days when you climbed the muddy stairs in a bitter winter, he admired the Chinese doctors and nurses, and he had a particular admiration for two doctors who had come up in 1938, after graduating from the Shantung Christian University, and remained ever since. There had been lonely desolate moments when they felt themselves ineffective because they were so completely cut off from the world. They had trained over 3,500 doctors in a short-term training course in the Border Areas, but they wished they had trained ten times as many. Now nearly every village possessed its doctor. There were co-operatives in everything: spinning and weaving co-operatives, farm co-operatives, teaching co-operatives and now there were medical co-operatives. "We try to teach the peasants not to live with their animals and to dig their latrines far from their houses. Ultimately, of course, the problem is economic. He will live with his animals, and catch all the diseases that come from living with his animals, until he can afford to build a separate house for the animals. We can't force them to do these things. We have to train them gradually. The tempo is slow. We try to educate the primary school children and the soldiers—especially the soldiers, because they are usually in close contact with the villagers, but we wish sometimes we were going faster."

We came down the slope, and looked up again at the two hundred caves in the cliff-wall and at the small grey-tiled building which had been built when the last bombings came to an end in 1943. The winter wheat was shining on the crown of the mountain. White-capped nurses with white blouses and white trousers were climbing down the loess paths. It was a good place to be in.

June 21st, The Poet . . . HE WORE his blue cotton coat like a cape, and though he must have been fifty, he walked with a swagger, his black beard coiling in the wind. He was K'e Chung-ping, the poet, a man who sang for the people and thought it was not worth while to write poetry unless the people sang it. He came from Yunnan, and may have had tribal blood in him, and when he sang his own poems or the poems he had learned from the peasants in the mountains, his red, bearded face took on an aspect of extraordinary gravity and repose.

There were many in Yenan who regarded him as the greatest of the popular poets because he had combined with his political opinions a lyric depth of feeling. Years ago, in Shanghai, he wrote

361

a long epic describing the Red Armies. It was before the Long March, yet the description of the hardships endured by the armies until they reached the Wind Fire Mountains was like the hardships Mao Tse-tung and Chu Teh had endured. No copies of the epic, which had 20,000 lines, have remained; all were confiscated, and the poet himself was imprisoned three times, once by the war-lord Sun Chuan-fang and twice by the Kuomintang. "The worst of it is that your teeth fall out, and your hair falls out, and it is years before you can forget the bite of the manacles on your legs. It was worse than Dante's *Inferno*. The food was bad, and mixed with gravel and chaff; the only vegetables I ate were dried cabbages."

He could not remember much of the poem—prison had put an almost blank wall between himself and the past. He could remember odd verses, which he was good enough to write down, and the verses he liked best he asked permission to sing. He sang them superbly, stopping half-way to ask if he was boring his audience; but the audience had long ago agreed that they had never known a poet who sang his own poetry so well. He had a great fund of folk-songs, and insisted that the real poetry of the country lay in the fields and villages. He liked particularly poems of love or utter grief, for grief digs deep roots in China; and these he would sing as though the grief had only that moment struck him, in a piercing voice, the eyes closed, the expression agonized. There was a Yunnanese song he had heard in his native village of Kuang-nang, nine days' journey from Kunming. He would begin slowly in a deep voice, but the last line he uttered in a grief-stricken falsetto:

> The sunset and the flowers fade,
> The bees come to taste the flowers,
> The bees come, and the flowers are faded.
> The elder brother looks at the sister's open grave.

Nothing could be simpler, and nothing could be more complex, for the elder brother and the sister were evidently lovers according to a Chinese poetic tradition: grief and love were inextricably combined. So had Hamlet sung over Ophelia's grave in the days when English poetry spoke of such elementary things.

In the long poem *Feng Ho San* (Wind Fire Mountain) he remembered most the lyrical songs. Like Goethe's *Faust* the poem seems to have contained innumerable short songs interspersed

362

with declamations and descriptions, battle-scenes and songs sung round camp-fires while the soldiers toiled towards the mysterious mountain where all their hopes would become real. It was significant that the title itself should come from an old Chinese ballad. There was, for example, the song of a drunken goat-herd:

> Drink down the fine sweet wine!
> Seal your hundred flower hearts.
> I am a wandering saint.
> May you laugh at the third watch of the night,
> On the fifth watch you may have tears.

> I ride on my black-headed horse
> Through forty li of roads,
> Past fifty li of mountain caves.
> O pluck the poppy flower,
> And be drunk with sleep!

> I am the saint of the south mountain.
> There are witches on the mountain of the north.
> There are dark caves.
> O brother, go to the north mountain.
> O sister, go to the south mountain.
> I am the saint from the south!

As he sung these songs, you had an extraordinary impression that he was singing an Elizabethan love-song. Grief, the lover's grief, entered into the songs sung by the soldiers after battle:

> Some day there will be judgement for the dead!
> We shall know who killed the headless corpse.
> Have the mountain spirits killed him?
> On the second moon they come to this boy's grave.
> Brothers and sisters come to look at the dead.
> O mountains filled with lamentation!

> No one must weep for the beloved,
> The tea-flowers are beginning to blossom.
> Why weep and destroy your eyes?
> The reeds flower on these white-haired nights.*
> The boy you dream of is still young. . . .

* At weddings in China the couples drink "white-haired wine" as a sign that they will grow old together.

It was no wonder that he was regarded as a great poet when he could turn the simple ballad rhythms and the ballad imagery into songs that could be still sung by the people. Ai Ching was a poet's poet, who knew his craft perfectly, but he did not *sing*. K'e Chung-ping sang because it was the only voice he possessed—he had been too long in prison to believe that there was anything else worth doing. He sings of his imaginary Red Army coming towards the end of its journey, the Wind Fire Mountain before them:

Now in April, with a thousand toils, ten thousand hardships,
We have come at last into our worldly inheritance.
O the great sons and great daughters!
The road shines with blood, yet we sing the war-song.
As long as the two ends of a wheat-stalk are pointed,
There will be pure springs on the high mountains.
O, our stomachs are full of noodles dipped in sauce.
The mountain roars, the wave surges.
Only when you work hard do you realize the taste of wine
    and meat!

There was a perfection in his work which was sometimes startling, and you wondered why, of all the books which have become lost, the long revolutionary epic with the glorious title *Wind Fire Mountain* should be among them.

June 27th, Kalgan . . . I CAME back to Pekin from Yenan a week ago. I remember there was sun every day in Yenan except on the last day. Mao Tse-tung and Chu Teh came down to the airfield in the rain, in their sandals and blue cotton clothes, while the sky looked utterly grey and the valley was lost in the rain-mist. For the first time in eleven days there was no sun on the valley; and somehow it seemed wrong. There is sun nearly all the year round in northern Shensi, a hard glittering baking sunlight, which hardly changes in its intensity, though the seasons change. I asked Mao again about his poems. He made the same handshake, smiled and said he still thought the poems were *ma-ma-hu-hu*, and meanwhile Chu Teh stood a little way away, lost in thought, the fine old face looking graver than ever in the rain. But in Kalgan it is all sunlight.

The valley of Kalgan is twenty times wider than the valley of Yenan, a great curving sweep of valley rising towards dark moun-
364

tains. The mountains were not close to you; they did not oppress you, and they were magnificently formed, with peaks and promontories and huge black buttresses which rose from the plain. There were two cities, the old dark walled city, tortuous and decaying, and the new city of reinforced concrete built largely by the Japanese. They had had eight years to build the place, but they had not finished when the three Communist columns came from north, east and south on August 27th, 1945, and threw the Japanese in confusion. The Japanese had left at last for Japan, but Kalgan was full of their traces—there were *tatamis* everywhere, there were gaunt grey buildings and factories, there was machinery in the printing works which was less than three years old. What was surprising was the newness of the Japanese town, and how incomplete it was; here there would be a building, and there a vegetable patch, and farther on another building. So it must have been in the American west in the early days. Kalgan was always a frontier town; it lay on the great wall; it had existed at least as long ago as the Han Dynasty, for a famous Han governor had inscribed on the city gateway in his own hand: "O good and great country," and the inscription remained. The Empress Dowager had passed through here on her return from exile in Sian. Feng Yu-hsiang had once made the city his headquarters. On the Nankao Pass, between Kalgan and Pekin, innumerable battles had been fought, and it was there that the last defenders of Pekin in 1937 had been mown down by the Japanese. But Kalgan had changed completely. Among these pepper-coloured plains and sharp-toothed hills, the impact of modern industrialism was being felt. At this time only one other industrial city was owned by the Communists—Harbin.

The farmers came in on their small carts, soldiers marched through the streets and sometimes, seeing those scattered and often half-finished buildings, you felt you were still in a country of farmers; but late at night you heard the roar of machinery. It was utterly unlike Yenan. Yenan might be more conscious of its responsibilities as an administrative centre, but Kalgan at the centre of the Chin-Cha-Chi area, was conscious of its industrial potential. The factories were everywhere, and smoke came from their chimneys. There were coal-mines on the hills, which the Japanese had worked savagely, surrounding them with electrified barbed wire; if a Chinese labourer fell ill, he was left to die. Iron ore was brought by railway, mica and asbestos were mined, there were cinemas and innumerable shops, there were palaces and memorials to the Japanese dead, there were broad paved streets which led out into open country and then continued—they did not become mule-tracks. The people walked twice as quickly as they walk in Pekin. And in spite of the Japanese occupation, the *tatamis* and the shrines and the constant invasions and civil wars, it seemed to belong perfectly to the Chinese, and you realized that all over China there would soon be cities like these. This was modern industrialism; this was railways and mining and reinforced concrete. It was a city of peasants and workmen, the shepherd boys tending their sheep on the sandhills in the shadow of a factory and at midday, in the shade of the poplars, the workmen in blue cotton were resting. The old Chinese walls were crumbling. From now on it would be concrete, not stone. And you had only to shut your eyes to see the same thing in the farthest provinces of China.

It was heady wine for the Chinese who came here for the first time after living in villages and fighting as guerrillas. An industrial city, white, clear and shining in the sun.

June 28th, The Palace of Prince Teh . . . THE palace lay under the shadow of Great Divine Son Mountain, a bleak blue range of mountains which straddled east of Kalgan, looking menacing enough in the rain. Even when the sun shone these savage cliffs looked menacing, and the small pagodas perched on the summits of its sheer foot-hills did not look like pleasure houses: they were pagodas of iron, starkly etched against the lowering sky, almost terrifying. But the palace, with its marble dragons and painted eaves and innumerable court-yards folding into one another, was completely delightful. Until he fled, it was occupied by Prince Teh, whose other titles were Prince Demchukdongrob, Lord of West Sunid, of the Silingol Banner in the north of Chahar. He had occupied the palace on the invitation of the Japanese, with his concubines and retainers, a tall man, with a close-cropped skull, already ageing; and they said he had the keenest eyes of anyone in Mongolia and the greatest ambition to imitate Genghiz Khan and carve out of Asia a new kingdom for the Mongols. Before the surrender of the Japanese, he had fled to Pekin and then to Chungking, where he was received with due ceremony as the leader of the Mongol Horde. The Communists said: "He lived here under the Japanese, therefore he was a traitor, and we would have killed
366

him if he had not fled."

The palace was now occupied by the Communist Governor of the province, a thickset man with fine mobile features and a reputation for good calligraphy, hardheaded and earnest. It was this man who had most of the responsibility for seeing that Chin-Cha-Chi suffered as few growing pains as possible. He was obviously overworked, but what was amazingly attractive was that he did not resemble in any way any preconceived idea of a governor. The mayor of Pekin, Hsiung Ping, looks like a governor—fat, and of course immensely wealthy. Governor Sung of Chin-Cha-Chi could have been a precision worker in a factory, a professor or a civil servant or anything you please. He had a heavy forehead; you could feel the power behind it; you were conscious that he would stand no nonsense; like Mao Tse-tung he had developed a curiously flamboyant calligraphy, but he spoke in a quiet slow voice which the interpreter found the greatest difficulty in understanding. He was amused with the idea of living in Prince Demchukdongrob's palace and sleeping in Prince Demchukdongrob's bed. He was amused, and he was a little sad, and he always looked slightly lost in the reception-room with the gilded pillars and the yellow satin embroidery on the chairs and sofas.

And then others came in, General Nieh, the military governor of the Border Area, and General Tsai—both had been on the Long March, but no two people could be more different. Nieh had studied in Paris and Belgium. For a while he studied chemical engineering at Charleroi University. He had a keen pale intelligent face, a good forehead, the manners of an eighteenth-century cavalier. He had directed with two others the operation over the Tatu Bridge. He laughed easily and splendidly, and he liked telling stories and possessed a quiet, mordant humour. (Someone asked him why there were so many aged American colonels in Executive Headquarters. He replied: "Perhaps the President of the United States has heard that we Chinese have a deep respect for age.") General Tsai looked like a factory worker. He had lost an arm in the Long March. The mouth was bitter and indrawn, but the eyes were large and transparently clear. He said very little, but what he said was always to the point. He was vice-chairman of the military-political bureau.

There were many others, but what was surprising was that they could easily be divided into two types—those who had returned from France or Belgium, and those who had remained in China.

367

You could distinguish the types at once. Neither looked like the current conception of what a Communist leader should look like. You would see these people in any American or English town, you would be friendly with them and get to like them. They felt that the government of the Kuomintang was a travesty of a government, but they knew that they were unprepared to take over the power. They were conscious—no one could be more conscious— of their limitations. They did not look sly, and not one of them resembled the pot-bellied compradore type which spills over Nanking. They would not beg for help, they did not care very much if they were misunderstood and they were about as independent as the Americans were during the war of independence. They liked good food, but they didn't care very much if there wasn't any. They liked good wine—there is excellent grape-wine produced in Huahsien on the road between Pekin and Kalgan— and they drank innumerable toasts for no particular reason except that there were a considerable number of bottles available. And then, when we went out into the court-yard, where it was still raining and the marble lions looked more arrogant than ever, you half expected to see Prince Demchukdongrob surrounded by his concubines and walking in the rain, for nothing can be more pleasurable to a Mongolian than to walk in the rain, and nothing fills him with a greater love for the vast plains. But instead there were Communist delegates in blue cotton suits, looking rather shabby except for General Nieh who wore a uniform captured from the stores left by the Japanese.

June 29th, More about Mao Tse-tung . . . IT WAS said all over Yenan that Mao hated to talk about himself. For four nights he had discussed his own biography with Edgar Snow. It was necessary at that time: the Long March of the Communist armies was unknown, its leaders were unknown, and even the objects of the Long March were unknown. But at that time Mao had said he would never write about himself again, he was not important, the movement among the peasants, the farmers and the factory-workers was far more important than any single man. Probably he meant all this. It was infinitely difficult to get any information about him.

But in Kalgan there lived a man who had known Mao Tse-tung since he was twelve years old. His name was Hsiao San, he was editor of a newspaper and looked like a professor at the Sorbonne.
368

He was born like Mao Tse-tung in Hsiang-tang in Hunan, and though he had left China for two long periods of study in France and Russia, he had kept up a correspondence with his childhood friend. He lived in a small Japanese house, with the usual patterned and uncomfortable sofas, the usual *tatamis* and sliding panels and rooms which were so small that they resembled wooden prisons. We had some friends in common who had taken part in the Spanish civil war, and I got him to talk about Mao Tse-tung.

"Mao is the most complex person we have," Hsiao San said, when I spoke about the incredible difference which existed between Mao bare-headed and Mao wearing a peasant cap—the scholar could so easily turn into a peasant, a schoolboy, the vicar at a harvest festival, the poet, the soldier and the political leader. "None of us have really understood him. I have known him longer than anyone else, but I have never got to the root of him.

"When he was sixteen and I was twelve, I met him for the first time. He was hurrying down a road with a parcel of books under his arm. I had seen him before—he always had books. A few days later I lent him a book about the great heroes of the world. It was a book with articles about Peter the Great, Wellington, Washington, Lincoln, Rousseau, Montesquieu and Napoleon and perhaps twenty others. He read the whole book in one night, and gave it back to me, saying: 'We need great people like these in China.'

"In those days when I remember him, it is always the scholar. There was a free library in Changsha. He would stay there all day, reading, reading, reading. He didn't read with any deliberate plan —he read everything, everything without exception, politics, economics, history, *The Dream of the Red Chamber* which he admired immensely, the histories of the famous generals like Yueh Fei. He noticed that in all the epics and legends of the past there were always victorious emperors and generals, but no victorious peasants. He was himself the son of a peasant. His father had been in the army. When he returned from the wars, he bought twelve *mou* of land and made young Mao work with him in the fields. The father was often brutal and cursed him, quoting Confucius and saying that the son should obey the father implicitly. In answer, Mao quoted another chapter from the *Analects* where the father is enjoined to treat the son mercifully. It was from that time, I think, that there dates Mao's implacable opposition to Confucianism.

"In 1911 he was eighteen, and had been for a short while conscripted in the army. He was still reading furiously, but now he was reading chiefly the works of Adam Smith, Darwin and Spencer, which had been all translated into classical Chinese by the celebrated translator Yen Fu. At this time he read a book by Chiang Kan-fu on socialism. If you read it now, you would think the book was ridiculous—it was a terribly muddle-headed book, but it contained some good quotations and it belonged to the school of thought which owed much to the Reform Party in China under Kang Yu-wei and Liang Ch'i-ch'iao. It was half-baked, like so much that was being written by Chinese at that time, but it was the first time Mao had heard of socialism. All his sympathies, all his scholarship, all his memories of life in the field and in the army seemed to lead to one conclusion—he would become a socialist. Later he read three books: the Communist Manifesto, Kautsky's *The Class-war* and a history of socialism by someone whose name I've forgotten. He was completely thunderstruck by these books.

"At that time he wanted to be a teacher—or rather, he did not know what he wanted to be, but he thought that if he was a teacher, he would have time for reading, and writing. He wanted passionately to be a writer. He still went to the library early in the morning, slipped out of the library for lunch and read again until the library closed. He had little money, and his parents were complaining. He entered the normal school. He passed through the entrance examination with flying colours—the principal of the school publicly posted his essay on the wall and commended him. At first the principal could hardly believe it could be written by one so young. At this time he was absorbed in Chinese history.

"It was the time of the European war. I still saw him nearly every day, and now I noticed that he was passionately reading every newspaper he could lay his hands on. The war fascinated him. He knew all kinds of details, and he could explain during our evening walks what it was all about, what important factors there were, and where it was leading. In 1920 I went to France. Mao himself had organized some of the groups which went to France—you could study and work for your living at the same time. Many of the people who went were his friends, and he begged them to go. For himself he preferred to remain in China where he could work out his own destiny. He was already conscious of his leadership.

"He has won battles, but his knowledge of war came from his wide reading, from his association with the peasants, with the
370

legends of the past and with an incident which occurred at the normal school. Soldiers came and wanted to take it over. This is the kind of thing that happens all over China—soldiers try to take over schools because they are the largest available buildings. It is happening now in Pekin. Mao organized the defence of the school. He drilled the students and the professors, and however unlikely it sounds, he gave orders to the senior professors which were instantly obeyed. We even bought arms in Changsha to defend the school, and medical supplies. We kept the soldiers out and Mao Tse-tung remarked: 'Well, this is the first time I have taken military command.' He seemed to know that it wouldn't be the last.

"He is fifty-three now, and he has been many things in his time. He has led armies, he has been secretary to the old reactionary Hu Han-min, he has been editor of an official Kuomintang newspaper—the *Political Daily* which was issued in Canton before the Northern Expedition, he has been director-general of propaganda under the Central Committee of the Kuomintang; but it was only this year that he assumed for the first time the acknowledged leadership of the Communist Party. There have been many changes within the party, many quarrels. But what he likes to remember most is the days when he wandered round the districts of Hunan in great poverty, wearing a sun-helmet, a white shirt, white trousers and sandals, and organized the peasants.

"Three or four times he nearly died of weakness during the Long March, which he directed with Chu Teh. They went through nine provinces, Kwangtung, Hunan, Kwangsi, Kweichow, Yunnan, Sikong, Szechuan, Kansu and Shensi. Many stronger men died on the journey. He was strong—he put tremendous significance on physical health in his youth, and liked wandering through the countryside in all weathers—but he looked ill when it was over. He still looks after his health carefully. He eats less pepper and smokes less cigarettes, and doesn't read late into the night any more, unless he has to. His speaking voice is not good, but when he makes speeches he has all the air of an old peasant —*un sage paysan,* and he is loved by them because he says, only more forcibly than they say them, the things that are on their minds. He is not an actor. He has no dramatic appeal. He talks simply. He delights in being as scientifically accurate as possible, but at the same time he is a dreamer and a poet. His poetry is a kind of secret vice. He won't show it to anyone except his closest intimates like Chu Teh or Lin Po-chu. I spent nearly ten years in

Russia, coming back in May, 1939, through Urumchi, Lanchow and Sian, and the odd thing was that he seemed hardly to have changed at all."

June 30th, Ku Yuan and the Woodcuts . . . He was well-built and though he was a Cantonese, he looked like a northerner, and there was a curious gentleness in his expression which suggested that he had recently been ill. He spoke very little, and then always to the point, and he lived like Ai Ching, the poet, and Ting Ling, the novelist, in one of those countless Japanese houses which are strewn around Kalgan, with *tatamis* and small sofas and low walls. The house was small, but not uncomfortable. There was a hedge outside, and you felt that it might be a suburban house in the centre of England except that it had shrunk inexplicably. He was Ku Yuan, the most famous of their woodcutters and almost certainly the best. He was thirty-five, but looked twenty-four.

From time to time he picked up the woodcutting instruments which resembled scalpels; he could not take his hands away from them, and when we were talking he would make little incisions on the wooden table. Most of his instruments were home-made; two had been sent from America recently, but bore German trade-marks. He was grateful for them, but he was even more grateful for the promise of some books on modern painting and design in Europe and America. "We've been cut off from books from abroad for so long—— When I started, I was influenced by Katte Kolowitz and then by Grosz. My peasants were always starving or being beaten to death. I drew them with enormous thick-veined hands which hung down limply. I drew them cowering and afraid, or being raped and beaten, or they were being tortured. It was true that these things were happening, but I left out the other truth—that in the war against the Japanese and in the war for production, they were living strenuously and in a sense happily. So now most of my drawings are not about their miseries but about their strenuous efforts to make a new world. Why should not my drawings glow with health when the world around me is glowing with health?"

He had been trained by Ma Ta and Woo Ch'a, two much older woodcutters, at the Lu Hsun Academy, but he had trained himself long before and soon excelled his masters. He had a natural talent, a natural itch for digging into wood and making patterns out of it. Recently he had made designs to replace the gate-gods
372

which appear on all doors on New Year's Day. His gate-gods were not the heroes of warrior epics; they were simple peasants, surrounded by their children and flocks. He found among the peasants a delight in making silhouettes and pasting them on paper windows. He employed their technique and drew designs like theirs, with effortless mastery of the method. He knew almost nothing about ancient Chinese art, but said that woodcutting in China was still in swaddling bands, it would grow up when they had learned more from the west and from their own past. It was the easiest art for the peasants to master, since it needed little more than a gravel and some wood. His woodcuttings were everywhere: you saw them in shops, in villages, in peasants' huts, in official residences. Oddly enough, two collections of his drawings were being printed in Pekin. He was a little sorry they were being printed, because the reproductions were never so good as the originals taken from the woodblock. You looked through the prints, and all of them had that glowing life—there were farm-carts loaded with wheat, peasants learning to read, there were scenes in village squares, there were the new and prouder gate-gods and drawings of old peasants and children and soldiers and boys and girls. They were clean-cut and he possessed an immense and satisfying sense of space, and afterwards you remembered them; but you remembered, too, the nervous beautiful hand on the table which was continually digging out new patterns from the wood.

July 1st, The Poet Ai Ching . . . THEY said in the south that he was a man of about forty, very rugged and bearded, who took no care of his clothes and wandered over the country singing his poems and never so happy as when talking with some other wandering peasant. It was all wrong; he was nothing like this, and yet it was easy to understand from his poetry how the legend arose. The poetry is robust, hard, filled with a kind of sunlit energy and defiance, and sometimes the hardness would disappear and in its place there was pure lyric feeling, a quietness like that which descends on ancient Chinese poetry. He was famous for the long poems on soldiers fighting against the Japanese—there was *The Trumpeter* and *The Man Who Died a Second Time,* and there were a host of others, which reflected the roughness and energy of the times. It was easy to imagine him tall and bearded, stalking over the northern plains, a Chinese Whitman who cared only for

373

the sufferings of the people.

In a sense the legend was true—he *was* the Chinese Whitman, and he had sung of the sufferings and deaths of the soldiers more than any other poet in China, and far better. He did not look like Whitman. He looked like a young scholar, perhaps twenty-five, with a brown sensitive mobile face, a fine forehead and immense eyes. Like almost everyone else in Kalgan he wore a thin blue cotton suit, and a blue cotton cap. The hair was long and blue-black; in immobility the lips seemed carved from red sandstone; he had almost no gestures, and carried himself with a natural grave dignity, though he often grinned like a schoolboy. You would say at first glance that he was a scholar, at second glance you were certain he was unlike any scholar you had ever seen.

I saw him nearly every day I was at Kalgan, and tried sometimes to discover the springs of his poetry, since he alone of all Chinese poets has sung perfectly of the war. I asked him whether he had seen war at close quarters, and he said he had seen it very rarely and then only accidentally when he was on some propaganda work near the front line. But he had seen drought and famine and the insides of prisons, and he had seen the new China growing up in the north; he had lived for years with the villagers and soldiers, and watched their sudden fury against the Japanese. "The best thing was the people. That was why I wanted to live among them, encouraging them to write and editing their magazines and writing for them—above all *for them*. We were cut off from the world. There was the blockade in the south, there was the Japanese blockade in the east, hardly anything came to us from Russia. And in a way it was good, for the writers had no other source than the people." Like others, he would say the word for people—*lao pai hsing*—with a special tenderness.

Most of the time during the war he had been at Yenan, living very quietly in a cave dug out of the loess mountain cliffs. There he had been an elected representative on the Shen-Kan-Ning Border Region Congress—hardly anything else in life had pleased him so much as his election as representative of a county in this parliament. He had written a lot, but not as much as he had hoped to write. "You are so damnably busy there, there were so few administrators, and sometimes I thought I would never be able to write poetry again—you get snowed under with details. The details are important—they have to be done because they concern the life of the people—but for the poet it is especially difficult: this

374

is one of the problems that remain unsolved. You need quiet for poetry. We were not living in quiet—we were living with annihilation campaigns directed all round us."

One morning, when he seemed less occupied than usual, I asked him for details of his life, saying that I had once written a short essay on him from the material that was available, but most of it was hearsay. He was not very worried about his biography, and seemed to think it was almost of no importance at all. "Not very much—just prison and painting a little, and working."

"Why did they send you to prison?"

"I was arrested in the French Concession, and they kept me in prison for nearly three years—dangerous thoughts, I suppose." And then a little later: "I was born in 1910 in Chinghua *hsien* in Chekiang. My father was a small landlord, who had graduated from a middle school and had a little modern education. I was born on the farm. I learned by heart all the classical things that were taught in the schools near the farm, then when I was fifteen I went to a middle school at Chinghua. After that, I thought I wanted to be a doctor and studied medicine for half a year. It was no good—I was not made to be a doctor, and by this time I had decided I wanted to be a painter. My parents did not want me to go abroad—they knew nothing of other countries, and besides it was a time when the Chinese still had little love for foreigners. It seemed monstrous to go and study painting in Paris. But still I went, and they sent me a little money, and I earned some more by drawing designs for Chinese porcelain in France. Yet I depended on my father's money, and in the end, when he sent an ultimatum—no more money if you stay abroad—I returned, very reluctantly. There were other reasons for returning. 1931 was the year of the Mukden incident and the beginning of the Japanese invasion. The French seemed to be in sympathy with the Japanese, and you felt as you walked around the streets of Paris that the Chinese were despised. But I had learned something—I knew how to paint a little, I had been to Arles, I had seen the paintings of van Gogh, I had read a great deal, chiefly in French. I was beginning to think I might be a poet and began to write seriously for the first time on the boat coming back to China—they were immature poems, and all of them are lost now.

"I left Marseilles on January 28th, 1932. I remember the date, because it was also the date of the Shanghai incident—the Japanese attacked Shanghai. The fighting had ended by the time I returned home. I went straight to my native home in Chekiang, and found that my parents still wanted me to become a high official; gradually, when they discovered that I had no intention of becoming an official, they began to hate me. In May I left them and went to Shanghai—it was useless to go on in the small village. In Shanghai I met Lu Hsun. I had studied the social revolution in France, and was becoming more and more a socialist, so I studied and taught in a small study group called—for all these study groups had that kind of name—the *Chun Ti* study group. *Chun* means spring and *Ti* means earth, and it meant 'the awakening of the earth in spring.' It was a rather mild group, but our thoughts were evidently 'dangerous thoughts.' It was banned on July 12th, and I was arrested.

"I had written a very little poetry in Paris, and more on the boat, but now in the prison in the French Concession in Shanghai I began to write in earnest. The French, mercifully, were not so strict as the Chinese. There was just enough food, and I could smuggle the poems out of the prison, and through friends we could get good food sometimes and magazines from outside. I was released in October, 1935.

"I had met Lu Hsun once before going to prison, and now I decided if it was humanly possible to be a professional writer. I gave up painting altogether, and plunged into poetry and literary magazines. It was a time of peace, though the peace was soon to be broken, and literary magazines were growing up like mushrooms. Now and then they would be suspended, or they would change their names. It was a time of awakening. I stayed most of the time in Shanghai, and developed a close friendship with Ho Feng, the theorist, and Tien Ch'ien, the poet, and then at the beginning of the war, in July, 1937, I went to Hankow and later I became a teacher in the National Revolutionary University in Shansi—this was an eminently respectable University, in spite of its name, sponsored by Marshal Yen Hsi-shan, the war-lord of Shansi.

"Meanwhile the war went on, and Marshal Yen Hsi-shan was not entirely the 'model governor' he pretends to be. Two months later I went to Sian and organized resistance groups against the Japanese. It was a time when the writers became organizers. They were propagandists—they had to be. They had to tell the people what they were fighting for, and never to stop fighting till the Japanese were out of China. Afterwards I returned to Hankow
376

and then to Kweilin, where for a while I edited the literary page of a newspaper.

"We were terribly unsettled in those days—always moving about. I stayed in Kweilin for a year, then I went to Hunan and taught Chinese in a middle school for another year. The school was very liberal; I was happy there. But gradually it became known that the school had liberal tendencies, and the Government became alarmed and closed up the school. The times were dangerous. We thought of what we should do, and decided to go to Chungking—the safest places are the large cities, where you can hide more easily. There, for a while, in Chungking I taught in the Yu Tsai School founded by Tao Hsin-tzu,* an American-returned student who is now a leading member of the Democratic League; and there in Chungking I met the great novelist Mao Tun.

"In January, 1941, there occurred the New Fourth Army Incident, when this Communist Army south of the Yangtse was ordered to move north of the Yangtse. It obeyed the order, but was surrounded by Kuomintang troops and 4,000 were killed. It was in this civil war fought in the midst of the war against Japan that General Yeh was captured—he was imprisoned for five years, and died, as you know, this year in an aeroplane crash not far from Yenan. Like hundreds of thousands of others, I began to wonder whether the Kuomintang was prepared to fight to the utmost against the Japanese. Partly with the help of General Chou En-lai, and partly with the help of one of my students who had become an officer in Marshal Yen Hsi-shan's army, I went to Yenan. The journey was dangerous. I was disguised as a staff-officer in Yen Hsi-shan's army. There were six or seven of us, and one famous writer was disguised as our batman. We had the right papers, but we didn't look very much like soldiers, and the worst moment came when one of the patrols discovered that we were carrying wooden tooth-picks—officers in Yen Hsi-shan's army were presumably supposed to carry silver ones. We passed altogether forty-seven sentries. In March we arrived in Yenan. Since then I seem to have lived continually in an atmosphere of annihilation campaigns."

He had shown no bitterness at all during this long account until he came to the end; he said "annihilation campaigns" like a rat-trap closing. He said nothing more for a long while.

* Died July, 1946.

"It was not so bad—we got down to the people at last. This was the important thing. You know, for years we had lived in cities. We wrote about the people, but we did not know the people. In Shensi we had time to learn the folk-songs of the people, I began to realize we were all too much influenced by western literature. We read Mayakovsky and the French poets, but they were not Chinese, and they were badly translated. They told us a great deal, but they did not tell us the thing we wanted to know most. Years before, I read Mayakovsky's *Cloud in Trousers* in a French translation. It was a tremendous shock. It opened up immense possibilities, but most of us copied the method too literally, and we did not realize that he was speaking about a particular Russian situation. Our own situation in China had little enough to correspond with the situation in Russia in 1916. When I was younger, I read Byron, Heine, Pushkin, Goethe, Whitman, Verhaeren—I translated *La Cité, La Plaine, Les Douze Mois*—Mayakovsky, Essenin, a hundred others. Some of the influences remain, particularly Verhaeren, but what I wanted in my poetry is that the greatest influence of all should be the Chinese people.

"I believe that art and the revolution must go together; they can never be separated. We are political animals, and sometimes we must write as political animals. *If the revolution fails, the art will fail, but in as far as is possible the artist must be a revolutionary. As a revolutionary and as an artist he must represent his times. Therefore he must write propaganda. One writes propaganda for the same reason that the Christian painters painted Madonnas—I write about the people and a particular social system, because I have faith in them. It is possible for us to have the same faith in democracy as the people in the mediæval Church had for their God.*

"Now more than ever I realize that we were wrong in our beginnings. The movement of May 4th went too far. It was too iconoclastic. We destroyed the images of the past entirely; now we must return to them. We thought we must write something entirely new, not knowing that the tradition remains, and we can never escape entirely from the tradition. We forgot that there must be *harmonie.*" When he said *"harmonie"* his face lit up; one derived the impression that all problems were resolved in this mysterious word, a word which possesses an almost Chinese significance and force. "It seems to me that in the future our poetry will change, and all our culture will change with our poetry. It will change in

378

three directions. We shall take the best, the most revolutionary poems of the past, we shall take the folk-songs of the people, we shall continue to take influences from the west. We need simpler tunes—tunes the people can sing. We do not need any longer the delicate fragile emotions of the intellectuals.

"So far in our new poetry we have not always succeeded—the best things we have produced in North China during the blockade were not poems, but *reportages* and woodcuts. These sprung from necessity. There had to be *reportages,* because the soldiers and the people wanted pictures. We did produce some illustrated books with photographs, but they were rarely good. We had expert cameramen, but we rarely had good materials. And so it was with everything—the men were good, but we were being besieged and the materials were bad, unless we captured them from the Japanese.

"We had at least one good poet—Tien Ch'ien. He has a more vigorous style than Mayakovsky's, a succession of rousing hammer-beats, and he has a tremendous gift for stating things simply. He is still very young, and unfortunately became famous too early, before he had matured. Occasionally he wrote love poems, but most of his poems were concerned with the war and problems of production—they were two very real things when we were fighting. Most of us at first tried to write as we had written before: it took a long time to realize what were the most important things. But Tien Ch'ien saw them at once, and it is only recently that he has taken a real interest in folk-songs. They say he is a propaganda poet. It is true. And why not? We had to win the war, and there were exactly two fundamental things—production, which meant our own survival, and our continual attacks against the Japanese. But sometimes Tien Ch'ien, using this new hammer-beat language he had invented, made terrible mistakes—he distorted Chinese phrases, and where the tone of a character should be soft, he made it hard, and where there might have been easily remembered rhythms, he deliberately distorted the sounds into hammer-beats; and you cannot remember his poems easily.

"Thinking about it now, it seems that we did what we could, and on the whole we were successful. We subordinated everything—our lives, our customs, our traditions—to winning the war. It had to be. We had everything to gain by organization. No one starved, and no one was without weapons. *We relied on ourselves, and we knew that China would have to rely on herself for victory.*

379

And gradually, over all those long years, we built up in the north a system of democracy which can never fail, because it represents so intimately the demands of the peasants, for after all we are a nation of peasants and will always be a nation of peasants, and this is what is important."

He had spoken very quietly, rarely using gestures, and sometimes his eyes would wander to the glass cases placed against the wall where there were buddha-heads and black-stained wooden goddesses which had come from abandoned temples. He had cut himself away from the past; now he was busy attempting to find the past again. For him most of the old Chinese poets I admired were worse than useless: they had no social message, no sense of political responsibility. There remained a few poets—Tu Fu and Po Chu-I were among them—who spoke of the sufferings and aspirations of the people. This was what was important. China was going through her revolution now, and until the revolution was accomplished, there was neither time nor energy left for sheer beauty. I said that at first I was shocked in the Communist areas by the drabness of the people, who all wore cotton-cloth and seemed so like each other. Gradually I noticed that the cotton uniform possessed vast advantages: you no longer looked at clothes—you looked at faces, and each face was different. It no longer became important that a girl should wear a coloured skirt, or paint her face. You saw the real face undisguised, and somehow, with all your attention concentrated on the face, she was displayed more nakedly than if she wore the close-fitting gowns of the Pekin girls.

"And besides," he went on, "what else can we wear? We have our uniforms, as you call them, though they are not uniforms; but if we wear the clothes you see in Pekin, how can we go among the peasants, how can we expect the peasants to tolerate us? It is important that we should be as like the peasants as possible. This is not a disguise. We take to it naturally. The body is not important, but the face tells everything—— We must learn once again to look directly at people's faces."

It seemed simple then to understand the strength of these people of northern China who had fought against the Japanese without aid from outside so long that they had developed a kind of instinctive pattern of behaviour, which depended only on fighting and production. In Kalgan you do not feel hemmed in as you do in Yenan: you felt that the future was there, and unconsciously
380

they had mapped out a future so self-reliant that it seemed youthful in comparison with anything I had seen in the south. In the north they were young and full of promise; in the south they were old men, who had long ago lost their youthful defiance. In Kalgan, in Yenan, in a hundred places in North China men had deep roots, for all were peasants or workers, all were brethren. There were no vast riches, even though a co-operative could pay a dividend of 70% in four months, and there was no poverty. In this world a man like Ai Ching could live at ease.

He spoke of many other things, of writers and the difficulties of printing, of his extraordinarily beautiful wife and children, of the horrors of living in a house which had been built by the Japanese and was cluttered with *tatamis* and sliding panels and labour-saving devices and little wooden platforms where you placed a solitary bowl of flowers if you were Japanese; but he preferred to have flowers all round him. He lived quietly and methodically. He was still editing magazines, still teaching, still writing, and sometimes he would wander off among the peasants and live with them, for fear that literature would claim him too ardently. His whole wealth consisted of his bed, some furniture, a chest littered with manuscripts, and a Japanese sword. He had killed the demon that desires money, and had only one belief: that at this period in China's history it was necessary to serve the people.

July 2nd, Ting Ling and the Blind Story Tellers . . . I HAD been wanting to see Ting Ling ever since I came to China, for of all the novelists since Lu Hsun she had seemed the best. She could describe lovers, the morning mists, the trials and strains of the young Chinese before the Japanese war with an immediacy which gave her writing a curious similarity with D. H. Lawrence. It was all there. She saw cleanly; and her lovers were as real as her landscapes. Yet during the whole course of the war we heard almost nothing about her, and some wondered whether she was dead. It was rumoured that she had published three or four books in Chungking under assumed names, that she had died in battle, that she had become the Red Commissar for something or other and lived in a state of free love. I sent a note round to say that I would like to see her. We had mutual friends. She came. I did not interview her; she interviewed me on all the writers I knew in the south.

She is hardly more than four feet six inches tall, but when she is sitting down she gives an extraordinary impression of height. She is Hunanese, and like most Hunanese almost expressionless until she smiles, and there is a special sweetness about the smiles of those who are born in Hunan. She spoke in a low voice, very feminine, without gestures, wearing the usual blue cotton coat and blue baggy trousers; but once again you noticed, in this country where clothes have always possessed such mysterious significance that even now clothes are emblems of rank, that the blue cotton sets off the face perfectly; and you are conscious only of face, hands, the curve of the shoulders. She looked thirty, but she is over forty. She had fine teeth, and her black hair was drawn straight back from the brow; you realized that she must have been an extraordinarily attractive girl, and that she is herself the heroine of most of her novels.

She spoke of the odd fate which her work has received abroad. A few of her short stories were published in translation by Edgar Snow, a play was translated into English and performed in India. *The Mother* had been translated into Japanese during the occupation, she had read the book again recently, it did not please her, she wanted to revise it, making it the first of a trilogy dealing with the women of North China. She was proudest of her plays, which had been performed close to the front lines, and of one play especially called *Wang Hsiang T'ai Pan,* which translated literally means: Seeing one's Native Home from beside the Execution Grounds, and refers to the ghosts who rise after their execution by the Japanese and gaze into the distance. She had published one book in Chungking during the war under an assumed name. She had never been a Red Commissar, and she was happily married and had two children. She had spent all her time during the war editing magazines, organizing drama groups and writing *reportages.*

"We didn't have time for other things—there were so few writers, and we had to write for the people. I wrote a lot, of course; but most of it somehow got lost during our journeys, and it doesn't matter. I wrote several plays, and in some of them I found myself attempting desperately to try to understand the Japanese character. There was a play called *Ho-nei-yi-lang,* which is simply a transliteration of a Japanese soldier's name, and there was another called *The Meeting Place of Lovers,* which was largely about death and the war. I wrote some short stories called *Living in Shatsung,* which was the name of a perfectly imaginary place in
382

northern Shensi, and another called *Scenes in Northern Shensi*, but best of all were the *reportages*.

"We had to write for the people, because we were living in a time of revolution, and nothing else was important. Most of my early writings are valueless. Those stories of the emotional crises of young women in Shanghai—they have little enough meaning for me now. What is important is to get the people on paper, to find out how they really behave, how they think and act and love one another, and above all how they fight, and to do this authentically, not relying on the imagination—to do it with real feeling and understanding. You cannot write about the peasants unless you have lived with them for years, and because China consists so largely of peasants, you cannot write about China at all unless you have lived with the peasants.

"When a writer sits down to write, he does not say: 'I shall write for the people or not for the people.' His characters, the people he describes, depend on his daily life, on his observation, on his love for them. He can write, if he pleases, about young women suffering emotional and spiritual crises in Shanghai, or about the habits of the cultured scholars, but the peasants will not read them or listen to them. We had to develop an understanding of them, to go down among them, to suffer with them; and their crises are not like the crises in Shanghai. They are made of simpler stuff, but how difficult to render them on paper!

"My early works were a kind of continual *Sorrows of Werther*. Sometimes, too, I wrote of the peasants, but reading these things now I realize how often I misunderstood them. Lu Hsun spoke of their faults, their lack of education, their pitiful obedience to feudal laws. It was true at the time. It is not true now. They are maturing incredibly quickly, and they know now that they have rights and duties, and that they will never again suffer under the old feudal forces. They are making a world good enough to live in. They are learning to read—every village has its reading classes—and they are learning to write. I spent as much time as I could trying to find young writers among the peasants. They were not many, but they were good.

"What I wrote about the peasants in the past lacks *life*. I had to begin to think how to write all over again. In 1942 Mao Tse-tung made a speech calling upon the writers to study the peasants, to move among them and to be as much at their service as the government administrators. I was doing this long before his speech,

383

but I still did not understand them, I was still partly the young woman who wrote about love affairs in Shanghai. I discovered some things. I discovered that style was not important, that it was dangerous to invent a style, that one should write in such a way that all writing is a mirror of the people. I tried to break my old style and create a new style, but even that was no good—style, too, must come from the people, from the rhythms and sounds of the voices you hear round you.

"If you write for the moment, it is called propaganda, it cannot last long, but even though you call it propaganda, it has its own validity. It is created by the moment. Best of all would be to have time to compose a historical novel, trying to bring together all the impressions of the time, all the moments, all the heroism and suffering of the people. But how? It is not yet time—we are still struggling.

"There are other things we learned: that nearly all past Chinese literature was divorced from the people. *The Book of Odes* contains songs sung by the people, but we are no longer the same people we were two thousand five hundred years ago; we are changed; our feelings have changed; conditions have changed; and only the scholars can read and understand the old terminology. When we write the new *Book of Odes,* it will be utterly different from anything that has gone before. We must go back to the songs of the people."

Wandering among the mountains of Shensi, disappearing for months on end in remote villages, or organizing dramatic groups, she had listened to the songs of the people and studied them until she could almost identify herself with the old singers. They had a naked, original strength, often satirical, occasionally brutal, but there at least she had heard the real voice of China. Her face lit up when she spoke of the blind singers in the villages—this was real, this at least was the word she had been listening for.

"And they were not what we expected at all—they were infinitely better than we expected. The songs were unstudied, natural, springing from the earth and from their lives. In my family no one could sing a peasant song—perhaps there was no need. But in northern Shensi, everyone, everyone without exception, could sing these songs. There were love-songs and labourers' songs and there were songs cursing the officials and scholars, and they were mostly anonymous songs. Also, there are story-tellers, who are also singers, and I think most of us learned more from these

384

old blind story-tellers than we had learned from anything we ever read.

"In every small district there were these story-tellers. They were professional story-tellers, supported by the villages. Their stories are sung to music. They have a *pipa,* a kind of guitar with four strings, and they have other instruments which they perform all at the same time. There is a kind of flat board laced to the leg beneath the knees—they can tap on it with their fingers to give an accompaniment to the *pipa,* or else they can beat on it with a bronze clapper, or else they have a sounding board above the knee to beat on. They sing without gestures, wholly absorbed in their song; and the song is very long, usually an interminable story of heroes in the past, of kings and the downfall of dynasties, of amazing battles and great deaths.

"The people knew the stories by heart, and sometimes, but very occasionally, these blind musicians used to invent new stories. There were hundreds of stories, and the people knew them all, and never tired of listening to them. The story-tellers would move from one family or one village to another—new ones were constantly coming in. We invited these story-tellers to Yenan. We took down their stories, and studied them, and we started to ask them to tell stories about the resistance of the peasants to the Japanese. It was propaganda, if you like, but the resistance had already led to innumerable good stories. We have sent writers to live with them and learn from them. We have sent other writers to get them to sing the new stories. They were men with fantastic memories, and fantastic imaginations. We found after a while that they could invent stories prodigiously—as much as ten stories in half a year. Then they went back to their villages.

"Now, all over Shensi, there are these story-tellers. In the evening, when the farmers have returned from the fields, they listen to the blind old men with the bronze clappers and the *pipas* telling stories of the old heroes like Chu-ko Liang or of the young soldiers who fought in tunnels and blew up the Japanese with land-mines. It is almost the same world—there is not so very great a distance separating the past and the present. The stories are told in dialect; they belong to the people; they are continually growing and budding, and forming new stories. We feel now that the art of the story-teller has never been richer than in the places we have liberated from the Japanese, and the writers from the coast-ports are humble before the achievements of the blind men who wander

385

from village to village. There, at last, is the intimacy between author and audience which we lack, the direct communication, the splendour of the legends which belong to the present time.

"We still need to study the West, but in the end we found the best story-tellers among our own people."

I saw her many times again in Kalgan, striding down the road or coming to the stuffy hotel to discuss the importance of India or the places where the most beautiful women were born or what had happened to the friends she had not seen for nearly ten years, but the impression that remains is of a woman who wanted to spend the rest of her life among the peasants, and perhaps even wishing that she was a blind musician wandering among the tented hills of Shensi. She hated to discuss politics, which was a pity; she had a fine clear-cut mind. She spoke of the *lao pai hsing* * as Ai Ching spoke of them, conscious of their enduring greatness and of all men's ignorance about them until the war made it possible for people to see and write about them clearly for the first time. They were there. She was one of them, born on a small river in northwestern Hunan.

"There are four hundred and fifty million of them," she said. "It is time we learned about them."

July 3rd, The Old Revolutionaries, I . . . He was as ugly as sin, and he was President of Hua-pei University, which had come from Fu-ping and Yenan to Kalgan when the Japanese were overthrown. He looked like a Hapsburg, with an enormous jutting chin and a narrow red-veined nose, and he was so small that he would pass easily in a crowd; yet he smiled delightfully, and though he was dogmatic in his opinions, and self-assured when he addressed the University students, it was all part of a necessary disguise. The vice-president of the University, Chow Yang, was a famous critic. The President was not famous, he had written very little, and you realized that he had been made President because he possessed excellent administrative ability.

We talked about the University, which has fine buildings left by the Japanese and seven or eight hundred students. I admired the students immensely. They were usually tall and well-built, they wore their blue cotton uniforms with a swagger and they looked as though they were not afraid of anything. Many of them had come from the Kuomintang areas in the south, either on foot

* The old hundred names, i.e., the people.

or on pony-back, often in disguise to pass the frontier posts, or else they had flown from Chungking. Nearly a hundred of them had flown secretly, with the help of the American army, in three plane-loads to Kalgan in April. There they joined the school of English language—the Communists had very few students who knew English well—and this was a godsend, for now they could build up their *cadres* of interpreters and translators. In general the Communists were bad propagandists, and seemed not to care very much what happened in other parts of the world, and they had paid almost no attention to the necessity of telling the outside world what they were doing. There was every day a quarter of an hour of Morse broadcast from Yenan, and this was about all—in Yenan they knew the broadcasts were received in the office of *Amerasia* in America, and also in the Philippines, but they had no idea whether they were received elsewhere. Now for the first time they were attempting to train interpreters.

He was a man of about fifty, and he had good reason to be pleased with the progress of his University. At Fu-ping there were sometimes three thousand students scattered over neighbouring villages. Many, far too many of their students had been killed in the war against the Japanese. There were four faculties—political science, education, literature and western languages. In the last seven years they had trained over ten thousand students. Sometimes the courses were deliberately made as short as possible. The first semester was usually given over to political training based on Mao Tse-tung's New Democracy, social science and the history of social development, and there were courses in contemporary Chinese history, the development of the liberated areas and methods of thinking. Marxism was not taught in these courses, and from what I saw of their books the teaching was somewhat akin to old-fashioned English liberalism. There were no technical colleges in the University—there was a science school and a technical college outside the town. This was a University for a purpose —to train as quickly as possible administrators and government officials, propaganda workers in the army and what they called *cadres*—trained and efficient boys and girls who would go among the peasants and organize them and find out what the peasants wanted.

I have never seen so many students looking so well-fed; all had red cheeks, and enjoyed life. Though all, boys and girls, wore blue cotton coats, blue cotton trousers, and blue cotton peaked caps, there was no impression of uniformity. There were an infinite number of gradations in the blue colour of their clothes, and seeing them all in the same uniform, you were not aware of oddities of dress and had time to look clear into their sunburnt faces. The students were expected not to marry while they were attending the University, but many of them were married. Nor were they asked to pay anything. Everything, food, paper, pencils, underwear, shoes, clothes, beds, blankets, all these were provided by the Government, and the Government guaranteed them jobs after graduation. They would get little money from their jobs, but they would be provided with everything they needed. They seemed, and were, students who were dedicated to serve the peasants.

The President complained a little of the students who had flocked in from Pekin and Tientsin after the downfall of the Japanese. Their morale was not high; they were grossly ignorant, and sometimes did not know who was the President of the United States or when the Boxer Rebellion took place. These students had an average age of about twenty, yet their mental age was considerably less. The time of the Japanese occupation had been sheer loss to them.

"And the worst of it is that their handwriting is mixed up with Japanese," he went on, "and when they first came they were always bowing tiresomely and sucking in the air between their teeth, exactly like the Japanese. Mostly they came from the senior middle schools, and very often we found they were the sons and daughters of traitors. They came here because they wanted to get away from the atmosphere of treachery which ran through Pekin and Tientsin for eight years. They had heard about our work, they knew we would look after them, but at first we wondered whether we could do anything with such amazingly poor material. It took three or four months for them to shake down, and now they have shaken down, and some of our best students are among them.

"They find it difficult, of course, to communicate with their parents, but there are ways and means, and we even give them the stamps. They have their baths and haircuts free, and they don't seem to worry very much about money, though we give them in money each month the equivalent of eight catties of millet. This pays for the small things they want, which the University doesn't provide. But under the present system we find that we save enormous sums of money by this kind of University co-operative, and enormous amounts of time. We still lack text-books, and have to
388

produce most of our text-books on mimeographing machines. But the printing-presses are beginning to turn out books on good paper, and we are no longer living in the time of short six-month courses. The average length of time the students will now spend in the University is three years, but sometimes even now we take them from the school and send them out into the field before they have graduated.

"My feeling is that they are enjoying themselves. The sense of dedication is there, and they know that within a few years or months they will be given responsible positions. We have far more jobs open for them than we have students. The University was founded in 1939—it is the oldest University in the liberated areas, for even Yenan University came afterwards. They like the patterns of behaviour which we try to inculcate in them—a pattern based on the utmost simplicity. They are to have government positions, but they must remain close to the peasants and the farmers, and they must live simply like the peasants and farmers. They cannot be corrupt, for in this area there are precious few advantages to be derived from money; and they are given heavy responsibilities so early that they will probably never fight for power. You fight for power only if you have never had it, and it brings advantages; but here it brings no advantages, only such vast responsibilities that they would quail before them. Ultimately, the important thing is that they learn here to live simply, to be honest and to serve the people as teachers or administrators or whatever work is given to them.

"They can choose their own work. There are six courses in the Department of Literature. Literature itself has most, but there are courses in drama, woodcutting and painting, music, journalism and dancing. Very few are now taking woodcutting or dancing, but there will be more later. A good number are taking drama—there is theory of drama, history of drama, methods of acting, and how to write plays. They write like mad, and perform their own plays. In Kalgan there are only six theatres but they are filled every night. The good actors have tremendous followings, though the plays are mostly propaganda plays. What we want them to do is to write their own plays, act their own plays, know everything about the drama from top to bottom; the best actors come mostly from this University."

I had seen a series of plays given by the University students the previous night. They had an almost professional competence, but

389

I had been struck most of all by the way in which the students acted peasants. There were two boys of seventeen or eighteen, and they took the parts of old peasants perfectly; they knew all the manners and gestures; they spoke as I have seen peasants speak; they tapped their long silver-stemmed pipes on the soles of their rice-straw sandals, and instead of looking seventeen or eighteen, they looked sixty. There was a Japanese officer, and this too was played perfectly; a man in khaki uniform, with a clubfoot and an insolent ragged contempt of the Chinese peasants who surrounded him on all sides, speaking Chinese with a Japanese accent, turning up the cuffs of his coat to strike the peasants and behaving with studied and bestial idiocy. But the effect was fantastic—it was a real Japanese, no longer acting, a man with a toothbrush moustache and a small perplexed mind. The Chinese peasants had run rings round him, they had almost laughed in his face, but every gesture gave the impression of accurate authenticity—this was the Japanese they had studied at close quarters for eight years. I remember, too, a Mongolian dance by two girls dressed in red, green and yellow silk; the dance was hieratic and essentially buddhist, and more a dance of weaving hands and slow-paced movements to the tune of a *pipa* than an invocation to any new age which the Communists were about to usher in; but how perfectly they had danced, how expressionless and yet full of expression were those silent faces and those gently accomplished young bodies! They did not sing. They wove, with pointing hands and with the folds of their silk gowns, a pattern of adoration across the stage.

It was this kind of thing that was so impressive, the way the curtain would draw back and you would see, here and there in the north, the permanent things revealed so simply and effortlessly that you remembered the greatness of the people who are as great as their land. The colours of mountains, the small Kansu ponies riding towards the distant gates between the mountains, the Great Wall itself, the odd depths which were sometimes surreptitiously displayed in the faces of the people, the white scars of the river beds and the curves of men's shoulders—these were permanent, and would remain long after the New Democracy of Mao Tse-tung was forgotten; but perhaps they were more splendid here, because the New Democracy, which has nothing to do with Communism, gave men a fervour and delight in life absent in all the other parts of China where I have been.

390

There were other plays, and the President discussed them professionally; he knew the actors, their private lives, their difficulties—even the difficulty of finding lipstick and rouge for their faces. The ugly face became less ugly after a while: you noticed the eyes, and forgot the large stained teeth and the Hapsburg chin. He was small and quiet, and spoke sometimes as though he was reading from a catalogue; but often the catalogue disappeared, and his intense pride in the University shone forth. This was not a University where scholars could study at their leisure, though there is a place for such Universities in China. It was a University of the people, for the people, by the people, and those broad northern faces had looked astonishingly pleasant and hopeful.

It was then, I think, that someone told me that the President had taken part in the Long March. I have spoken of the Long March before, and met at least twenty people who had taken part in it, and in Kalgan as elsewhere it was noticeable how the Long Marchers were treated with deep respect. The President was delighted to have an opportunity of talking about it. His memory was fading. He could not remember all of it, and besides, in the early stages, he had been suffering from malaria—he remembered the early nightmare journeys only through the scorching fever of malaria. There were no doctors. He had taken part in the Long March because there was no other alternative, and as soon as he came out of the hospital he was placed in one of the two companies of sick men which staggered behind the fighters. It was not a glorious position, but at least these two companies had fought bravely at times.

"What I remember now are certain incidents—the crossing of the Tatu Bridge, quick sudden engagements with the enemy, our sufferings and our poverty. I remember particularly the weather, how it rained during the first two months in Kiangsi and Hunan, and how foggy it was in Kweichow. We started in October, which was the worst time for starting a long journey. When we came to Kwangsi, it was already hot and we abandoned our padded clothes by the roadside. When we passed through the Man-tzu territories of Szechuan, it was windy; and in May the snow had never been deeper on the *Ta Hsueh San*—the Great Snow Mountain. It is a very slow slope, but nothing could be more difficult to cross—there was almost no air there. We would pass the night in ruined temples, and we could not sleep because we were all crowded together

391

and our clothing was wet through. We went on. The advance guard could not get through to the top. We camped that night half-way up, and then when we did reach the top of the mountain at dawn, it *hailed*. It was the last thing we expected—thick lumps of hail as large as your finger-nail.

"Men died on the top of the mountain. They would be standing next to you and talking to you, and then their faces took on a sudden frozen look, they swayed and they were dead; and what was extraordinary was that some of the strongest men died on the mountain. In the morning we raced down to the valley."

As he said this his eyes gleamed, and you realized then how these men, who have fought the Japanese for so long, still dreamed of the Long March, which was so fantastic and unbelievable a thing that it assumed the colours of legend. You could hardly believe you had taken part in it. And gradually, as I collected stories from them about the march, it became evident that there were twenty thousand different stories, for every man had seen the march through his own emotions. General Peng Teh-huei had told me about the crossing of the Tatu Bridge; Chu Teh had said a few words; the President and others were to tell me more, but though the stories could easily be reconciled, I was struck with the essential differences. Each man had remained himself, and saw things which no others had seen.

"And after we crossed the Great Snow Mountain things grew better. We came to the grasslands—it was all plain and swamp, the earth soft, with no trees and the grass about a foot high. There were bogs where men died, but not all of us travelled through the centre of the grasslands—others travelled in long columns along the edge of the grasslands, and that was better. We got milk and butter from the tribesmen, and most of us survived; and later on we came to the Yi tribespeople.

"It was the strangest of all journeys. We had seen Kweiyang in the distance, at a time when the Generalissimo was staying there. Some of us saw Kunming, but we had no time to stay there or capture it—we had to cross the Golden Sand River as quickly as possible to avoid the enemy. The Kuomintang knew we intended to cross the river and took all the ferry-boats to the other side. We made a forced march in three columns across the plain till we reached the river, trying to find a place where we could get through, and we sent another column walking backwards and forwards between Kunming and the river to put the enemy off the scent. The middle column was the first to reach the river—they walked 140 *li* in one day. We found a single boat tethered to the south side of the river, and some of the soldiers boarded it, disguised as civilians. The enemy were in no hurry, they thought we were still far away. On the other side of the river our soldiers, disguised as civilians, found a tax officer. They explained they were Kuomintang troops in disguise and wanted the boats sent hurriedly to the south bank, and they wanted fuel and food. The tax-inspector agreed with alacrity, and invited them to dinner with the local landlords. It was not a trap—the tax-inspector really believed we were Kuomintang troops, and while the dinner went on, and our own soldiers cursed the Reds, our troops were being ferried over.

"It was dusk when they crossed the river. They encamped on the bank, and the next day at dawn they climbed a mountain. By this time the landlords and the tax-inspector were beginning to doubt we were really Kuomintang troops; they fired a few ineffective shots at us, and we returned their fire.

"On the top of the mountain there was a plain. We marched along the plain for about thirty *li* and came to Tungchow, which was guarded by two battalions of Kuomintang troops. We found them sleeping, with their arms scattered all round them—we took all their weapons, and some good machine-guns. It was the easiest of all our victories, and there we waited, while the rest of the Red Army, numbering perhaps 60,000, came up with us—some of them had crossed the river at further points down south.

"Things were getting curiouser and curiouser, for we had had to fight stern battles with them in the past, but now they seemed to have lost heart. A column of Szechuanese soldiers found our hiding-place and attacked, but what was surprising was that they had lost all vestiges of *morale*, they shouted at us and screamed at us, but they weren't very effective soldiers and soon surrendered all their equipment. It was as though the gods were beginning to favour our side. Later, we destroyed the boats and fortified our position. We needed a rest. There was a long journey ahead. At one time General Hsueh Yueh's army was a day's march behind us; now we learned that the Kuomintang forces were at least a month's journey behind us. This heartened us. We took a long rest. We still had the Tatu River to cross.

"The Tatu River was not easy to cross. General Shih Tai-k'ai had been surrounded there during the Taiping Rebellion, his forces cut up and none left to survive. He lost his armies in a place close to the bridge where we crossed. We made forced marches to the river-bank, but found no boats there. One Szechuanese Kuomintang officer had come to the south side of the river by boat to see his father-in-law. We captured the boat. About nineteen soldiers crossed over in it, and on the other side of the river there were two Kuomintang battalions waiting for us. These nineteen soldiers in turn captured more boats and returned, but the river was desperately rapid and dangerous. Yet we got two companies across unhurt, and these defeated many of the Kuomintang soldiers on the north bank.

"We heard that the enemy was delighted with their success at trapping us at the defiles of the river. They never calculated worse. We had two columns marching along both sides of the river. There were no good roads—just stepping-stones and paths scratched out of the rock, so that we were for ever jumping from rock to rock or putting down planks between them. Then in the end, we captured the bridge from both sides, we cut down the Kuomintang defenders and the two columns met together at last."

And then as we rose for dinner, he smiled his quiet Hapsburg smile and said: "I can't remember all of it, but it was as simple as that."

July 4th, The Old Revolutionaries, II . . . THERE was excellent beer, and on the label there was printed in large florid characters: Five Star Brand Lager Beer Shinohin Brewery Pekin. It was Japanese beer, but it tasted in those hot days in summer like good English beer, and we kept drinking it till four o'clock in the morning. The building was in the old city, belonged to the Field Team and had once belonged to a Japanese general; the sofas were small, and were delicately patterned: the tall Communist general found himself imprisoned within the arm-rests. He looked like a peasant, with a close-cropped skull which shone like gold in the light of the electric lamps; he possessed an infectious laugh; it was only rarely that he showed any signs of bitterness. He had been a supply officer during the Long March. He had taken an important part in the campaign called the Hundred Regiments Campaign which Chu Teh had organized, all over North China, against the Japanese, and you derived the impression that he preferred fighting or farming to doing paper work in the Field Team.

I asked him whether there was any real hope that the war might be stopped. He grinned and poured out another glass of beer. "We're doing our best," he said. "No one wants this war. The *lao pai hsing* don't want the war. We're all so desperately tired of war, but we'll fight for democracy against dictatorship. There are good people in the Kuomintang, but they don't want democracy apparently. We fought against the dictatorship of the Japanese under conditions of blockade from the Kuomintang. We were surrounded with 'ramparts of copper and iron.' We are bound to be bitter against them, and they are bound to want to conserve their power. Best of all would be to go back to the agreements already made, call a National Assembly and have a real democratic China —as democratic as America or England."

But he could see little hope for the moment. The balance was weighted for war. American intervention was probably insufficient: the issues at stake were so great that it needed the intervention of Soviet Russia and Britain, yet they had kept silent and aloof. Both would be immeasurably affected by the decisions made in China. The Americans were mediators, but they were also technically and factually at the service of the Nationalist Government, and the Nationalist Government was no longer representative of the people. "It's all dictatorship—a one-man government—and we are so tired and sick of it." He was violent about the corruption in the south and asked whether I had seen any in the north. I said I had been there too little a time to be sure, but it seemed in the highest degree unlikely that anyone on the Communist side was corrupt. There were no advantages that money could bring in the northern areas. I said I had read some reports written and broadcast by the Communists about Kalgan, saying that there were no ricksha-pullers, no prostitutes, no beggars in the capital of the Chin-Cha-Chi area. It was untrue. I had seen two prostitutes, one beggar and three ricksha-pullers. He laughed.

"But you don't know what it was like before the war. This was a Japanese city—there were prostitutes everywhere. How many have you seen?"

"Two."

"When?"

"At four o'clock this morning."

"What the devil were you doing in the streets at four o'clock in the morning?"

"I had been talking with the Kuomintang general. We came back by car. They were standing on a street corner. I can't think who else would be standing at street corners at four o'clock in the morning."

He agreed that some of the Communist claims were exaggerated, though for some reason (it may have been a perfectly good reason) he was inclined to think that the beggars were Kuomintang agents in disguise. "Half the beggars in China are in the secret service. We swept the beggars off the streets and put them into trade, and two months later they started coming back again from the south." A little later he said: "There's nothing worse than these exaggerated claims for the Communist areas. We're doing the job well, we are organizing administrations and factories, but we haven't got enough trained men. In the war everyone was fighting, and fighting with inadequate equipment. In the peace we find we have inadequate numbers of trained men."

It was getting late. He had discussed the ways in which the war might be brought to an end—a *coup d'état*, manifestations by the students everywhere, the retirement of the leaders of both sides from the scene, a prolongation of the truce. For some reason all of these seemed unlikely to succeed. We were waiting for the miracle; and now, as often, the miracle was simply democracy. He was bitter about the Kuomintang as the Kuomintang general had been bitter about the Communists the previous night. Was there any way in which the bitterness could be bridged? He shook his head. "It's a question of waiting and hoping—that's all."

We had come down to that. There seemed in those days to be no hope at all—and within ten hours the truce would end, and the war would be aflame all over China. It was two o'clock in the morning, and the truce would end at midday on the last day in June. What would happen? There might be general offensives everywhere, with the Kuomintang capturing many large towns and the Communists growing stronger and stronger in the villages. There could be no victory. China would be split, not horizontally or vertically, but into urban and rural areas, according to the pattern already visible in Shantung, where the Kuomintang possessed Tsingtao and Tsinan and the Communists claimed to possess all the surrounding areas. This was not civil war like the war in Spain; it resembled more than anything else the kind of undeclared war which took place in Germany after 1918 between the villages and the towns, and for some of the same reasons. A kind of utter despair settled on us, and it was then that I asked him to talk about the Long March. In this world, where everything seemed to be failing, where no one was thinking clear-headedly, where the stakes were so large that nearly everyone was overwhelmed by them, the epic journey remained. It was perhaps the centre-pole round which one could think a little more clearly about the future.

It was half-past two, and we had been talking since nine o'clock —two of the interpreters were asleep, and it would be necessary to hurry for fear that the third would fall asleep, too. But the general looked fresh and gleaming, the bronze skull caught the light and the immensely mobile peasant face, which possessed craft and intelligence and an extraordinary youthfulness for one so old—he was forty, and he had been fighting continuously since he was nineteen—seemed to grow into even greater life as he spoke of the past. The magic worked. It was a very potent magic. It was only a moment before he was once more a strippling youth just out of military college.

"It happened very quickly. There was the march to the north, a tremendous democratic fervour in the country and then suddenly, so it seemed to us, there was an end to it—the Generalissimo came out on the side of the reaction, and there was the inevitable and necessary uprising at Nanchang.

"We fought stubbornly, even though we were small in numbers, because we knew that we could save the country from the reaction if we succeeded in our aim. I was a supply officer. That meant that ammunition, clothing, medicines, everything had somehow to be obtained, listed and placed in the proper hands. There are things I remember well, but some of it is forgotten—when you have been fighting for so long, all the wars and battles seem to have the same colour. I remember a forced march near the Gold Sand River, on the boundary of Yunnan and Szechuan. We sent a small army to the river. The Kuomintang thought we would fight for passage at the place where this army came, but suddenly we moved away secretly and marched for two days and one night without stopping towards another crossing. It was the hardest thing we ever did. We were worn out. We dared not fail. We had no time to eat, and we had to eat as we walked, without rest, taking our drinking water from the river. We marched two or three hundred *li*, and crossed at the new crossing.

"I remember many other things, but most of all I remember the crossing of the Tatu Bridge. We had defeated several armies after crossing the Gold Sand River, we had climbed over mountains and then we saw in the distance the defiles of the Tatu. The current

397

was unbelievably swift. We came to a town called An-shun-ch'ang. There we found an old man who told us frankly that the crossing was impossible, and a great Taiping general had lost all his forces there. We knew nothing of this war. We asked him for details, and he said that General Shih Ta-kai's wife had given birth to a child, his soldiers were allowed to rest and feast for two days, and then it was too late for the crossing—they were encircled and defeated. So we thanked the old man, telling him there was no danger we should rest and feast for two days, and we had no wives on the Long March.

"At Tatu River we could capture only three boats. We tried to make a bridge, but failed. With the three boats we sent over about 500 men, and then two of the boats overturned and it was decided not to send any more. Along both sides of the river we approached Liutingchiao, the Bridge Made by Liu, the only bridge lying on the frontier of Sikong and Szechuan. The Kuomintang guarded the bridge with one regiment of soldiers. We selected about a hundred young soldiers to try to get across the iron bridge, and at the same time, to distract their attention, we sent bursts of machine-gun fire across the river. Some of our soldiers fell a hundred feet below into the river—there was no help for them, and there was nothing we could do to save them. In the end we wiped out the regiment. At that time those in command were Lin Piao, who is now in Manchuria, Liu Po-ch'eng, and General Nieh.

"There was a great deal of fighting in north-western Szechuan. We fought rivers and we fought marshes and we fought mountains —it was more difficult to fight nature than to fight men. On the Great Snow Mountain the snow never melts; there is so little air that you can hardly breathe. Lin Piao's * heart was bad. They carried him half-way up the mountain, and then they had to rest, and it was only much later that he reached the summit. The tribes-people here told us that we should cross before noon, because in the afternoons there are high winds and the air pressure becomes mysteriously changeful. After crossing the Great Snow Mountain we found that the troops of Hu Tso-nan, which had come down from Shensi and Hunan, were waiting for us. We defeated them, and then came to the grasslands—we walked for a whole week through mud and grass. The mud-holes were terrible—we had to

* In 1946 Commander-in-Chief of the New Democratic Army in Manchuria.

rely on the tribespeople to lead the way. There were no houses, no villages, where we could pass the night, but sometimes we came upon ancient forests—they were so ancient that beneath the trees there were layer upon layer of fallen leaves; and these were drier than the grasslands, and better than any house. We had eaten up all our foodstuffs by this time, and we were starving. The tribespeople raised cattle, but hid them when they saw us approaching. We ate hides, searched for mushrooms, anything.

"This was the worst time, for we felt lost, we did not know the language of the tribespeople, the terrain failed us, and many of us died. There was only the small straggling columns on the grass plains.

"It all happened a long time ago, and many who took part in it are dead. We lost heavily during the journey. There were originally five commanders of the four armies which took part in the march—Lin Piao, Liu Po-ch'eng, Peng Teh-huei, Lo Ping-huei and Tung Chen-tang. Lin Piao and Peng Teh-huei were the best. Liu Po-ch'eng later became Chief-of-Staff, but Tung Chen-tang died some years ago and Lo Ping-huei died recently. Soon, of all that vast army, there will be only a few leaders left, for you could not live through those hardships and come through them unharmed. We were an army without a uniform, without marks of rank, living on the land, wandering through nine provinces, always fighting— has it ever happened before that an army has made such a journey?"

There was no need to answer him, for only Cortes and the Torguts had travelled over such vast spaces and with such great difficulty surrounded by enemies. The young general had changed during the course of the conversation. Tired now, he looked magnificent, the smile disappeared, the small mouth was set in a firm line and the close-shaven head began to look for the first time commanding and even forbidding. We went out at last into the courtyard where on the wall there was written in blood-red the Chinese character for "happiness." The stars glittered. Somewhere in the great house we could hear a Morse tapper. The war was still going on.

July 5th, Tunnels and Land-Mines . . . HE WAS tall and swarthy, and though he wore impeccable uniform and had spent long periods during the war against the Japanese in the headquarters of the Eighth Route Army at Fuping, he looked what he was

—a fighter. I knew him as Colonel Ma. It was probably his real name, for he looked as though he had Mohammedan blood and Ma is a common name for the descendants of the old Mohammedan invaders. He smiled easily; he spoke English nearly perfectly; he liked nothing better than telling stories, and above all he liked telling stories about land-mines and tunnels. There were even moments when it seemed as though Colonel Ma regarded the whole eight-year war as a rather delightful pastime in hoodwinking the Japanese by burrowing under them or away from them, or blowing them up nastily and efficiently. And he would roar with laughter at some particularly nasty and efficient trickery. Writing this now, I remember him smiling mysteriously, gazing at the ceiling, absorbed in a kind of conjuring trick, effortlessly filling the room with the vision of the plains of North China where the farmers of the small scattered villages were vigorously plotting against the three-pronged columns of the Japanese annihilation campaigns, and doing this so superbly that you almost forgot the legendary terror—burn all, kill all, loot all.

He had a quiet voice, well modulated, and he would speak very slowly as he described the sudden merciless attacks just before dawn, or the enemy's amazing delight in murder, and their methods of rape. These things occurred. Their memory could not be stamped out. Hatred for the Japanese still burned among these people, who were so accustomed to long years of hatred that there was almost a vacuum in their lives now that the Japanese had gone. Sometimes we would go outside the city and see the fortresses on the distant hills, and he would talk of the time when the Japanese began to build fortresses in every village and on every mountain in great rings and circles which became smaller and smaller as they advanced towards the centre.

"It was all they could do," he said. "They had so many enemies that they had to exterminate us to survive, and they could only exterminate us by drawing a vast circle of blockhouses round us, and then narrowing towards the centre. They were desperately afraid. They had the railroads and the towns, but every village and every field belonged to us, and in every village and every field there were traps laid for them. The traps were everywhere—inside houses, along the roads, under railroad lines, in trees, in stones. There came a time when they would not even dare to enter our houses, even after they had murdered everyone in the village they could lay their hands on—they would send puppet troops into
400

the houses instead. The floors were dangerous, the walls were dangerous, the brick bed was dangerous and the roof was dangerous. A stone on the floor might explode if you stepped on it, there might be a false wall and suddenly a brick would move and they would be killed by revolver fire from a man hiding behind the wall. The brick bed was dangerous, and they began to learn to regard brick beds with horror—people could hide there, and it was very easy to put explosives there. If they climbed on the roof, all the tiles might explode in their faces.

"They didn't like it, but they had to take it. They preferred not to march or ride along the roads: you would see them going through flooded fields or along the slopes of the mountains—it was safer there. Or better still they rode their horses along river-beds. But all places were dangerous for them; there were land-mines in rivers, and even on the mountains an unsuspected stone might explode and kill them.

"In this area, Chin-Cha-Chi, we had a land-mine hero called Li Yun. He thought about land-mines all day and all night. He was puzzled by one thing. You could put a land-mine on the road and blow up a Japanese motor-car, but often the Japanese inside the motor-car survived. He kept thinking about it. How the devil to kill the Japanese in the car? In the end he decided to put a small land-mine in the road, and two large ones on each side of the road which exploded when the Japanese came out of the car.

"Land-mines were the easiest things to make. You could make them out of anything. We had the nitre and saltpetre, and we had stones in abundance. In the end half of our land-mines were simply stones, bored out, with a cardboard or glass tube like a cartridge inserted in them, and connected by a lanyard or a trip-wire to some hiding-place where a soldier was watching, or just simply left there to explode when anything touched it. The Japanese might come into a peasant house and pick up some turnips —the turnips would explode; or they would lift up the wooden cover over the stove, and the cover would explode. When the Japanese occupied a village in the early days they always did two things—they held a mass meeting of the villagers in the village square, and they took over the best houses; so we put land-mines under the village square and arranged that under the beds of the best houses there should be more land-mines. After that they did not hold meetings in the village square, and they did not take over the best houses.

"We made their lives miserable with land-mines. We were very successful with them, and when we captured their reports, we found that they were frightened to the marrow by every stone and every blade of grass in North China. We would use land-mines in combination with ambush—very effective, and the wounds caused by splinters of stone are much worse than shrapnel. They tried to use land-mines against us, but it wasn't very effective—we were rarely in the places where their land-mines were. But still they were powerful, they could build blockhouses and try to narrow us down.

"This is where the tunnels came in. They came in gradually, and we learned how to make them and use them only after bitter experience. Generally speaking, there were two kinds of tunnel—a tunnel built from village to village underneath the fields for the purpose of saving the lives of the villagers when the Japanese attacked, and a tunnel built deliberately for fighting in. The tunnels did not necessarily run directly between the villages. There were side-turnings, blank alleys, and in the fighting tunnels all kinds of tricks were employed. We used land-mines in the tunnels, too. And some of the most bitter fighting in the war in North China took place six or seven feet underneath the earth.

"We had to excavate the tunnels secretly; we would take the earth away to the foot of a mountain and bury it again. When it was raining, we would take it to the fields and sprinkle it there. We had to be careful—there must be no tell-tale marks of earth, and they must never know whether we had tunnels or not. It was a game of nerves—we wanted them to believe that there were tunnels everywhere. It was true in the later stages of the war, but not in the beginning.

"There were all kinds of problems, and we solved them very, very gradually. The entrance to a tunnel might be anywhere— under a bed, behind a false wall, anywhere, and always it was carefully concealed, so that if you went into the room you wouldn't find it in less than ten minutes. There was a time when half the population of Chin-Cha-Chi was digging tunnels, and the other half was trying to hide the earth. Why not? It had to be done. It was the only way we could safeguard our lives. There were some beautiful tricks. A tunnel might begin in the side of the well. Excellent. We would drop down on to a wooden board, and make our way through the tunnel, but if the Japanese followed us, we
402

would arrange that the wooden board would tip up—the Japanese would fall into the well-water, and just beneath the surface of the water there were bayonets and sharp-pointed sticks. This worked beautifully. Or else the entrance to the tunnel would be beneath the *k'ang*, and when the Japanese entered the house they would find an old lady sitting on the *k'ang*. She could communicate with the people in the tunnel below by pulling on a string concealed in the bed-covers. She could tell them when the Japanese had come, and when they were gone, and many other things about them.

"We had trouble with ventilation, of course. It can be very damp and dark in the tunnels—not pleasant. Sometimes the tunnel would pass beneath the wall of a house: then we could arrange an air-let. Or else it would pass near an old well, and we could arrange another air-let. But it was not always easy. Sometimes, too, we arranged that the tunnels should utilize old wells. Suddenly, where the tunnel passed through the well, there would be a drop of twenty or thirty feet. For ourselves we put boards over the place where the tunnel passed through the well, but the boards were removed if the Japanese were following. Then, too, sometimes the tunnel would narrow down till it was so small that only one man could worm his way through: at such places, if the Japanese were following, we put mill-stones bored through with a hole in the centre: through the hole we could fire at them. In the darkness they never knew what hit them. But generally they did not follow us through the tunnels—they contented themselves with digging outside the village, hoping to cut through the tunnel-lines. It wasn't much use to them. The tunnels were complicated affairs. If they were cut in one place, we still had branch tunnels going to other places. The only way they could stop the peasants using tunnels would have been to dig a vast circular trench round the village and put sentries at all the tunnel exits. It wouldn't have worked. They didn't have enough sentries.

"The earth is firm in central Hopei, and this is where most of the best tunnels were—it is not loess, as in Yenan. We didn't need roof supports: six or seven feet under the earth the tunnels were firm, and there was no danger of the roof falling in. We would arrange little sidings, where we could rest or ambush the Japanese or pass one another. There are a lot of dead Japanese in these tunnels still—it saves the trouble of burying them. But mostly they did not get into the tunnels—if they tried to, they were

403

blown up with land-mines the moment they dropped into the tunnel entrance. Sometimes they used poison gas. It was very effective at first, until we learned to put up cotton quilted blankets soaked with water inside the tunnels—it kept the gas out. We were fighting on our own middens, and against all tricks, but the tunnel was the best trick we had; the Japanese would come and occupy a village, but the villagers had fled. The Three Alls—Burn All, Kill All, Loot All—were excellent in theory, but we hid the grain and we hid ourselves, and we could always rebuild our houses afterwards.

"We hid the grain in the tunnels or in specially prepared pits. They rarely found it; and the grain keeps perfectly if you take certain precautions. They wanted grain badly—it was the best kind of plunder, and there was a time when they thought they could starve us out. But the peasants for centuries have learned to hide grain from the tax-inspectors. They usually arranged that their annual annihilation campaigns would take place in the autumn, when we were harvesting. They could destroy some of the crops, but they could not destroy all of it, and they could always kill a few people. They killed a lot of old women, who could not run fast enough. They were stupid people, and they did not understand us, and we were better organized than they were."

He had spoken of the tunnels and the land-mines as though nothing could be more pleasant than outwitting the Japanese; but evidently it was not all pleasant. There were tragedies, too. A tunnel with hundreds of people in it would be blown up with dynamite, or poison gas would be thrown in at the right time and the right place. There are ghost villages where no one has survived. There are areas where they had succeeded in destroying every living thing. And there were minor tragedies, more poignant because they concerned individual people, which he told sadly and slowly, as though he could reproduce with his slow, deliberate voice the tension of the days of the past.

"It was two years ago, somewhere in central Hopei. We had come to a small village, with our six or seven bodyguards. We heard that the Japanese were about to attack a village about ten *li* to the north, but we were desperately weary and slept without adequate precautions, though some of the bodyguards remained awake. The Japanese did attack the village ten *li* to the north, but they also attacked us. They came by forced marches suddenly from the south, and they reached us just before dawn. This was

404

their favourite manœuvre, for just before dawn is the time when it is most difficult to resist them.

"My bodyguard woke me up and told me the Japanese were already in the main street of the village. There was just time to throw our documents and ammunition down the tunnel-well, and clamber in. They knew we were there. They had spies—mostly traitors, and besides they had passed through this village only a little while before. Some Japanese soldiers climbed up on the roof of a neighbouring house and fired down on us, but by that time we were struggling through the entrance of the tunnel, ten or twelve of us, and the documents were still in the well, and we had no time to hide the entrance. They came into the room. A puppet soldier jumped down the well when he saw the documents. We wounded him in the thigh, but not seriously—he climbed up again, bringing some of the documents with him. It didn't matter so much—they were in code.

"The house where we were staying belonged to an old woman. They went to her, and asked her who we were. She said there were no soldiers there. They answered by hacking off one of the fingers of her left hand with a meat-axe, and then asked her again. She gave the same answer five times, and they cut off all five fingers. What made things so difficult was that we were accompanying a general who was bringing with him his wife and a six-months-old girl-child. We were all making our way through the tunnel. It was muddy, the tunnel was small, and we crawled forward on hands and knees. We could hear the Japs just above our heads digging trenches. They dug more than ten trenches, and when they came to a tunnel they poured in poison gas. The general and his wife were slightly poisoned, and the baby began crying. This was dangerous. You couldn't ordinarily hear the sounds of a baby crying six or seven feet underground, but the sound might be heard near an air-let. The Japanese were determined to get us. We could hear the horses above us, and sometimes we heard their officers—that meant we were near an air-let. And then suddenly the baby stopped crying. We went on. It was so dark and so miserable, and the air was full of the smell of poison gas, which had soaked into our clothes. We had wet cloths over our mouths, and we were terribly cramped. We stayed in the tunnel thirteen hours, always moving about. Then we heard them go away, and climbed out. It was night. We discovered then, not before, that the general's wife had smothered the baby to death for fear that the Japanese would hear her cries. She said nothing about the killing to the general. It was just there—the dead child, covered with mud, the face blue, and the woman was weeping."

July 6th, The Desert and the Sown . . . THE aeroplane left Kalgan one burning summer day and headed for Mongolia. Once again there were the bronze mountains in the sun, no clouds, the white scars of the unflowing rivers and here and there on the mountain slopes were small temples among green trees. No day could have been brighter and nothing could have been smoother than the flight of the aeroplane. The pilot said they were going to Suiyuan, the most northerly of the provinces of China proper, in the direction of the Ordos plains; but when you looked for the plains you saw only the sweep of the mountains going on for ever, till at last you came to a region of yellow-blue earth which seemed even at that height to be barren and uninhabited. We were already in Suiyuan. From the air you saw the railway line, the green fields and nothing else.

Chi-ning is a small walled town on the railway to Pailingmiao. It stands in the middle of a vast plain, dominated by the immense power-station and water-tower of white concrete—you can see only the walls, the station, the tower and the railway station, and for the first time it occurs to you that all over Asia there are towns like this along all the railway lines. There had been no need to make an air-strip; the plain was enough, a plain where there are few roads, no animals, the only signs that people once passed by here were the hillocks of stone erected for the dead. I hoped to see camels, but none came. The air was pure, and the sky was touched with the green grass, which went on for ever. In the distance were the faint blue mountains low on the horizon. The town was in the hands of the Communists; the first Field Team had come here.

It was comfortable there, lying under the shadow of the plane with a great wolf-hound which had appeared from nowhere, or talking to a girl student who had walked from Yenan two weeks before, a bad journey, without compass or maps, always a little afraid of straying into enemy territory. She had come with three or four others. It had rained often. Kweihua, the capital of the province, was in Kuomintang hands. There was still the possibility that Kuomintang troops might attack Chi-ling. Even while we were there two P-38s came high over the city and circled round.
406

One of the Americans in the Field Team shook his fist at them. "Jesus, they look as though they're going to strafe our plane." He ducked when they came lower. They were Kuomintang planes out on a mission of observation. It had happened before, it would probably happen many times again, and always there were complaints sent into Executive Headquarters. "The goddam bitches," he said, and the smile broadened on his face when they disappeared at last in the direction of Kweihua.

It was poor country, growing only sheep-grass and *yu mei,* and it was deathly still during that long morning of full sunlight. The girl said: "In winter it is desperately cold. There is snow on the ground, but the skies will clear." And you wondered whether the Field Team would still be there, and what fortunes of war there were for this small brown city on the plains.*

Later . . . THE plains came to an end, and the russet-red mountains with their green shadows returned again. There were no rivers, almost no farmsteads, there were a few trees near the monasteries, but the whole earth seemed broken up with the white cracked fissures of rivers which have long ago been forgotten. It is one of the dominant impressions which remain of northern China—the rivers have gone, and they have left in their places only the salt-white tracks where they once rode. It was midsummer. They would flow again in autumn, but they would not flow as they did once before desiccation had affected those great buttressed plains.

It was wild, and it was sad. The chequered fields, with their millet, their winter wheat and corn and vegetables—there was no sign of them. Perhaps there were farmsteads huddled at the foot of the mountains in the shadows, but you could not see them, though we were flying low, perhaps not more than 5,000 feet. China is a hard-bitten land. She never looked so hard-bitten as when we flew south-east from the beginning of the Ordos plain.

And then suddenly—it was the last thing you expected, for your eyes were so accustomed to the yellow mountains and the cracked earth that you forgot there were other mountains—you come to the foot-hills and see before you, covered in cloud, the great blue hills that guard Pekin. They are sharp-peaked, wild, and they rise

* Chi-ning was captured by Kuomintang forces in September, 1946. Kalgan fell, after a brief and fierce battle, early in October, 1946. The Field Teams were dissolved in February, 1947, under Secretary Marshall's orders.

up like the serrated teeth of some mythological animal to guard the Pekin plain. In this light they were cobalt blue, and sometimes resembled waves, though here and there green pines covered the lower reaches of the mountains. The white and broken waterways were no longer visible. The faint greenness was pleasing. You saw no roads. Flying low over the mountains, it seemed that there were mountains for ever, no end to them, and some were white-capped, not with snow, but with some glancing light from the sun. And there in the distance, like a mysterious thin white thread colouring the peaks of the mountains was the Great Wall. I had not seen it before. I must have dozed or slept when we were crossing it before, or perhaps there were mists. But now, as it grew larger and more definite—the thin cotton thread taking on the texture of a thin fine-spun rope—you noticed how closely it kept to the highest peaks, and how often there were precipitous slopes to the north of it. From the air it looked perfect. They could not have chosen better. The small white square guard-houses were perfectly spaced. You could make out the inner and outer walls, and you could follow the line of the wall to the horizon, so that even when the mountains disappeared in haze, you thought you could see the thin stretch of white walled road going beyond. But from the air the wall gave no impression of power. On the contrary it looked fragile, delicate as lace, powerless to stem invaders, a deliberate and artificial colouring of the peaks, as artificial indeed as the marble bridges in Pekin.

They say the wall is crumbling, and perhaps in five hundred years' time the bricks will all have been washed away by the rains and shrivelled by the frosts. It may be true. But like the tumuli and the cities whose outlines can still be seen from the air though wheat-fields ride over them, the walls will remain; and probably as long as men live on the planet there will be seen this thin delicate white lace which was once powerful enough to resist all invaders. They will not be walls any longer, but the whiteness of the bricks will have left its trace on the blue mountains, and men will remember, uncomfortably and vaguely, that battles were fought there.

There are only a few more mountains till you come to the plain. The plain shone like beaten bronze that afternoon all the way up to the gates of Pekin. The bronze was chequered and pat-terned, but dead level; there were farmsteads, clusters of dark-roofed villages, there were roads and railway lines. We flew low

408

over the West Field, over the pagodas and temples which cluster
the western hills, over the curving lake of the Summer Palace
dominated by yellow-roofed temples squatting in grottoes and
hills, but the lake was empty and the marble bridge looked like
one of those miniature Japanese toys and the palaces were dying
for lack of gold paint. Then, perhaps because there were so many
aeroplanes in the air, the pilot decided to fly low over Pekin.

It was all over. Yenan, Kalgan, Chi-ning, the vast experiments,
Mao Tse-tung leaning forward heavily, Chu Teh's red face in the
light of the oil-lamp, the soldiers riding up the valley in clouds
of dust with the Persian patterns on their saddle-bows, the loess
caves and the pagodas and the ten thousand buddhas and the intensity and seriousness of these people—these you could remember, as you remember legends, but like all legends they belonged
to the past. Once there was the legend of the Long March. Later
there was the legend of the Border Areas, when farmers and soldiers fought off the Japanese for eight barren years. New legends
would come—men prayed and hoped so much for a coalition
government that when this happens it will become as legendary as
the rest, and still later there will be the legend which will come
when the Chinese have understood themselves and how to behave among all the conflicting values of the modern world. But
to possess legends at all, a country must be active, its people physi-
cally strong, its aim defined as sharply as the contours of the Great
Wall. What was astonishing in Yenan and Kalgan—I felt the same
thing in Barcelona during the civil war—was that you believed
you were living in a legendary present, and when the present becomes legendary, it is worth living in. It is worth living in Pekin,
for there the legends of the past are insistent and without the
slightest difficulty you can believe yourself a part of the old Ming
conquerors, and slide easily into a life where legend is dominant;
but this was a new legend—this legend which was being hammered out in caves, in industrial cities, on battlefields by these
men who call themselves Communists and hope perhaps to realize
Communism in ten thousand years.

As the aeroplane flew low over Pekin, throwing its shadow on
the vast square golden-tiled roofs of the palaces, on the budding
lotuses in the ponds and into the depths of the green lake, you
realized that it was part of the same splendour—the imperial city
reflected the colour of the people in tiles and stone. The people
were changing, but they were still the same. Somewhere in the

north of China an upheaval was taking place, comparable with the upheavals at the end of the Han and Sung Dynasties, and no one could foretell its end, except that one could say that China was at last coming into its own, conscious of herself, and superbly contemptuous of her past. The experiment was being made. For the first time in known history the peasants, the farmers and the soldiers were learning to read and to think, and to exert power. The feudal age was passing before your eyes. For a few more years the tide could be stemmed, but sooner than most of us believe she will grow into maturity. There was inexperience in Red China, they had made many blunders, they were hardly at all aware of the existence of an outside world because they had been hemmed in for so long and possessed at times an ingrown character, so that they seemed content to be withdrawn into themselves, but they were educating the peasants and they were on the side of the people. The Kuomintang would remain, shorn of its unnecessary cruelties, but between them it was in their power to make a China worth living in—a China where the dying soldiers did not rot on the wayside, and no one needed to starve any more, and there were no requisitions by bandit armies, and no corruption. It was not a dream. It had been done. And because it had been done in one part of China, it could be done in other parts. And as the aeroplane circled over Pekin in the gold sunlight, and the hammered yellow of the imperial roofs shone so splendidly, there seemed no reason why its splendours should not be shared by all China. For this was at least certain—China was coming into her own.

July 15th, Pekin . . . THERE are no wise old women in Chinese mythology; I cannot understand why, because there are no women so wise as old Chinese women. When I stumble at night through all the immense courtyards of this house and grope my way through the dark to the small grass-covered shop where a woman sells me cigarettes, and suddenly see her there, detached from everything else, the face red and deeply wrinkled, the loose blue gown reflecting the light from all the strange bottles and paper packets on the wooden tray, I am convinced that she is three thousand years old and has her place in all men's dreams, so unchanging she is. The shop stands under an immense banyan tree; from one of the branches there descends, as a sign that she
410

owns the place, a circle of red hair and a gold trinket shaped like a fish.

July 16th . . . Every night I must tell Jacqueline a fairy story about the princesses of Persia. I do not know why it must be Persia, though she insists upon it, though she knows perfectly well that the Persia I have to describe for her is her own Pekin. She comes in her pyjamas and snuggles into my arms, fantastically certain of her place, even though I am working or reading; and then we must argue about the names of the princesses, and she will insist on the most ridiculous names of all, and then go to sleep—or so I think, until she wakes up when I am gazing down at her, quite silent before her beauty, the faintly Chinese eyes, the faintly yellow skin, the mouth and cheekbones which are wholly European. I know sometimes that I love her more than I love anyone, and love her most because her father was French and her mother Chinese, so that she has been brought to life in the best of both worlds, and has the gaiety of the French and the intolerable wisdom of the Chinese.

In this old ruined palace there are so many courtyards that I am continually losing myself. To enter the house at all one must step through mountains of debris, for the great gates and porticos were burnt this January; over the high walls you can see the brick pillars still supporting the charred *nanmu* wood, and I have such a horror of this stupid destruction that I cannot enter the palace without a sense of revolt. K., who stayed here throughout the war, says that when the front courtyard went up in flames because the electrical connections were out of order, there was a most brilliant scarlet flame and even better than the flame was the scent of the wood, which was first placed here when the palace was built to the glory of one of the eight iron-capped princes, who were the sons of the Emperor Chien Lung. I confess I envy him. I should have liked to see the moment when these things happened, but it seems absurdly unfair that after all this waiting in exile in the south of China, this amazingly beautiful entrance should be denied to us. And now the whole palace is crumbling to ruins, and the Japanese have littered some of the smaller courtyards with their *tatamis* and the boll weevil is at work and the plaster ceilings are falling down on us, and there is so much corruption among the estate officers that we dream only of having a small house

411

somewhere in the west city, for fear that we shall live, like the author of *The Dream of the Red Chamber*, in a place where "all order is perishing and only vice survives." The strangest people live here. Old women peer out of gnarled courtyards, among the wistaria trees. At night I have come across immense stores of UNRAA flour which are being sent—heaven knows where. The ancestral altar has lost its glory; there are times when the old grandfatherly face which peers down at us has a look of feverish disgust, and those immense window-cases in the room, filled with the costumes of the Ch'ing Dynasty, seem already in decay. This palace could tell many things if it spoke, and I suspect that it would speak most often of the terror it feels at its own decay. Once through all these courtyards officers of state came to lay their petitions before the Prime Minister of China, who worked in a room which is now haunted by crumbling chairs and an untuned piano and the relics of a children's playroom. Once, too, there was vast wealth here, but that has been stolen by the same estate officers who now hide their stores of flour in the darkest alleyways. There seems to be no hope for the palace of the iron-capped princes. It will go on decaying, the tiles will continue to fall from the roof, the servants will continue to steal and the old relatives of the Prime Minister will continue to make their living by cheating at mah-jong parties and by taking service with corrupt officials. So it is perhaps with everything in Pekin. There are only a few places where the glory remains, but how prodigious a glory it must have been before the speculators and the usurers and the officials took pride in defeating one of the loveliest works of men!

July 18th . . . YELLOW dust, the roofs sparkling yellow, the pure intoxication of walking alone for the last time through the courtyards of the Tai Miao, the old ancestral buildings of the Ch'ing Emperors. There were lovers on the marble balustrades, and a great falcon was hovering among the trees. I have never seen it so beautiful, or so quiet. The trees were greener than ever, the proportions of the great gables were (as always) astonishing in their perfection, in their solidity of line; and I remember now not the horror of walking through those immense halls where the yellow silk and the halberds and the armour are all crumbling, but the enduring pleasure of the summer—the deep green of the ilex trees against the gold bosses of imperial roofs, and the still
412

greater pleasure of coming through the last of the halls into a small courtyard with a door which opened out on the green moat and the huge walls of the Imperial City. And every way you turned there were lovers on the grass or on the marble balustrades, and the birds were singing.

Here there are moments when the dream comes singularly to life, when the illusion gives place to a more tangible reality. Suddenly, like a girl's face coming across a room, the heart of Pekin is seen—a gesture of a beggar, the curve of a coolie's naked back between rickshas as he turns into a sidestreet with yellow roofs flashing, the sudden perfection of music and vision which comes when you hear the fluted doves playing in some deserted courtyard, or best of all those moments when you wander alone in the hot sunlight around the Altar of Heaven, knowing that the marble altar has no relevance to our present mechanical life, though it reflects our desires and belongs to all our legends. I shall never go again to the tawdry Legation Quarter, but I know now that I could spend my life wandering through these dusty streets, waiting for winter and spring.

July 19th, The Hunting Park . . . THERE are some cities whose light comes to us like the light of the stars—it takes a long time to reach us and is faint when it arrives; but Pekin is like a meteor which comes swimming into our consciousness, blazing with its tail of lights. Leningrad, London, Vienna and Paris have the colour and the texture of stone, uncoloured except by the seasons; Pekin is the colour of yellow porcelain, and the seasons can hardly change it, though the trees wither, and there are snows. But when we drove out to the Hunting Park this morning, the knee-high maize on both sides of the road, the blue hills and the white statues of ministers and tortoises and the deep green of the yews and tamarisks, all these possessed their own colours, but you saw them so blinded by the predominant yellow tones of Pekin that they were unlike any colours you have ever seen. The yellow of Pekin is not gold, nor bronze, nor the colour of the sun, though it is nearest to those yellows van Gogh discovered in the south of France; it is all these, and more, and most of all it is like the yellow you can imagine if a gold plate were seen in a stream with the water foaming over it, a yellow so rich and deep that it seems to possess many depths, and all are changing. And so it was this

413

morning when, coming through the abandoned fields, we saw the yellow roofs of the Empress Dowager's summer palace above the mist.

When you travel outside Pekin, you are at once at the mercy of ghosts. There is nothing in Pekin as old as the Tower of London, but the past is more visible here than in any city I have ever known; for six hundred years there has been a settled condition of living, an unchanging ritual of life comparable only with the unchanging ritual of the Balinese. But the Chinese are wanderers; whole villages and towns have been built on the great plain which stretches to the western hills, they have been allowed to fall into ruin, nothing remains except the broken walls or the pillars of temples. We passed an immense fortress, with moat, drawbridge and gates, with grass growing all over it. They say it was there that the Emperors inspected their personal guards. We passed a mausoleum built by the Japanese in honour of one of the Chinese collaborators. It was all bright red and gold, with flaring roofs and marble steps, but the ruins showed the graver taste of men who lived before collaboration had become an art, and what was strange was that you could see at once, from the shape of the guardian lions and the shape of the roofs, how much had been lost. "We shall not recapture it again, we are no longer an imperial power." It may be true, but I do not see why, with so much wealth of architecture still available, we should not discover those old proportions. Certainly they were present at the entrance to the Hunting Park, the great studded gates and bronze dragons protecting it as majestically as the Imperial City is protected by its cloud-pillars. Nothing had been lost. Skill, proportion, the sense of fitness—they were all there, though no huntsmen ride through the park and the old pleasure-palaces are covered with weeds.

When Hsiung Hsi-ling was Prime Minister, he asked the Emperor Pu Yi for a grant of the western quarter of the Hunting Park to build an orphanage. There were famines in Honan, and great floods. He was a poor man, but he collected three hundred thousand taels from his friends and built an orphanage here with his own architects, and made it one of the best in the Far East. The children were well cared-for. The most modern equipment was installed. There were workshops, porcelain kilns, a printing-shop, three churches; he sent the supervisors to America, and himself studied during all his journeys to America and Europe how best to create an orphanage. Under the Empress Dowager, before he

414

became Governor-General of Jehol, he was sent on a mission to the west, with the humble aim of learning what would be of most use to China, and though his days as Prime Minister have been forgotten, and the wild scheming of his friends, the Reformers, is old history, he made this orphanage, which remains. He was evidently proud of his work, for here and there you will come upon the scrolls he wrote, or his own calligraphy outlined in stone above the lintels, and sometimes there is his photograph, an old man with a small white beard and heavy eyelids, not frail, not determined, not even conscious of his dignity as Prime Minister, not weary or broken, though he was broken many times by affections which were never returned, a man who gives an impression of abiding honesty and simplicity, himself the last of the rulers of China to have believed faithfully in the past. He was a buddhist scholar with a deep reverence for the imperial tradition and with a great loathing for the Empress Dowager, who ordered his execution, so that he was compelled to go into exile in Japan. He hid the Reformers of 1898 in his own house, and accepted no bribes, and died poor, having given everything he possessed to the orphanage except a part of his old house in Pekin. In his will he says that he bought his palace out of his hard-earned savings and only once received a gift from Yuan Shih-kai; and it is clear that he loved nothing except that the orphanage should survive.

It had survived well enough, through wars and civil wars, but when we reached it this morning, we wondered whether he would have approved of the changes. At the entrance to the Hunting Park there were Kuomintang soldiers, trigger-happy. It was not difficult to believe that somewhere in the Hunting Park there were also communist soldiers, for the western hills mark the frontiers of Kuomintang control and fierce battles have been waged here at night against the Japanese. But the Hunting Park was unchanged. There were the forests of white pines, the acacias and the pears, the small lakes, the stone plinths from which palaces once arose, a confusion of brambles and arching trees, all sweet-scented. The orphanage looks new, though the children have scabies and are not well cared for. Hsiung Hsi-ling built houses on the sloping shores of the forest at a time when houses cost hardly more than a labourer's monthly hire; he could get away from the fret of his palace in Pekin and gaze at the goldfish in the pool or dig for buried treasure—there was one superb green vase

415

which had come from some princess's grave he found in the park. He set it beside a pool full of reeds and fishes, and shaded by acacia trees, near a small one-storied hunting lodge where he often stayed. I shall never forget this place for the quiet and the gleam of gold in the pool and the serenity of the forest, and most of all I shall remember it for the exquisite good taste of this man who was almost the last cultured ruler of the Chinese Empire. One can see him so perfectly in this setting, an old man in a maroon gown, who came here as often as possible to drink the spring water which bubbles from a black cave. The orphanage is corrupt now; there seems to be no one with power to put it on its feet again; there are far too many teachers for far too few orphans; too much of the food brought from America is going to the supervisors; the flour for the children is mixed with bran, as we discovered when we entered unannounced in one of the small buildings, while the flour for the supervisors is clean and white. Worse was to come later when the old Prime Minister's servant confessed that he had let the hunting-lodge on his own authority and taken the money for himself and wept and knelt at the feet of the Prime Minister's daughter, and at that moment we were conscious, not only of the depths of corruption but also of its inevitability whenever there is no strong government in control and no settled behaviour of living.

Among these lakes and mountain streams, the enchantment remains, an enchantment which is not overpowering like the gold tiles and the proportions of Pekin, but shadowy and insubstantial as a dream. Once, near the shaded hunting lodge, a shadow came from behind the trees and walked in the direction of the green bronze vase which is set on a square stone, and suddenly the whole place came to life, and there was the sound of singing, and my step-daughter was skipping beside the lake in slacks, but she looked like a princess who has returned to her accustomed lake. The old boat quivered in the wind as it lodged among reeds. The tall green pillars engraved with buddhist sutras gleamed in the sun. The ice-cold bubbling spring was boiling over. A shadow darkened the sun, and as we wandered down the steps to the car and saw the great plain stretching yellow to the walls of Pekin, we knew we were determined to come again and live here and try to make the orphanage once again the perfect thing it was in the past.

July 20, Nightmares . . . DREAMING of Chen Kung-p'o, who was executed last month. We have all been dreaming about it, because the details in the Chinese newspapers were so completely authentic. The strange intolerable disease of the Chinese for the facts of death, which they know only too well. Everything about the last hours of the traitor was recorded—how he stayed awake on his last night and wrote one more letter to the Generalissimo, and then when they came in the morning, he asked that the letter should be sent, though it was unfinished, and arranged to pay the executioner for a speedy death and went in his stockinged feet to see some others who were awaiting trial, saying nothing, but holding their hands and looking into their faces, while the tears fell endlessly from his eyes. He desired that his body should not be allowed to putrefy, and he requested that after his death his body should be enclosed in ice. The way he walked slowly across the prison yard, and how he was shot by a single bullet from a Mauser which killed him before he reached the wall. We know these things only too well, for too many people knew Chen Kung-p'o and there is still some doubt whether Wang Ching-wei was any worse than many members of the government who made fortunes during the war. They say that Chen Kung-p'o died poor. It may be true, because he belonged to the old order and did his best according to shifting lights. But what is intolerable is that his death has suddenly brought us face to face with one of the insoluble problems of the Chinese scene: we see in him a small man, caught up in the stupid miseries of the war, a man without will, with a perverted sense of patriotism, and though we shall shed no tears for him at all, his execution has shown us inevitably that we are living in an age of calm and controlled violence. The field of events in China is so vast that we cannot think of it without symbols—we need our witless soldier-heroes as focal points, so that we can take our bearings. And so we have added one more focal point in the death of this scholar.

Five days ago, in a street in Kunming, the cold and abstract violence of the Kuomintang military clique led to the death of another scholar, who was my friend. I dare not dream of him; if I do, all dreams forever will be shadowed by him. I have not written about his death before, because I could not. He was the greatest man I ever met in China, the most scrupulous, the most happy

417

in his work, the most popular of all the professors at Lienta, the man with the sweetest smile and the most mature brain. His name was Wen Yi-tuo, which means "the one and the many of learning," and hence by implication all that can be understood by learning. He started life with an intense desire to paint, went to America, returned with his mind full of colours, helped to build up the architectonics of modern Chinese verse and having written two slim books of poems, decided to dedicate the rest of his life to an examination of the ancient Chinese classics in the light of modern criticism. We were so often together that I cannot remember when we first met. At the time when I knew him first he wore a gold-brown beard, and he would explain, as though excusing the colour of his hair, that he thought he was descended from tribesmen. His body was frail. He had starved during the war, and taken while Dean of the College of Chinese Literature, so many various odd-jobs in Middle Schools that he had no time for himself. When the students were murdered in December, he did his best to make sure that justice would be done, and in doing this incurred so much enmity that we knew even then that his life was at stake. He had a fine speaking voice which would sometimes become dark with passionate remonstrance. He cared nothing for his own life, and on March 17th this year marched at the head of the funeral procession of the students through the streets of Kunming and gave the saddest of all the farewells at the grave. He was a man born to command, whose children loved him, though he insisted continually that the position of the father under the Confucian system was pure tyranny. He would say: "The family must be destroyed —we must follow the west," and though these words have none of the overtones of meaning in English which they possess in China, and though he was the wisest among the Chinese I knew in his discrimination between the good and bad things of the west, he remains more than any other the forerunner of the new China which will soon be born.

I would wander round the lake with him, and sometimes in the early afternoon or late at night I would come upon him at his table, his head bent over the seals which he was carving against time, so that he could feed his children—he hated this waste of time, even though the seals sometimes brought good money, and he would say he preferred to be teaching for eighteen hours a week in the middle schools, where at least he could inculcate a fervour for Chinese traditions. And there was nothing at all

418

strange in the fact that he more than anyone else in this great complex of Universities was overthrowing those traditions.

He was ill last year of typhus, after a journey to the petrified rocks in the south of Yunnan; and then I would see him in his ragged blue gown walking slowly with a stick through the campus. Students would run up to him asking for interpretations of the classics; always he spoke to them with especial sweetness. His classrooms were always filled to overflowing, and there would be perhaps forty students listening through the windows. He had a quiet contempt for the professors who thought it unnecessary to speak with students about political problems. He believed the present government of China to be corrupt, and said so openly, with no shadow of fear on the fine high-boned face. I took him once to see the American Consul, and what was most delightful was Wen's unspoken delight in being in an American home. He had a hard-bitten mind and was obsessed by the poverty and degradation all round him; once he nearly broke under the strain; he recovered easily, and never showed the least sign of strain afterwards. He led the long march of the students from Pekin to the southwest at the beginning of the war, and we had thought of him always as the man who lead them back again. It was no more than we expected of him. But we did not expect him to die in the way he did, returning after a meeting, shot down in cold blood by four gangsters with American silent revolvers. He received six bullet wounds, and was dead almost immediately. His son, who was standing a little away from him, saw the father fall and threw himself over his father's body, crying "Let me die for you, father," and then fell unconscious, for the gangsters put four more bullets into him. They say the father's body will be cremated, and he will be buried near the students who died last December. The son has recovered, though he is still not out of danger. From his hospital bed he has told a strange story of how the assassins stood over him and said before shooting him: "We must shoot you to save our lives, but we will not kill you. Later, when you have recovered, you may take revenge on us."

The death of Chen Kung-p'o was a small thing compared to the death of China's greatest scholar.

July 23rd . . . IN THREE days I shall leave China and then fly home. I thought, after five years, I had roots here, but the roots are drying up and I know there will not be peace for many years.

419

Death and corruption and unimaginable beauty, and the lion awake at last, and yet not sufficiently awake, and the worst is the evil all round us, and the best lies with the young. I am glad I lived with them, and yet not sorry now to leave, for there must be other countries as good. I saw the landscape and very nearly exercised a childhood dream, and lived for a while in the valley of Yenan, and knew Wen Yi-tuo, and helped a few, and was helped by many; and what was left, except the pain, can never be put on paper, or even dreamed on. The beauty lay everywhere, and most of all in the faces of the children. And it was kind of whatever fates control us to leave the best to the end—Kunming, Yenan, gold roofs of Pekin.

July 28th, On the plane to Shanghai . . . THIS morning, the ultimate day, Pekin was the same, a mist rising, dust whirling along the ground, an awful feeling of heaviness, as though one wanted to stay here forever.

Writing this in the aeroplane, drowsy in the overheated cabin, not caring, knowing that the best is over and Shanghai is a nightmare, not caring, and yet angry a little, because this time we did not fly directly over Pekin but skirted round the walls and flew directly south. The last we saw of Pekin was the gold glow in the sky, as of a burning, above the city.

Nanking. A red gash in a purple hill, where Sun Yat-sen lies at the top of far too many steps, the city black as ants, floods all round; no yellow tiles, only dark roads, bleak and miserable, criss-crossing interminably. And then to Shanghai again, seven hours after leaving Pekin, an eternity of mist and rain, bumping, the rain discolouring everything—even, at last, the sea.

July 30th, Shanghai . . . So OVERWHELMINGLY tired that I locked the door of the hotel bedroom and went to sleep after wandering round the city all day in a relentless pursuit of tickets, visas, passports. Someone must have opened it with an outside key. A shaft of orange light; a girl and a hotel coolie come in noisily.

"Want girl?"

"No."

"Want boy?"

"No."

"You American?"

"No."

420

He pushed the girl towards the bed; she wore a flowered dress, and pulled her skirt above her knee.

He said: "$75,000 dollars. You pay me now."

I tried to push him away.

"Okay—$50,000 dollars. You ask for girl, eh?"

"No."

"Okay—$40,000 dollars. You see."

Somehow they were pushed out, but someone was playing on a Chinese violin in the next room, and somewhere across the landing someone was screaming; and in the morning it was worse still, the hotel unswept, the boys grey and colourless, the prostitutes still wandering round the evil-smelling building. And then all day at CNRAA offices claims and counter-claims—it is the fault of UNRAA, it is the fault of someone else, we can't get the food shipped outside of Shanghai, God knows where it disappears to, the police take ten per cent, and someone else takes fifty per cent, and the whole of Shanghai is living on UNRAA supplies, and no one else at all gets any supplies whatsoever. Corruption, the smell of corruption, the loaded goods on the walls marked UNRAA —the menace in the letters, which should have brought blessing —and everywhere a feeling of seething unrest, ambulances at every street-corner, soldiers everywhere. I took a ricksha out into the country, as far away as possible from the Bund and the sweating grey skyscrapers; and there were small villages, and the sunflowers were growing on the gravemounds, and the people looked thin and worn, and the smoke belched from Shanghai in the distance. It is not true that Chungking is the sheer antipodes of Pekin. J. said: "The people were better fed under the Japanese— prices were controlled. Now Shanghai holds the rest of China in fee." Escaped at last to stay with the Indian Agent, far from the centre of the city, grateful for his calm, his dark eager humorous face and the quietness which, like all Indians, he carries with him as we carry clothes.

August 1st, Nanking . . . I FLEW this morning to Nanking to say farewell to Feng Yu-hsiang. Nanking was quiet, dust-laden, bathed in heat and silence, the streets wide and clean; impossible to understand why it had looked so black and menacing when I saw it from the aeroplane on my way to Shanghai. It is his birthday. He said sadly that because he has reached the age of sixty-five, he had today been removed from the active list—he would have preferred to be a soldier to the end. In the heat and the dust we went out onto the Lotos Lake, Feng sitting in the prow, his servant fanning him, and then one by one the red lanterns came out, bobbing over the rushes and lotoses. He said quietly, looking up at the first stars: "There is an old proverb. A clean sky and lotoses are like scholars," and then he went on to talk of Wen Yi-tuo's death and his plans of going to America. He looked older now, limping a little, the eyes half-closed, the great head red in the light of the lanterns. "A clean sky and lotoses—those are the most beautiful physical things, but more beautiful still are the great scholars, and this man who was killed——"

August 2nd . . . As you fly from Nanking to Shanghai, you see everywhere the remains of villages which have gone forever. Across the ploughed ricefields, you see the faint lines which tell you that there were streets there once, and watch-towers, and great shaded avenues. Slow green mountains rise, with sulphur-white outcrops, valleys full of lakes, floods, almost no trees. Down below a serpentine railway, recently cut by the Communists, takes its toy train to Shanghai. Best of all are the small dark villages with their surrounding lakes full of duckweed, and worst is that the land changes colour as you approach Shanghai: the rich green disappears, and everything turns the colour of ash, greyish-white; as though the poison was driving the fields away, making everything the same colour as the grey city.

August 3rd, Mme Sun Yat-sen . . . Wondering what would happen if I stayed longer in Shanghai, for there are some things in this huge, grimy, domineering, relentless, noisy and bloodshot city which should not even be contemplated, we came at dusk to the gates of Mme Sun Yat-sen's house. Guards with fixed bayonets stood at sentry-go. There were chains on the great iron gates, and three bars; but once you are allowed inside the gates, everything is peaceful again, there are flowers everywhere and the house stands among trees.

She wore a white gown, her face very pale and unbelievably beautiful. There were lilies in a Chinese jar on the table, and a painting of Dr. Sun Yat-sen looked down from the wall. She looked twenty, and there were moments when she gestured or pursed her lips and looked eighteen. She talked of her Peace Hospitals and of her recent statement, calling upon both sides to cease

422

their conflict, and of the Chinese general who had accused her of communism in a deliberate and unavailing effort to incriminate her. She complained against the censorship, the terrors to which so many Chinese, and so many foreigners, bowed; and she spoke most softly when she mentioned the secret police. "It was not like this before. Dr. Sun would not approved of them." And then again: "I had looked forward so much to the end of the war—now I am ashamed." Nobility was there, and grace, and goodness. The pale face, the sleek shining hair, the long white gown, and the girl's smile over the polished table. The rain thundered and roared beyond the quiet room, but in the centre of the room, pouring tea, smiling faintly and not in the least mysteriously, she spoke of the time when peace would come, or frowned because there was still war. "In my mind for a very long time the hospitals have been first. This is how it must be—but why, when we think of the health of children, do those others think of guns?"

August 4th . . . No MAN is lonelier than on an airfield in the morning mist; the aeroplanes half hidden, the clouds low, the sun breaking, and everything is fresh, but the aeroplanes look like prehistoric monsters unmoving on the sandy field. I am haunted still by Mme Sun Yat-sen, and shall be for ever. I have seen a photograph taken twenty five years ago; nothing has changed, the lines of the face as unchanging as the eyes, the sleekness of the hair as unchanging as the expression of the pursed lips. She spoke, I remember, not with bitterness, but with a kind of terrible Chinese despair, seeing no hope unless there was a coalition government, knowing that her husband was being forgotten by those in power.

Shivering here on the airfield, seeing the mist rising, the sun flooding across sand, deadened almost by the weight of these last five tragic years, it seems unthinkable that this evening I shall be in India, where life may be no better but at least there are no civil wars. All human wars are victories for the sun and the rain; famine and floods come, and the ravelled earth grows weeds where there was once corn; and sooner or later if these wars endure, China will become a desert. For twenty years after the Taiping rebellion there were deserts in the Yangste valley, the land which was most tamed became the most barren. War destroys men, but worse than anything else it destroys the things men have made; and the war is here, on the airfield, for here in the rising mist are

423

Kuomintang planes with machine-guns.

We had hoped for so much. We did not know or guess that this would happen. We lived among simplicities, the Japanese the only enemy; and then at last we found the enemies among ourselves. The naked game of the world is being played in China. On this ravaged country we can see better than elsewhere the forces at work—the decay of the old religious systems, the terrible dangers which accompany the introduction of industrialization in an agricultural community, and the final birth of a new social consciousness, slow and groping, but clean and vigorous, healthy with the health of the young. We have seen these things through eyes shadowed by tragedy, and no place on earth can be so tragic as China.

Clean-cut, silvered with clouds, the river ran below, and the floods came like a sea, and the red hills, and the river widening, flowing over the land, more beautiful than ever among the rich ricefields of Hunan, till the gaunt blue mountains rose again in Szechuan, and at the end of the journey Burma was dark with immense green shadowy forests, and India grew out of the dusk, like an evening cloud. For five years of war I had been in China, and now as we come down on the airstrip above Calcutta it seems like a moment of time, no longer than it takes for lightning to score a dark land, where men are seized in terrible gestures of war and the lakes are shining and somewhere among the suddenly illuminated temples beside the shore there are lovers and scholars; and this too remains. The best were the scholars, the farmers and the soldiers; the worst were worse than anything one can imagine. The best remains.

THE END

424

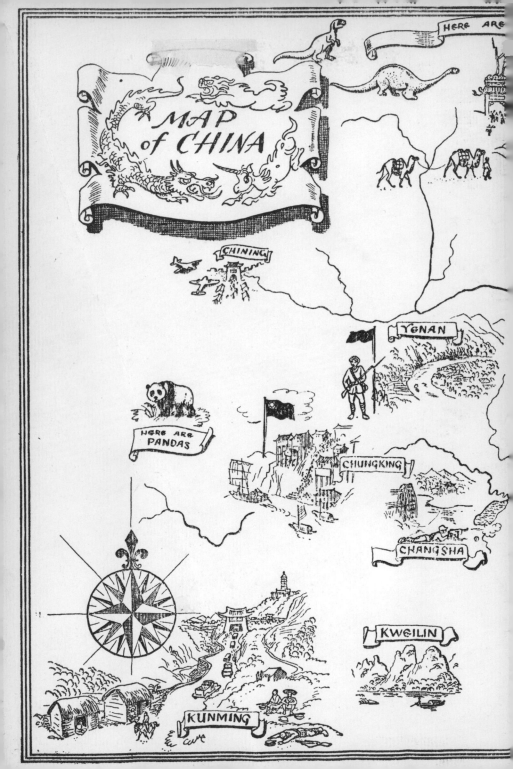